D0396077

Total War and Historical Change

Total War and Historical Change
Europe 1914–1955

Edited by
ARTHUR MARWICK, CLIVE EMSLEY AND
WENDY SIMPSON

Open University Press
Buckingham · Philadelphia

Open University Press
Celtic Court
22 Ballmoor
Buckingham
MK18 1XW

email: enquiries@openup.co.uk
world wide web: www.openup.co.uk

and
325 Chestnut Street
Philadelphia, PA 19106, USA

First published 2001

Selection and editorial material
Copyright © The Open University 2001

All rights reserved. Except for the quotation of short passages for the purpose of
criticism and review, no part of this publication may be reproduced, stored in a
retrieval system, or transmitted, in any form or by any means, electronic,
mechanical, photocopying, recording or otherwise, without the prior written
permission of the publisher or a licence from the Copyright Licensing Agency
Limited. Details of such licences (for reprographic reproduction) may be obtained
from the Copyright Licensing Agency Ltd of 90 Tottenham Court Road, London,
W1P 0LP.

A catalogue record of this book is available from the British Library

ISBN 0 335 20793 6 (pbk)   0 335 20794 4 (hbk)

Library of Congress Cataloging-in-Publication Data
Total war and historical change: Europe, 1914–1955/edited by Arthur Marwick,
Clive Emsley and Wendy Simpson.
        p. cm.
    Chiefly collections of previously published extracts, articles, etc.
    Includes bibliographical references and index.
    ISBN 0-335-20794-4 – ISBN 0-335-20793-6 (pbk.)
    1. World War, 1914–1918 – Influence.   2. World War, 1939–1945 – Influence.
3. Europe – History – 20th century.   4. World War, 1914–1918 – Social aspects –
Europe.   5. World War, 1939–1945 – Social aspects – Europe.   I. Marwick,
Arthur, 1936–   II. Simpson, Wendy, 1941–
    D523.T47 2001
    940.5 – dc21   00-055054

Typeset by Type Study, Scarborough, North Yorkshire
Printed in Great Britain by St Edmundsbury Press, Bury St Edmunds, Suffolk

HOUSTON PUBLIC LIBRARY

R01208 80247

Contents

Acknowledgements

Open University Press would like to make grateful acknowledgement for permission to reproduce the following material.

1 Ian F. W. Beckett, 'Total War', *Warfare in the Twentieth Century: Theory and Practice* edited by Colin MacInnes and Y. D. Sheffield, pp. 1–23, London, Routledge.
2 Arno J. Mayer (1981). *The Persistence of the Old Regime*. Copyright © 1981 by Arno J. Mayer. All rights reserved. First published in the United States by Pantheon Books a division of Random House Inc., New York City.
3 G. D. Josipovici, 'The Birth of the Modern: 1885–1914' © Oxford University Press 1970. Reprinted from *French Literature and Its Background, Volume 6 – The Twentieth Century* edited by John Cruickshank (1970) by permission of Oxford University Press.
4 Samuel R. Williamson Jr, 'The Origins of the War' © Oxford University Press 1998. Reprinted from *The Oxford Illustrated History of the First World War* edited by Hew Strachan (1998) by permission of Oxford University Press.
5 Anna Bravo (1982). 'Italian Peasant Women and the First World War', *Our Common History: The Transformation of Europe* edited by Paul Thompson and N. Burcharat, pp. 157–70, London, Pluto Press.
6 Richard Bessel, 'Demobilization and Labour' © Oxford University Press 1993. Reprinted from *Germany After the First World War* edited by Richard Bessel (1993) by permission of Oxford University Press.
7 Charles S. Maier (1975). *Recasting Bourgeois Europe: Stabilization in France, Germany and Italy in the Decade after World War I*, pp. 3–15 and 579–93, Princeton, Princeton University Press.
8 Norman Rich (1986). 'Hitler's Foreign Policy', *The Origins of the Second World War Reconsidered* edited by G. Martell, pp. 119–39, London, Routledge.

9 R. J. Overy (1982). 'Hitler's War and the German Economy: A Reinterpretation', *Economic History Review*, 2nd Series, Vol. XXXV, No. 2, pp. 272–91.

10 Christopher R. Browning (1994). 'One Day in Józefów: Initiation to Mass Murder', *Lessons and Legacies III: The Meaning of the Holocaust in a Changing World* edited by Donald G. Schilling, pp. 169–83, Evanston, Northwestern University Press.

11 Stanley Hoffman (1961). 'The Effects of World War II on French Society and Politics', *French Historical Studies*, Vol. 2:1 (Spring 1961), pp. 28–63. Copyright 1961, Society for French Historical Studies. All rights reserved. Reprinted by permission of Duke University Press.

12 Penny Summerfield (1986). 'The Levelling of Class', *War and Social Change, British Society in the Second World War* edited by Harold L. Smith, pp. 179–207, Manchester, Manchester University Press.

13 Mark Harrison,' "Barbarossa", The Soviet Response, 1941', *From Peace to War: Germany, Soviet Russia, and the World, 1939–1941* edited by Bernd Wegner, Oxford, Berghahn Books.

14 Mark Roseman (1988). 'World War II and Social Change in Germany', *Total War and Social Change* edited by Arthur Marwick, pp. 58–78, London, Macmillan.

15 Hew Strachan (2000). 'Total War in the Twentieth Century'. This chapter was specially commissioned by the AA312 Course Team, but has also been published in *International History Review*, June 2000.

Introduction

ARTHUR MARWICK AND CLIVE EMSLEY

What do we mean by social change? Some historians conceive the answer in quite broad terms, in terms, indeed, of shifting patterns of dominance, of changing structures of power, of groups and classes overthrowing or replacing or reaching accommodations with each other, of, perhaps, a bourgeois class replacing a landed class and then, say, of the bourgeois class skilfully fending off the claims of a 'rising' working class. The Introduction to the Open University course *Total War and Social Change: Europe 1914–1955*, in conjunction with which this Reader has been designed, suggests a different approach which, rather than dealing with broad shifts in power relationships, tries to get at the detail of social change by defining ten overlapping areas: social geography (including basic population statistics, distribution of urban and rural populations, etc.); economic and technological change; social structure (including questions of 'class' etc.); national cohesion (questions of ethnic composition, etc.); social reform and welfare policies; material conditions; customs and behaviour; the role and status of women; high and popular culture; institutions and values.[1]

What do we mean by total war? How is total war distinguished from other kinds of war? It is common practice to refer to both 'the Great War' of 1914–18 and the 'Second World War' of 1939–45 as total wars, and to see the former as the first total war in history. Questions then arise about how true the second generalization is, and about how far there were critical differences between these two wars. What is the relationship, if any, between the Great War and the revolutions which broke out in various countries towards the end of it? Between that war and the rise of Fascism and of Nazism? What are the differences, and what are the links, between total war, other international wars, revolutions, civil war and 'internal war' and genocide?

How do wars come about? As total wars, did the two major wars of the twentieth century have essentially similar origins? Were they perhaps just two instalments of one massive conflict? Or were the assumptions and conditions obtaining in 1914 very different from those of 1939? Can we make a distinction between long-term 'structural', 'ideological' and 'institutional' forces making for war, and more immediate political and military decisions? What are the possibilities, if any, of a negotiated peace during the course of a total war?

In the popular mind, the two world wars loom large: to many in the 1920s, the world of 1914 and before seemed very remote; people in the 1940s, too, had the feeling of having lived through cataclysmic change. What exactly is the relationship, if any, between these wars and social change? To give a rigorous answer it is not good enough simply to list changes that took place during or after the wars. It is first of all vital to identify the other forces which, entirely independently of war, were making for social change. And, if we are to get an accurate assessment of the effects of war, we have to be absolutely clear what the various European countries were like in 1914, and again in 1939, *before* each war. Whether the wars did have significant consequences within any, or all, of the ten areas of social change already identified, and, if so, how much, is a matter for careful exploration. So too is the question, if the wars did have social consequences, *why* exactly was this so? Can it be possible that wars (which, after all, are in their very nature immensely destructive and negative) touch off processes which do actually bring about social change? Social change apart, obviously the wars have had important geopolitical consequences: the First World War, for example, greatly reduced the power of Russia in Europe; the Second World War greatly increased it. All over Europe, at the end of each war, boundaries were redrawn.

In effect, these opening paragraphs have identified four themes (each containing further sub-themes): the nature of social change and the form it takes in different countries; the nature of total war, other kinds of war, war's relationship to revolution, civil war and genocide; the causes of war; the consequences of war. In this Introduction we shall be attempting to indicate the ways in which each of the essays which follow contributes to one or more of these themes. But there is something else. Right at the start it was suggested that there are two rather different ways of looking at the question of social change. Now, it is the case that historians often do bring different approaches to bear on the sorts of issue with which this book is concerned. One hallowed way (it goes back to the late nineteenth century) of defining the way approaches differ is to say that some historians adopt a *nomothetic* approach (one which, rather in the manner of the natural sciences, seeks to advance and refine theory and tends to make use of broad explanatory categories), while others prefer the *idiographic* approach (one which stresses the uniqueness of historical events and developments and tends to stress precise detail). The division is not a hard-and-fast one; most historians recognize that their subject does differ significantly from any of the natural sciences, while, at the same time, most of those who avoid general theories do recognize the need for generalization and the exploration of structural interrelationships: many historians, it could be said, incorporate elements from both approaches.

Thus, a simpler and less rigid way of identifying differences of approach might be to speak, on the one hand, of historians who are 'more-theoretical', and, on the other, of historians who are 'less-theoretical'. Still another way would be to distinguish between historians who are *strongly* influenced by the ideas of Karl Marx, or the ideas of Max Weber, or perhaps by elements from both, and historians who, while probably recognizing the important intellectual contributions made by both Marx and Weber, do not give any special weighting to their theories about social change or structures of power, preferring to follow where their primary sources lead them. (Thus this latter approach might also be described as 'source-based', save that most Marxist historians would claim, very reasonably, that they too place great emphasis on the primary sources; as a further alternative to 'less-theoretical' or 'source-based', there is the label 'liberal humanist', usually used by critics of this approach.) This elaborate discussion has been necessary because although differences of approach are widely recognized to exist, there is no agreement on how they are best defined, *nomothetic* and *idiographic* being at best very crude labels. Yet it can be absolutely crucial to know what kind of approach a particular historian is following, since the approach may very well determine the assumptions attaching to such terms as 'class conflict' or 'corporatism', or, for example, influence what conclusions are presented about the significance, or otherwise, of war. A historian who gives greatest weight to long-term structural change may well play down such short-term influences as those brought about by a particular war. However one defines the differences, there can be no denying that the distinguished authors of the essays that make up this book do differ in their approaches to historical study. 'Know your historian' is always good advice to any student of history. Thus for the purposes of this Introduction we have a fifth theme, the 'historiographical' one, the question of the different approaches followed by the different authors. In following up this theme, we hope to bring out particular points of originality or utility in the essays which might otherwise be missed, and, as relevant, to indicate where issue may be taken with their authors. It is also very important that you note carefully the original date of publication of each chapter (for example when Charles Maier, writing in 1975, refers to 'the last quarter century's stability', first check whether it would be more appropriate now to say 'the last half century's stability').

The first essay in this volume, 'Total War', is by a military historian. However, Ian Beckett's concerns are not those of the traditional military historian; battles, campaigns and generalship are replaced here by a broad introduction to current debates among historians about the nature of 'total war' and its effect on social change. This puts the focus of the essay directly on the second and the fourth of our themes. Beckett begins by charting the way in which the study of war had changed over the previous thirty years; before the 1960s war was generally conceived as having a negative or retarding impact on social development. It might be noted as illustrative of this point how many history courses, and how many history books, used peace treaties as their opening paragraphs and wars as their full stops. But increasingly from the 1960s, war, in Beckett's words, has been perceived 'as a determinant of major social change'. It is flattering to see the prominence given to the History Department of the Open University here, and particularly to one of the editors of this book, but perhaps we should not be too bashful and seek to hide our lights under a bushel.[2] Of course there is a difference between accepting that war can produce major social change and agreeing with each and every analysis of the kind of social change brought about by war; controversy and debate are central to the practice of history. Having described the way in which historical thinking has focused on war, Beckett goes on, in the meat of his essay, to discuss some of the new areas of research and some of the current controversies. He suggests that, while the scale and impact of twentieth-century total wars are new, yet these wars are, in many respects, a natural progression from earlier conflicts. What is central to the new studies of war and society is the insistence that war, however appalling, cannot be considered purely in terms of disaster. Beckett notes some of the research which indicates that, in some places, war led to increased living standards and decreases in infant and maternal mortality. The demands of twentieth-century wartime economies have produced changes within the labour forces of the combatant states: often more women have been employed; trade unions have increased their bargaining powers; but, at the same time, skilled labour has found itself diluted. All of these are issues which are touched on again in some of the essays that follow in this volume. Finally, Beckett provides a word of warning about some of the shibboleths which have emerged from the two world wars: the 'war generation' and the 'people's war' are both evocative terms utilized by politicians and adopted, at times rather uncritically, by historians, but what do they really mean when analysed?

The second reading in the volume is extracted from Professor Arno Mayer's challenging monograph *The Persistence of the Old Regime*, a work conceived as 'a Marxist history from the top down . . . with the focus on the upper rather than the lower classes'.[3] The extracts included here touch on almost all of our themes, but primarily we have included them for the way that they address the nature of social change in Europe before the First World War, and thus lay the bases for an assessment of the effects of the war. Mayer believes that the two world wars of 1914–18 and 1939–45 are best understood as 'The Thirty Years' War of the general crisis of the twentieth century' (p. 42); it was only as a result of these wars that the old order reconstituted itself in 1918. This is asserted rather than discussed in relation to the evidence, and a later chapter in this collection offers a very different interpretation. Central to the argument of this book is Mayer's insistence that historians have concentrated too much on the modernizing elements within European society before 1914 and have consistently ignored the strength of the pre-industrial, pre-bourgeois order which constitutes his 'old regime'. While considerable historical research has concentrated on tracing industrialization in nineteenth-century Europe and on charting the growth of an industrial and financial bourgeoisie, Mayer points out that the European economies of 1914 were grounded in petty commerce, consumer manufacture and, above all, in labour-intensive agriculture. Moreover it was landownership which provided most of the wealth, and landowners, drawn predominantly from old-regime families, who dominated society and the organs of government. Far from challenging the cohesive and self-confident old regimes, the rising bourgeoisies were divided among themselves and the most successful individuals among them generally sought to emulate their social superiors or to worm their way into their ranks. Of course there were national differences: France had abolished her monarchy; and Britain was exceptional in not having the largest proportion of her labour force engaged in the agricultural sector of the economy. There were also regional differences, with varieties of constitutional monarchy in Britain and Italy contrasting with the rigid, absolutist monarchies of eastern and central Europe. Yet the underlying structures, Mayer insists, were the same; even in the realms of art, the avant-garde and various modernist movements 'were effectively bridled and isolated' by the cultural establishments which both leaned on and propped up the old regime.

Mayer's work falls within the *nomothetic* approach which we outlined above, and he believes that 'no comprehensive historical vision is possible without recourse to organizing generalizations and principles'.[4] The inclusion of these extracts thus relates as much to the fifth as to the first of our themes, while the concluding pages address directly the causes of war – our third theme. It is a pity that Mayer chose to eschew footnotes and references in the book, yet to employ so many apparent quotations; nevertheless, he writes with considerable rhetorical power and he deploys formidable knowledge in describing both Europe on the eve of the First World War and the forces operating within it both for and against social change. Yet even the most brilliant works of history, however good at setting a scene and persuasive in argument, need to be approached with caution. The view that Mayer puts forward about the persistence of the old regime has already been proposed by others, though generally within the context of a single national experience and without his authoritative and comparative sweep of the whole continent including Britain[5] – and as a Scot and an Englishman we feel duty bound to criticize his use of 'England' in place of 'Britain'. The principal problem with the book is that, writing a 'Marxist history', Mayer understands classes as essentially factors of production, and while this is a perfectly respectable stance both within, and outside of, a Marxian tradition, it leads him to persist in describing aristocracy and bourgeoisie as inherently separate classes, even when discussing the interpenetration between them, as for example on p. 44 and especially on p. 45. It also leads him, from time to time, to address what the European bourgeoisies ought to have done in fulfilling some predestined historical role, and, at one point he writes of their impairing 'their own class formation and class consciousness', and again on p. 46 where he implies that the leaders of the class should have done something other than line up with the nobility. Similarly, towards the end of the extracts, he seems to be addressing culture as something linked directly to class, a view which is challenged in the third chapter here.

The third essay, 'The Birth of the Modern: 1885–1914' by G. D. Josipovici, may seem an eccentric choice in at least two respects. First, with regard to the period covered: while, as the title makes clear, the essay delves far back into the nineteenth century, it terminates in 1914 and thus does not even touch upon either of the two world wars. Second, since it is exclusively concerned with trends in high art (in particular, poetry, music and painting), it may seem very remote from the central concerns of the student of history. There is possibly a third oddity in that the essay is reprinted from a collection entitled *French Literature and its Background*. Let us take these three points in reverse order. First of all, although Josipovici was providing background for a book on French literature, in fact he covers the whole of Europe. The arts are international: even if one were to be so parochial as to wish to study only British high culture, one would still have to discuss the Europe-wide antecedents of modernism. This is exactly what Josipovici does. On the second point, the riposte is simple: if we are to have a full understanding of the development of Europe in the twentieth century, we must have a grasp of the main lines of cultural change. There are various ways in which one evaluates a society, or a continent: by its political institutions, by its economic achievements, for instance; but not least is the evaluation of its products in the realms of high art. If we are to assess the significance of the two world wars, we must make an assessment of their effects on culture. This takes us back to the first point. If we are to assess the influences of war, we must, as has already been said, have a clear understanding of the base-line. In the textbooks you will find all kinds of sweeping statements about war poets, war novelists, Nielsen's 'Inextinguishable' Symphony, Elgar's Cello Concerto, Britten's 'War Requiem', German Expressionism as it developed immediately after the First World War, and so on; but we cannot pin down the influences of war (if any) until we know how the arts were developing in the period before the war. In a nutshell, modernism, the key movement in the arts in the twentieth century, was not initiated by the First World War. This, with rigour and clarity, is explained by Josipovici. That is why his contribution is so important to the study of war, peace and social change. It is, let this be admitted frankly, only a preliminary to the studies with which we are concerned: but angels get the preliminaries sorted out first, while fools rush in regardless.

The central sentence with regard to our concerns (in this case, the fourth theme, the consequences of war) occurs on the second page of Josopovici's chapter (p. 57):

Although the First World War effectively marks the break between the world of the nineteenth century and our own – both in the minds of those who lived through it and of those of us who read about it in the history books – the modern revolution in the arts did not take place during the war or immediately after it, but a decade or so before it.

But that is not the end of it. Historical writing should be a dialogue between reader and historian. Josipovici makes his case most efficiently. Unlike many writers, he sets up a clear question (in his second sentence, devoting the rest of the essay to answering it):

What are the specific features of the [modern] movement, and how are we to account for its emergence?

We as readers may well feel bound to accept Josipovici's account, but while it would be difficult to argue that the modern movement in the arts was created by the First World War, that does not mean that, within the framework set by modernism, it is not possible to tease out specific developments affected by the war. To do this, of course, we would have to turn both to primary sources (artistic works and contextual documents relating to them) and to secondary authorities dealing with the effects of the war. Many such secondary authorities have indeed suggested that the First World War was so catastrophic, so disillusioning for humanitarian liberals believing in the inevitability of human progress, that it had a 'scorching' effect on intellectuals and artists; the American literary critic Paul Fussel has stressed how the tragic irony of the First World War entered into literary consciousness.[6] All this needs further study far beyond the scope of this collection; but – and this is the point – any such study needs to be conceived within an analysis of modernism such as that provided by Josipovici.

Josipovici's analysis, readers will surely not be surprised to learn, is far from uncontroversial. Josipovici does not fall into the *nomothetic*, more theoretical, or, to look the matter in the eye, the Marxist tradition. What he does do is exemplify certain methodological points which readers, whatever tradition they favour, should grasp to their bosoms. Ponder over Josipovici's second paragraph: he fully admits that there is no specific thing called 'modernity', yet through setting up a 'frame of reference' it is possible to identify something important which quite appropriately can be called 'modernism', even if it is something as much reacted against as accepted (third paragraph), even if individual exponents of modernism loathed, or ignored, or never knew, each other (p. 63). When Josipovici speaks of being wary 'of too facile an identification of art with the culture and society out of which it springs', the implicit criticism is of certain Marxist writers: he emphasizes the unchanging *forms* of art – very important again if we are to make a genuine assessment of the influences of war on the arts.

The importance of Chapter 3 in this collection, then, is that it provides a basic understanding of the nature of modernism in the arts against which one can assess the influences of the two world wars, and also that it offers some general reflections on the relationship between the arts and society, helpful also for this particular endeavour. It is in the context of these two points that, first, some comments on Josipovici's text will be made; the discussion will be concluded with some further general points on the relationship between total war and the arts. Essentially what Josipovici is arguing is that modernism is both a *development* of Romanticism, and a *reaction against* certain aspects of latter-day, or decadent, Romanticism. Thus, of course, he has to say quite a deal about Romanticism, and particularly its later forms. To develop his arguments about late Romanticism he, very properly, quotes in the original French from some key primary sources: you may not find the translations we have inserted particularly clear, but, read on – the confused expression of these utterances is exactly the point Josipovici is about to make. As a reaction against Romanticism (p. 64), and indeed a reaction against four centuries of western artistic tradition (p. 65) modernism stresses the *limitations* of the arts. In summary:

1 Art is simply itself, not a key to the universe – brush-strokes on a canvas, notes played in certain combinations, etc. (p. 63).
2 Art is 'a pair of spectacles' helping us to see things in a different way from the lazy, unthinking, habitual way in which we see them – it 'makes the spectator work' (p. 65).
3 Art no longer claims to be 'magical', but simply represents itself as a 'game' with its own rules (p. 66).
4 While art is recognized as being supremely important, it is recognized that it is helpless to change the world – this is all part of a 'modest' retreat from the exaggerated claims for art made by the Romantics (p. 68).

Furthermore:

5 Modern art breaks with a long tradition in which art had simply attempted imitation (or, to use a posh word, *mimesis* – a most important point taken up by Paul Fussel in his study of literature and the First World War). Thus there tends to be a break with the anecdotal tradition.

Some of the later Romantics believed that music somehow had a freedom which language did not have. Josipovici makes a valuable point on p. 61 when he remarks that 'music is nearly as conventional as speech': when discussing the relationship between society, wars, revolutions, etc. and the arts, it is always important to consider the particular 'languages' of the different arts. Josipovici brings out the long-term significance of modernism (which extends far beyond the chronological framework of our own studies) when he says it is 'first and foremost a rethinking of the whole field of aesthetics as it had been seen in the West since the time of Plato and Aristotle' (p. 69). If that seems a little removed from the concerns of the student of history, consider what Josipovici says on p. 62 where he speaks of 'the connection between decadent Romanticism and the rise of totalitarianism'. Josipovici is referring to Stalin's Russia, Hitler's Germany, and Mussolini's Italy. He is pointing to another element; certainly it is true that the 'totalitarian' regimes were very hostile to modernism. One cannot refrain from commenting that Josipovici is grossly unfair to Wagner: however it remains a legitimate question whether there is a link between Romantic mysticism, the exploration of ancient folk legends, central to many of the operas of Wagner, and the mystique of Hitler's Nazi philosophy.

On p. 62 there is a highly quotable, though fictional, phrase which captures the essence of the decadent, and rather arrogant Romanticism of some elements in upper-crust society at the end of the nineteenth century – 'as for living [as distinct from experiencing art], our servants can do that for us'. Could such an attitude persist after the First World War? After the Second World War? On p. 70 Josipovici refers to the pessimism of the twentieth-century artist (however much he may hark back to the wit of the eighteenth century). A major question which Josipovici doesn't go into is whether, in so far as artists show a sensitivity to horror, violence, and evil, this is a reaction to general developments in the twentieth century, rather than just to war: a question that has to be asked is whether artists respond directly to the evil of war, or whether they simply see war as part of a wider evil characteristic of the twentieth century as a whole. Perhaps the greatest literary parable of German history in the twentieth century is Günther Grass's *The Tin Drum* (1959). Is the Second World War central, or is it simply a facet of the whole nightmare of twentieth-century German history? If one is to analyse the relationship between war, peace, and social change, that is the sort of issue one must pin down. Although, as noted, the dates appended to Josipovici's title confine the essay to the period before the First World War, he does in fact refer to later writers: Joyce and Proust, whose great works straddled the First World War, Virginia Woolf, whose main works came in the aftermath of the First World War, Robbe-Grillet, one of the pioneers of the 'new novel' of the 1950s and 1960s, Picasso, at work all through the horrors of the twentieth century, and Francis Bacon, whose international successes as a British artist came only after the Second World War. (Can it be, perhaps, that while wars do not affect artistic styles, they may help to make 'modern' styles acceptable to a wider audience? Is it true that the Second World War – the 'people's war' – brought a reaction away from modernism towards realism?) Josipovici also refers on his first page to Stravinsky, and on his last to the Russian Ballet: reminders again that modernism in music had hit Paris some years before the First World War broke out. At the end of the essay, Josipovici identifies Paris as a uniquely important cultural centre, different, it would seem, from London, or Berlin, or Vienna, or Rome (a later essay mentions the significance of Leningrad). Occupied Paris in the Second World War was the setting for the very close interpenetration between war and culture represented in the poems of Louis Aragon and the short novel by 'Vercors', *Le Silence de la mer* [*The Silence of the Sea*].[7] Cultural studies, indeed, keep bringing us back to historical 'reality' as more conventionally understood.

The origins and immediate causes of the First World War have long exercised a fascination for historians, both those who relish the detailed scrutiny of diplomatic and military decision-making, and those who, like Arno Mayer, focus on long-term structural trends. German guilt was written into the Treaty of Versailles, and was raised again after the Second World War most notably in the work of the German scholar Fritz Fischer. Fischer's book, *Griff nach der Weltmacht*, translated into English as *Germany's Aims in the First World War*, created a storm in Germany, arguing that the Wilhelmine Empire, a new nation with a burgeoning economy, was prepared to risk war in order to establish herself as a world power on a level with much older established powers like Britain and France.[8] In the pursuit of this aim the Kaiser and his advisers encouraged Austria-Hungary to take a strong line against Serbia, fully conscious that this could lead to war. Indeed, according to Fischer, rather than seeking to alleviate the tensions, the government in Berlin impeded last-minute attempts at mediation. The fourth essay in this collection, by Samuel R. Williamson Jr., adopts a different, broader perspective. Williamson is conscious of the 'bombastic behaviour' of much of German foreign policy under Wilhelm II from the closing years of the nineteenth century, and of the German army's 'simple, dangerous and exceptionally mechanical' war plans. But he is far more liberal in the way that he apportions blame. Williamson chronicles a succession of incidents and diplomatic decisions throughout the July crisis of 1914 stressing how, at almost any moment, a different decision or another response might have brought a different outcome. The system of alliances which, like German bombast, has been credited with increasing anxieties and tensions in the decade before the war, restricted the decisions that governments could take. Yet the alliances could show themselves to be feeble, and the crisis of 1914 was not especially different from those that had preceded it, except in its outcome. A final point emerges almost tangentially from Williamson's account: the outbreak of war in 1914 has tended to overshadow subsequent perceptions of that summer, yet there were issues other than the assassination of a Habsburg Archduke which seemed closer to home and which created anxiety or excited fascination – the British, for example, looked anxiously towards trouble brewing in Ireland, while the French were preoccupied with the scandal surrounding Madame Caillaux's trial for murder.

Chapter 5, 'Italian Peasant Women and the First World War' by Anna Bravo, fits firmly into our fourth theme, the consequences of war. Indeed, the argument over whether or not twentieth-century wars have, or have not, resulted in improvements in the conditions and status of women is one of the most intense in the whole area of war and society studies. With regard to our fifth, historiographical, theme, Bravo's essay is also important as an example of the feminist influence on historical writing (in her very first paragraph she announces a general theme, 'the relationship between women's conditions and external historical moments – between women's history and "great" history') and, also very important, as an example of a very effective use of 'oral history'. If you turn to the notes, you will see that apart from the very few references to secondary sources, this essay is entirely based on the oral accounts of women interviewed by the author and her collaborator; the account given in note 1 should be read carefully. At first sight it seems almost astonishing that this method could be employed for events as remote as the First World War and, of course, from the dates of birth given in the notes we can see that the women interviewed were very old. It is a fact encountered in research of this type that elderly women tend to be much more coherent in recounting their memories than men of similar age. Certainly the quotations cited in the text seem very clear and offer convincing testimony to the value of the oral approach. The fundamental consideration is that for this particular sort of topic – dealing with the poor, who leave few written sources – very little other evidence exists.

In general (though, of course, the complete picture is more complex and nuanced than that) feminist writers have tended to contest the thesis that wars bring opportunities and gains for women: overall, understandably enough, feminist writers have been concerned to stress the continuing sub-jugation of women, to argue that the main trend in wartime was the further exploitation of women in the interest of the war effort, that hard manual work for women was nothing new, and that even if there were some changes during the war, these were always short-lived. Where women have made gains, these are usually attributed by feminists to the activities of politically conscious women's movements (the suffragettes, for instance) or to longer-term economic and technological changes which were in any case drawing women into new forms of employment. As is often the case with carefully argued and well-documented pieces of historical writing, Anna Bravo's essay does not point conclusively in one direction or the other. She speaks boldly in the opening paragraphs of 'the transformation of women's social con-ditions in the countryside during the First World War' and of the war appear-ing 'as a moment of primary importance', and she certainly demonstrates conclusively that women did take on new tasks and new responsibilities. With regard to long-term effects she seems to be indicating that while many changes were temporary, some were permanent, while there were perhaps also losses. Bravo speaks of a growth in 'self-realization' and here fixes on a point which other writers, both feminist and non-feminist, have agreed to be important, the change in 'mentalities', the way in which women gained in self-confidence because of their war experience. The answer Bravo seems to be giving is that outside of their community, in dealing with state officials in par-ticular, the role of women did expand permanently, but that within the com-munity they were 'forced back into traditional peasant silence'. Read the article very carefully, try to let the evidence of the women themselves speak directly to you, and decide which side of this equation presented by Bravo carries the greater weight. You will need, of course, to set this study within the wider context where, for instance, Italian women, unlike those in many other European countries, did not gain the vote at the end of the war. You might wish to ask how far the forces of traditional Catholicism served in Italy to hold back progress which women elsewhere were beginning to make.

Chapter 6, 'Demobilization and Labour' from *Germany After the First World War*, unlike Chapters 3, 4 and 5, is not a self-standing, self-contained essay, but like Chapter 2 has been extracted from a substantial book, Richard Bessel's celebrated study, based on massive original research, *Germany After the First World War*, published in 1993. We have printed about half of his Chapter 5, 'Demobilization and Labour'. The main focus of the chapter is on the relatively successful way in which demobilization, in all the circum-stances, was carried out. Clearly we are here concerned with the fourth theme, the consequences of war; and, much more indirectly, the second theme, the relationship of war to revolution and, within that, the nature of the revolution as it actually took place in Germany. The overall conclusion is that the consequences of the war were very severe for the German people, the negative effects far outweighing any positive ones. Bessel brings out very well that for both male workers, and some female ones, there were some direct positive effects of the war; but then when we take into account the great hyper-inflation and industrial depression and unemployment (which we have to account as, at the very least, indirect consequences of the war) these gains were swept away. Bessel sets out for you very clearly seven reasons for the relative success of demobilization, and these points, which you should note very carefully, form a kind of framework for much of the rest of the chapter. We are going to pick out points made with regard to labour organization and conditions and then, in turn, look at social policy in regard to unemployment, changes in attitudes and values, the position of women, the position of white-collar workers, and then, finally, the general question of wages.

Trade union membership declined during the First World War, but then had reached double its pre-war level by the end of March 1919. Bessel twice mentions the crucial agreement concluded in November 1918 between Hugo Stinnes, leader of the employers, and Carl Legine, a Social Democrat deputy in the *Reichstag* and chairman of the General Commission of Trade Unions, which recognized the unions as collective bargaining partners. It also, we learn later, established the eight-hour working day, 'the most significant achievement of the labour movement in 1918', according to Bessel. The union bureaucracy greatly expanded and (more important) trade union leaders became active participants in various kinds of tribunals and in local and regional legislatures. Bessel explains the motivations of the employers as basically to curry favour with the government and to strengthen moderate labour leaders against the threat of revolution.

The government both instituted unemployment relief (to the cost of which the central government contributed one half, the state governments one third and the local councils one sixth) and directly intervened in relations between employers and employees to protect men's jobs. Bessel says of Employment Relief that, despite its later collapse under the heavy pressure of depression, 'it marked a major turning point'. Of government intervention to maintain employment he says: 'This marked a major new incursion of the state into the workings of the labour market'. With regard to changed attitudes and values, Bessel speaks of a 'relaxation of the old authoritarian system and the patterns of discipline and deference which it had sustained'. With regard to women workers the situation fluctuated greatly. Both at the end of the war, and later, there was great pressure for women in employment to give way to men. But in the period of full employment during 1920–21 there were jobs for women (as for young people and, above all, skilled workers). Bessel makes an important point, which echoes what happened in other countries, where women who had escaped from domestic service during the war were very reluctant to return to it: 'the wartime experience . . . had changed the ideas of many women about the sorts of work they were willing to accept'. While at least some opportunities had opened up for women, we learn that generally prospects for white-collar workers were not good in the years after the war. Finally, in looking at one of the best indicators of losses and gains, real wages, it is salutary to note that even in the boom of 1919–20 wages rose to only within 10 per cent of pre-war levels (this contrasts very sharply with the British experience). Nonetheless the combination of the need for labour, and the fear of revolution, did work in favour of the workers, and Bessel borrows from the famous US expert Gerald Feldman the phrase 'bribery through wage concessions'. In the end, though, we have to keep uppermost in our minds the concluding words from the extracts of the chapter which we have printed. By the end of March 1924, 'the labour market was in retreat, real wages were substantially below pre-war levels, and unemployment was at dizzying heights'.

Like Arno Mayer, Professor Charles Maier (Chapter 7) believes that the social hierarchies of twentieth-century Europe have proved to be remarkably tenacious. But Maier is concerned with a 'twentieth-century capitalist order' which is very different from the old order based on landholding discussed by Mayer. Maier defines the conservatives who wrested security from disorder in the aftermath of the First World War as 'bourgeois', and, again in contrast to Mayer, he stresses how, during the nineteenth century, these bourgeois had achieved social rights and a close association with the old elite. European society in 1914 was, according to Maier, essentially bourgeois – and he gives a careful discussion of the relevance and meaning of the word. In the aftermath of the war this bourgeois society was not restored, as some had hoped, but recast in a mould which owed much to the pressures of war. Like Mayer, Maier deploys and advances a broad conceptual framework, but while Arno Mayer claims to be writing a form of Marxist history, Charles Maier's angle of vision might best be labelled as Weberian. The focus of Maier's *Recasting Bourgeois Europe* – a book based on enormous and highly original pioneering work in primary archives published, note carefully, in 1975 – is on France, Germany and Italy; the extracts we print, drawn from the introduction also contain a few references to Britain and the USA. For our purpose, the extracts included here are of particular relevance to the fourth theme, the consequences of war, yet Maier's discussion also raises issues about the general pattern of social change and broad historical conceptualization, our first and fifth themes. Maier argues that the pressures of war in Europe led to an integration of organized labour into state-supervised bargaining systems and to an erosion of the distinction between the private and the public sectors, a process he describes as corporatism. The idea of corporatism has also been deployed by British historian Keith Middlemas with reference to the development of twentieth-century British society; according to Middlemas, as a result of the First World War 'what had been merely interest groups [trade unions and employer associations] crossed the political threshold and became part of the extended state'.[9] Maier's new corporatism, similarly, did not come to an end with the war but continued to develop after it; as a consequence, he argues, during the 1920s, parliaments declined in power and authority and the nature of representative government altered. In the first half of the decade the prime object of Maier's bourgeois forces was to keep the socialists out of power; at the same time they transformed the principles of class division, making social consensus more possible. Nazism and Fascism, in Maier's view, were the responses of extreme radicals of the right to the corporatist collaboration of industry and organized labour; but the forms of these responses differed in Germany and Italy as a result of their different social and economic structures. France escaped a similar fate partly because she had a less developed corporate structure and thus experienced a less serious challenge from the radical right.

Again, as with Arno Mayer's book, we are confronted by a text written with tremendous force and erudition, but which contains certain basic assumptions that are not universally accepted. Most notably, the whole of Maier's analysis is based on a Weberian conception of 'emerging structures of power', and he uses the word 'corporatism' explicitly in the Weberian style of an 'ideal type' against which events in France, Germany and Italy can be assessed, rather than as an actual description. Even though the word has been used by Feldman[10] and Middlemas in similar contexts, this is not the only way to approach interrelationships between the state and interest groups such as trade unions and employers' associations in the period of the First World War and its aftermath. Moreover, while Maier believes that corporatism was less advanced in France than in Germany and Italy, many historians would challenge the extent of 'a decay of parliamentary influence' in post-war France, and even more in post-war Britain. Might not Maier's 'relative backwardness in terms of corporate organization' be another man's effective pluralism? Might not the more empirical historian replace Maier's notions of rescuing bourgeois Europe through recasting with the simple recognition that societies had to be reorganized for peace after five years of total war? Going back to 1914 was impossible; the empiricist, searching in vain for monolithic social classes, might argue that pragmatism and the various pressures on different governments and administrations meant simply that some wartime practices were kept and others discarded.

In the eighth essay Norman Rich begins with a devastating attack on A. J. P. Taylor's *The Origins of the Second World War*, first published in 1961.[11] This was the same year as Fischer's *Griff nach der Weltmacht*, and Taylor's book created something of a similar furore. Taylor insisted that the war was not brought about by megalomania on Hitler's part; Hitler was an opportunist politician simply following the traditional line of foreign policy pursued by German statesmen, and in 1939 he miscalculated the response of the British and French to his Polish adventure. The work of Fischer and Taylor suggests a continuity in German expansionist foreign policy within Europe, and they have both been criticized for this. But Taylor's book was largely a reworking of well-known sources rather than a study based on the kind of detailed archival research undertaken by Fischer, and while Taylor had, in an earlier book,[12] traced a pattern in a united Germany that was dangerous for European peace he did not detail any precise links between Hitler, Bismarck, Kaiser Wilhelm and his advisers in *The Origins*. Rich is especially critical of Taylor's description of Hitler as both a typical German politician in his foreign policy and an opportunist. While it is wrong to think that Hitler had a blueprint and a precise timetable for his actions, and while it is right to emphasize the accidental and improvised nature of the execution of Nazi foreign policy, neither of these mean that Hitler had no policies and no intentions. In the second half of the essay, Rich provides a concise survey of the main interpretations and debates over Hitler's foreign policy, ranging from those who argue over the extent to which this policy was rooted in the German historical experience, to those who debate the role of domestic problems in formulating Nazi policy abroad – the latter has been especially popular with Marxist historians who have seen the causes of war as fundamentally economic even if the economic aspects enter the picture in a mediated form. In conclusion Rich draws on the work of the German historian Eberhard Jäckel, to portray Hitler as a man who had a very precise list of objectives and priorities in foreign affairs; but Rich parts company with Jäckel where the latter implies that Hitler was continuing a long-standing tendency in German history, on the grounds that this effectively denies the significance of both individuals and accidents.

Richard Overy's essay, 'Hitler's War and the German Economy: A Reinterpretation' (Chapter 9), focuses on Nazi preparations for war from an economic perspective; and perhaps it should be stressed at the outset that this is, of course, very different from seeing the fundamental cause of the war as economic.[13] Ian Beckett stresses that control of the economy 'lies at the heart of the concept of total war' and he notes the controversy over when, and the extent to which, the economy of Nazi Germany was organized for war. The essay by Overy is his first reappraisal of the notion of the *Blitzkrieg* economy developed by economic historians who have suggested that, until 1942, Germany was organized only for *Blitzkrieg* wars, having built up armaments in breadth rather than in depth. Like most historians challenging an orthodoxy Overy does tend to make his target appear rather less substantial than it was: Alan Milward's original research in this area was both pioneering and persuasive;[14] moreover it should be noted that Mark Roseman's essay later in this volume largely accepts the *Blitzkrieg* thesis. Overy confronts the thesis with a detailed analysis of German economic life between 1936 and 1942. Along with the other critics of Taylor, Overy considers that Hitler was planning a large-scale war of conquest, and while the Führer may have had only a weak grasp of the facts of economic life, nevertheless both he and his subordinates were contemplating a war which would last a long while and which would require a massive economic effort directed by the state – from the beginning they were thinking in terms of 'total war', and they had a model in the experience of the First World War. Overy shows that Germany was spending enormous sums on armaments before 1941, that the workforce employed on military projects increased from 20 per cent of the total in 1939 to 60 per cent in 1941, and that as early as 1937–8 a large state-owned and state-operated industrial structure was being built up. There were problems in all of this: Goering was incapable of the task of supervising the organization for war, and civilian and military economic leaders disliked having to work under him, and went out of their way to avoid his jurisdiction; much of the expenditure had to be used for rebuilding the military infrastructure; there was conservatism among both workers and employers militating against necessary changes; and the German military insisted on the highest quality of equipment when something cheaper, quicker and easier to produce would probably have served. But perhaps most significantly, the economic preparations for war were out of step with the events of foreign policy: Hitler was planning his big war for some time in the 1940s; he did not expect that his adventure in Poland would be the cause of war against Britain and France.

War, whether it be 'limited' or 'total', involves killing people. Indeed, one social historian has recently gone so far as to write a long, well received book specifically designed to put the killing back into the history of war and to emphasize that, even the soldiers caught up in the slaughter of the Western Front between 1914 and 1918 should not be considered always simply as victims.[15] During the Second World War there was, in the Holocaust, an example of killing on an unprecedented scale with industrial means deployed for genocidal ends and with victims who were not in any way soldiers on the other side. Christopher Browning's 'One Day in Jósefów' (Chapter 10) describes the mass murder of around 1500 Jews – women, children and elderly – by the men of Reserve Police Battalion 101 on 13 July 1942. This was not the mechanized or industrial killing of the Auschwitz crematoria, but close range, often very clumsy and messy killing with rifles. How could such ordinary, generally middle-aged men, from one of the least Nazified cities in Germany, cold-bloodedly shoot so many defenceless people? What happened to the men who either refused the 'duty', or who became so revolted after the first shots that they were unable to continue? Browning's chapter is based on the judicial investigations carried out in post-war Germany, some twenty years after the events described. His account and conclusions are chilling, and suggest how men, especially perhaps men in uniform, will yield to human weakness when under orders, and when they feel the need to stand by their comrades and/or conform with their peer group.

The title of Chapter 11, 'The Effects of World War II on French Society and Politics' by Stanley Hoffmann, firmly places it in the fourth theme. In fact, since the article both discusses the nature of French society as it had developed by the 1930s, what Hoffmann calls the 'Republican synthesis', and looks in detail at developments between 1934 and 1940, it also belongs to our first theme of general social change. All in all, Hoffmann's piece is a good example of the methodological principle which argues that you cannot properly assess the effects of a war on a particular society without first defining the nature of that society and the processes of change already at work in it, before the war. Many academics, including quite a proportion of those who deny any connection between war and social change, stress the influence of politics: at its simplest, a left-wing government will introduce social change, a conservative one will tend to resist it. Hoffmann's paper, delivered as long ago as April 1960, was genuinely casting new light on events in France when, instead of making a rigid distinction between the right-wing Vichy regime installed in France by the Germans between 1940 and 1944, and the Liberation regime which came into power in the final stages of the war, and to which, traditionally, all the major social changes associated with the war were attributed, Hoffmann suggested some continuity as between the two regimes. Thus, though this was not his deliberate intention, he was directing attention away from guided political action, and focusing on war itself as a complex experience which tends to bring about social change whatever the deliberate intentions of politicians. Hoffmann (an American, like so many of our authors) was a political scientist as well as a historian much interested in developments in contemporary French politics, particularly at a time when the Fifth Republic under De Gaulle had just come into existence (in this reprint of his paper some of the detailed political material has been omitted).

The paper is not based on detailed historical research, though Hoffmann was able to draw upon his own considerable expertise as well as on the mainly secondary sources cited in the footnotes: his paper, as he says at the beginning, consists of 'a number of hypotheses' which 'need further study and qualification'. The article, then, presents many generalizations, sometimes in the form of quite striking metaphors. Yet it does not reflect the sociological or nomothetic tradition in the way that, say, Maier does: Hoffmann explicitly disavows attributing a 'revolutionary tradition' to the French workers, preferring what he calls the clumsy but more accurate expression, a 'tradition of non-cooperation'. Hoffmann makes few value judgements, and clearly does not see the advance of the working class as something which 'ought' to happen; he simply records, as he sees them, the consequences, often unintended, of the actions of politicians of different persuasions.

In the first numbered section of the chapter (pp. 177–80) Hoffmann provides a very useful summary of what he terms the Republican synthesis. The first paragraph contains a good brief explanation of the nature of class in France (and one which could well also be applied to Britain at this time). While one could at times challenge the way in which Hoffmann summarizes quite complex material, he does give a persuasive view of how France, with the working class effectively excluded from the mainstream of French life, was both a contented and a 'stalemate' society (the main influence of the First World War, he suggests, had been to foster complacency). The second section discusses the 'destruction of the Republican synthesis' in the period 1934–40. Now, almost certainly, Hoffmann makes too rigid a break at 1934; he also underestimates the amount of economic progress which, recent research has shown, was being made in France during both the 1920s and the 1930s. It may be that he exaggerates the forces of change in the 1930s, and thus overall underestimates the significance of the Second World War; or it may be that in underestimating developments throughout the inter-war period he actually ends up exaggerating the effects of the Second World War. These are propositions that could be evaluated only in the light of a good deal of further reading. Here what it is important to concentrate on is the way in which Hoffmann brings out how developments under Vichy (which many in the past had considered purely regressive, and 'corporatist' – here is that concept again, though Hoffmann only once refers to 'Vichy corporatism') formed the basis for social advances under the Liberation. The interconnections are often complex, and it is worth spending time working carefully through Hoffmann's arguments; one does, it could be maintained, get quite a strong impression of the various accidents and necessities of war being more important than the deliberate decisions of politicians. The general conclusion Hoffmann presents is of a France more dynamic and more united after the Second World War than it had been previously, though he does not really go into much detail. In assessing society at the end of the war, Hoffmann speaks of 'both major innovations and a few sharp limits'; he spends some time going into these limits, particularly as he sees it, the continuing isolation of the French working class. That an independent French working class has continued to exist has been demonstrated in many social surveys; but arguably Hoffmann, perhaps because he happened to be writing in the aftermath of De Gaulle's 1959 victory, exaggerates the isolation of the working class and its distance from the rest of French society. Two critical points that really do have to be made about post-war France are the granting, for the first time, of votes for women, and the development of advanced social insurance, medical and other welfare services.[16]

In contrast to the sweeping hypotheses of Hoffmann's article, Penny Summerfield in Chapter 12, 'The "Levelling of Class" ', builds up a meticulous analysis from detailed statistical sources. Summerfield's article, indeed, is a model example of the rigorous and relentless development of historical arguments, carefully considering at each stage the cases which have been put forward in support of there having been changes in the condition of the British working class brought about by the war, then with clarity and thoroughness exposing the weaknesses in these cases. This chapter, then, is firmly related to the fourth theme, the social consequences of war, and, with respect to the particular instance of the position of the working class in Britain, is very strongly arguing against the thesis that war helps to bring about social change. It may be noted that the phrase 'levelling' is an unsatisfactory one, often used in a vague way. Summerfield is certainly right that classes were not levelled, which would imply class distinctions being removed altogether (this did not happen anywhere, apart from the countries that fell under Russian Communist influence, and even what happened there is open to some debate). The debate with regard to class in Britain (and indeed in France, Italy and Germany) centres on whether or not, given that the basic framework of the class structure remained the same, there were significant changes in the relationships between classes and attitudes about class. Although Summerfield's article is basically an empirical study without anything in the way of sociological theorizing, her basic definitions of class are essentially the economic ones derived from Marxism. As with most studies in that tradition, she is concerned solely with the relations between working class and middle class and does not consider the possibility of there being a significant distinction between a middle class on one side, and an upper class on the other. In fact, she finds herself in contention with the view of class which attempts to integrate the perceptions and images of class which people hold with the realities of differing life-styles and of economic and political inequality, though she dismisses that view somewhat cursorily. Summerfield's article is also distinguished by the great attention she gives to both the earnings of women and the conditions under which they had to support their families during the war: this is a most important dimension which gives a tremendous sense of practical reality to the article, and is entirely in keeping with the fact that Summerfield is one of the pioneering feminist historians in Britain. Overall, it can be said of the article that it is a most effective antidote to those who have romanticized about the war having transformed the British class structure and transformed the position of the working class within it. But it is not by any means the last word on this subject.

Chapter 13 takes us back to our second theme, focusing on the nature of total war – in particular, the devastatingly brutal war launched by Hitler against the Soviet Union; there are also some references to the fourth theme, to the consequences of the war for Russia. The first section details the appalling toll of the war, ending by pointing at the immeasurable significance for the course of the war (and world history) of the eventually successful Soviet resistance. In the second section we learn of the severe impact of rearmament on the civilian economy and living standards, and of the poor quality of both soldiers and their weapons. In the third section we learn of some of the immediate (and largely temporary) transforming effects of the war: informal leadership took over and there were initiatives from below. It is hinted that, under the pressures of war, Stalin eventually learned to act less like a dictator, but in 1941 he remained in brutal control. In the following section we get details of the Soviet Union's 'fantastic' contribution to Allied munitions. Against that was the 'unprecedented expenditure of combat equipment'; then comes one of the key points in the article, vital in assessing the different nature of the different war fronts:

> More than the British and the Americans, the Russians were faced with a war of national extermination. They carried on fighting under conditions in which soldiers of other nations might have given ground; and their losses were correspondingly heavy.

Note that, apart from the unrestrained brutality of the Germans towards the Russians, the *Luftwaffe* used the poor skills of Russian pilots as providing the opportunity of practice for their own inexperienced pilots. Stalin himself, we learn, was completely callous in sending untrained industrial workers to the front to be slaughtered. Equipment was also squandered.

In the fifth section, we are informed of the heavy damage to the economy caused by the acceleration of war production. Decline in industrial production and, in particular agricultural production, was also caused by the loss of territory to the Germans. Yet the civilian economy was absolutely crucial to the continued waging of war. This takes us into a section which gives us a clear sense of some of the main effects on the civilian population, 'mobilised to the maximum extent through universal liability to perform either military or civilian service'. After a period of chaos, new centralized institutional controls were introduced, which were only operating properly at the end of 1942. Food rations, which depended on the function the individual was serving in the war, were extremely meagre, particularly when many of the new war workers had to be recruited from the countryside.

Much special interest attaches to the seventh section on 'National Feeling'. Many ethnic minorities welcomed the Germans, who, however, quickly alienated these potential allies. Harrison several times mentions the particularly appalling conditions suffered during the long siege of Leningrad: 'but civic morale did not crack'. Another of the transforming effects of war is apparent in the way in which the regime softened pre-war policies in order to unify society. The concluding section makes it clear that while 1941 was certainly a key year, things in many ways then got worse for the Russians. What Harrison stresses is the 'huge Soviet civilian sacrifice'. In 1943 there came more rational central organizations, and also massive resources from the USA. One cannot discuss the Second World War without giving detailed attention to the Russian front: Harrison gives us key insights into that most horribly destructive of war theatres.

It is worth noting that Mark Harrison is actually an economist, rather than a historian, teaching at Warwick University, UK, editor of and contributor to *The Economics of World War II: Six Great Powers in International Comparison* (Cambridge University Press, 1998), and joint author with John Barber of *The Soviet Homefront 1941–1945: The Social and Economic History of the USSR in World War II* (Longman, 1991).

Chapter 14 'World War II and Social Change in Germany' by Mark Roseman, concludes this clutch of articles devoted to the controversial question of the social consequences of war. Roseman's article is the only one to be reprinted here from the collection of papers delivered in January 1987 to the Open University Conference on 'Total War and Social Change'. It is in many respects a perfect example of how to go about answering the question presented to the contributors to that conference: 'What if any, social change is brought about by war?' Roseman points out that most of the relevant historical writing concentrates on the Nazi period as a whole, rather than singling out the experience of war. In his pioneering study he points out, first, that great weight must be given to the transformations already carried out by the Nazis in the period (which he wittily defines as one of 'total peace') *before* the war, and to the fact that with German military defeat the shaping of German society was very much influenced by the nature and policies of the occupying powers – Roseman is dealing essentially with West Germany and the influence of the Americans. This actually takes us to one of the major debates within the whole question of the effects of war. Is it perhaps the case that rather than social change developing out of the war experience itself, its character is essentially determined by the geopolitical situation obtaining at the end of the war?

This is the position taken, in particular, by many latter-day Marxists who, conceiving of social change in the very broad manner indicated in the opening sentences of this Introduction, see social structure and social life in one half of Europe as being dominated by Russian Communism, while that in the other half is dominated by Americanization. It may be, indeed, that Roseman's article lends some support to this thesis. However, it is also of great significance for the painstaking way in which it does tease out a number of changes attributed to the war experience itself, of which the new self-confidence engendered in the working class is perhaps the most important.

Our collection ends with an essay specially written for us by Hew Strachan, Britain's leading military historian today, co-founding editor of the journal *War in History*, and Professor of History at Glasgow university. Echoing the title of Chapter 1, Chapter 15 makes an excellent counterpart to it. However, it should be stated right away that this chapter is not related so closely to our themes as the other chapters: it, rather, serves the function of setting your studies in a much wider context, wider both in that it takes a world perspective (rather than the purely European one of our course) and in that it comes practically up to the end of the twentieth century (and also goes back into the nineteenth and even eighteenth centuries), while we end quite sharply in 1955. We would recommend that you read it fairly rapidly before embarking on your studies, and preferably immediately after reading Chapter 1. You will then, during the course, need to pay particular attention to what Strachan says about whether what we tend to call 'total war' might not better be described as 'modern war'.

In the second paragraph, the German word *Sonderweg* means 'special' or 'unique', 'route' or 'way'. Strachan is challenging the view that total war was a special invention of the Germans. In the second sentence of the third paragraph, Strachan, as a military historian, is making a perhaps slightly critical reference to a course such as our own which does feature the 'cultural and political baggage' of total war. Much of what follows is concerned with theories of war, of which the eighteenth-century writer Clausewitz is usually taken as the pioneer, and Strachan introduces Clausewitz's concept of 'absolute war'. Strachan, to repeat, is interested in 'total war' as a military concept – the emphasis is on the *destruction* of the enemy, military *and civilian*, while our emphasis is on the way in which total war *involves* civilians, and in the social changes this brings about.

The chapter begins direct engagement with our subject matter in the middle of p. 260: 'As the twentieth century ended . . .'. The crucial distinction Strachan wants to make is between 'total' war, which, roughly, is absolute or all-out war conducted by whatever means are available, and 'modern' war, which is war using all the devices of industrialized technology. The suggestion, then, is that the two world wars of the twentieth century are better described as 'modern' wars rather than 'total' wars. There were, Strachan says, linking up to some extent with Beckett in Chapter 1, earlier total wars, though they were not necessarily modern wars. Strachan, further, suggests that the elements which give the First World War, and still more the Second World War, qualities of being total, are ideological: they are total to the extent to which they are wars of ideas.

Since this book is focused on what we call the two total wars, it is important that you should be aware of the latest ideas military historians have about the nature of total war. Really, it is a matter of whether you are fundamentally interested in the nature of warfare, including warfare right up to the present, or whether you are interested in the effects of war on society. Our book (and our Open University course) is concerned with a particular period in history, that running from 1914-55; it is not concerned with the way warfare has developed *since* 1955. It makes sense to refer to the two wars which dominated the period of our study as 'total wars', when the emphasis is on the impact on civilians. But it is important that you should have the wider perspective: that is why you have this very rich and challenging article by Hew Strachan.

This Introduction has simply sought to show where the essays which make up this book fit into the broad themes associated with the topic *Total War and Historical Change*. The essays themselves have been chosen for the major contributions they make on these themes, and for the variety of methodological approaches and broad 'philosophies' (Marxist, non-Marxist, feminist, etc.) they present. Our complex topic serves to raise some of the most important problems and debates in the study of twentieth-century European history. Together, the essays which follow offer no simple conclusions, save that of the outstanding importance of the subject itself. These essays must now be left to speak for themselves, the reader always bearing in mind that in reading the work of a historian it does pay to know just a little bit about the attitudes and approaches of that historian. Readers should also remember that the best historians often make important points which may actually fall outside the basic theses which they were intending to present in their writing.

Notes

1 See Arthur Marwick, 'Introducing the course', in A. Marwick and C. Emsley, *Europe in 1914*, Book 1 of *Total War and Social Change*, Milton Keynes, 2001.
2 Perhaps it should be noted here that Arthur Marwick does not speak of a 'model' or 'four dimensions of war' in *The Deluge*, London, 1965, as Beckett maintains. This was a later formulation used in Arthur Marwick, *War and Social Change in the Twentieth Century*, London, 1974, and in the Open University Course, A301, *War and Society*, Milton Keynes, 1973. The most up-to-date statements of Marwick's thinking are to be found in his Introductions to *Total War and Social Change*, London, 1988, and the new edition of his *The Deluge: British Society and the First World War*, London, 1991.
3 Arno J. Mayer, *The Persistence of the Old Regime: Europe and the Great War*, London, 1981, p. x.
4 Ibid.
5 See for example, for England, F. M. L. Thompson, *English Landed Society in the Nineteenth Century*, London, 1963; and for France, Maurice Halbwachs, *Les Classes Sociales*, Paris, 1937.

6 Paul Fussel, *The Great War and Modern Memory* (1975). See also Barry Cadwallader, *Crisis of the European Mind* (1981) and John Cruickshank, *Variations on Catastrophe* (1982).

7 See Arthur Marwick, 'The debate over the impact of World War II: high and popular culture', in C. Emsley, A. Marwick, W. Purdue and A. Aldgate, *World War II*, Book 4 of *War, Peace and Social Change*, Milton Keynes, 1990.

8 Fritz Fischer, *Germany's Aims in the First World War*, London, 1966.

9 Keith Middlemas, *Politics in Industrial Society: The Experience of the British System since 1911*, London, 1979, p. 373.

10 Gerald Feldman, *Army, Industry and Labor in Germany, 1914-1918*, Princeton, NJ, 1966.

11 A. J. P. Taylor, *The Origins of the Second World War*, London, 1961.

12 A. J. P. Taylor, *The Course of German History*, London, 1945.

13 Indeed Overy has subsequently debated vigorously with one of the leading Marxist historians of Nazi Germany over the economic origins of the war. R. J. Overy and T. W. Mason, 'Debate', *Past and Present*, 1989.

14 See especially Alan Milward, *The German Economy at War*, London, 1965.

15 Joanna Bourke, *An Intimate History of Killing: Face-to-Face Killing in Twentieth-Century Warfare*, London, 1999.

16 *Total War and Social Change: Europe 1914-1955*, Book 4, Units 21-5, Milton Keynes, 2001.

CHAPTER 1

Total War

IAN F. W. BECKETT

The historiography of total war

In the past twenty years, historians have come increasingly to recognize the often pivotal role played by war and conflict in historical developments. In the process, the interpretation and understanding of the impact of war upon states, societies and individuals have been transformed. In particular, the concept of 'total war', as applied to the two world wars of the twentieth century, has become a familiar one and a matter for modern historiographical debate. Generally, the term 'total war' is used by historians not only to describe the nature of the world wars but also to differentiate such wars from other conflicts. The study of total war within the context of war studies or studies of war and society is largely a product of the 1960s, but the term itself is older. Ludendorff appears to have used the term first in his memoirs, published in 1919, but it was also employed in a ritualistic fashion during the Second World War. Josef Goebbels, for example, threatened the Western Allies with 'total war' in a celebrated speech in February 1943 and was himself appointed Reich Plenipotentiary for the Mobilization of Total War in July 1944; Winston Churchill also used the phrase in an address to the United States Congress in May 1943. Now, the term has become almost synonymous with the concept of war as a catalyst of far-reaching social change, and it is in precisely that sense that total war is a subject of continuing historical debate.

The American scholar, J. U. Nef, whose *War and Human Progress* was published in 1950,[1] may stand perhaps as representative of an earlier period of historiography, when war was regarded as having a purely negative impact, in so far as it was at all relevant to historical development. However, there were other scholars in the 1950s whose work was suggestive of the future approach to the question of war and social change. Richard Titmuss made a connection in 1950 between the two in his volume, *Problems of Social*

Policy, for the British official history of the Second World War[2] while Stanislas Andrzejewski offered the 'military participation ratio' in 1954,[3] which postulated a firm correlation between the extent of wartime participation by society in the war effort and the amount of subsequent levelling of social inequalities. The English historian, G. N. Clark, also produced during the 1950s a pioneering study of war and society in the seventeenth century,[4] but the real broadening of historical perspectives with regard to what became known as war studies came in the following decade. A comparison of Michael Howard's classic military history of the Franco-Prussian War, published in 1961,[5] with his *War in European History*[6] fifteen years later may serve to indicate the profound historiographical change that occurred.

In the forefront of that change was Arthur Marwick, whose study of British society in the First World War, *The Deluge,*[7] published in 1965, was followed by *Britain in the Century of Total War* in 1968 and *War and Social Change in the Twentieth Century* in 1974.[8] Marwick was not the only historian in the field and the titles of Gordon Wright's *The Ordeal of Total War* in 1968 and Peter Calvocoressi's and Guy Wint's *Total War* in 1972 were also indicative of the new approach.[9] However, it was largely Marwick who established the framework for the study of total war. Four 'modes' put forward in *Britain in the Century of Total War* had become a 'four-tier model' in *War and Social Change in the Twentieth Century,* by which the changes effected by total war might be gauged and compared between different states. Thus, for Marwick, total war implied disruption and destruction on a vast and unprecedented scale; the testing of the existing social and political structures of states and societies; the participation, in the context of the total mobilization of a state's resources, of previously disadvantaged groups in the war effort; and, lastly, a 'colossal psychological experience'. The cumulative effect would be real and enduring social change. The model became familiar to a wide readership through the 'War and Society' course introduced by Marwick and his colleagues at the Open University in the 1970s.[10]

To be fair to Marwick, the model was offered only as a 'rough tool', but it is undeniable that the idea of war as a determinant of major change has had a profound impact during the past decade. Indeed, this concept has been described recently by Michael Bentley as one of the most common 'misapprehensions' in the perception of modern British social history.[11] From the beginning, too, some historians were far more cautious than Marwick in their appraisal of the impact of total war upon society. Examples are Angus Calders *The People's War*[12] – a title itself derived from a British propaganda slogan in the Second World War and echoed in a 1986 television series and accompanying book on Britain at war[13] – which was published in 1969, and Henry Pelling's *Britain in the Second World War,* published two years later.[14] More recently, Brian Bond has described total war as being as great a myth as the idea of total victory or total defeat[15] and, while the debate has continued to be waged within the context of parameters laid down by Marwick, recent and current research has done much to suggest that the social impact of total war in the twentieth century should not be overstated.

The emergence of total war

A preliminary consideration is that the acceptance of the periods between 1914 and 1918 and between 1939 and 1945 as those of total war implies that conflicts prior to the twentieth century were more limited. Traditionally, historians have described the late eighteenth century as a classic era of 'limited war', in which armies were relatively small in size and would manoeuvre with the intention of avoiding rather than engaging in battle. Campaigns would be designed to exhaust an opponent's economy by occupation, in search of strictly limited political and dynastic aims. Societies as a whole would hardly be touched by the impact of war and, indeed, a prevailing bourgeois assumption that military activity was not the destiny of mankind ensured that trade flourished between states at war. Examples usually cited of the normality of social intercourse include Laurence Sterne's visit to Paris during the Seven Years' War (1756-63) and the continuance of the Dover to Calais packet service for a year after France in 1778 had joined the United States in the American War of Independence (1774-83). Closer analysis, however, reveals that war between 1648 and 1789 was limited, in the words of John Childs, 'only when it was compared with the holocaust that had gone before and the new totality of the Napoleonic wars'.[16] As surely as the Thirty Years' War (1618-48) had devastated Germany, reducing its urban population by 33 per cent and its rural population by 45 per cent, so incipient warfare during the next 120 years laid waste much of central Europe and the Low Countries at regular intervals. Conventions applied by armies in relation to each other did not extend to civilian populations, as the French army's ravages in the Palatinate in 1688 and 1689 or both the Russian and Swedish armies' depredations in the Great Northern War (1700-21) well illustrate. In any case, for all their balletic appearance, battles were murderous affairs, the 'butcher's bill' at Malplaquet in 1709 of an estimated 36,000 casualties not being surpassed until the Battle of Borodino in 1812. Borodino itself was then exceeded by the 127,000 casualties at the four-day 'Battle of the Nations' at Leipzig in 1813. The cumulative effect of such conflict upon areas that were fought over was considerable. Equally, participation in five major wars between 1689 and 1783 was a major stimulus for English industry and trade at a crucial early stage in the world's first industrial revolution.

None the less, warfare was to become increasingly more total in its impact during the course of the nineteenth century, which can be taken as representing an extended transitional period. During the French Revolutionary and Napoleonic wars (1792-1815), the motive forces of nationalism and democracy combined to create a mass French citizen army through the introduction of, universal male conscription. The success of this 'nation in arms' or 'armed horde' resulted in the example being emulated elsewhere, notably in Prussia. Although the concept of the nation in arms came under sustained attack after 1815 from monarchs and restored monarchs, who distrusted its social and political implications, the actual system of short-service conscription survived in Prussia. The military victories then won by Prussia in the

German wars of unification of 1864, 1866 and 1870 and the ability of short-service conscription to produce large numbers of trained reserves upon mobilization encouraged European states – with the exception of Britain – to reintroduce Prussian-style conscription. Although the forms of universal service adopted were necessarily selective in practice, states were rapidly accepting the national birthrate as an index of military power. Moreover, the transformation wrought by the technological innovations of the industrial age, particularly the development of the railway, ensured that ever larger armies could be mobilized theoretically more quickly than hitherto and sustained in the field for far longer.

At the same time, industrialization dramatically increased the destructive capacity of armies by providing them with weapons of enhanced range, accuracy and rate of fire. By 1870, a firefight between opposing infantry, which might have been conducted at 60 yards range seventy years before, had now stretched to a possible 1,600 yards and a breech-loading rifle such as the Prussian Dreyse now fired seven rounds for every one from a smoothbore musket of the Napoleonic era. By the 1880s and 1890s magazine rifles, quick-firing artillery and machine guns had all entered service with major European armies. Just before the First World War, most armies were also experimenting with aircraft, even if it appeared to require a considerable feat of imagination to conceive that airmen could offer any valuable intelligence while flying over the ground at speeds approaching 30 mph. At sea, too, wood, sail and round shot had given way to iron and steel, steam and screw propellor, and shell, while mines, submarines and torpedoes all threatened the traditional supremacy of the capital ship.

Through the innate conservatism of European military and naval officer corps, the significance of much of the change that had taken place during the nineteenth century was misinterpreted. Contrary to popular belief, soldiers did recognize the problems inherent in crossing the so-called 'empty battlefield' in the face of modern firepower, but they believed mistakenly that they could solve the difficulty simply by closing with an enemy more rapidly. Moreover, the use of bayonet, lance and sabre implicit in this 'offensive spirit' ideally complemented traditional military ideals of honour and glory, which some feared devalued by the unwelcome intrusion of technology and professionalism into an overwhelmingly aristocratic occupation. While soldiers conspired to discount the more uncomfortable evidence of such conflicts as the American Civil War (1861–5), Franco-Prussian War (1870–1) and Russo-Japanese War (1904–5), civilians were equally seduced by the general trend in the later nineteenth century towards popular nationalism, imperialism, militarism and crude social Darwinism into a more ready acceptance of war and conflict as an appropriate test of nationhood and national virility. There were pacifists but, in 1914, it was nationalism and not internationalism that triumphed across Europe. Similarly, a succession of international conferences, such as those at St Petersburg in 1868 or at the Hague in 1899 and 1907, failed to find a universal readiness among nation states to compromise their future freedom of manoeuvre by accepting meaningful limitations on the actual conduct of war.

Wars between 1789 and 1914, while such developments were occurring, were hardly devoid of impact upon those societies that waged them. In the case of Britain, for example, the manpower problems experienced during the Crimean War (1854–6) were very similar to those encountered in the First World War, and losses sustained in the twenty years of almost continuous warfare between 1793 and 1815 were almost certainly proportionately higher in terms of men under arms than in the First World War.[17] Military participation in Britain was also probably greater in proportion to the male population between 1793 and 1815, and it is at least arguable that the resulting social, economic and political upheaval in the immediate post-war period was of more significance for the future pattern of British society and democracy than developments in the aftermath of either of the world wars. Of course, the wars of German and Italian unification were of very limited duration, but they still had profound political consequences for Europe.

There was once a tendency to view the American Civil War largely in terms of its military developments and to focus upon such innovations as armoured trains, the first clash of armoured warships, the first loss of ships to mines and submarine torpedoes, the first extensive use of the telegraph, and so on. In fact, the largely amateur armies fought the war on the battlefield as if it were the last Napoleonic encounter rather than the 'first modern war' but it is now recognized widely that the war was truly modern in terms of its impact upon society. Both the northern states of the Union and the southern states of the Confederacy deployed large numbers of men in the field but, for the predominantly agricultural Confederacy, war also demanded efforts to create an industrial economy to challenge the far greater manufacturing potential of the North. It had become essential to outproduce as well as to outfight an opponent. Despite its efforts at industrialization, the mobilization of 75 per cent of its white male population, and unprecedented participation by white women and blacks in industry and agriculture, the Confederacy was doomed to defeat by the superiority of the North's numbers and resources. The inescapable logic of the attempt to create a war economy was the recognition that a society that sustained a war became as much a legitimate target for military action as an army that waged war on its behalf. Thus, in the autumn of 1864, Sheridan's Union forces swept down the southern 'bread basket' of the Shenandoah valley while Sherman's armies wrought equal destruction in cutting a swathe from Atlanta to the sea in November and December 1864 and through the Carolinas in the following months in a determination to expose the Confederacy to the 'hard hand of war'.[18]

The world wars

Thus, there are sufficient examples of the way in which the impact of war upon society was increasing through the nineteenth century to suggest that the world wars should be regarded as a natural progression from earlier conflicts rather than as unique. But, of course, this is not to suggest that the impact of world war was not greater than that of earlier wars through the sheer scale of conflict enhancing the effect. Quite obviously, both world wars were global in scope, although both began as European conflicts. In the First World War, the Central Powers comprised Imperial Germany, Austria–Hungary, Ottoman Turkey (from October 1914) and Bulgaria (from October 1915), but the Allies eventually embraced twenty-two states including the major European powers of Britain, France, Imperial Russia and Italy (from May 1915) and their colonies and dependencies, and also Japan, the United States (from March 1917), Liberia (from August 1917) and Brazil (from October 1917). Similarly, the Second World War widened with the aggression of Germany, Italy (from June 1940 to September 1943) and Japan (from December 1941) bringing in the Soviet Union (from June 1941) and the United States (from December 1941), although the Soviet Union did not join in the war against Japan until August 1945. Successive German and Soviet occupation contributed to a bewildering proliferation of contradictory declarations of war by many eastern European states during the war, while, between February and March 1945, no less than ten states ranging from Peru to Saudi Arabia declared war on both Germany and Japan and a further two on Japan alone.

Total war therefore implies a far wider global conflict than previous wars and, while limited war suggests a degree of constraint, self-imposed or otherwise, total war implies a lack of constraint. In practice, total war was still a relative concept in both world wars since, as an absolute, it was unrealizable through a lack of instantaneously destructive weapons. Nevertheless, belligerents could not be accused of failing to attempt the absolute even if they were unable to mobilize all their resources at the same time and at the same point. In effect, they employed all the weapons they felt appropriate rather than all the weapons available in every case. The array and potential of weapons increased dramatically over previous wars. For example, in eight days before the opening of the British offensive on the Somme on the Western Front on 1 July 1916, British artillery fired 1.7 million shells at German positions. In fourteen days preceding the opening of the Passchendaele offensive on 31 July 1917, the British fired 4.2 million shells. In addition to the weight of shell, horrendous new weapons were introduced in search of an elusive breakthrough. Gas was first used on the Western Front at Langemarck near Ypres on 22 April 1915, although it had previously been used by the Germans at Bolimov on the Eastern Front, and, in July 1915, flamethrowers were used effectively for the first time by the Germans at Hooge near Ypres. In all, over 150,000 tons of varying gases were produced during the First World War and caused an estimated 1.2 million casualties, of which more than 91,000 proved fatal. Tanks were also introduced for the first time by the British on the Somme on 15 September 1916.

Although gas was not used in the Second World War other than in the context of Nazi genocide, its military use was pressed by a powerful military–industrial lobby in Germany. There were also considerable technological advances that further enhanced the destructive power of the belligerents. Paradoxically, the speed of the early German *Blitzkriegs* actually made these operations less costly in terms of casualties than trench warfare during the First World War but, equally, there was the development in the capacity to bring aerial destruction to civilian populations. Ultimately, Germany utilized its V1 and V2 rockets and the Allies, of course, dropped the first atomic weapons on Japan.

The conscious abandonment of most if not all restraints was paralleled by the wider war aims adopted by belligerents in total war. Limited dynastic aims had given way to sweeping territorial aggrandisement and the total destruction of states and of peoples. It could be argued in this respect that the necessary manipulation of the population of democratic states through propaganda and other means, in so far as this proved possible, in order to sustain the war effort, introduced as great a push towards total war aims as the attempt by authoritarian or totalitarian states to impose their ideologies on others. Thus, on the one hand, the Germans pursued total domination in the Second World War, while Britain and the United States adopted a declaration of the need for the unconditional surrender of Germany at the Casablanca conference in January 1943. At Cairo in November and December 1943, Britain, the United States and nationalist China also agreed to strip Japan of all those overseas possessions taken by her forces since 1894.

Quite clearly, the participation of many states and their willingness to use extreme means to achieve wide aims resulted in destruction of life and property on an unprecedented scale compared with previous wars. In all, the First World War is thought to have resulted in 10 million dead and 20 million maimed or seriously wounded, leaving 5 million women widows and 9 million children orphans. The Second World War may have cost 30 million dead in Europe, although other estimates put Soviet losses alone at well over 20 million dead. Although figures for the First World War usually exclude an estimated 1.5 million Armenians exterminated by the Turks in 1915, those for the Second World War do include an estimated 5.9 million Jewish victims of Nazi genocide. More-over, as many as 26 million people may have become displaced from their country of origin during the Second World War through forced transportation or other reasons: in Britain alone, which did not suffer such displacement, there were still 60 million changes of address during the Second World War. Compared with previous wars, also, civilians had become subject to sustained and deliberate attack to an unprecedented degree. During the First World War, some 1,413 British civilians were killed by aerial attack, but, between 1939 and 1945, German bombers and rockets accounted for 51,509 civilian deaths in Britain. Hamburg suffered approximately 50,000 dead in a week in July and August 1943, and calculations of the loss of life at Dresden on a single night in February 1945 range from 35,000 to 135,000. In all, total German civilian losses to aerial bombardment may have been 593,000 during the Second World War. USAAF 'fire raids' on Japan caused an estimated 100,000 deaths in Tokyo on one night in March 1945, or approximately the same number of immediate deaths at both Hiroshima and Nagasaki combined in August 1945.

The loss of life in individual states could be grave, but total war was not necessarily a cause of demographic loss overall. In France, the loss of life during the First World War did cast a long shadow, at least in political terms, and draconian laws were introduced against birth control and abortion in the inter-war period. Yet, it would appear that more men and women married than might otherwise have been the case. In Britain, as Jay Winter has pointed out, the war was dysgenic in that some sectors of society volunteered for war service in larger numbers than others and many of the working class were physically unfit for service through pre-war deprivation. Hence, the idea of a 'lost generation' current in Britain in the 1920s and 1930s had some basis in fact. But, as Jay Winter has also demonstrated, infant mortality declined through the improvement in the nutrition of mothers and children with the redistribution of food and increased family income consequent upon wartime changes in public health policy. These, paradoxically healthier, standards of living were not eroded by the depression years.[19] Similarly, J. J Becker has concluded that standards of living were not materially diminished in France during the First World War.[20] Unexpectedly, too, there was a close correlation during the Second World War between Britain, which suffered little real violence and deprivation, and most other European countries in terms of more and earlier marriages, increased fertility, and decreased infant and maternal mortality. Such demographic gains were achieved despite the estimated 27 million deaths worldwide from the Spanish influenza pandemic of 1918 and 1919. The latter in itself was once attributed to war-related conditions of less resistance to infection and easier transmission of disease through armies but, in fact, it hit neutrals as hard if not worse than belligerents and the highest mortality rates were recorded in the United States and India. Advances in medicine were of considerable account in preventing disease during and after the Second World War. It must also be borne in mind that total war is a stimulus to medical development and, even in the First World War, soldiers were far more likely to survive serious wounds than any of their predecessors on countless battlefields in the past.

The reduction of suffering and much else to statistics is unfortunate but unavoidable in conveying the totality of the world wars. Similar repetitive statistics are available to compute the undoubted losses of property and of manufacturing and agricultural production as a result either of direct attack or of occupation. Certainly, the cost of waging war had increased spectacularly. In 1870, for example, it has been suggested that the Franco–Prussian War cost Prussia and the other German states some 7 million marks a day, whereas the First World War cost Imperial Germany an estimated 146 million marks a day in 1918. Just 18 months' participation in the First World War cost the United States $112 billion, but the Second World War cost the United States some $664 billion. In fact, such exact calculations of the direct and indirect costs of war are notoriously difficult to make and quantitative evaluations may not in themselves be particularly helpful in suggesting the impact of war upon the economy. Structural changes are far more significant and, in this regard, both world wars were of unquestionable importance as economic events. As a result of the First World War, there was not only a global depreciation in the value of currencies, which had repercussions in terms of currency instability in the inter-war years, but also a decentralization of the international economy. Europe's share of world production and trade fell through the stimulus afforded non-European competitors. Much the same effect was reproduced during and after the Second World War with the growth of manufacturing capacity outside Europe and a legacy of post-war economic planning very different from the policies followed prior to the war.[21]

The primary beneficiary of the stimulus to non-European economies in both world wars was the United States, which moved from being an international debtor before 1914 to an international creditor on a large scale. In the process, the United States also emerged as a global power, even if subsequently choosing isolation for another twenty years. The First World War also destroyed four empires – those of Imperial Germany, Austria-Hungary, Tsarist Russia and Ottoman Turkey. It left a legacy of new states in eastern Europe, such as Poland, Czechoslovakia, Hungary and Yugoslavia, with significant racial minorities. It directly fostered the growth of nationalism among subject peoples in those empires that did survive. The British, whose empire reached its greatest extent in 1919 with the acquisition of former German colonies and custody of new Middle Eastern territories, encountered nationalism in such areas as Palestine, India and Ireland. Later, the Second World War made a significant contribution to the further decline of western Europe *vis-à-vis* the United States and the Soviet Union. Moreover, the occupation of much of South-East Asia by the Japanese struck severely at the hold of the remaining European colonial powers. Nationalism was fostered both through the establishment by the Japanese of puppet governments and quasi-nationalist organizations and also through the emergence of anti-Japanese opposition movements, such as the Viet Minh in French Indochina and the Malayan Peoples' Anti-Japanese Army (MPAJA) in Malaya, which proved equally opposed to the return of former colonial administrations once the Japanese had been defeated. It would be difficult to argue that such global changes in the balance of power would not have occurred but for the world wars. Both wars also saw some attempt at a new internationalism in the shape of institutional mechanisms for world order – the League of Nations and the United Nations – although such ideals were not entirely novel.

The growth of state control

The collapse of some states and the post-war political challenges to others suggests that Marwick is perfectly correct in postulating total war as a testing experience for the institutions of state. Certainly, the world wars did promote far greater state control in its broadest sense as a response to wartime challenges. In 1914 a spate of emergency legislation, such as the revived Prussian Law of Siege of 1851 in Imperial Germany and the Defence of the Realm Act (DORA) in Britain, enabled the state to assume wide powers. In all cases the railways were swiftly nationalized and, in Britain and France, this was followed by state control of mines and the shipbuilding industry. Precisely the same pattern occurred in the United States in 1917 and key areas such as munitions, food and manpower policies were submitted to intervention and control by new governmental agencies. In Britain, the Ministry of Munitions was created in May 1915 with an accompanying Munitions of War Act extending state control to munitions factories to prevent strikes, suspend trade union activities and to prevent free movement of labour. More new creations followed Lloyd George's appointment as prime minister in December 1916 (such as the Ministry of Labour and Ministry of Food), although often with ill-defined responsibilities. Canada created an Imperial Munitions Board; Austria-Hungary, a Joint Food Committee; the United States, a War Industries Board and a Fuel and Food Administration; Imperial Germany's new agencies included the War Wheat Corporation, the War Food Office and the splendidly named Imperial Potato Office. In the Second World War, Britain established new ministries of supply, home security, economic warfare, information, food and shipping, and aircraft production. New executive agencies wielding wide powers in areas previously untouched by the state appeared in the United States as well, the number of government employees there increasing from 1 million in 1940 to 3.8 million by 1946. Even the Vichy regime in France experienced the growth of organization committees in the supervision of the wartime economy.

In essence, it is this control of the economy that lies at the heart of the concept of total war, because it is assumed that a state is required to mobilize all its resources in order to survive. However, it has become increasingly apparent that many of the wartime creations did not necessarily alter the pre-war structure. Much of the dramatic change once attributed to Lloyd George's premiership in Britain during the latter stages of the First World War is now seen more in terms of administrative continuities with that of his predecessor, Asquith.[22] The new centralized War Cabinet was not the administrative revolution Lloyd George claimed, many of its functions being hived off to *ad hoc* subcommittees in the manner of the War Committee it replaced. In terms of manpower policy at least, co-ordinated manipulation and distribution of mobilized resources was not effected until late 1917[23] and, in many respects, similar effective control of food production and distribution was achieved only in July 1918. Businessmen were introduced to government by Lloyd George and they also featured in the United States, where Wall Street broker Bernard Baruch headed the War Industries Board, and even in Imperial Germany, where Moellendorf and Rathenau of the electrical giant, AEG, were early appointees to the raw materials section of the war ministry. However, businessmen in government and the failure of the British Treasury to secure wartime control of the new ministerial creations were but temporary phenomena, with wartime controls speedily divested in Britain after the armistice.

In the case of Nazi Germany, there has been a lively debate on the extent to which Germany was already or became a total war economy during the Second World War. An earlier interpretation associated with Alan Milward postulated an economy designed for swift and lightning *Blitzkrieg,* which was then required to be converted into a total war economy from 1942 onwards under the guiding hand of Albert Speer. By contrast, Richard Overy has argued that fewer changes were required early in the war because the logic of Goering's Four-Year Plan Office of 1936 was the creation of a total war economy, and that what Milward has seen as rhetoric prior to 1942 was rhetoric applied. This should be seen within the context of competing agencies and interests that promoted gross inefficiency rather than effective preparation for war, and also in the context of German miscalculations as to the likely starting date for that war. Thus, Speer's efforts should be regarded as an attempt to improve the performance of an economy already geared for total war rather than to initiate the process in the first place.[24]

Undoubtedly, however, total war did result in increased state control over the individual. Some state systems already involved a degree of coercion, citizens of Nazi Germany and Soviet Russia having relatively little choice as to the degree of their participation in the war effort. But increased state control was equally a feature of democracies. During the First World War, both British and United States citizens were exposed to military conscription for the first time in many generations. The restrictions of DORA in 1914 were easily exceeded by the theoretical powers of the British government under the Emergency Powers (Defence) Act of 1939 and its revised version in May 1940. However, there were few compulsory labour directions in Britain and, although Britain also went further than any other belligerent in taking powers for the conscription of women, the legislation was again used sparingly. But there was compulsory direction of men to serve in the mining industry – the so-called Bevin Boys – in 1943 and, following a spate of unofficial strikes, it became an indictable offence in April 1944 to instigate or incite industrial stoppages in essential war work. Canada compulsorily transferred 127,000 workers from low to high priority employment under its National Service Civilian Regulations of January 1943 and, in the United States, the War Labor Disputes Act of the same year enabled government to conscript strikers. In the First World War, both British and American governments had contemplated conscripting striking Midlands engineering employees and copper miners respectively. At a lower level too, government impinged on everyday life in new ways, although in the United States the population tended to fight the wars, to use J.M. Blum's words, 'in imagination only'.[25] Bread was rationed in Imperial Germany in the First World War as early as January 1915, and meat rationing was introduced in Britain in February 1918. In the Second World War commodities such as butter, bacon, sugar, meat, tea, cooking fats and margarine were all rationed in Britain before July 1940. Both wars saw the imposition of a blackout in Britain and the licensing laws and summer time of modern Britain remain legacies of the First World War.

War and social change

Military and industrial conscription also reflected the greater demands made

upon manpower in total war. Just as pre-war soldiers in 1914 had not anticipated the kind of warfare that was to be waged on the Western Front, few
politicians or soldiers had estimated correctly the extent of the demands
which would be made upon industry. Britain, France and Imperial Russia all
suffered 'shell shortages' in 1915, as did Germany in the following year. Part
of the problem derived from the way in which skilled workers had been
either conscripted or allowed to volunteer for war service in 1914 but, in any
case, industries such as munitions expanded to such an extent that there was
a massive growth in the labour force. In Italy, for example, those involved in
war industries increased from 20 to 64 per cent of the industrial working
force during the First World War, and in Imperial Russia there was a stagger-
ing increase from 24 to 76 per cent of the working force. Precisely the same
happened in the Second World War. The shipbuilding industry in Canada, for
example, alone increased its work-force from 4,000 in 1939 to 126,000 in
1943 and the United States labour force as a whole increased from 54 million
to 64 million. Such increased demands provided new opportunities, not only
for unskilled male labour, but for groups previously under-represented in
the industrial labour force. In Imperial Germany, the number of women
employed in industry increased from 1.4 million in 1914 to 2.1 million by
1918, and there were 800,000 more women in British industry in 1918 than
in 1914 and two and a half times the number of women in United States
industry in 1918 than a year previously. In the Second World War, there were
3 million more women in full or part-time employment in Britain in 1943 than
in 1939 and 4.5 million more in the United States in 1945 than in 1940. In the
United States, a parallel can be drawn with Negro employment in both world
wars, the number employed in industry increasing from 2.9 million in 1940
to 3.2 million in 1944, for instance.

Particular attention has been devoted by historians to the condition of
labour and to the question of the employment of women in total war. Total
war invariably effected a stimulus for those sectors of the economy considered especially vital to war production: heavy industries such as coal,
shipping and heavy metals, but also newer lighter industries such as chemicals, electrical goods and motors. In the United States, there was a boom in
synthetic rubber manufacture during the Second World War owing to the
loss of South-East Asian sources. As a result of such trends, unemployment
declined rapidly and the position of labour generally was liable to be improved. One manifestation was the increase in trade union membership. In
the United States this rose from 2 million in 1917 to 3.25 million in 1918 and
from 10.5 million in 1941 to 14.75 million in 1945. In Britain, the increase was
from 4 million to 8 million between 1914 and 1918 and by one-third – to 8
million – during the Second World War. Through enhanced union strength,
continued militancy on the shopfloor and the need of government to ensure
a better relationship with labour, total war would then generally result in
lower working hours and higher wages in real terms. In Britain, it is estimated
that average working hours fell from 50 hours to 48 hours a week between
1914 and 1918 and, although they increased from 48 hours in 1939 to 54.1

hours for men and between 44.2 and 46.9 hours for women by 1943, they declined to an average 44–5 hours in 1945.

However, average figures do not always reflect reality. In British industry during the First World War, for example, much of the earlier interpretation of the effect of dilution of trade and the narrowing of differentials within and between differing sectors of industry was based on the experience of engineering. Further research has indicated that the experience of labour employed in other sectors such as shipbuilding was very different. Calculations were also made in terms of differences between wage rates and earnings, a presumption being made that skilled men paid by the hour would not benefit to the same extent as 'unskilled men paid by piecework rates, but this ignored the widespread official and unofficial bonuses and incentives provided for skilled labour during the First World War. In any case, there was no substantial reorganization of British industry in either of the world wars, pre-war differentials being restored in 1918 so that, if labour could be said to have gained generally, most groups moved up together in broadly the same relationship as previously. In Britain, too, trade union membership declined rapidly in the 1920s and 1930s. In the Second World War, industrial wage differentials in Britain widened to such an extent that there was official concern at the level of wages in Midlands engineering and aircraft factories.

Another factor to be taken into account is wartime inflation: while, on average, wages in real terms kept ahead of inflation in Britain in both world wars, this was far from true in other states such as Imperial Germany. There, real wages fell and, although it can be said that the working class did relatively well, with unions forging a new partnership with employers in 1918, it did so only in the context of losing less than other social groups, which were affected even more in a society impoverished by wartime inflation. Similarly, although wages kept ahead of inflation in the United States in the Second World War, this was not the case in France. Generalization, therefore, is exceptionally hazardous and wide differences must be expected between and within varying social groups, not all of which might be in the position to benefit from the opportunities afforded by wartime participation in the labour market. Much remains to be done on the experience of social and occupational groups other than the working class and the unskilled – to give but one example, some of the most profound social changes in Britain in both wars took place not in industry but in the agricultural sector.

The judgement of the impact of total war upon the position of women is equally beset with difficulties of interpretation. As already indicated, there were measurable increases in female employment in most belligerents in both wars, Nazi Germany being the most notable exception. In many cases, however, it is the increase of women in areas such as transport or white-collar employment that is more significant than increases in the numbers in manufacturing industry, because the former employment was more likely to endure after the end of hostilities. The degree of female dilution in the munitions industry in both Britain and France in the First World War has been exaggerated, because most women were employed for specific functions and did not supplant skilled male labour. Equally, during the Second World War, British trade unions negotiated dilution agreements that protected male jobs. In many cases, many women may not have perceived wartime employment either as permanent or as an expression of long-term emancipation, and it can be argued that there was a significant revival of domesticity in Britain in 1945. Some trends can be perceived in Britain in terms of the increase in part-time female employment during the Second World War and the greater employment of married women and older women, although the proportion of married women within the female labour force as a whole was still relatively small. Clearly, however, wartime employment neither implied equality of pay nor an erosion of the sexual divisions of labour. It is also arguable how far the extension of the suffrage in Britain after the First World War reflected an appreciation of female participation in the war effort. The enfranchisement of women aged over 30 in 1918 compensated for that of the 40 per cent of the adult male population, mostly working class, who had not been able to vote prior to the war. Moreover, in France, although the Chamber of Deputies voted for female suffrage in 1919, the Senate repeatedly rejected it. It has been argued that the final conceding of the principle of female suffrage in France in 1944 reflected the role of women in the resistance movement, but, in fact, the leftward turn in the indirectly elected Senate – especially among radicals, who had previously opposed the vote for women – guaranteed such an outcome anyway. Yet, if the world wars did not improve the status of women, they did perhaps offer some women wider opportunities and freedoms. Again, generalization about the perceptions or expectations of women is no easy task.[26]

It is also largely in terms of perception that social change as a result of total war must be gauged. Of course, the tendency of the modern state to collect statistics ensures that there are some measurable social trends. In both world wars, there were likely to be more marriages, more divorces and more illegitimate births. In Britain, attendance at the cinema rose in both world wars and, in the Second World War, 'eating out' increased with the 79 million meals per week of May 1941 increasing to 170 million meals a week by December 1944. Crime rose also in both world wars, although this included offences against wartime regulations. In the United States and Britain, for example, juvenile delinquency increased in both wars. There was also enhanced urbanization. In Imperial Russia, the urban proletariat grew from 22 million in 1914 to 28 million by 1916, one-third of the increase taking place in St Petersburg, with particular repercussions when the widespread failure of the transportation system contributed to the hunger and unrest in the cities in 1917. In the United States, the First World War saw the beginnings of a large-scale migration of the Negro population from the rural south to the industrial north, and this continued both through the interwar period and the Second World War. The Willow Run township in Detroit increased its population by 32,000 during the Second World War owing to the location of production of B-24 bombers there, and Detroit as a whole increased by 500,000 inhabitants, of whom 12 per cent were blacks. Changes in occupation can also be measured, such as the permanent decline in the number of domestic servants in Britain during and after the First World War and, in Britain, it is also possible to measure the changes in the numbers paying income tax. In the First World War, this increased from 1.5 million in 1914 to 7.75 million in 1918 and from 1 million to 7 million among manual workers between 1939 and 1944.

The measurement of quantifiable trends contributes to some extent to an understanding of those that cannot be so calculated, such as the degree to which total war resulted in greater social homogeneity and the breakdown of class distinctions through participation. Two commonly expressed vestiges of this are the concepts of a 'war generation', emerging from the shared experiences of the trenches in the First World War, and the idea of a 'people's war' during the Second World War. In terms of the former, it appears doubtful that shared experience between officers and men in the front line brought a greater understanding between different classes in the post-war period, not least because of the considerable distinctions that were preserved in the relationship of officer and man. Richard Bessel and David Englander have concluded from a survey of the literature in this field that the war generation lasted 'only as long as it remained under fire'.[27]

The identification of a 'people's war' by contemporary socialist, and invariably middle-class, intellectuals in Britain during the Second World War has tended to disguise the persistence of class differences. A significant change was the post-war bargaining power of labour through trade unions, but this occurred within the existing structure of social consciousness and the structure of the trade union movement itself was also unchanged. The image of the happy communion of the London underground shelters during the Blitz and much else in popular mythology does not bear close investigation.[28] Much was made by Titmuss, for example, of the wartime reformist consensus that was said to have emerged as a result of the compulsory wartime evacuation of 1.75 million persons, mainly women and children, from inner cities and coastal towns in Britain in 1939. In fact, it would appear that most hosts were as working class as the evacuees themselves and the experience merely reinforced existing pre-war analyses among middle-class observers of the nature of the working class. In any case, the great majority of the evacuees had returned to the cities by 1940.[29] In general, therefore, although there may have been some changes in social stratification during wartime, a temporary equalizing effect upon income had little impact upon class differences or the ownership of property. Nevertheless, total war does imply at least a temporary throwing together of different social groups, and it would be hazardous to deny altogether the impact of evacuation upon individuals or, for example, the presence in Britain during the Second World War of some 1.5 million foreign servicemen.

At the same time, although states did not go to war to transform their societies, total war did produce the ideals if not the reality of post-war social change and guided reconstruction. In the United States, the housing shortages resulting from the growth in urban population during the First World

War and the attendant social problems did establish a precedent for federal intervention, which foreshadowed the programmes of the 1930s. Britain also experienced the intention for reconstruction through such measures as the Ministry of Health Act and the Housing and Town Planning Act of 1919. Economic depression left such promise unfulfilled but, during and after the Second World War, an apparent wartime consensus on guided change bore fruit in such measures as the Town and Country Planning Act, the Education Act, Keynesian declarations of full employment and the establishment of a welfare state along the lines of the Beveridge report of December 1942. Again, however, care must be exercised in interpreting post-war changes as novel. A broad consensus on such matters as family allowance provision and the principle of a National Health Service had existed before the war, and the 1944 Education Act did not materially affect the pre-war status quo. Full employment rested upon the assumption that a condition already arrived at in wartime would be maintained, and the war generally created a false impression that emergency apparatus would also be maintained to ensure the preservation of social solidarity and the unchallenged consensus on a welfare state. Some changes resulted from the electoral success of the Labour party in 1945, itself arguably a result of the unguided change in popular expectation through enforced egalitarianism and creeping collectivization. But the Labour party had moderated during the war through participation in coalition government; in the United States, there was actually a shift to the right rather than the political left despite equal measures of guided social change. Though not rivalling the far-reaching provisions of Canada's Marsh report of March 1943, both Negroes and ex-servicemen were the theoretical beneficiaries of social measures in the United States. In reality, of course, discrimination against blacks continued, irrespective of presidential executive orders to the contrary, although the US Servicemen's Readjustment Act of 1944 – the 'GI Bill' – illustrated the ability of veterans' organizations to achieve far more through the power of pressure-group lobbies in the American system than through comparable veterans' organizations elsewhere.

In effect, wartime changes may not mean much in practical terms thereafter and the lack of success of British veterans' organizations merely illustrates how far change depended upon the political system of the state waging total war. Clearly, too, changes were potentially greater where a state collapsed under the strain of war, as in Imperial Russia in 1917, or suffered total defeat as in Germany and Japan in 1945. Generally, however, it would appear that institutional mechanisms are more liable to change than social structures, although here, too, the example of the British army as an institution in the First World War is instructive. In theory, it ought to provide clear evidence of the impact of total war, since a small pre-war regular cadre of 250,000 officers and men expanded to almost 6 million in the course of the war, becoming theoretically more representative of society than ever before. In fact, the army remained unrepresentative of British society through the unequable distribution of war service and, in the long term, there was little or no change in its social structure or ethos owing to the survival of the pre-war officer corps. Even the impact of service life may be challenged, since the popular image of men such as Robert Graves or Siegfried Sassoon as representative of the thousands who served in the army is hardly compatible with the reality.[30] In short, armies as institutions do not seem to change to the same extent as society is said to change as the result of total war.

Furthermore, it is also necessary to place wartime change and development within the context of long-term social trends, which often suggest evolutionary rather than revolutionary change during the course of the longer period. This would suggest, for example, that female suffrage would have come to Britain irrespective of the impact of the First World War, although that experience may have accelerated changes already taking place. Total war could not fail to generate some change through its sheer scale, but it is important to judge how far changes survived the immediate postwar situation that generated them and, indeed, how far such changes would have occurred in any case. In conclusion, therefore, it might be suggested that total war is an important and largely instructive concept, provided that its limitations are kept in mind.

Notes

1 J. U. Nef, *War and Human Progress*, London, Routledge & Kegan Paul, 1950.
2 R. Titmuss, *Problems of Social Policy*, London, HMSO and Longman, 1950.
3 S. Andrzejewski, *Military Organisation and Society*, London, Routledge & Kegan Paul, 1954.
4 G. N. Clark, *War and Society in the Seventeenth Century,* London, Cambridge University Press, 1958.
5 M. E. Howard, *The Franco-Prussian War*, London, Hart-Davis, 1961.
6 M. E. Howard, *War in European History*, Oxford, Oxford University Press, 1976.
7 A. Marwick, *The Deluge*, London, Bodley Head, 1965.
8 A. Marwick, *Britain in the Century of Total War*, London, Bodley Head, 1968; Marwick, *War and Social Change in the Twentieth Century*, London, Macmillan, 1974.
9 G. Wright, *The Ordeal of Total War*, New York, Harper Torchbooks, 1968; P. Calvocoressi and G. Wint, *Total War*, London, Allen Lane, 1972.
10 Open University, A301 *War and Society*, Milton Keynes, Open University Press, 1973.
11 M. Bentley, 'Social change: appearance and reality', in C. Haigh (ed.) *The Cambridge Historical Encyclopedia of Great Britain and Ireland*, Cambridge University Press, 1985, p. 327.
12 A. Calder, *The People's War*, London, Cape, 1969.
13 P. Lewis, *A People's War*, London, Thames Methuen, 1986.
14 H. Pelling, *Britain in the Second World War*, London, Collins/Fontana, 1971.
15 B. Bond, *War and Society in Europe, 1870-1970*, London, Fontana, 1984, p. 168.
16 J. Childs, *Armies and Warfare in Europe, 1648-1789*, Manchester, Manchester University Press, 1982, p. 2.
17 C. Emsley, *British Society and the French Wars 1793-1815*, London, Macmillan, 1979, p. 169.
18 P. J. Parish, *The American Civil War*, London, Eyre Methuen, 1975.

19 J. M. Winter, *The Great War and the British People*, London, Macmillan, 1986.

20 J. J. Becker, *The Great War and the French People*, Leamington Spa, Berg, 1985.

21 G. Hardach, *The First World War, 1914–1918*, London, Allen Lane, 1977; A. S. Milward, *War, Economy and Society, 1939–1945*, London, Allen Lane, 1977; A. S. Milward, *The Economic Effects of the Two World Wars on Britain*, 2nd edn, London, Macmillan, 1984.

22 K. Burk (ed.) *War and the State: The Transformation of British Government, 1914–1918*, London, Allen & Unwin, 1982.

23 K. R. Grieves, *The Politics of Manpower, 1914–1918*, Manchester, Manchester University Press, 1988.

24 A. S. Milward, *The German Economy at War*, London, Athlone Press, 1965; R. J. Overy, *The Air War, 1939–1945*, London, Europa, 1980; R. J. Overy, *Goering: The Iron Man*, London, Routledge & Kegan Paul, 1984.

25 J. M. Blum, *V was for Victory*, New York, Harcourt Brace Jovanovich, 1976.

26 P. Summerfield, *Women Workers in the Second World War*, London, Croom Helm, 1984; G. Braybon, *Women Workers in the First World War*, London, Croom Helm, 1981; A Marwick, *Women at War, 1914–1918*, London, Croom Helm, 1977.

27 R. Bessel and D. Englander, 'Up from the trenches: some recent writing on the soldiers of the Great War', *European Studies Review*, vol. 1, no. 3, 1981, pp. 387–95.

28 T. Harrisson, *Living through the Blitz*, London, Collins, 1976.

29 T. C. Crosby, *The Impact of Civilian Evacuation in the Second World War*, London, Croom Helm, 1986; B. S. Johnson, *The Evacuees*, London, Gollancz, 1968.

30 I. F. W. Beckett and K. Simpson (eds) *A Nation in Arms: A Social Study of the British Army in the First World War*, Manchester, Manchester University Press, 1985.

CHAPTER 2

The Persistence of the Old Regime

ARNO J. MAYER

Introduction

Even with the passage of time the first half of the twentieth century stands out for having witnessed an unprecedented cataclysm and a major watershed in the history of Europe...

[*The Persistence of the Old Regime*] is intended as a contribution to the discussion of the *causa causans* [ultimate cause] and inner nature of Europe's recent 'sea of troubles'. It starts with the premise that the World War of 1939–45 was umbilically tied to the Great War of 1914–18, and that these two conflicts were nothing less than the Thirty Years' War of the general crisis of the twentieth century.

The second premise is that the Great War of 1914, or the first and proto-genic phase of this general crisis, was an outgrowth of the latterday remobiliz-ation of Europe's *anciens régimes*. Though losing ground to the forces of industrial capitalism, the forces of the old order were still sufficiently willful and powerful to resist and slow down the course of history, if necessary by recourse to violence. The Great War was an expression of the decline and fall of the old order fighting to prolong its life rather than of the explosive rise of industrial capitalism bent on imposing its primacy. Throughout Europe the strains of protracted warfare finally, as of 1917, shook and cracked the foun-dations of the embattled old order, which had been its incubator. Even so, except in Russia, where the most unreconstructed of the old regimes came crashing down, after 1918–19 the forces of perseverance recovered suf-ficiently to aggravate Europe's general crisis, sponsor fascism, and contribute to the resumption of total war in 1939.

The third and major premise of [this] book is that Europe's old order was thoroughly preindustrial and prebourgeois...

... The conventional wisdom is still that Europe broke out of its *ancien régime* and approached or crossed the threshold of modernity well before 1914. Scholars of all ideological persuasions have downgraded the importance of preindustrial economic interests, prebourgeois elites, predemocratic authority systems, premodernist artistic idioms, and 'archaic' mentalities. They have done so by treating them as expiring remnants, not to say relics, in rapidly modernizing civil and political societies. They have vastly overdrawn the decline of land, noble, and peasant; the contraction of traditional manufacture and trade, provincial burghers, and artisanal workers; the derogation of kings, public service nobilities, and upper chambers; the weakening of organized religion; and the atrophy of classical high culture. To the extent that economic, social and political historians accord any vitality to these vestiges of a dying past, they present them as using or misusing that vitality to delay, derange, and complicate the ultimately inevitable growth of capitalist industrialization, social leveling, and political liberalization. In this same teleological spirit, cultural historians have pored over the accomplishments of the artistic avant-garde while curtly dismissing academic cultures for being exhausted and for obstructing the preordained march to modernism.

In order to reconstruct the historical matrix in which the general crisis and Thirty Years' War of the twentieth century originated, it may be necessary to reconceive and perhaps even totally reverse this picture of a modern world commanding a recessive and crumbling old order. At any rate, it is the thesis of [the] book that the 'premodern' elements were not the decaying and fragile remnants of an all but vanished past but the very essence of Europe's incumbent civil and political societies. This is not to deny the growing importance of the modern forces that undermined and challenged the old order. But it is to argue that until 1914 the forces of inertia and resistance contained and curbed this dynamic and expansive new society within the *anciens régimes* that dominated Europe's historical landscape . . .

Europe's old regimes were civil and political societies with distinct powers, traditions, customs and conventions. Precisely because they were such integral and coherent social, economic, and cultural systems, they were exceptionally resilient. Even in France, where the *ancien régime* was pronounced legally dead between 1789 and 1793, it kept resurfacing violently and lived on in many ways for more than a century. Of course, Europe was not a single entity. There were vast national and regional variations of economy, social structure, legal tradition and mental outlook, and these historical singularities cannot be ignored or minimized. Nonetheless, in its prime as well as in its perdurable extension into modern times, the *ancien régime* was a distinctly pan-European phenomenon.

The old order's civil society was first and foremost a peasant economy and rural society dominated by hereditary and privileged nobilities. Except for a few bankers, merchants and shipowners, the large fortunes and incomes were based in land. Across Europe the landed nobilities occupied first place not only in economic, social and cultural terms but also politically.

In fact, political society was the linchpin of this agrarian society of orders. Everywhere it took the form of absolutist authority systems of different degrees of enlightenment and headed by hereditary monarchs. The crowns reigned and governed with the support of extended royal families and court parties as well as compliant ministers, generals, and bureaucrats.

The Church was another vital constituent and pillar of the *ancien régime*. Closely tied to both the crown and the nobility, it was, like them, rooted in land, which was its principal source of revenue. The upper clergy was of distinguished social provenance, exercised far-reaching influence, and enjoyed important fiscal and legal exemptions. As a great corporate institution the Church exerted considerable sway through its quasi-monopoly of education and social services and its exclusive control of the sacred rites of birth, marriage and death . . .

Just as there was no complete or model feudal society, so there was no archetypal postfeudal or preindustrial *ancien régime*. England was only one of its variants. Although England's economy was dominated by manufactural and merchant capitalism, the aristocracy continued to be paramount. This was so because land remained the chief source of wealth and income despite the radical contraction of British agriculture in the course of the nineteenth century. In other words, the monarchy and landed elite tamed the industrialization of England without succumbing to it . . .

. . . The major Continental powers, except for France, had none of Britain's advantages: the landed elites were intact, agriculture remained a major social activity, and insecure frontiers justified the military presumption of kings and nobles. This explains, in part, why Russia, Austria-Hungary and Germany persisted as absolutist monarchies.

France alone among the major powers finally became a republic in 1875. But except for no longer having a king and for now being governed by a *petit bourgeois* political class, France stayed in tune with the rest of the Continent, its economy dominated by agriculture and traditional manufacture. Ironically, an excess of agrarian and political democracy impeded French industrialization, notably after the onset of the second industrial revolution in the late nineteenth century. If France became 'a half-hearted republic in continual crisis', it was because its bourgeoisie was too weak and divided to steady it.

In any case, neither England nor France had become industrial-capitalist and bourgeois civil and political societies by 1914. Their polities were as 'obviously outdated' and 'stubbornly concerned with their longevity' as the polities of the other four big powers. All alike were *anciens régimes* grounded in the continued predominance of landed elites, agriculture, or both.

As Joseph Schumpeter saw so clearly,[1] except in France the kings remained the divinely ordained 'centerpieces' of Europe's authority systems. Their position was feudal in both 'the historical and the sociological sense', not least because 'the human material of feudal society' continued to 'fill the offices of state, officer the army, and devise policies'. Although capitalist processes, both national and international, generated ever larger shares of government revenue – for the 'tax-collecting state' – the feudal element remained a '*classe dirigente*' [directing class] that behaved 'according to precapitalist patterns'. While the entrenched upper classes took account of 'bourgeois interests' and availed themselves of the 'economic possibilities offered by capitalism', they were careful 'to distance themselves from the bourgeoisie'. This arrangement was not an 'atavism . . . but an *active symbiosis* of two social strata' in which the old elites retained their political, social and cultural primacy. In exchange they let the bourgeoisie make money and pay taxes. In Schumpeter's judgment, even in England 'the aristocratic element continued to rule the roost *right to the end of the period of intact and vital capitalism'*.

By controlling what Schumpeter called the 'steel frame' or 'political engine' of the *ancien régime,* the feudal elements were in a position to set the terms for the implantation of manufactural and industrial capitalism, thereby making it serve their own purposes. They forced industry to fit itself into pre-existing social, class and ideological structures. Admittedly, industrial capitalism distorted and strained these structures in the process, but not beyond recognition or to the breaking point. The old governing class was both resilient and flexible. It had the support of the landed nobilities and interests, which quite rightly considered the steel frame of the *ancien régime* to be the protective armor for their privileged but exposed positions. In addition, the managers of the state won the loyalty of the bourgeoisie by furthering or safeguarding their economic interests with government contracts, protective tariffs and colonial preferments.

If the feudal elements in both political and civil society perpetuated their dominance so effectively, it was largely because they knew how to adapt and renew themselves. The public service nobilities, both civil and military, took in qualified and ambitious scions of business and the liberal professions, though they were careful to regulate closely this infusion of new blood and talent. Newcomers had to pass through elite schools, ingest the corporate ethos, and demonstrate fealty to the old order as a precondition for advancement. Besides, the highest ranks of the state bureaucracy and military services continued to be reserved for men of high birth and proven assimilation.

The landed magnates were no less effective in adjusting to changing times. Above all, they absorbed and practiced the principles of capitalism and interest politics without, however, derogating their aristocratic world-view, bearing and connections. Some noble proprietors became improving landlords. Others combined the rationalized exploitation of the soil and agrarian labor with large-scale milling, distilling, brewing and dairying. Still others turned to extracting timber, coal and minerals from their lands and invested in industrial ventures. Moreover, all learned alike to resort to lobbying and log-rolling as well as pressure and partisan politics to protect or promote their interests. Increasingly, the landed estate assumed the attributes of class and class consciousness, and acted accordingly.

This extensive and many-sided adaptation is usually considered evidence for the de-noblement and de-aristocratization of the old order, for the inevitable if gradual *embourgeoisement,* or bourgeoisification, of Europe's ruling and governing classes. But there is another way of viewing this accommodation. Just as industrialization was grafted on to pre-established societal and political structures, so the feudal elements reconciled their rationalized bureaucratic and economic behavior with their pre-existent social and cultural praxis and mind-set. In other words, the old elites excelled at selectively ingesting, adapting and assimilating new ideas and practices without seriously endangering their traditional status, temperament and outlook. Whatever the dilution and cheapening of nobility, it was gradual and benign.

This prudential and circumscribed adjustment was facilitated by the bourgeoisie's rage for co-optation and ennoblement. Whereas the nobility was skilled at adaptation, the bourgeoisie excelled at emulation. Throughout the nineteenth and early twentieth centuries the *grands bourgeois* kept denying themselves by imitating and appropriating the ways of the nobility in the hope of climbing into it. The grandees of business and finance bought landed estates, built country houses, sent their sons to elite higher schools, and assumed aristocratic poses and life-styles. They also strained to break into aristocratic and court circles and to marry into the titled nobility. Last but not least, they solicited decorations and, above all, patents of nobility. These aristocratizing barons of industry and commerce were not simply supercilious parvenus or arrivistes who bowed and scraped for fatuous honors from the parasitic leisure class of a decaying old order. On the contrary, their obsequiousness was highly practical and consequential. The bourgeois sought social advancement for reasons of material benefit, social status and psychic income. In addition, and no less important, by disavowing themselves in order to court membership in the old establishment, the aristocratizing bourgeois impaired their own class formation and class consciousness and accepted and prolonged their subordinate place in the 'active symbiosis of the two social strata'.

But there was another result as well. As part of their effort to scale the social pyramid and to demonstrate their political loyalty, the bourgeois embraced the historicist high culture and patronized the hegemonic institutions that were dominated by the old elites. The result was that they strengthened classical and academic idioms, conventions, and symbols in the arts and letters instead of encouraging modernist impulses. The bourgeois allowed themselves to be ensnared in a cultural and educational system that bolstered and reproduced the *ancien régime*. In the process they sapped their own potential to inspire the conception of a new aesthetic and intellection.

Indeed, the self-abnegating bourgeois were among the most enthusiastic champions of traditional architecture, statuary, painting and performing arts. This high classical culture had formidable state support. Academies, conservatories and museums provided training, access to careers and official prizes. The governments financed most of these institutions, awarded commissions, and sponsored individual and collective artistic activities. The churches and universities were part of this towering hegemonic edifice.

But to say that the conventions and idioms of high culture remained traditional and classical is not to say that they were archaic and lifeless. To the extent that Europe was an old order, its official high culture was congruent with it. It might even be said that some of Europe's finest cultural achievements were and continued to be 'inseparable from the milieu of absolutism, of extreme social injustice, even of gross violence, in which they flourished'. No doubt, judging by the tendency to formalist replication, overdecoration, and monumentalization, some of the arts were becoming sclerotic and trailed behind their times. But cultural productions were no less effective for being turgid and specious. Certainly the official cultures were not about to be subverted or toppled by the modernist avant-garde, which kept being assimilated, defused and turned back.

The ruling classes: *the bourgeoisie defers*

The rising business and professional classes were in no position to challenge the landed and public service elites for parity or first place in Europe's ruling classes, let alone in its governing classes. Quite apart from their numerical and economic disadvantage, the rising bourgeoisies were weakened by internal cleavages between heavy industry and large-scale consumer manufacture and their respective banking associates. They were also estranged from petty manufacture and commerce, which left them without much of a popular base. But most important, the new-fledged industrial and financial bourgeoisies as well as the subaltern free professions lacked a coherent and firm social and cultural footing of their own. Unsure of themselves, they remained obsequious in their relations with the venerable notables of land and office . . .

Evidently the old nobility of the land and the new magnates of capital never really embarked on a collision course. At most they jostled each other as they maneuvered for position in ruling classes in which the bourgeoisie remained liegelike suitors and claimants. Inveterate nobles firmly occupied and controlled access to the high social, cultural and political terrain to which the bourgeoisie aspired. With characteristic flexibility and adaptability, and capitalizing on the bourgeois element's craving for social status and advancement, the grand notables admitted individual postulants from business and the professions into their midst. Rather than yield institutional ground, they opted for this selective co-optation, confident of their ability to contain and defuse its attendant ideological and cultural contamination. This strategy or gamble paid off, for the fusion of the two strata remained manifestly asymmetrical: the aristocratization or nobilization of the obeisant bourgeoisie was far more pervasive than the bourgeoisification of the imperious nobility.

Except in France, anointed dynasts and royal courts were the apex and fulcrum of Europe's stratified nobilities. Kings, emperors and tsars alone could legally confer new and higher titles, and throughout Europe landed estates provided the required nimbus. In descending order the noble estate comprised, on the Continent this side of Russia, dukes, princes, marquises, counts, viscounts, barons and knights; across the Channel in England, dukes, marquesses, earls, viscounts and barons. Although the various ranks no longer reflected distinctions in wealth and status as accurately as in the past, they nevertheless remained an approximate index of grandeur and influence. The high aristocracy combined blue blood with enormous wealth in land, including urban real estate, and with considerable political influence or power. These peerless peers, many of them courtiers, had privileged relations with the royal families, who shared their concern for not diluting the status of their rarefied caste with needless ennoblements. Moreover, the extended royal and aristocratic families shared a pan-European predilection for the French language, the English hunt and the Prussian monocle, which they displayed at the Continent's fashionable resorts. Yet while Europe may be said to have had a single aristocracy, it had as many nobilities as there were nations.

There is no disputing the sempiternal *rise* of the bourgeoisie. Instead, what remains problematical is the congenital inability of the grandees of business and the professions to fuse into a cohesive estate or class of more than local dimension. As Schumpeter noted, although 'the bourgeoisie produced individuals who made a success at political leadership upon entering a political class of nonbourgeois origin, it did not produce a successful political stratum of its own'. Through the centuries rich and wealth-accumulating commoners of the cities and of the nonagrarian economic sectors were bent upon rising out of their 'bourgeois' stations into the nobility that was their archetypal model.

[. . .]

On this score England was typical of much of Europe. Until the early twentieth century the new magnate of money who did not invest in a landed estate with a country house was the exception. Because of the limited supply of old and sought-after country houses in prestigious locations, would-be nobles had architects build new ones, invariably in traditional styles. To be sure, country houses with time expressed social status stripped of political pretension, and therefore came to be less stately. Even so, by purchasing or building country houses girded by extensive lands, England's merchants, bankers and industrialists struck an aristocratic rather than a bourgeois pose as they steered their sons away from the world of business.

On both sides of the Channel new wealth-holders climbed the irregularly spaced steps of the social ladder to ever higher noble stations. Once there, many of the novices became snobbish purists, leaving it to more poised and accomplished – and perhaps also wealthier – social transvestites and their patrons to admit new men and ideas into the time-honored establishment. Down to 1914 even the most zealous and brazen social climbers were rarely satirized as vainglorious fools, there being few Figaros to taunt and trick counterfeit nobles without falling prey to their wiles.

Of course not all nonlanded magnates aspired to pass, there being men of great new fortunes who proudly spurned the aristocratic embrace. Immune to the lures of high society, they declined official honors and ennoblement. But quite apart from being rare exceptions, even these self-conscious and self-willed recusants were more nobiliar than bourgeois in mentality and demeanor. Besides, since their children were educated and socialized in elite schools and cultural institutions, many of these resistant families could not help but drift into the orbit of the old establishment, a movement that more often than not was intergenerational. Perhaps it should be added that the mounting need for economic preferment from the state made the bourgeois element that much more disposed to pay homage to the noble element which dominated civil and political society.

[. . .]

It would appear, then, that down to 1914 the interwoven landed and service nobilities throughout Europe continued to be dominant in the ruling classes. Except in England and France, they also maintained their primacy in political society. Their position was solid and awesome, not precarious and quaint, precisely because their immense capital was not only cultural and symbolic but also economic. To be sure, their time-tested and resilient material base was being impaired because of the relative decline of the agrarian sector. But the nobilities, especially the magnates among them, bolstered their failing economic fortunes by securing government supports, by investing in the non-agrarian sector, and by adopting clever marriage strategies.

The ascendant and claimant *grands bourgeois* had little beyond their economic capital with which to challenge this comprehensive, coherent and formidable upper establishment. They were at a disadvantage in every major respect: social, cultural and political. The future was acknowledged to be theirs, but the nobilities, for the present, blocked their path. Doubting their own legitimacy and in no position to subvert or conquer the old ruling classes, the new big businessmen and professionals decided to imitate, cajole and join them.

[. . .]

Political society and the governing classes

In 1914 the kings were still 'the centerpiece' of civil and political society 'by the grace of God, and the root of [their] position was feudal, not only in the historical but also in the sociological sense'. Certainly there is no denying that following the preventive 'regicide' at Sarajevo the sovereigns of the Hohenzollern, Habsburg and Romanov empires – William II, Francis Joseph I, Nicholas II – played a crucial role in pushing Europe over the brink of war. As autocratic rulers all three commanded ministers and advisers who were nobles of one sort or another and who were creatures not of party, parliament, or movable capital but of the inveterate public service estate. As for George V of England and Victor Emmanuel III of Italy, they were more than reigning figureheads, although their prerogatives and powers were rigorously and constitutionally limited. Neither of them exerted himself to dampen the fires of war. Of course, being a republic, France had no king, though the incumbent president, Raymond Poincaré, increasingly acted like one. Abetted by aristocratized *notables,* he adopted a military and bellicose posture considerably ahead of the Chamber of Deputies and the cabinet.

But between 1848 and 1914, whatever the differences in their powers and prerogatives, all the kings exercised grave and impressive ceremonial and representational functions which heavily benefitted the hereditary leisure class, including the dynasties themselves. King, emperor and tsar remained the focus of dazzling and minutely choreographed public rituals that rekindled deep-seated royalist sentiments while simultaneously exalting and relegitimating the old order as a whole. The coronation was the most solemn and resplendent of these studied spectacles of power, and it was saturated with historical and religious symbolism. Although the relationship of throne and altar was left studiedly ambiguous in this supreme ceremony, a high priest – appointed or approved by the sovereign – solemnly administered the oath of office and consecrated the initiate's crown, scepter, and sword. At the same time, this elaborate inaugural pageant, though centered on the king, displayed and ratified the latest ranking of status and influence in civil and political society at large. There were, of course, other rites of passage and rededication of comparable pomp, display and mystery: the christenings, weddings, funerals and jubilees of the ruling houses. At all these punctiliously staged sociodramas the grand, costumed and rankordered nobles of blood, land, office and church totally eclipsed even the most prominent un-uniformed commoners. Foreign royalty and nobility which invested these occasions with a cosmic aura and sanction also overshadowed them.

Nor did the kings hesitate to appropriate the highest religious and national holidays for the benefit of the feudalistic elements in the *anciens régimes*. In addition, as the incarnation of the warrior tradition, they flaunted their martial powers at infantry and naval maneuvers, military parades and the changing of elite guards. Last but not least, the crowned heads dominated the social scene with their grand receptions, soirées and hunts.

All these civil and social rituals invigorated the monarchy, cemented the discordant nobilities, and heralded the latest changes in the order of precedence. This ceremonial rearticulation of calibrated cohesion in the upper class was as significant as the institutional enaction of laws and forewarnings to control counter-elites and underclasses. The populace, high and low, was to be awed rather than cowed by the effulgent uniforms, vestments and decorations that intensified the magic and mystery of rites in which the kings lorded over the fusion of the scepter, the altar, the sword and the national flag. Furthermore, the kings embodied and sustained this conflated potence during the state visits they paid one another.

These king-centered ceremonial rounds may appear stilted and contrived because of the ebbing of public ritual in recent decades. At the time, however, they were still very much alive and genuine. If anything, the use of old-world attire, transport and splendor intensified the spell of meticulously staged pageants in tradition-soaked societies. Except in France, the royal family and the nobiliar notables dominated the nation's ceremonial calendar, which remained linked to high rather than low culture. The succession of spectacular civic rites reinforced hegemonic ideas, values and feelings that braced the prebourgeois elites. This political ritual also integrated the lower orders by catering to their craving for dazzling spectacles, which was the counterpart of the passion for strict hierarchy among the upper orders.

[. . .]

Down to 1914 the 'steel frame' of Europe's political societies continued to be heavily feudal and nobilitarian. In spite of vast national and constitutional variations, there were significant family resemblances among all the regimes. Perhaps this affinity was rooted first and foremost in the enduring importance of landed interests and of rural society throughout Europe. While in England land was more a source of social status and political ascendancy than of economic and financial power, in France it provided the principal material understructure of the Third Republic, and most notably of its ruling and governing class. Although the Revolution of 1789–94 had swept away the monarchy, it had reinvigorated the agricultural estate: quite apart from leaving many of the landed notables as well as the praedial Catholic Church in place, it expanded and strengthened small and medium peasant holdings. Throughout Europe upper houses, legislatures, bureaucracies and armies drew their life-blood from land-enveloped villages, towns and provinces rather than from industrializing cities or regions. Moreover, except in France, king and court, like the nobilities, were inconceivable without the wealth, income and nimbus generated by large landed proprietorship.

To the extent that this landed society was in relative economic decline, political society was there to brace it. King and court served an overall agglutinating function in the politics of economic, social and cultural defense, France being the exception that proved the rule. By virtue of ancient custom or constitutional convention, or both, the strength of the old ruling class was magnified not only in local and provincial councils but above all in central government. The two houses of parliament and the public service nobilities worked to preserve or reinforce the preindustrial civil society. They passed protective tariffs for uncompetitive agriculture and manufacture everywhere except in England and provided prestigious government positions for embattled nobles and aspiring commoners. No less important, they blocked tax, suffrage, educational and social reforms that threatened to hasten the erosion of the old order.

Official high cultures and the avant-garde

Europe's official cultures conspicuously mirrored the tenacious perseverance of preindustrial civil and political societies. In form, content and style the artifacts of high culture continued to be anchored and swathed in conventions that relayed and celebrated traditions supportive of the old order. The eclectic revival and reproduction of time-honored and venerable styles dominated not only in architecture and statuary but also in painting, sculpture and the performing arts. Museums, academies, churches and universities actively promoted this congruent academic historicism, and so did the state, which enlisted historicism to articulate national and regional purposes. Overall, the hegemonic arts and institutions maintained sufficient inner vitality and synoptic coherence to invigorate the *anciens régimes*.

Of course, between 1848 and 1914 Europe's official cultures experienced discordant modernist movements in the arts as well as in the churches and higher schools. But these defections were easily contained, above all because they were no match for the reigning cultural centers. Admittedly, most defectors were young, spirited and aggressive experimentalists and innovators, and many of them eventually won recognition. Even so, successive waves of the avant-garde hit against the official cultures, which, like breakwaters, survived intact. In the long run the victory of the modernists may have been inevitable. In the short run, however, the modernists were effectively bridled and isolated, if need be with legal and administrative controls. Despite or because of relentless challenges and gibes from the avant-garde, the producers and guardians of official academic traditions remained at once imperious and adaptive. Like kings and nobles, they learned to defuse ascending rivals through calibrated assimilation and co-optation. And just as outworn economic interests made the most of their political leverage to secure protective tariffs and fiscal preferments, so eminent artists used their influence in key hegemonic institutions – academies, salons, museums, ministries of culture – to rally support for their timeworn idioms.

Compared to the vanguard, the cultural establishment and its rear guard were above all protective. But even though the historicist legacy for and with which they did battle was aesthetically impoverished, it was far from spent. Historicism was not an archaic, lifeless and inert accretion that trailed far behind the economic and social developments of the nineteenth century. In fact, between 1848 and 1914 historic academicism declined no further than the rest of preindustrial civil society. To be sure, it lost in vitality as fixed form prevailed over idea, imitation over authenticity, ornateness over artlessness, and pomp over sobriety. But historicism was no less useful and effective for being turgid and specious.

The major historical styles – classical, medieval, Renaissance, Baroque, rococo – were part of the storehouse of symbols and images that served to thwart, dignify and disguise the present. Historicism provided critics of modernity with an inexhaustible reservoir of representations with which not only to glorify and reinvigorate their own privileged though beleaguered world but also to censure and traduce the rival new society. Landed and service nobilities, political catonists and Arcadian social critics each had their own reasons for harking back to time-honored metaphors and emblems.

But the makers and bards of modernity also had recourse to ancient tropes as they set out to justify their project and make it fathomable. While capitalist entrepreneurs excelled at creative destruction in the economic sphere, they took care not to tear the inherited cultural fabric. Indeed, in their quest for divine sanction and social recognition they enveloped their exploits and themselves with historical screens. This use of and solicitude for historical culture substantially mitigated and disguised the stress of fitting modernity into pre-existing civil and political society.

For the political classes high culture was an important ideological instrument. Not only public buildings, statues and spaces but also the pictorial, plastic and performing arts were expected to exalt the old regimes and revalidate their moral claims. The ruling classes took an equally functional view of the arts. Whereas new men enlisted them to display their wealth, taste and aspiration, well-established families used them to reaffirm their fortune and status. For the two factions the consumption of high art and culture was both badge and sacrament of achieved or coveted positions of class, prestige and influence in what remained distinctly traditional societies. Having assigned art such practical functions, the governing and ruling classes were disinclined to sponsor vanguards that balked at ratifying and extolling the *anciens régimes* and their elites in the accustomed ways.

In an age in which the declining old order easily held down the rising new society, traditional conventions, tastes and styles only gradually yielded to breakaway visions and representations. [. . .]

World view

The upper classes of Europe were prepared to take their peoples into a catastrophe from which they hoped against hope to draw benefits for themselves. In other words, though unprecedented, the catastrophe was not expected to be total. To be sure, there might be millions of victims, massive devastation and severe unsettlement. Even so, a general war would not turn out to be 'the end of history', though it would overload the circuits of military planning and control. Certainly the politicians and generals of the aristocratic reaction were accomplices rather than adversaries or rivals in the march to the brink. This is not to deny that there were strains between civil and military leaders and that the military plans, including their operational provisions, limited the freedom of action of politicians and diplomats. But these civil-military tensions were embedded in factional battles over means, not ends, within conservatism and the governing classes. Once the ultraconservative resurgence lifted the soldiers into the highest levels of government, the generals militarized the civilians no more than the civilians politicized the warriors. The latter left their mark not because of their expertise but because the civilians were in search of military solutions to political problems. What tied them together, quite apart from shared social and political attitudes, interests and objectives, was a common commitment to struggle against political democracy, social leveling, industrial development and cultural modernism. These *idées-forces* [key ideas], wrapped in pugnacious patriotism, significantly influenced the making of strategic and tactical plans. To be sure, these required the expertise of generals. But military know-how alone did not dictate the stress on mass assault *à outrance* in pursuit of a swift battlefield victory, regardless of human cost. Besides, that know-how was obsolete. The generals meant to re-enact the lightning campaign of 1870, in which the first Moltke had overwhelmed France with his pioneering speed and concentration of infantry divisions, having over-looked the fact that since then Moltke's formula had been assimilated by all the general staffs. Furthermore, they deceived themselves into thinking that by using the railroads they were appropriating the latest technology for their own purposes, when as a military technique the rails for troop trains, immovably fixed in space, were nearly as much a legacy of the first industrial revolution as the officers were of feudalism.

At any rate, the civilian governors were not disposed to scrutinize the military's strategic and operational schemes. Not that they lacked the intelligence and knowledge to do so. But the statesmen were locked into the same impetuous worldview and political project as the generals. Accordingly, they screened out other options, such as defensive strategies which would have reduced the pressures of timetables and mutual fear. Clearly, the rigidity of diplomatic and military master plans was 'as much in the mind as it was in the railway timetables'. In addition, Europe's politician-statesmen refrained from questioning the wisdom of the quick and massive strike because of their gnawing realization that the *anciens régimes* were too fragile to support the burdens of a protracted war of attrition. In sum, their position was highly paradoxical, and more than likely they knew it.

Eventually, in July–August 1914 the governors of the major powers, all but a few of them thoroughly nobilitarian, marched over the precipice of war with their eyes wide open, with calculating heads, and exempt from mass pressures. Along the way not a single major actor panicked or was motivated by narrow personal, bureaucratic and partisan concerns. Among the switchmen of war there were no petty improvisers, no romantic dilettantes, no reckless adventurers. Whatever the profile of their populist helpers or harassers, they were men of high social standing, education and wealth, determined to maintain or recapture an idealized world of yesterday. But these politician–statesmen and generals also knew that to achieve their project they would have to resort to force and violence. Under the aegis of the scepter and the miter, the old elites, unrestrained by the bourgeoisie, systematically prepared their drive for retrogression, to be executed with what they considered irresistible armies. They, the horsemen of the apocalypse, were ready to crash into the past not only with swords and cavalry charges but also with the artillery and railroads of the modern world that besieged them.

For its own reasons and interests the capitalist bourgeoisie, symbiotically linked to the old elites, was ready and willing, if not eager, to serve as quartermaster for this perilous enterprise. The magnates of movable wealth calculated that the requisites of warfare would intensify the *ancien régime's* need for the 'economic services of capitalism'. Like their senior partners, the bourgeois did not shy away from what they too knew would be absolute war, confident that it would be a forcing house for the expansion of industry, finance and commerce and an improvement of their status and power. As for the industrial workers, they were too weak and too well integrated into nation and society to resist impressment, though theirs was the only class in which there was any marked disposition to do so.

[. . .]

Notes

1   Joseph Schumpeter: economist and economic historian, born in Austria–Hungary, moving to the USA in the 1930s.

CHAPTER 3

The Birth of the Modern: 1885–1914

G. D. JOSIPOVICI

The problem to be dealt with in this chapter can be formulated quite simply: the years 1885-1914 saw the birth of the modern movement in the arts.[1] What are the specific features of the movement, and how are we to account for its emergence?

Three points have to be made before we start. First of all we must be clear that from one point of view our inquiry is nonsensical. There is no specific thing called 'modernity' which we can extract from the variety of individual works of art and hold up for inspection. Every modern artist worth his salt is good precisely because he has found his own individual voice and because this voice is distinct from that of his fellows. And yet it cannot be denied that something did happen to art, to all the arts, some time around the turn of the century, and that Proust, Joyce, Picasso, Klee, Schoenberg and Stravinsky, for all their manifest individuality, do have something in common. Before we plunge into a study of individual artists and works it may be useful to have a frame of reference, a set of common assumptions, which will stop us asking the wrong kinds of questions or looking for the wrong sorts of answers.

This leads to the second point, which is that such an inquiry is far more than an academic exercise, the reconstruction of the past for its own sake. Although more than half a century has passed since those decisive years, the majority of people who are interested in the arts have still not come to terms with what happened then. The indiscriminate abuse of Picasso and Schoenberg may have ceased, but it has merely given way to equally indiscriminate praise. Great artists create their own posterity, said Proust; but though it may be fashionable to enthuse over the latest avant-garde music and painting, there is everywhere – among professional reviewers as well as academic critics – a real failure to understand the premises upon which the great artists of the turn of the century based their works. And until such an understanding has been arrived at, the serious artists of today, who are their heirs, are bound to be misjudged – though not necessarily to go unrecognized. It is thus of paramount importance for us today that we should make sense of the great change that came over the arts at the turn of the century.

The third point is merely a reminder of a historical fact which, if rightly interpreted, should serve as a guide and a warning throughout this investigation. Although the First World War effectively marks the break between the world of the nineteenth century and our own – both in the minds of those who lived through it and of those of us who read about it in the history books – the modern revolution in the arts did not take place during the war or immediately after it, but a decade or so before it. This should make us wary of too facile an identification of art with the culture and society out of which it springs. For, paradoxically, while artists have always been ahead of their times, art has always fulfilled the same basic needs, and men have not fundamentally altered since the days of Homer. It is with the changing *forms* of art and not with what one might call the furniture of art – the props and backdrops which it borrows from the world around it – that we will be concerned in the pages that follow.

The modern movement in the arts cannot be understood in isolation. It must be seen as a reaction to the decadent Romanticism that was prevalent in Europe at the turn of the century. Some of the theoreticians of modernism, such as T. E. Hulme in England, tried to argue that it was nothing other than a wholesale rejection of Romanticism and all it stood for, and a return to a new classicism. Looking back at those pre-war decades from our vantage-point in the mid-century, however, we can see that the matter was considerably more complex than Hulme suggests; that it was more a question of redefining Romanticism, of stressing some of those aspects of it which the nineteenth century had neglected and discarding some of those it had most strongly emphasized, than of rejecting it outright. If we are to understand what the founders of modern art were doing it will be necessary to grasp the premises and implications of Romanticism itself.

Romanticism was first and foremost a movement of liberation – liberation from religious tradition, political absolutism, an hierarchical social system, and a universe conceived on the model of the exact sciences. Reason and scientific laws, the Romantics felt, might allow man to control his environment, but they formed a sieve through which the living, breathing individual slipped, and which retained only the dead matter of generality. What man had in common with other men, what this landscape had in common with other landscapes, was the least important thing about them. What was important was the uniqueness of men and the uniqueness of everything in the world around us, be it a leaf, a sparrow or a mountain range. There were moments, they felt, when man was far from the distractions of the city and of society, and when the reasoning, conceptualizing mind was still, when life seemed suddenly to reveal itself in all its beauty, mystery and terror. In such moments man felt himself restored to his true self, able to grasp the meaning of life and of his own existence. It is to experience and express such moments, both in our lives and in our art, that we should strive, for these are the moments when we throw off the shackles of generality and are restored to our unique selves.

The function of art thus becomes that of digging deep down into those areas of the mind and the world which lie beyond the confines of rational thought and ordinary consciousness; and the hero of Romantic art becomes none other than the artist himself, who is both the explorer of this unknown realm and the priestly mediator between it and his audience. Something of this is suggested by August Wilhelm Schlegel, who is most probably responsible for introducing the term 'Romantic' as a description of the age:

> Ancient poetry and art is rhythmical *nomos*, a harmonious promulgation of the eternal legislation of a beautifully ordered world mirroring the eternal Ideas of things. Romantic poetry, on the other hand, is the expression of a secret longing for the chaos . . . which lies hidden in the very womb of orderly creation . . . [Greek art] is simpler, cleaner, more like nature in the independent perfection of its separate works: [Romantic art], in spite of its fragmentary appearance, is nearer to the mystery of the universe.

Schlegel, it is true, is not here talking only of the nineteenth century; he is contrasting the whole 'modern' or Christian era with the Classical age of Greece and Rome. But his stress on the transcending impulse of Romanticism, on the aspiration towards the mystery of the universe, is taken up by Baudelaire nearly half a century later, in a discussion of the 'Salon' of 1846: 'Qui dit romantisme dit art moderne, -c'est-à-dire intimité, spiritualité, couleur, aspiration vers l'infini, exprimées par tous les moyens que contiennent les arts' [He who speaks of Romanticism speaks of modern art – that is to say intimacy, spirituality, colour, aspiration towards the infinite, expressed by every means at the disposal of the arts].

But here a curious contradiction begins to emerge, a contradiction that lies at the heart of the whole Romantic endeavour, and on that was to determine its future course. One final quotation, from the theologian Schleiermacher, will bring it out into the open:

> I am lying in the bosom of the infinite universe, I am at this moment its soul, because I feel all its force and its infinite life as my own. It is at this moment my own body, because I penetrate all its limbs as if they were my own, and its innermost nerves move like my own . . . . Try out of love for the universe to give up your own life. Strive already here to destroy your own individuality and to live in the One and in the All . . . fused with the Universe.

Romanticism had begun as a movement of rebellion against the arbitrary authorities of the eighteenth century and its abstract laws, a rebellion undertaken in the name of the freedom of the individual. But this freedom, which, as we saw, involves the suppression of the tyrannical intellect, now appears to be synonymous with the loss of individuality as most men conceive it; thus the ultimate freedom, according to the Romantic logic, is death.

Where consciousness itself is felt to be an imprisoning factor, keeping man from his true self, freedom must lie in transcending it. Yet the only times we escape from consciousness for more than a brief moment are in sleep, under the influence of alcohol and drugs, or in madness, while the only total escape is death; hence the key place accorded by Romanticism to dreams, to various forms of addiction, to madness, and to the death-wish. In all these cases the result is, of course, extremely ambiguous. The freedom from consciousness and from social convention does often result in deeper insight, but it results also in the destruction of the individual. Hence the general tone of Romantic art and literature is one of melancholy gloom, for there seems to be no way of resolving the contradiction.

This pull between freedom and annihilation is even easier to discern in the sphere of art itself. The task of the poet, as the Romantics saw it, was to communicate those moments of visionary intensity which only he could experience, moments in which the meaning and value of life were revealed to him. But the poet's only means of expression is language, and language belongs almost by definition to the realm of consciousness and of social intercourse. For language, as Plato had already noted, only exists at a certain degree of abstraction and universality; it takes for granted that there is some sort of social agreement as to the referents of words: we can use the word 'tree' or 'man' only because we all agree roughly what these two words stand for. But if we feel that what is important is the individuality, the 'instress' as Hopkins called it, of this tree or this man – what essentially differentiates it from all other trees or men – then clearly words are going to be a hindrance rather than a help. How then are we to express this insight? The Romantic poet finds himself struggling to express by means of language precisely that which it lies beyond the power of language to express. He is a man desperately trying to get away from his own shadow.

Only one poet in the nineteenth century was fully aware of the implications of the Romantic endeavour, and was prepared to accept and try to overcome them. In Rimbaud's famous letter to Paul Demeny of 15 May 1871, we can see that he had fully understood the problem and had decided on a radical solution:

Donc le poète est vraiment voleur de feu.

Il est chargé de l'humanité, des *animaux* même; il devra faire sentir, palper, écouter ses inventions; si ce qu'il rapporte de *là-bas* a forme, il donne forme; si c'est informe, il donne de l'informe. Trouver une langue; – du reste, toute parole étant idée, le temps d'un langage universel viendra! Il faut être académicien – plus mort qu'un fossile – pour parfaire un dictionnaire, de quelque langue que ce soit. Des faibles se mettraient *à penser* sur la première lettre de l'alphabet, qui pourraient vite ruer dans la folie!

Cette langue sera de l'âme pour l'âme, résumant tout, parfums, sons, couleurs, de la pensée accrochant la pensée et tirant. Le poète définirait la quantité d'inconnu s'éveillant en son temps dans l'âme universelle: il

donnerait plus - que la formule de sa pensée, que l'annotation *de sa marche au Progrès!* Énormité devenant norme, absorbée par tous, il serait vraiment *un multiplicateur de progrès!*
[Thus the poet is truly a plunderer of fire.

He is responsible for humanity, for the *animals* even; he must produce creations which can be felt, touched, heard; if what he brings back from *beyond* has a shape, he gives it shape; if it is shapeless, he gives it shapelessness. He must find a voice - so all speech being idea, the era of universal language will come! One needs to be an academician - deader than a dodo - to fuss over a dictionary confined to a single national tongue. The feeble-minded apply themselves to *pondering* the first letter of the alphabet, quickly ending up in foolery!

That voice will come from the soul for the soul, embracing everything, scents, sounds, colours, and from thought linking and drawing upon thought. The poet will explain the great awakening in his own time of the unknown in the universal spirit: he will provide more - more than the expression of his thought, more than the account *of his march towards Progress!* As infinitude becomes commonplace, imbibed by all, he would truly be *a multiplicator of progress!*]

The failure of this ideal can be traced through the poems themselves, and forms the explicit content of *Une Saison en enfer.* And, indeed, how could he succeed? What he desires is not communication but communion, the direct and total contact of one person with another through a language so charged that it will act without needing to pass by way of the mind at all. Such a language can never be more than a Utopian dream, for to give words the meaning we want them to have, regardless of the socially accepted meaning they already have, is tantamount to abolishing language altogether. When Rimbaud recognized this, with admirable logic, he gave up writing poetry.

But just because he was so ready to push the premisses of Romanticism to their ultimate conclusion, Rimbaud remains one of the key figures of the nineteenth century, marking for ever one of the two poles within which modern art is to move. His contemporaries (Mallarmé excepted - but see below), both in England and in France, chose a somewhat less arduous and therefore less interesting path. They tried to solve the problem by making their verse approximate as closely as possible to their own conception of music - which had, naturally enough, become for the Romantics the artistic language *par excellence,* since it appeared to have none of the disadvantages of speech. To this end they made their verse as mellifluous as possible, stressing its incantatory qualities, smoothing out all harshness of diction, minimizing its referential content, and rigidly excluding all forms of wit and humour for fear these would break their fragile spell. The result was aptly described by T.S. Eliot in a famous essay on Swinburne:

Language in a healthy state presents the object, is so close to the object that the two are identified. They are identified in the verse of Swinburne only because the object has ceased to exist, because the meaning is merely the hallucination of meaning, because language, uprooted, has adapted itself to an independent life of atmospheric nourishment.

So, as with Rimbaud, we see the normal function of language being denied and words taking on an independent meaning. But here the meaning is not just independent of general usage, but of the poet's own will into the bargain. The result is not insight into the mystery of the universe but empty cliché, not the articulation of what lies beyond the confines of rationality, but simple reflex, the verbal equivalent of the canine dribble. For language has a way of getting its own back on those who try to step over it in this manner, and just as the Romantic dreamer found that he escaped from the bonds of his intellect at the cost of his life, so the Romantic poet, trying to escape from the bonds of language, found himself its prisoner, uttering platitudes in the voice of prophet.

But if the poets dreamt of living in a world freed from the stifling restrictions of language, and looked with envy to the composers, these, had the poets but known it, were no freer than themselves. For if language is not natural, that is if words are not inherently expressive, as Rimbaud had thought, the same is true of music. Although Hoffmann wrote enthusiastically about the inherent qualities of a chord of A flat minor, the truth of the matter is that music is nearly as conventional as speech. We find it difficult to grasp music which is distant from us in space or time (Indian or Japanese music, or Gregorian chant, for instance); to know when it is 'cheerful', when 'sad'. Musical instruments, too, have different and highly specialized functions in other societies, and so are associated with different things than they are for us. It is only through frequent hearing, through a familiarization with its 'language', that we can come to appreciate Indian music; the composer, no less than the poet, works in a language which is largely the product of convention, and according to rules to which he voluntarily submits in order to master the world of sounds. Thus, when the initial impetus of Romanticism starts to peter out, we find a development in music parallel to that we traced in poetry – a slackening of formal control, a loosening of the harmonic texture, and the emergence of a soulful, cliché-ridden style that strives to lull the listener into a trance as the music struggles to express the world of the infinite which Baudelaire had urged the artist to seek with every means at his disposal. Naturally enough the piano, instrument of the half-echo, the indefinite, the suggestive, becomes the favourite of artist and public alike. And in music, as in poetry, the attempt to express everything, the totality of experience, unfettered by the rules and limitations of convention or consciousness, leads to its own destruction. More than any of the other arts Romantic music is imbued with the melancholy which stems from the knowledge that to achieve its goal is to expire.

The apotheosis of Romantic art, as all his contemporaries recognized, is to be found in the operas of Richard Wagner. These vast music-dramas seemed to be the perfect answer to Baudelaire's plea for a work of art that would make use of all the arts, thus finally lifting the spectator into the realm of the infinite, the very heart of the mystery of the universe. And we are fortunate in possessing a critique of Wagner by one of the few men who was really aware of the implications of Romanticism because he was so much of a Romantic himself: Friedrich Nietzsche. Nietzsche's analysis of the 'decadent' style sums up some of the points already made:

> What is common to both Wagner and 'the others' consists in this: the decline of all organizing power; the abuse of traditional means, without the capacity or the aim that would justify this; the counterfeit imitation of grand forms . . .; excessive vitality in small details; passion at all costs; refinement as an expression of impoverished life, ever more nerves in the place of muscle.

But Nietzsche is not content with a simple catalogue of Wagner's characteristics: he wants to understand what lies behind this, and to try to account for Wagner's enormous popularity. He sees first of all that for Wagner music is only a means to an end: 'As a matter of fact his whole life long he did nothing but repeat one proposition: that his music did not mean music alone. But something more! Something immeasurably more! . . . "Not music alone" – no musician would speak in this way.' And he explains what this 'more' is: 'Wagner pondered over nothing so deeply as over salvation: his opera is the opera of salvation.' And this, thinks Nietzsche, is the source of Wagner's power, that what he offered was nothing less than the hope of personal salvation to a Europe – and especially a Germany – bewildered by the rapid social and technological changes of the previous forty or so years: 'How intimately related must Wagner be to the entire decadence of Europe for her not to have felt that he was decadent!' And again: 'People actually kiss that which plunges them more quickly into the abyss.' We remember that Schlegel had already talked about a 'secret longing for the chaos . . . which lies hidden in the very womb of orderly creation', and that this longing was nothing other than the Romantic desire for a total and absolute freedom. Nietzsche's suggestion that with Wagner this longing spills out of the realm of art into that of politics and society allows us to glimpse the connection between decadent Romanticism and the rise of totalitarianism. The cataclysmic events of the first half of the present century would have occasioned him little surprise.

What Nietzsche particularly objects to in Wagner is precisely the fact that by trying to turn his music into a religion he debases both music and religion; by trying to turn the entire world into a music-drama, drawing the audience up into the music until they shed their dull everyday lives and come into contact with the heart of the mystery, he dangerously distorts both the life of every day and the nature of art; by blurring the outlines between life and art he turns art into a tool and life into an aesthetic phenomenon, that is, into something which is to be judged entirely by aesthetic criteria and where the rules of morality no longer apply. In so doing Wagner is typical of decadent Romanticism in general, of Huysmans and Swinburne and all those who took to heart Axël's dictum that, as for living, our servants can do that for us.[2] The end of the nineteenth century is the great era of the *poète maudit* [accursed poet], of the dandy, of the Romantic agony. It marks the final bankruptcy of the Romantic revolt.

But even as Wagnerism swept through Europe and Nietzsche sank into his final madness the reaction to Romantic decadence had already begun. This did not take the form of a movement in the sense that surrealism, say, was a movement, with polemical manifestos and self-appointed leaders and spokesmen. It was not even a movement of like-minded men holding the same beliefs about human liberty and the function of the artist in society, as Romanticism, in its early phases, had been. Proust and Joyce met once and barely spoke to one another; Schoenberg loathed Stravinsky; Eliot was more interested in Laforgue than in Mallarmé or Valéry; and Kafka ignored them all. Yet it is easy for us today to see that all these artists were united by one common attitude, albeit a negative one: they all insisted on the *limitations* of the sphere of art. More than that, they all stressed, in the art itself, that what they had created was only art and nothing more: that a painting was nothing except a series of brush-strokes on a flat canvas; that music was nothing except certain notes played by certain combinations of instruments; that poetry was nothing except a grouping of words on the page; that prose fiction was fiction and not reality.

Since the Romantics had regarded art as simply a means to a transcendental end, they naturally tended to see all the arts as more or less interchangeable – it doesn't matter what train you take since they're all going to the same place. The insistence on the part of the moderns that their work was art and not something else, their stress on the particular *medium* in which they were working, was not meant to be a denial of art but rather a reassertion of its crucial function. Art, they argued, was not a means of piercing the sensible veil of the universe, of getting at the 'unknown', as Rimbaud and others had claimed, for there was nothing beyond the world that lay all round us. The whole mystery was there, right in front of us, where everybody could see it – except for the fact that normally men are too blind or lazy to do so. What most of us tend to do in front of the world, of ourselves, of works of art, is to neutralize what is before us by reducing it to something we know already. Thus we are for ever shut up inside our preconceived notions, reacting only to that which makes no demands that we should really see. As Giacometti put it:

> Où y a-t-il plus de monde? Devant le 'Sacre de Napoléon'. Pourquoi les gens regardent-ils justement ce tableau? Parce qu'ils imaginent d'abord assister à la scène, y participer. Ils deviennent des 'petits Napoléons'. En même temps le spectacle devient l'équivalent de la lecture d'un roman. [Where is the biggest crowd to be found? In front of the 'coronation of Napoleon'. Why exactly do people look at this painting? Because, first of all they imagine that they are present at the scene, are taking part in it, they become 'little Napoleons'. Simultaneously, the viewing becomes the equivalent of reading a novel.]

Like the library novel, it becomes an excuse for daydreaming. The modern artist, on the other hand, holds that the work of art is meaningful precisely because it reveals to us the 'otherness' of the world – it shocks us out of our natural sloth and the force of habit, making us 'see' for the first time what we have looked at a hundred times but never really noticed. Art is not a key to the universe but a pair of spectacles, as Valéry, echoing Proust's Elstir, points out:

> Nous devinons ou prévoyons, en général, plus que nous ne voyons, et les impressions de l'œil sont pour nous des signes, et non des *présences singulières,* antérieures à tous les arrangements, les résumés, les raccourcis, les substitutions immédiates, que l'éducation première nous a inculqués.
>
> Comme le penseur essaie de se défendre contre les *mots* et les expressions toutes prêtes qui dispensent les esprits de s'étonner de tout et rendent possible la vie pratique, ainsi l'artiste peut, par l'étude des choses informes,[3] c'est-à-dire de forme *singulière,* essayer de retrouver sa propre singularité . . .
>
> [In general, we guess or imagine rather than see, and the impressions our eyes take in are signs, not *unique presences* with a real existence prior to all the instant arrangements, summaries, foreshortenings, and representations instilled in us by previous education.
>
> Just as the thinker tries to avoid the sayings and ready-made expressions which destroy the possibilities of surprise but may make everyday life possible, so the artist may, by studying disordered items, that is to say of *unique* form, try to rediscover his own uniqueness . . .].

Art, then, does not feed us information, nor does it give us a glimpse of a world beyond or above this one. What it does is to open our eyes by removing the film of habit which we normally carry around with us. It does this by shocking us into awareness through its insistence on itself as an object in its own right, irreducible to anything we could see or think in the normal course of affairs. The cubist picture, for instance, teases the eye as we follow shape after shape on the canvas, always on the verge of understanding it, yet never quite allowed to do so. And because we cannot step back and say: 'Ah, yes, a mandolin, a glass of wine, a table', etc., we go on looking at the canvas and in time learn to accept its own reality instead of reducing it to our own preconceived idea of what a mandolin or a glass of wine looks like. Thus Braque can say: 'le tableau est fini quand l'idée a disparu' [the painting is complete when the idea has vanished], and Valéry, elsewhere in the essay on Degas quoted earlier: 'Regarder, c'est-à-dire oublier les noms des choses que l'on voit.' [to look is to forget the names of the things one is looking at]. Proust's whole novel can be seen as an attempt to substitute the object for the name, to render the uniqueness of the feeling by recreating it rather than simply by naming it.

An art of this kind clearly makes the spectator work. It does not, like Wagnerian opera, claim to provide a passport to salvation, nor, like the 'Sacre de Napoléon', allow each of us to indulge his daydreams. What it does claim to do is to recreate within the willing reader or spectator the liberating experience of the artist himself. When Picasso said, of his famous sculpture of the bull's head made out of the seat and handlebars of a bicycle, that the whole point would be lost if the viewer, through excessive familiarity with it, were to see *only* a bull's head, he neatly illustrated this aspect of modern art. What is important is not the finished product, but the *process*. Picasso wants us to be aware of the fact that what is in front of us is not a bull's head but a man-made object. The product is not there to be contemplated for its own sake but to stimulate the viewer's own perception and to allow him to relive the act of creative discovery for himself. In the same way Proust's novel does not so much tell a story as create within the reader the potentiality for telling the story Marcel is about to set down as the work ends. Thus, paradoxically again, the artist's very acceptance of limitation, his open acknowledgement of the medium in which he is working, leads beyond art to alter the very life of the reader or viewer.

We have been looking at the modern revolution in the arts as a reaction to decadent Romanticism, but if we look at it in a larger perspective it becomes clear that this reaction entailed a radical break with four centuries of the Western artistic tradition. Shifts in taste and forms of expression had occurred at regular intervals in those four centuries, of course, but these were really modifications within a fixed framework. Romanticism, by trying to give full expression to the individual, burst this framework and so made it possible for the moderns to step out of it and see that the frame enclosed not the whole universe but only a restricted area of it. Perhaps a more accurate way of describing the change would be to say that what the artists of the previous four centuries had taken to be the limits of the universe were now discovered to be only the limitations imposed by spectacles they had not realized they were wearing. It is not by chance that the birth of the modern coincides with the discovery or rediscovery of Japanese art, African sculpture, Romanesque painting, the musical instruments of the Far East, and the poetry of the troubadours. This was no simple widening of the cultural horizons; it was the momentous discovery that what had been taken as *the* way of seeing was really only one way among many; that perspective and harmony, far from being in each case a datum of experience, were almost as conventional as the sonnet form and, unlike the latter, were the product of certain metaphysical assumptions which began to emerge in the West at the time of the Renaissance.

All art, since the Renaissance, had been based on the twin concepts of expression and imitation. In an earlier chapter,[4] I suggested why these two should always go hand in hand, and why they should have emerged as the primary criteria of art at the time when medieval notions of analogy could no longer be accepted. It seems appropriate to conclude this brief analysis of modernity by looking at it from the point of view of each of these concepts in turn.

The artist expresses himself and he imitates external reality. For three centuries there was an uneasy compromise between these two notions, until the Romantics, by stressing the first of these aspects to the exclusion of the second, brought the hidden assumptions of both out into the open and showed how unsatisfactory they both were. Writing again about the 'Salon' of 1846, Baudelaire quotes at some length from the German Romantic writer, E. T. A. Hoffmann. The passage, as will readily be seen, is central not only to Baudelaire's whole aesthetic, but to that of Romanticism in general:

> Ce n'est pas seulement en. rêve, et dans le lèger délire qui précède le sommeil, c'est encore éveillé, lorsque j'entends de la musique, que je trouve une analogie et une réunion intime entre les couleurs, les sons et les parfums. Il me semble que toutes ces choses ont été engendrées par un même rayon de lumière, et qu'elles doivent se réunir dans un merveilleux concert. L'odeur des soucis bruns et rouges produit surtout un effet magique sur ma personne. Elle me fait tomber dans une profonde rêverie, et j'entends alors comme dans le lointain les sons graves et profonds du hautbois.

> [It is not only while dreaming, nor in the gentle delirium which precedes sleep, it is also evoked when I listen to music, in which I find an analogy and an intimate conjunction of colours, sounds and scents. It seems to me that all of these things have been engendered by the same ray of light, and that they have to come together in marvellous concert. The scent of brown and red marigolds above all has a magical effect on me. It makes me fall into a deep reverie, and then I hear as if in the distance the dark and solemn tones of the oboe.]

The implicit belief behind this passage is that individual sights, sounds, smells and tastes touch each one of us in the same way and are themselves interchangeable. In other words, that each speaks a natural language. In a similar way the poet has simply to reach down into himself and pour out what he feels, while the reader allows this to enter into his own soul. We have seen how this grossly oversimplified view of the poetic process led to the breakdown of art into a series of utterances so individual that they no longer made sense, or else turned into the banal expression not of vision but of cliché. This failure showed the moderns that the work of art is not simply the expression of some inner feeling, but the creation of a structure which will 'hold' this feeling for the poet as well as for the reader. Hence the insistence on the impersonality of the poet, the radical distinction between the artist and the man made by Proust and Rilke and Eliot. For the artist *qua* man is no different from the reader; the difference lies in the fact that he is a craftsman who can 'catch' the fleeting sensation and make it communicable in the form of a poem or a painting. The work of art, to use a famous phrase of Archibald MacLeish, no longer says, but is.

This is really only another way of making the point discussed earlier about the modern artist's emphasis on the limitations of his medium. To draw these two together it may be useful to look at the change from Romanticism to modernity from a slightly different point of view, that of the change from a view of art as magic to a view of art as game.

The Romantic artist, as we saw, be he Rimbaud or Wagner, claimed, in some way, to be a magician. He claimed, that is, that words and sounds hide within themselves certain magical properties over which the artist alone has power. Through this power that artist can confer salvation upon the rest of mankind. The reader or listener has simply to submit to the words or sounds in order to shed the pains and frustrations of daily living and to emerge reborn. The consequences of such a view were quickly seen by Nietzsche in connection with Wagner, and his description of the Wagnerian style can be paralleled in all the other arts: there is everywhere a solemnity, a pompousness, the stifling feeling of a magical ritual no longer quite under control. In contrast to this view, the moderns sought to instil the notion of art as a game. The work of art does not offer permanent salvation, its function is to increase the reader's own powers of imagination. This requires his active participation and he can, if he wishes, withdraw from the game – no one is forcing him to take part. If he agrees to go on, however, he must abide by the rules laid down by the artist. Again it is not a matter of what the work is saying, but rather of what it is doing. This notion of art as game, moreover, lays stress on the essential modesty of the modern artist, and his awareness that though art has a supremely important place in life, it is helpless to change the world. The rediscovery of the hieratic and stylized arts of other periods and cultures, we must remember, went hand in hand with the rediscovery of genres and forms of art which had not been considered serious enough to form part of the mainstream of European art: the puppet-play, the shadow-play, children's games of all sorts, used to such good effect by Jarry and a little later by Stravinsky, Picasso, Satie, and Debussy. The latter's *Jeux*, a ballet performed by the Diaghilev company in Paris in 1913, and one of the most subtle and inventive works of the period, is 'about' nothing other than a game of tennis!

If all art is a game with its own rules – something that happens between the author and the reader, viewer, or listener – then what is important is the mastery of convention, not the accuracy with which either external reality or the author's own emotions are depicted. And this, leads us to the final and most obvious aspect of the modernist revolution: its break with four centuries of mimesis.

Because all Western art since the Renaissance had been essentially an imitation of reality, it was necessarily anecdotal. Paintings have been concerned with subjects such as coronations, battles, weddings, landscapes, and so on. Novels have told stories, and so have all but the shortest lyrical poems. But, as the Romantics realized, to tell one story, to describe one scene, is at once to cut out the possibility of telling a lot of other stories, of describing quite other scenes. Why should the artist paint this rather than that? Why should the novelist tell this story rather than that, put in this incident rather than another? It is not enough to say: 'Because he feels like it', since this feeling is itself in need of justification – why does he feel like it? Since everything is possible, everything is equally arbitrary, as the hero of Kafka's *The Castle* recognizes:

> It seemed to K. as if at last those people had broken off all relations with him, and as if now in reality he were freer than he had ever been, and at

liberty to wait here in this place usually forbidden to him as long as he desired, and had won a freedom such as hardly anybody else had ever succeeded in winning, and as if nobody could dare to touch him or drive him away, or even speak to him; but – this conviction was at least equally strong – as if at the same time there was nothing more senseless, nothing more hopeless, than this freedom, this waiting, this inviolability.

The problem already haunted the Romantics, and we find its echoes everywhere in their poetry. But so long as they held to any expressive theory of art they could never solve it, however hard they tried to blur the outlines of their fictions, their music, their painting, until it merged with the surrounding world. The paintings of Cézanne mark the decisive break, and his phrase 'Je pars neutre' [I set out neutral] is the key one for this aspect of modernist aesthetics. What he meant was that he tried to paint, eliminating the inevitable personal slant in both subject and object, seeking instead to discover the general laws of light and space in the scene before him, rather than reproducing that particular scene on his canvas. Proust, whose design is similar, makes the point again and again in *Le Temps retrouvé* [Time rediscovered]: he is not interested in imitating a flat reality but in drawing out the general laws inherent in love, in perception, in speech. And thinking perhaps of a Cézanne and of one of those society portraits even more popular then than now, he says:

> Si l'un dans le domaine de la peinture, met en évidence certaines vérités relatives au volume, à la lumière, au mouvement, cela fait-il qu'il soit nécessairement inférieur à tel portrait ne lui ressemblant aucunement de la même personne, dans lequel mille détails qui sont omis dans le premier seront minutieusement relatés, deuxième portrait d'où l'on pourra conclure que le modèle était ravissant tandis qu'on l'eût cru laid dans le premier, ce qui peut avoir une importance documentaire et même historique mais n'est pas nécessairement une vérité d'art.

> [If one example in the domain of painting demonstrated certain truths relative to volume, to light, to movement, it would not necessarily be inferior to a totally different portrait of the same person in which a thousand details omitted in the first painting are meticulously rendered, this second portrait allowing one to conclude that the model was ravishing while one would, on the basis of the first one, have believed her to be ugly, this being a matter of documentary or even historical importance, but not necessarily an artistic truth.]

In other words the work of art does not convey a fixed meaning from the artist to the reader or viewer: rather, it creates an object which did not exist before in either the one or the other, an object which both gives joy and uncovers a truth about the world hitherto hidden. The work of art becomes necessary rather than arbitrary because it is, rather than simply tells. The words in a novel by Joyce, Virginia Woolf, Proust, Robbe-Grillet, Claude Simon, do not enclose a content which the reader simply takes in as he takes in a telephone message, they live and function within the whole work asking the reader to reactivate them within himself as he reads. Ultimately we cannot extract a meaning from the painting or poem or novel, the meaning is the work itself, to be re-experienced every time the reader or viewer wishes to renew the experience.

It might be thought that the search for an art of total potentiality, an art of laws rather than things, would lead to a complete abstraction. Certainly the danger is there and one could say that, if Rimbaud forms one of the poles within which modern art moves, Mallarmé forms the other; for both took to their limits the implications of the Romantic revolt. To go too far in the direction of one or the other is to burst the bonds of art; it leads to either total noise or total silence, either total randomness or total organization. The artist then either plunges in and relies on the honesty of his gesture, on the spontaneity of his response to the paint he handles or the words or notes he puts down, or he organizes his work so rigidly that it might as well be – and often is – produced by a machine. Both points of view are prevalent in so-called avant-garde circles today, and both would have been anathema to the great modern revolutionaries, since both do away with the artist's most precious possession, his individual freedom of choice. As we have seen, this is a limited freedom, and to imagine that it is total is to lose what little there is. But it is essential to maintain it if art is going to survive.

Two quotations from painters would seem to sum up admirably the central features of the modernist movement. The first is from Picasso, who, it will be remembered, broke away from the strict cubism of his early period when he felt he had subjected himself sufficiently to its discipline. Talking to his friend, the photographer Brassai, he said:

> I always aim at the resemblance. An artist should observe nature but never confuse it with painting. It is only translatable into painting by signs . . . . But such signs are not invented. To arrive at the sign you have to concentrate hard on the resemblance. To me surreality is nothing and never has been anything but this profound resemblance, something deeper than the forms and colours in which objects present themselves.

The second is from the English painter, Francis Bacon:

> Art is a method of opening up areas of feeling rather than merely an illustration of an object . . . . A picture should be a re-creation of an event rather than an illustration of an object; but there is no tension in the picture unless there is the struggle with the object.

The preceding pages are an attempt to sketch out some of the characteristics and implications of the modernist revolution and to account for its sudden outbreak at the turn of the present century. Inevitably we have been involved in a discussion which has moved backwards and forwards from the sphere of history to that of aesthetics – inevitably because modernism is first and foremost a rethinking of the whole field of aesthetics as it had been seen in the West since the time of Plato and Aristotle. But this is not to say that this was a mere revolution in the theory of art, for, if the moderns have grown more modest than the Romantics in their view of the function of the artist, they are even more firmly convinced of the crucial place of art in human life.

It has also been necessary, as a matter of strategy, to make the division between the Romantics and the moderns sharper than it really is. For however much the modernist movement is a reaction to a decadent Romanticism, its basic assumptions are still the Romantic ones; a refusal to rely on any external system of values, moral or epistemological, the attempt to discover and communicate the uniqueness of the individual and of each object. If the modern artist frequently harks back to the wit, irony and sophistication of the eighteenth century, it is always a wit tinged with anguish, an irony that is mainly self-protective, a sophistication that has in it the stoic desire for evil to destroy itself mixed with the gnawing certainty that it is far more likely to destroy the good.

Finally, this chapter has deliberately not been confined to French artists because the modern movement was above all an international one. More specifically, and again in implicit reaction to Romanticism, it was an urban movement, one whose exponents are to be found in all great cosmopolitan centres of Europe: Vienna, Munich, Prague, and especially Paris. It was to Paris that the painters and sculptors who formed the backbone of the movement came; in Paris that Proust, Valéry and Joyce published their work; in Paris that Diaghilev's Russian Ballet burst upon the world as the modernist answer to the Wagnerian *Gesamtkunstwerk*. For this reason the modernist revolution has affected the cultural life of France more than that of any other country. In England and Germany the public remembers the leaders of the movement much as they remember all their classical writers – distant and embalmed, standard editions and dreary hours in the classroom. Only in France are they still the mentors of every aspiring artist, the source of all that is most alive in the intellectual life of the country. The history of French literature in the twentieth century is the history of the fortune of one or other of the modernist discoveries. And such was the richness and importance of these discoveries that we are only now beginning to realize their full implications.

Notes

1   The best introduction to 'modernism' is to be found in certain major modern novels, particularly those of Proust and Thomas Mann, but also those of Joyce, Virginia Woolf, Musil, Broch, etc. Other key texts are: T. S. Eliot, *The Sacred Wood* (1920), Valéry's essay 'Poésie et pensée abstraite' (a lecture delivered in Oxford in 1939 and reprinted in *Variété V* (1944)), and Hofmannsthal's 'The Letter of Lord Chandos' (first publ. as 'Ein Brief,' in 1902; transl. in Hugo von Hofmannsthal, *Selected Prose*, publ. in the Bollingen Series XXXIII in 1952). A selection of views by modern painters on their art is to be found in G. Charbonnier, *Le Monologue du peintre* (1959), and R. L. Herbert (ed.) *Modern Artists on Art* (1964). To these should be added Brassai, *Conversations avec Picasso* (1964), and Françoise Gilot and Carleton Lake, *Vivre avec Picasso* (1965). Important views by modern composers on music will be found in Schoenberg, *Letters* (1964), and the conversations between

Stravinsky and Robert Craft: *Stravinsky in Conversation with Robert Craft* (a Pelican book of 1962 containing *Conversations with Igor Stravinsky* (1958) and *Memoirs and Commentaries* (1959)), *Expositions and Developments* (1962), and *Dialogues and a Diary* (1968). A varied selection of texts on 'modernism' by writers, painters, and musicians will be found in H. M. Block and H. Salinger, *The Creative Vision: Modern European Writers on their Art* (1960); R. Ellmann and C. Feidelson, *The Modern Tradition* (1965); J. Cruickshank, *Aspects of the Modern European Mind* (1969).

Criticism. Even a selective bibliography of interesting secondary works would quickly reach enormous proportions. The following books are in the nature of a few tentative suggestions:

R. Barthes, *Le Degré zéro de l'écriture* (1953);

M. Blanchot, *L'Espace littéraire* (1955) and *Le Livre à venir* (1959);

M. Butor, *Répertoire* (to date 3 vols.: 1960, 1964, 1968);

G. Hartman, *The Unmediated Vision: an Interpretation of Wordsworth, Hopkins, Rilke and* Valéry (1966);

F. Kermode, *Romantic Image* (1957);

W. Mellers, *Caliban Reborn: Renewal in Twentieth-Century Music* (1968);

D. Mitchell, *The Language of Modern Music* (1963; paperback 1966);

Marthe Robert, *L'Ancien et le nouveau: de Don Quichotte à Franz Kafka* (1963).

2   Axël: fictional character in the drama *Axël* (1890) by the French symbolist writer Villiers de l'Isle-Adam.

3   A lump of coal, a handkerchief thrown anyhow on to a table.

4   'From analogy to scepticism', Chapter 1 in *French Literature and its Background: 1, The Sixteenth Century.*

CHAPTER 4

The Origins of the War

SAMUEL R. WILLIAMSON JR.

Košutnjak Park, Belgrade, mid-May 1914: Gavrilo Princip fires his revolver at an oak tree, training for his part in the plot. Those practice rounds were the first shots of what would become the First World War. Princip, a Bosnian Serb student, wanted to murder Archduke Franz Ferdinand, heir to the Habsburg throne, when the latter visited the Bosnian capital of Sarajevo. Princip had become involved with a Serbian terrorist group – the Black Hand. Directed by the head of Serbian military intelligence, Colonel Dragutin Dimitrijević (nicknamed Apis, 'the Bull'), the Black Hand advocated violence in the creation of a Greater Serbia. For Princip and Apis, this meant ending Austria-Hungary's rule over Bosnia-Hercegovina through any means possible.

Princip proved an apt pupil. If his co-conspirators flinched or failed on Sunday, 28 June 1914, he did not. Thanks to confusion in the archduke's entourage after an initial bomb attack, the young Bosnian Serb discovered the official touring car stopped within 6 feet of his location. Princip fired two quick shots. Within minutes the archduke and his wife Sophie were dead in Sarajevo.

Exactly one month later, on 28 July, Austria-Hungary declared war on Serbia. What began as the third Balkan war would, within a week, become the First World War. Why did the murders unleash first a local and then a wider war? What were the longer-term, the mid-range, and the tactical issues that brought Europe into conflict? What follows is a summary of current historical thinking about the July crisis, while also suggesting some different perspectives on the much studied origins of the First World War.

After 1905, Europe's diplomats, strategic planners, and political leaders confronted a series of interlocking issues: some had long troubled the continent, others were by-products of still older problems that had either been resolved or evaded. A major issue centred on the perennial Eastern Question. Since 1878 the European powers had helped themselves to large portions of the Ottoman empire, the so-called 'Sick Man of Europe': Egypt and Cyprus had gone to Britain. Morocco and Tunisia to France, Tripoli (Libya) to Italy, and Bosnia-Hercegovina to Austria-Hungary. The Balkan wars of 1912–13 had seen Turkish holdings in the Balkans disappear. But struggle over the Balkans had not ended, as Russia, Serbia, and the Habsburgs still contended for ascendancy. Russia wanted a dominant voice in the name of Slavic brotherhood: Austria-Hungary wanted to continue its historic mission as a bridge to the east through the Balkans: and the Serbs wanted access to the sea.

A second major issue focused upon the Habsburg monarchy, also considered 'sick'. The question for many was whether Europe's third largest state with 50 million citizens could survive as a multinational, dynastic state in an age of increasing nationalism and democracy. While most of its neighbours looked covetously at Austria-Hungary, one desperately wanted it to survive: its northern neighbour and ally since 1879, the German Reich.

Unified by Otto von Bismarck in the 1860s and the Franco Prussian War of 1870, Germany occupied a pivotal geographic and political position in Europe. A growing economic power and already a formidable military power, Berlin's aggressive policy of *Weltpolitik* and unrestrained navalism after 1900 had alarmed most of Europe. For many, German ambitions constituted a third major European problem. To complicate matters, no German government could easily accept the possibility that Russia might gain from the collapse of the Habsburg monarchy and thus become a still greater threat to Germany's eastern frontier. Germany's very strength would prompt the British and French, for balance of power reasons, to seek Russian help as a way to deter and threaten Berlin.

There were additional contextual issues that shaped the framework of international politics in the last year before 1914. These included alliance alignments, the arms race, imperialism's legacies, economic rivalries, and virulent nationalism. By 1914 Europe had become divided into two diplomatic groupings, loose to be sure but distinct. One, the Triple Alliance, was centred on Berlin and included Austria-Hungary, Italy, and, by secret protocol, Romania. Yet by the summer of 1914 few statesmen believed that Italy and Romania were reliable allies or likely ever to help Vienna. On the other side was the Triple Entente, centred on the Franco-Russian alliance and with Britain as *entente* partner of both. The British had detailed military arrangements, furthermore, with the French in the event of a German attack in the west. But the British never had a formal treaty commitment with France or with Russia, only the far more dangerous one of memories and emotions.

Despite the inherently hostile possibilities between the two alliance alignments, the great powers had managed to maintain the peace through three major international confrontations (two Morocco crises and repeated Bosnian tensions). In 1914, when the three central players – Austria-Hungary, Russia, and Germany – moved to mobilize, the earlier restraints fell away. If the alliance/*entente* structure *per se* did not cause the war, its very existence ensured that the conflict would become a wider war the moment the rigid military mobilization schedules became the ruling logic.

Closely linked to the alliance/*entente* diplomatic arrangements were their strategic and military-naval aspects. The years before 1914 had seen unprecedented arms races, most conspicuously the Anglo-German naval race after 1898. Every member of the alliance/*entente* system participated in the naval competition, but its most dramatic impact had been upon Anglo-German relations. No other issue had such a negative impact upon bilateral ties: no other issue proved such a stumbling block to efforts for restraint. Britain matched the German build-up which Admiral Alfred von Tirpitz had hoped would influence British foreign policy to give more respect to Germany. More radically, London introduced the all-big gun dreadnought class of battleships and thus revolutionized the entire race.

The very fact of the German threat also forced Britain to move its principal naval forces northward. This in turn gave France the ability to argue that its naval forces were protecting British interests in the Mediterranean. This issue decisively influenced Britain's sense of obligation to its principal *entente* partner, France.

Other powers also spent extravagant sums on battleships, as each sought to match its local neighbour. Ironically, as subsequent chapters in this volume will show, the large capital ships were almost irrelevant to the actual conduct of the naval war, while the submarine and the protected convoy would play a far more decisive role.

The more important arms race has often been overlooked: the sharp increases in continental military manpower after 1911. Except for Britain, every country already had male conscription. Even if not all males actually served, conscription provided a sizeable manpower pool. Each of the great powers counted their standing armies in the hundreds of thousands. For instance, in 1912 the German forces numbered 646,000, the French 611,000, and the Russian 1,332,000. Yet there could never be too many men, or so the Prussian general staff concluded after the second Moroccan crisis of 1911. In late 1912 the Germans would increase their standing army by more than 130,000 and the French would raise theirs by nearly 90,000. Austria-Hungary would increase its forces as well and Russia began plans for still more troops. By July 1914 there were, even before the mobilizations began, approximately 3.6 million men on active duty among the allied/*entente* states.

Buttressing the military and naval preparations was the legacy of decades of imperial rivalry. The scramble for colonies and imperial influence had shaped the agenda of late nineteenth century international politics. Tensions did not ease in the early twentieth century. The two Moroccan crises and the Bosnian annexation tension of 1908 brought the dangers closer to the continent: the Eastern Question remained as dangerous as ever. The Italian invasion of Tripoli in September 1911 had reinforced this point. The imperial rivalries had, moreover, exacerbated relations between Britain and Germany, Britain and France, Britain and Russia, and between Austria-Hungary and Serbia and Italy and Russia.

For Britain the Boer War (1899–1902) against the Dutch South Africans had exposed the risks of a policy of splendid isolation. Hence, the British government began to search for partners. Its first success came in 1902 with the Japanese alliance to protect Britain's Far Eastern holdings against Russia. Then in 1904 and 1907 there were the *entente* arrangements with France and Russia, each agreement seeking to contain or end imperial rivalries. With these treaties, Britain's imperial and continental politics became fatefully entangled even if technically London retained a free hand.

Imperial frictions were both reinforced and transcended by the economic rivalry among the great powers. Generally, trade flowed easily among the group save for tariff issues. The Austrians would order weapons from the Russians, the British would build ships on demand, the Germans would sell to the Russians, and the French sold weapons wherever possible. Yet the governments became progressively less flexible about their lending policies, as the French gradually moved to exclude the Habsburgs from the Paris money markets in an effort to appease the Russians. Even the usually generous British were less forthcoming with Vienna. Still Vienna found funds in Berlin and New York City without much trouble. The international trading and banking fraternity, Marxist rhetoric notwithstanding, remained international in outlook and was always alarmed at the prospect of war. For the financial community, peace appeared the only rational policy.

Among the tectonic plates shaping the context of international politics, none loomed as dangerous and irrational as rampant, virulent, passion-filled nationalism. Spurred by the French Revolution, the spread of literacy, and the growth of historical mythologies, by 1914 nationalism had become the plaything of politicians and the intelligentsia. After 1900 each country had its own shrill nationalism, but it reached new heights after 1911 and the second Moroccan crisis. Under the leadership of Raymond Poincaré, first as foreign minister and then as president, France had a veritable nationalistic revival. In Britain the Irish Question flamed to new peaks, as the Ulster Protestants refused to accept the prospect of Irish home rule. The German variety was no less strident, often blended with the myopia of Prussian militarism. In Italy, rabid nationalists fixated on Austria-Hungary's possession of the Tyrol and the Dalmatian coast. For Russia, every Balkan issue became a test of Slavic fraternalism and aggressive Russian nationalism. Nationalism had turned much of Europe into a veritable box of inflammable tinder.

But no place matched the Habsburg monarchy, where eleven nationalities competed, struggled, and yet finally managed to live together. Thanks to the Dual Monarchy's constitutional arrangements of 1867, the German-Austrians and the Hungarians controlled the political apparatus in the two states. Yet they had to accommodate the various nationalities and to adjust their internal and external policies accordingly. In fact, the Habsburg leadership struggled to make concessions to the Czechs and Poles and others inside the monarchy. Some leaders, including the Archduke Franz Ferdinand, were prepared to go even further, only to face the intransigent Magyar élites who refused to diminish their political power for other groups. The Habsburg neighbours were less benign. The Romanians wanted Transylvania, the Italians at least the Tyrol, the Russians the breakup of the entire monarchy, and the Serbs in Belgrade a Greater Serbia at Habsburg expense. Others, sparked by the Croatians and the Slovenians, talked of a new south Slav, Yugoslav state.

After the 1903 palace coup brought the Obrenović dynasty to power in Belgrade, Serbia gradually became Vienna's most implacable foe, anxious to accelerate the demise of the Habsburgs. The Bosnian crisis of 1908, the Balkan wars, and the increase of Serbian territory and population poisoned the relationship still more. And the Serbian government tolerated or encouraged groups who wanted to end Habsburg rule in all of the Balkans. The most dangerous of these societies was Apis's Black Hand. After 1908 Habsburg policy-makers would view Serbia as the major threat to the monarchy's survival in a democratic age. Vienna saw the Serbs, as the west would in the 1990s, as leaders for whom duplicity and evasion were staples of political and diplomatic behaviour. By June 1914 the Habsburg leadership had come to believe that a final reckoning with the Serb menace could not be postponed much longer.

Still, in the spring of 1914 the European scene appeared less volatile than at any point in the past four years. To be sure, the Germans and Russians had quarrelled over a German military mission to Turkey, and the military press in both countries had taunted each other. Rome and Vienna, two erstwhile allies, exchanged acrimonious notes over the future of Albania, which both wanted to control. And Vienna also had to face the fact that Romania was apparently drifting away from the Triple Alliance. By contrast, however, Belgrade and Vienna were involved in a set of economic negotiations that appeared promising. More surprisingly, Anglo-German relations appeared almost serene, with the British navy in late June paying a call on the German fleet at Kiel.

The major issues in each country were domestic. In France the prospect of Madame Henriette Caillaux's trial for the murder of the editor of *Le Figaro* over his slanderous attacks on her husband dominated the public agenda. In Britain the perennial Irish Question had prompted a near mutiny of senior British army officers over the prospect of enforcing a policy of home rule. In Russia the greatest strikes of the pre-war years threatened to paralyse the major cities. In Germany fears mounted about the surging power of the socialists. In Austria the parliament had been adjourned in March because of Czech-German clashes. In Hungary tensions were increasing between the Magyars and the Romanians in Transylvania.

But possibly the most dangerous situation existed in Serbia, where the civilian government (backed by Russia) found itself under assault from the Serbian military who wanted to become a virtual state within a state. The situation worsened when the military pushed Prime Minister Nikolai Pašić from office in early June, only to have the Russians insist on and achieve his restoration. Throughout Europe, these domestic, internal issues were troubling but not inherently dangerous to the international peace. Indeed, Arthur Nicolson, the long-time British under-secretary of state for foreign affairs, asserted in early May 1914 that he had not seen the international scene so calm in years.

Two shots in Sarajevo on Sunday 28 June shattered that illusion. Those shots had the ineluctable effect of converging all of the danger points of European foreign and domestic policies. The First World War would be the result.

The Serbian terrorist plot had succeeded. But that very success also threatened Pašić's civilian government. Already at odds with Apis and his Black Hand associates, Pašić now found himself compromised by his own earlier failure to investigate allegations about the secret society. In early June 1914, the minister had heard vague rumours of an assassination plot. He even sought to make inquiries, only to have Apis stonewall him about details. Whether Belgrade actually sought to alert Vienna about the plot remains uncertain. In any event, once the murders occurred, the premier could not admit his prior knowledge nor allow any Austro-Hungarian action that might unravel the details of the conspiracy. Not only would any compromise threaten his political position, it could lead Apis and his army associates to attempt a coup or worse.

After 28 June Pašić tried, without much success, to moderate the Serbian press's glee over the archduke's death. He also sought to appear conciliatory and gracious towards Vienna. But he knew that the Habsburg authorities believed that Princip had ties to Belgrade. He only hoped that the Habsburg investigators could not make a direct, incontrovertible connection to Apis and others.

Pašić resolved early, moreover, that he would not allow any Habsburg infringement of Serbian sovereignty or any commission that would implicate him or the military authorities. If he made any concession, his political opponents would attack and he might expose himself and the other civilian ministers to unacceptable personal risks. Thus Serbia's policy throughout the July crisis would be apparently conciliatory, deftly evasive, and ultimately intractable. It did not require, as the inter-war historians believed, the Russian government to stiffen the Serbian position. Once confronted with the fact of Sarajevo, the Serbian leadership charted its own course, one which guaranteed a definitive confrontation with Vienna.

The deaths of Franz Ferdinand and Sophie stunned the Habsburg leadership. While there were only modest public shows of sympathy, limited by the court's calculation to play down the funeral, all of the senior leaders wanted some action against Belgrade. None doubted that Serbia bore responsibility for the attacks. The 84 year old emperor, Franz Joseph, returned hurriedly to Vienna from his hunting lodge at Bad Ischl. Over the next six days to 4 July 1914 all of the Habsburg leaders met in pairs and threes to discuss the monarchy's reaction to the deaths and to assess the extensive political unrest in Bosnia Hercegovina in the wake of the assassinations. Nor could the discussions ignore the earlier tensions of 1912 and 1913 when the monarchy had three times nearly gone to war with Serbia and/or Montenegro. Each time militant diplomacy had prevailed and each time Russia had accepted the outcome.

The most aggressive of the Habsburg leaders, indeed the single individual probably most responsible for the war in 1914 was General Franz Conrad von Hötzendorf, chief of the Austro-Hungarian general staff. In the previous crises he had called for war against Serbia more than fifty times. He constantly lamented that the monarchy had not attacked Serbia in 1908 when the odds would have been far better. In the July crisis Conrad would argue vehemently and repeatedly that the time for a final reckoning had come. His cries for war in 1912 and 1913 had been checked by Archduke Franz Ferdinand and the foreign minister, Leopold Berchtold. Now, with the archduke gone and Berchtold converted to a policy of action, all of the civilian leaders, except the Hungarian prime minister Istvàn Tisza wanted to resolve the Serbian issue. To retain international credibility the monarchy had to show that there were limits beyond which the south Slav movement could not go without repercussions.

The Habsburg resolve intensified with reports from Sarajevo that indicated that the trail of conspiracy did indeed lead back to at least one minor Serbian official in Belgrade. While the evidence in 1914 never constituted a 'smoking gun', the officials correctly surmised that the Serbian government must have tolerated and possibly assisted in the planning of the deed. Given this evidence, the Habsburg leaders soon focused on three options: a severe diplomatic humiliation of Serbia; quick, decisive military action against Serbia; or a diplomatic ultimatum that, if rejected, would be followed by military action. Pressed by Conrad and the military leadership, by 3 July even Franz Joseph had agreed on the need for stern action, including the possibility of war. Only one leader resisted a military solution: Istvàn Tisza. Yet his consent was absolutely required for any military action. Tisza preferred the diplomatic option and wanted assurances of German support before the government made a final decision. His resistance to any quick military action effectively foreclosed that option, leaving either the diplomatic one or the diplomatic/military combination. Not surprisingly, those anxious for military action shifted to the latter alternative.

The Austro-Hungarian foreign minister, Berchtold, made the next move on 4 July, sending his belligerent subordinate Alexander Hoyos to Berlin to seek a pledge of German support. Armed with a personal letter from Franz Joseph to Wilhelm II and a long memorandum on the need for resolute action against Serbia, Hoyos got a cordial reception. The Germans fully understood Vienna's intentions: the Habsburg leadership wanted a military reckoning with Belgrade. The German leadership (for reasons to be explored later) agreed to the Habsburg request, fully realizing that it might mean a general war with Russia as Serbia's protector.

With assurances of German support, the leaders in Vienna met on 7 July to formulate their plan. General Conrad gave confident assessments of military success and the civilian ministers attempted to persuade Tisza to accept a belligerent approach. At the same time the preliminary diplomatic manoeuvres were planned. Finally, on 13–14 July Hungarian Prime Minister Tisza accepted strong action and possible war with Serbia. He did so largely because of new fears that a possible Serbian Romanian alignment would threaten Magyar overlordship of the 3 million Romanians living in Transylvania. Drafts of the ultimatum, meanwhile, were prepared in Vienna. Deception tactics to lull the rest of Europe were arranged and some military leaves were cancelled.

But there remained a major problem: when to deliver the ultimatum? The long-scheduled French state visit to Russia of President Raymond Poincaré and Premier René Viviani from 20 July to 23 July thoroughly complicated the delivery of the ultimatum. Berchtold, understandably, did not want to hand over the demands while the French leaders were still in St Petersburg. Yet to avoid that possibility meant a further delay until late afternoon, 23 July. At that point the forty-eight-hour ultimatum, with its demands that clearly could not be met, would be delivered in Belgrade.

Germany's decision of 5–6 July to assure full support to Vienna ranks among the most discussed issues in modern European history. A strong, belligerent German response came as no surprise. After all, Wilhelm II and Franz Ferdinand had just visited each other, were close ideologically, and had since 1900 developed a strong personal friendship. Chancellor Theobald von Bethmann Hollweg, moreover, believed that Berlin must show Vienna that Germany supported its most loyal ally. Far more controversial is whether the civilian leaders in Berlin, pressured by the German military, viewed the Sarajevo murders as a 'heaven-sent' opportunity to launch a preventive war against Russia. This interpretation points to increasing German apprehension about a Russian military colossus, allegedly to achieve peak strength in 1917. And Russo-German military relations were in early 1914 certainly at their worst in decades. Nor did Kaiser Wilhelm II's military advisers urge any modicum of restraint on Vienna, unlike previous Balkans episodes. An increasingly competitive European military environment now spilled over into the July crisis.

However explained, the German leadership reached a rare degree of consensus: it would support Vienna in a showdown with Serbia. Thus the German kaiser and chancellor gave formal assurances (the so-called 'blank cheque') to Vienna. From that moment, Austria-Hungary proceeded to exploit this decision and to march toward war with Serbia. Berlin would find itself – for better or worse – at the mercy of its reliable ally as the next stages of the crisis unfolded.

For two weeks and more Berlin waited, first for the Habsburg leadership to make its final decisions and then for their implementation. During this time the German kaiser sailed in the North Sea and the German military and naval high command, confident of their own arrangements, took leaves at various German spas. Bethmann Hollweg, meanwhile, fretted over the lengthy delays in Vienna. He also began to fear the consequences of the 'calculated risk' and his 'leap into the dark' for German foreign policy. But his moody retrospection brought no changes in his determination to back Vienna; he only wished the Habsburg monarchy would act soon and decisively.

By Monday 20 July, Europe buzzed with rumours of a pending Habsburg *démarche* in Belgrade. While the Irish Question continued to dominate

British political concerns and the French public focused on the Caillaux murder trial, Vienna moved to act against Belgrade. Remarkably, no Triple Entente power directly challenged Berchtold before 23 July, and the foreign minister for his part remained inconspicuous. Then, as instructed, at 6 p.m. on 23 July Wladimir Giesl, the Habsburg minister in Belgrade, delivered the ultimatum to the Serbian foreign ministry. Sir Edward Grey, the British foreign secretary, would immediately brand it as 'the most formidable document ever addressed by one State to another that was independent'.

With its forty-eight-hour deadline, the ultimatum demanded a series of Serbian concessions and a commission to investigate the plot. Pašić, away from Belgrade on an election campaign tour, returned to draft the response. This reply conceded some points but was wholly unyielding on Vienna's key demand, which would have allowed the Austrians to discover Pašić's and his government's general complicity in the murders.

News of the Habsburg ultimatum struck Europe with as much force as the Sarajevo murders. If the public did not immediately recognize the dangers to the peace, the European diplomats (and their military and naval associates) did. The most significant, immediate, and dangerous response came not from the Germans, but from the Russians. Upon learning of the ultimatum, Foreign Minister Serge Sazonov declared war inevitable. His actions thereafter did much to ensure a general European war.

At a meeting of the Council of State on 24 July, even before the Serbians responded, Sazonov and others pressed for strong Russian support for Serbia. Fearful of losing Russian leadership of the pan-Slavic movement, he urged resolute behaviour. His senior military leaders backed this view, even though Russia's military reforms were still incomplete. The recently concluded French state visit had given the Russians new confidence that Paris would support Russia if war came.

At Sazonov's urgings, the Council agreed, with the tsar approving the next day, to initiate various military measures preparing for partial or full mobilization. The Council agreed further to partial mobilization as a possible deterrent to stop Austria-Hungary from attacking the Serbs. These Russian military measures were among the very first of the entire July crisis: their impact would be profound. The measures were not only extensive, they abutted German as well as Austrian territory. Not surprisingly, the Russian actions would be interpreted by German military intelligence as tantamount to some form of mobilization. No other actions in the crisis, beyond Vienna's resolute determination for war, were so provocative or disturbing as Russia's preliminary steps of enhanced border security and the recall of certain troops.

Elsewhere, Sir Edward Grey sought desperately to repeat his 1912 role as peacemaker in the Balkans. He failed. He could not get Vienna to extend the forty-eight hour deadline. Thus at 6 p.m. on 25 July, Giesl glanced at the Serbian reply, deemed it insufficient, broke diplomatic relations, and left immediately for nearby Habsburg territory. The crisis had escalated to a new, more dangerous level.

Grey did not, however, desist in his efforts for peace. He now tried to initiate a set of four power discussions to ease the mounting crisis. Yet he could never get St Petersburg or Berlin to accept the same proposal for some type of mediation or diplomatic discussions. A partial reason for his failure came from Berlin's two continuing assumptions: that Britain might ultimately stand aside and that Russia would eventually be deterred by Germany's strong unequivocal support of Vienna.

Each of Grey's international efforts, ironically, alarmed Berchtold. He now became determined to press for a declaration of war, thus thwarting any intervention in the local conflict. In fact, the Habsburg foreign minister had trouble getting General Conrad's reluctant agreement to a declaration of war on Tuesday 28 July. This declaration, followed by some desultory gunfire between Serbian and Austro-Hungarian troops that night, would thoroughly inflame the situation. The Serbs naturally magnified the gunfire incident into a larger Austrian attack. This in turn meant that the Russians would use the casual shooting to justify still stronger support for Serbia and to initiate still more far reaching military measures of their own.

By 28 July every European state had taken some military and/or naval precautions. The French recalled some frontier troops, the Germans did the same, and the Austro-Hungarians began their mobilization against the Serbs. In Britain, Winston Churchill, First Lord of the Admiralty, secured cabinet approval to keep the British fleet intact after it had completed manoeuvres. Then on the night of 29 July he ordered the naval vessels to proceed through the English Channel to their North Sea battle stations. It could be argued that thanks to Churchill Britain became the first power prepared to protect its vital interests in a European war.

Grey still searched for a solution. But his efforts were severely hampered by the continuing impact of the Irish Question and the deep divisions within the cabinet over any policy that appeared to align Britain too closely with France. Throughout the last week of July, Grey tried repeatedly to gain cabinet consent to threaten Germany with British intervention. The radicals in the cabinet refused. They wanted no British participation in a continental war.

Grey now turned his attention to the possible fate of Belgium and Britain's venerable treaty commitments to protect Belgian neutrality. As he did so, the German diplomats committed a massive blunder by attempting to win British neutrality with an assurance that Belgium and France would revert to the status quo ante after a war. Not only did Grey brusquely reject this crude bribery, he turned it back against Berlin. On 31 July, with cabinet approval Grey asked Paris and Berlin to guarantee Belgium's status. France did so at once: the Germans did not. Grey had scored an important moral and tactical victory.

In St Petersburg meanwhile, decisions were taken, rescinded, then taken again that assured that the peace would not be kept. By 28 July Sazonov had concluded that a partial mobilization against Austria-Hungary would never deter Vienna. Indeed his own generals argued that a partial step would complicate a general mobilization. Sazonov therefore got the generals' support for full mobilization. He then won the Tsar's approval only to see Nicholas II hesitate after receiving a message from his cousin, Kaiser Wilhelm II. The so called 'Willy Nicky' telegrams came to nothing, however. On 30 July the tsar ordered general mobilization, with a clear recognition that Germany would probably respond and that a German attack would be aimed at Russia's French ally.

The Russian general mobilization resolved a number of problems for the German high command. First, it meant that no negotiations, including the proposal for an Austrian 'Halt in Belgrade', would come to anything. Second, it allowed Berlin to declare a 'defensive war' of protection against an aggressive Russia, a tactic that immeasurably aided Bethmann Hollweg's efforts to achieve domestic consensus. And, third, it meant that the chancellor could no longer resist General Helmuth von Moltke's demands for German mobilization and the implementation of German war plans. Alone of the great powers, mobilization for Germany equalled war. Bethmann Hollweg realized this. Yet once the German mobilization began, the chancellor lost effective control of the situation.

At 7 p.m. on Saturday, 1 August 1914, Germany declared war on Russia. The next day German forces invaded Luxembourg. Later that night Germany demanded that Belgium allow German troops to march through the neutral state on their way to France. The Belgian cabinet met and concluded that it would resist the German attack.

In France general mobilization began. But the French government, ever anxious to secure British intervention, kept French forces 6 miles away from the French border. In London Paul Cambon, the French ambassador, importuned the British government to uphold the unwritten moral and military obligations of the Anglo-French *entente*. Still, even on Saturday 1 August the British cabinet refused to agree to any commitment to France. Then on Sunday 2 August Grey finally won cabinet approval for two significant steps. Britain would protect France's northern coasts against any German naval attack and London would demand that Germany renounce any intention of attacking Belgium. Britain had edged closer to war.

On Monday 3 August, the British cabinet reviewed the outline of Grey's speech to parliament that afternoon. His peroration, remarkable for its candour and its disingenuousness about the secret Anglo-French military and naval arrangements left no doubt that London would intervene to preserve the balance of power against Germany; that it would defend Belgium and France; and that it would go to war if Germany failed to stop the offensive in the west. This last demand, sent from London to Berlin on 4 August, would be rejected. At 11 p.m. (GMT) on 4 August 1914 Britain and Germany were at war.

With the declarations of war the focus shifted to the elaborate pre-arranged mobilization plans of the great powers. For the naval forces the issues were relatively straightforward: prepare for the great naval battle, impose or thwart a policy of naval blockade, protect your coastlines, and keep the shipping lanes open. For the continental armies, the stakes were far greater. If an army were defeated, the war might well be over. Committed to offensive strategies, dependent on the hope that any war would be short and reliant on the implementation of their carefully developed plans, the general staffs believed they had prepared for almost every possible contingency.

In each country the war plans contained elaborate mobilization schedules which the generals wanted to put into action at the earliest possible moment. While mobilization raised the risks of war in only two cases did it absolutely guarantee a generalized engagement: (1) if Russia mobilized, Germany would do so and move at once to attack Belgium and France; (2) if Germany mobilized without Russian provocation, the results were the same. Any full Russian mobilization would trigger a complete German response and, for Germany, mobilization meant war. Very few, if any, civilian leaders fully comprehended these fateful interconnections and even the military planners were uncertain about them.

The German war plans in 1914 were simple, dangerous and exceptionally mechanical. To overcome the threat of being trapped in a two front war between France and Russia, Germany would attack first in the west, violating Belgian neutrality in a massive sweeping movement that would envelop and then crush the French forces. Once the French were defeated, the Germans would redeploy their main forces against Russia and with Austro-Hungarian help conclude the war. The Russian war plans sought to provide immediate assistance to France and thereby disrupt the expected German attack in the west. The Russians would attack German troops in East Prussia, while other Russian forces moved southward into Galicia against the Habsburg armies. But to achieve their goals the Russians had to mobilize immediately, hence their escalatory decisions early in the crisis, with fateful consequences for the peace of Europe.

The Italians, it should be noted, took some preliminary measures in August 1914 but deferred general mobilization until later. Otherwise Rome took no further action to intervene. Rather the Italian government soon became involved in an elaborate bargaining game over its entry into the fray. Not until April 1915 would this last of the major pre-war allies enter into the fighting, not on the side of their former allies but in opposition with the Triple Entente.

By 10 August 1914 Europe was at war. What had started as the third Balkan war had rapidly become the First World War. How can one assess responsibility for these events? Who caused it? What could have been done differently to have prevented it? Such questions have troubled generations of historians since 1914. There are no clear answers. But the following observations may put the questions into context. The alliance/*entente* system created linking mechanisms that allowed the control of a state's strategic destiny to pass into a broader arena, one which the individual government could manage but not always totally control. Most specifically, this meant that any Russo-German quarrel would see France involved because of the very nature of Germany's offensive war plans. Until 1914 the alliance/*entente* partners had disagreed just enough among themselves to conceal the true impact of the alliance arrangements.

The legacy of Germany's bombastic behaviour, so characteristic of much of German *Weltpolitik* and *Europolitik* after 1898, also meant that Berlin was thoroughly mistrusted. Its behaviour created a tone, indeed an edginess, that introduced fear into the international system, since only for Germany did mobilization equal war. Ironically, and not all historians agree, the German policy in 1914 may have been less provocative than earlier. But that summer Berlin paid the price for its earlier aggressiveness.

Serbia allowed a terrorist act to proceed, then sought to evade the consequences of its action. It would gain, after 1918, the most from the war with the creation of the Yugoslav state. Paradoxically, however, the very ethnic rivalries that brought Austria-Hungary to collapse would also plague the new state and its post-1945 successor.

Austria-Hungary feared the threat posed by the emergence of the south Slavs as a political force. But the Dual Monarchy could not reform itself sufficiently to blunt the challenge. With the death of the Archduke Franz Ferdinand, who had always favoured peace, the monarchy lost the one person who could check the ambitions of General Conrad and mute the fears of the civilians. While harsh, Ottokar Czernin's epitaph has a certain truth to it: 'We were compelled to die: we could only choose the manner of our death and we have chosen the most terrible.'

Germany believed that it must support its Danubian ally. This in turn influenced Berlin's position towards Russia and France. Without German backing, Vienna would probably have hesitated or been more conciliatory toward Belgrade. But, anxious to support Vienna and possibly to detach Russia from the Triple Entente, Berlin would risk a continental war to achieve its short and long-term objectives. Berlin and Vienna bear more responsibility for starting the crisis and then making it very hard to control.

Nevertheless, the Russians must also share some significant responsibility for the final outcome. St Petersburg's unwavering support of Serbia, its unwillingness to negotiate with Berlin and Vienna, and then its precipitant preparatory military measures escalated the crisis beyond control. Russia's general mobilization on 30 July guaranteed a disaster.

Those Russian decisions would in turn confront the French with the full ramifications of their alliance with Russia. Despite French expectations, the alliance with Russia had in fact become less salvation for Paris and more assuredly doom. France became the victim in the Russo-German fight. Throughout the crisis French leaders could only hope to convince Russia to be careful and simultaneously work to ensure that Britain come to their assistance. Paris failed in the first requirement and succeeded in the second.

The decisions of August 1914 did not come easily for the British government. Grey could not rush the sharply divided cabinet. The decade-old *entente* ties to the French were vague and unwritten and had a history of deception and deviousness. Nor did the vicious political atmosphere created by Ireland help. Grey desperately hoped that the threat of British intervention would deter Germany; it did not. Could Grey have done more? Probably not, given the British political system and the precarious hold the Liberal Party had on power. Only a large standing British army would have deterred Germany, and that prospect, despite some recent assertions, simply did not exist.

In July 1914 one or two key decisions taken differently might well have seen the war averted. As it was, the July crisis became a model of escalation and inadvertent consequences. The expectation of a short war, the ideology of offensive warfare, and continuing faith in war as an instrument of policy: all would soon prove illusory and wishful. The cold, hard, unyielding reality of modern warfare soon replaced the romantic, dashing legends of the popular press. The élite decision-makers (monarchs, civilian ministers, admirals, and generals) had started the war: the larger public would die in it and ultimately, finish it.

CHAPTER 5

Italian Peasant Women and the First World War

ANNA BRAVO

The topic of this chapter – part of a larger research project on the role and identity of peasant and working class women[1] – is the transformation of women's social conditions in the countryside during the First World War. At the same time I shall be looking at the processes of adaptation and the elements of conflict present in the way in which women experienced these changes. In this way we shall be examining a specific example of the broader problem of the relationship between women's conditions and external historical moments – between women's history and 'great' history.

Among the various significant events which have affected Italian peasant society, the First World War appears as a moment of primary importance. Indeed, the war's importance as representing one of the central elements of popular memory has recently been re-emphasized in Nuto Revelli's great collection of life stories from the countryside around Cuneo, south of Turin, *Il Mondo dei vinti*. However, until now research has been primarily focused on the figure of the peasant soldier and the conflictual relationship between resignation and dissent which characterize his behaviour.[2] Much less attention has been given to analysing the impact of the war on the rural communities themselves, whose life was thrown into disorder by the massive call-to-arms, by material difficulties, and by the increased interference of state authorities in the fabric of daily life.

As for women, while some attention has been given to female workers in their role as labour power, which was of primary importance in this period, and as the subjects of a significant process of social activation, peasant women have been considered only as silent victims of poverty or as protagonists of sporadic and spontaneous outbursts of struggle against the war.[3]

Between these two extremes, which represent the two sides of an existence of radical oppression and exclusion, there is nothing: these women have a past, but not a history.

In a similar way, the researcher whose interest is women's social conditions, faces a central problem: the risk of oscillating between a narrowly specialized and 'ghettoized' understanding, and an understanding that results in a subsidiary inclusion of women with a larger predetermined framework of interpretation. We do not want to create a separate history which makes no sense of history as a whole, nor do we wish to see ourselves relegated to a small women's section – no more important than many other sub-sections – in 'great' history.

The current interest in the use of oral sources – linked to a growing attention now being given to the methodological and analytical categories of social science disciplines like anthropology, sociology and psychoanalysis – can bring a significant contribution to the redefinition of this problem. New areas of research, new keys to interpretation, different measures of social changes and continuities are now all suggested to the historian. Furthermore, the political and cultural presence of feminism has contributed to a better understanding of the theoretical and methodological complexities of research, and has made clear the inadequacy of some of the conceptual systems now used in social science: for example, the inadequacy of concepts of the social division of labour which deny the social and ideological relevance of the condition of women, or of a history seen as the development of Reason, which entails a radical exclusion of women, identified as irrational, subjective, 'different'.

To overcome this exclusion, it is necessary to reaffirm the specific centrality of women in any attempt to reach an understanding of social structures and social and political processes. Thus, the analysis of the workings of mature capitalist societies remains not only incomplete, but also profoundly falsified, if the importance of the economic and social role and the cultural significance of women's condition is not considered. But even this approach still risks establishing the centrality of women simply in their old role as symbols of the particular cultural level reached by society – as the passive 'stepping stones' which mark the stages of historical development: restored to the centre of attention, but of a broadened, all-encompassing 'great' history, rather than a history of women.

Although we still lack the fully developed theory and concepts which such a true history of women demands, we can at least attempt to penetrate behind the fixed image of women's 'nature' which culture has produced and history documented. We can try to see how at different times this 'nature' of women is socially constructed, by examining the connections between women's roles and ideology, the elements of consciousness and false consciousness, the non-rational aspects and subconscious impulses. In other words, we can interpret consciousness and subjectivity as a historically determined reality – but with stages of development and causal processes of its own.[4]

Within this perspective, oral sources become essential, precisely for the very specific richness they offer for an understanding, not only of daily experience, but also of processes of adaptation and resistance to social and structural transformations. In other words, oral sources can contribute to a project of women's history which lays the foundation for the recovery of different times and spaces, of different and hidden historical facts.

The territory which we have been studying, the Langhe, is a hilly region of extremely poor countryside to the south of Turin, with a great predominance of small, or extremely small, family-run farms. Only marginally influenced by industrialization, these communities have been marked by a sense of exclusion and a close-knit defensiveness towards the outside world. Inside the communities, life has been dominated by the struggle for survival, by the hunger for land and the conflict to possess it. Land is what unites but can also divide the community and the family.[5]

The women work both in the house and in the fields. Their existence is characterized, on the one hand, by the centrality of their family and work roles which makes their presence indispensable, and, on the other hand, by the delimited nature of their recognized rights.

The hereditary system excludes them from land ownership; the dowry consists exclusively of items of clothes and furniture. Therefore, women have value, in the matrimonial market and the social life of the community alike, only as labour power and reproductive power; and, along with this, to fulfil the demand for a psychological and moral force which guarantees the cohesion of the family. The space for women's social life is severely restricted both by the characteristics of their role and by the moral rigidity of the community. Sexual alienation is generalized and brutal. Their identity is marked by the contradiction between the image of strength and indispensability which they hold of themselves, and their acceptance of the weakness of their social conditions.[6]

The intervention of the war made its mark, first, on the women's relationship to both agricultural and domestic work. The delicate balance between consumers and producers upon which the peasant family is based was disrupted by the disappearance of the most active section of the male labour force. The women found their work cycle expanded even more: small baby girls and old women now had to work; the work day grew longer; and the variety of their tasks increased until it included all of those formerly held by men.

This meant the end of the traditional division of labour in which the men performed the heavier and, in some ways, more exacting jobs, such as manoeuvring the threshing machines. All of the oral accounts insist on this point:

> I had to do all the tasks the men used to do. I even had to unload the wheat, spread the wheatsheaves, help to thresh when the machine came around. And then, I was always looking after the animals. We even took the hoes and weeded the corn, the beans, everything.[7]

> They didn't give me any easy jobs just because I was a girl. I hoed, watered the vines, cleaned the stalls, looked after the animals.[8]

The marks that this excessive exertion left on the women's bodies are emphasized, and so is the women's capacity to resist and adapt:

> I had to do everything that a man does. My brothers were in the war. We watered the fields barefoot. It was bad for our health. We ate badly, but

we would have eaten anything . . . I got married when I was twenty; no doctor had ever touched me.[9]

The hired boy was in front watering the vines. I came behind spreading the sulphur. When I came home in the evening my eyes were burning. I washed and washed. But when I went to bed I didn't even want to sleep any more because if I closed my eyes they watered all night long . . . I weighed only 45 kilograms.[9] [My brother] always said: 'You look like the living death' . . . Well, I'm still here: I've always been healthy.[10]

When this redistribution of work was not sufficient to ensure the family's survival and the continued possession of the land, the women returned temporarily to the nearby factories or to some other type of work outside the family, including, in some cases, semi-clandestine seasonal emigration to France. This migratory work even involved married women with children, and thus disrupted the tradition whereby such experiences ended at marriage.

Beyond these cases of forced absence, there was also a reorganization of family life and domestic activity. Mothers devoted themselves almost entirely to work in the fields, while the weight of the house and the care of the children fell on the daughters who were often only slightly older. In some cases a daughter looked after the children from several families, so that the other girls could work in the factories or as servants. In any case, daily household tasks – cleaning, cooking – were reduced to a minimum. There was a parallel growth in the time devoted to the tasks which external changes imposed, in particular to those imposed by rationing and by intensified forms of immediate family consumption of production:

We made oil by crushing the nuts and sunflower seeds in the wine press.[11]

We dealt with the problems ourselves. We milked the cows to make butter because what they gave out for the rations was meagre and awful. We made our own bread.[12]

We had rationing cards, but we made a type of bread mixed with potatoes.[13]

In spite of the quantity of these efforts, the situation of certain families became so desperate that some were forced to eat animal feed and others even to stealing. Two women openly admit it:

We stole . . . Well, if you wanted to eat . . .[14]

My mother, your grandmother Antonietta, Carolina, eight or ten women altogether, you know what they did? They stole at night; potatoes, onions; they stole firewood together. They did all these things just to keep going.[15]

These women justify these small-scale thefts and other illegal activities by their families' need to survive. But the unambiguous social and cultural rejection of these women by others is a stark confirmation of community disapproval:

The wife would take a large apron, roll it up, and walk around the streets. In one place, potatoes, in another, beans. She stole a little here, a little there, and came home with the apron full. That woman was looked down on.[16]

In all oral accounts, the women's acceptance of such a vast array of responsibilities appears both as out of the ordinary and also as a duty almost as if it were natural for women to make themselves responsible for exceptional tasks, tasks which were accepted as the utmost expansion of a multiform and never-ending role.

This attitude seems accurately to reflect the meaning of matrimonial exchange in the community, and the conditions which had to be endured in order to be accepted in the new family. The man brought the land, which was a quantifiable good, always equal to itself; the woman brought a subjective capacity to work which was indeterminate. This capacity of hers had to be adapted to the family's life cycle and needs. The woman realized that she was accepted – and could feel her own value – only through her own capability and this willingness to adapt. Hence, there were no special compensations envisaged for her efforts. The few attempts to rebalance the family relationship in her favour tended primarily to improve her own condition only within the traditional family structure. The situation was perhaps slightly different for unmarried girls who worked within their original families, where the promise of some small rewards in exchange for longer and heavier work[17] was not merely a sign of consideration for their youth as such, but also an indication that their obligation to show unconditional willingness to work was less institutionalized and less general.

In the life of these communities, the war manifested itself above all through an increase in the presence and power of the state; in inspections, requisitions, forced hoarding, rationing; and the introduction of difficult procedures for obtaining benefits, exemptions from the draft, and military leave. This new relationship with authority fell on the women, as the only remaining young section of the population. But the new responsibility was also asked of them by their husbands at the war-front.[18] The women's lives, previously restricted to the house and community, were now filled with new tasks; going to government offices, discussing with local administrators and officials, travelling as far as provincial capitals to follow through these extended chores. Thus greater contact was established with the outside world, with new places, with a new environment of different experiences, with the public sphere of life. The women now had a direct relationship with the activities of a state authority which they also identified as responsible for the war. When the oral accounts deal with these themes, they are given great emphasis:

When my husband was a soldier, they sent a letter to my mother-in-law saying that she had to pay a certain amount because he was unfit for war duty. The poor old woman paid, and then wanted me to pay her back. 'I'm not paying. He may be unfit for war, but he sure isn't at home, he's off in the army.' I said it to the police too. I went to talk to the city officer. Other notices of payment due arrived. They told me to go to the tax office here in Caraglio. There they told me to pay and then to sue to get back my mother-in-law's and my money. 'Thanks, I have my money in my pocket and I'm keeping it. My mother-in-law paid her own money. I don't want it.'[19]

I was in bed with the six-year-old baby, and I caught the Spanish 'flu too. One day the marshal comes; I was in bed. He wanted me to give some hay to the government. I told him: 'Doesn't it seem disgraceful to you that they ask me for hay; me, here in bed, with my husband a soldier, and young as he is they've never given him an hour's leave; and I'm here in bed with nobody to help me. Aren't you ashamed?' Finally they sent my husband a telegram and gave him a ten-day leave.[20]

Attitudes of this type were an integral part of a more general estrangement from the state and of peasant society's opposition to the war. Furthermore, the encounter with the state occurred with the woman acting as representative and defender of the family, and this role appeared as a necessary extension of her function as guardian of the common interests. There are, however, other elements which suggest additional interpretative keys. It would be reasonable to expect that these women's behaviour would be marked by a combination of both insecurity and aggressiveness. The oral account, however, emphasizes only the latter aspect, often presenting a kind of drama in which the woman actively sets herself against arrogance and arbitrariness. This strong element of self-affirmation suggests the hypothesis that we are also dealing with the dynamics of a more general conflict with authority. Repressed and forbidden expression inside the family, these dynamics of conflict were shifted outside against a socially shared enemy, against an authority experienced as pure abuse of power, against an authority which could not, therefore, kindle processes of identification and complicity.

Furthermore, if we examine the special emphasis given in the oral accounts to other war-imposed encounters with the external world – the purchase of a pair of oxen, buying and selling at the market in the husband's absence – we discover that each of these episodes, beyond the particularities of the conflict with authority, is also experienced as a moment of self-realization, of individualization in the social world and the public sphere. The women seem only partially conscious of this stimulus, but as they tell their stories, one senses resonances of emotional involvement, not only in the goal they had in each encounter, but also of a hidden ability and quiescent desire which they had at last found acceptable ways of realizing.

The war affected relations between the sexes in contradictory ways. It opened – as we shall see – spaces for a less restricted and less orthodox sexuality. However, given that the peasant models of morality and the power relationships did not undergo any change, the position of women, already structurally fragile, appears to have been further weakened. In this society the women were not only productive and reproductive power, but were also sexual objects to be used as freely and brutally as the weakness of their social and personal position permitted. Their only defence was the family's control or protection. When this was lacking – something which coincided with extreme poverty or internal disintegration – violence, incest, the cheap sale of children and child prostitution, and persecution endured as farm hands and servants, were not uncommon.

The departure of husbands and brothers left the women weaker and more exposed. Furthermore, with the war women had increased contact with the external world; they needed masculine help for certain agricultural operations; local officials and police entered their houses to identify animals and goods to be requisitioned; deserters and draft-dodgers sought refuge in their barns. Certain oral accounts – only a few, probably because of a form of self-censure–document the spread of a threatening and predatory attitude. The man takes it for granted that the woman is suffering from male absence and aggressively proposes himself. The accounts speak of cases of rape and murder.[21]

In most of the accounts it appears that the women experienced this situation by a strong denial of their own sexuality: those accounts that deal with the problem do so only in order to reject its existence, and, at the same time, to re-confirm their own adherence to the model of wife and mother:

> My head was filled with other things. I swear that I never even thought about 'that' because I had so many other worries. I thought about him off in the war, and the children, the animals, the land, everything, and the debts to pay.[22]

Male sexual proposals were experienced without gratification, and the only emotional agitation was in the expression of harsh disapproval for an initiative considered 'shameful'. The women's refusals never betray an effort to control themselves, never show anything like the rejection of 'temptation'. The episodes take on the character of simply dealing successfully with a difficult moment, with a dangerous or socially embarrassing situation. Only the male has sexual impulses – and those that chase women are *lurdun* – good-for-nothings and pigs – because women have more important things to do.

Only through the women's references to deviants – from whom they rigidly distinguish themselves – do they let us see that the war had introduced specific kinds of disturbance in their sexual behaviour:

> There was one . . . The marshal always went to see her . . . I wasn't one of those that they could go to bed with.[23]

> There are women who had a hard life. And there were those who used their husband's absence, but you certainly had to have a lot of courage![24]

> The woman wanted to enjoy herself, and neglected the house, or else gave up the land and everything, and when the husband came back he didn't find anything.[25]

Certainly, this subject is influenced by the demands of social and self-respect and the need to reaffirm the values of their own past against the greater permissiveness attributed to the present. However, when evaluating this model of behaviour it is necessary to keep in mind that the acceptance of a subordinate and restricted sexuality in marriage is a 'natural' fact of these women's experience, and is closely linked to the other aspects of their roles. It is not a coincidence that sexual transgression is associated with the spectre of the loss of the land and the ruin of the household. Since the husband's absence created new material problems of solidarity and respect, the women had an even stronger stimulus to hold on to the models they had been socialized to accept. This stimulus was further strengthened both by the intensified control or protection exercised by the community and neighbourhood, and by the woman's understanding of the weakness of her social position, a weakness based on her exclusion from landownership. This understanding makes the risk of destroying the marriage unthinkable.

In this situation – in which the stimulus to maintain the established order went hand in hand with increased opportunities to violate it – the traditionally marginal dimension of sexuality in women's lives and self-identity presumably favoured the mechanism of self-repression and, beyond that, of total denial, which controlled the women's sexual behaviour and judgment.

The changes that the war created in social life are seen with particular prominence in the social life of women which was, until then, tied to very rigidly traditional and limited relationships. The time and space for the old forms of social life became even more restricted with the war:

> Life changed a lot during the war . . . To think that I hardly learned how to dance. Before the war people often danced during the festivals. But we didn't dance very much. People were worried. We still spent the evenings together in the barns, but we laughed and joked a lot less. [26]

In this exceptional situation, new, infrequent and 'unorthodox' parallel forms of social life began to develop. Many were directly linked both to the reorganization of agricultural and domestic work, and to the new solidarity created among the peasants:

> In Rivera, I remember, we were all women who threshed the wheat. There were a few machinists . . . but we did everything else ourselves: some of us spread the sheaves, others cut the wheat. We were all young girls and we enjoyed ourselves. There was a steam engine we called the 'black locomotive' because it seemed like the old train locomotives you had to feed with coal.[27]

> In Albaretto, everyone who lives in that farmhouse there is still called 'oilman', 'cause we all used to take our walnuts up there to be pressed.[28]

> In the evening we would help the women who had small babies. We did some of their work for them . . . One of them had her husband off in the

war. She wasn't very quick, so we went and did her sewing and knitting. She made us a plate of fritters, and we ate![29]

New relationships were also formed as a result of those created at the war-front:

> I had all the addresses of his companions: one from Mondovi, another from Garessio, and many more. Afterwards, they all came by to see me and bring me the war news.[30]

But the most significant element for understanding the transformation of both the women's daily social life and their subjective attitudes is the presence of small bands of deserters and draft-dodgers who moved from one hillside to another. This extremely important development was dependent on a conspiracy of silence and on the solidarity of the peasants.[31]

The subject is often discussed in the oral accounts. This presence of so many unknown young men, who lived clandestinely and suddenly appeared – perhaps in the middle of the night – in the barns or courtyards of a farmhouse, became a part of daily life, and enlivened it. For women, stuck to the old-established system of relationships, it was an entirely new experience:

> They wandered around at night and came to ask for something to eat . . . then others came on Sunday. They slept wherever they could, in hay-lofts, under the porch. Sometimes we'd see one come down from the loft, and we hadn't even realized he was up there. Once I got frightened: my father sent me to throw down some hay from the loft, and I uncovered one who was half asleep.[32]

In this extremely closed and suspicious society, the new situation was experienced with a tolerance and sympathy that cannot be fully explained, either by the fact that some of the deserters came from the villages under discussion, or by the generally exceptional situation. The young men helped the women with their field chores, and, although their lives were semi-clandestine, in some cases they became so integrated into the peasant family's life that they were allowed to organize football matches, festivals, and barn dances:

> They said to my father: 'Bastiano, let us dance a little.' He replied: 'Oh sure! If I let you dance, the police will arrive tomorrow!' Meanwhile, one of them began to play the accordion, and we started dancing.[33]

> Sometimes they sent around trying to find a house they could dance in, and then invited everybody. They always did the organizing. I remember that there were some who could really dance!![34]

The opinion of the women is explicitly positive, and contains none of the rumours of rape and other forms of violence which are present in some of the men's oral accounts.[35] On the contrary, the women's opinion emphasizes that the deserters were good people, who worked, who moved from one hillside to another in order not to weigh too heavily on the peasants, who never did anyone any wrong, and with whom it was perhaps even pleasant to talk and dance.

This evaluation is clearly influenced by the implicit comparison with the partisans of 1943–5 who are remembered in this region in a more conflictual manner.[36] However, the approval and emotional involvement are too strong to be tied only to this negative comparison: the personalities, the nicknames – one is found in a number of different accounts – are recalled with precision; the dangers faced to give them hospitality are emphasized; their courage is exalted:

> They sure were courageous! They weren't scared of anything; played football in San Sabastiano village. One always kept guard in case some-one arrived. We helped them, but if the police found us with deserters in the house, we were in for a lot of trouble. But the police weren't in any hurry to come to this region, because there were a lot of deserters, even if they weren't armed. I never saw them armed.[37]

The accounts emphasize the continuous cycle of escapes and arrests in the life of the deserters. They are recalled as the protagonists of an unfought war with the 'carabinieri' which in reality was probably less intense than this would suggest. The regret that some relative who died in the war did not follow their example is present in almost all of the oral accounts.

The role of positive hero given to the deserter springs above all from the tradition of peasant estrangement from the state and opposition to the war already mentioned. The deserter incarnates the most explicit opposition to the war which was achieved within this culture. But for the women there were probably additional aspects to the question: not so much elements of specific sexual and emotional tension – hinted at in the male accounts – which would have set off conflictual dynamics among the women; but rather, the presence of a desire for a less restricted social life, for a way out of daily routine, for affection. This gives the entire experience more complex emotional content and significance.

The deserter became a part of daily life and brought with him new, less 'orthodox' relationships; at the same time, however, he did not violently dis-rupt this existence. It was a parenthesis that was, at any rate, destined to end. It was danger, adventure, disorder, but it was also the denial of a rule imposed by the outside world. It was a transgression which could be identified with, a symbol of a conflict of values in which everybody was involved. The deserter was a young man, courageous but needing protection, afraid of noth-ing, but evoking pity.

The relationship was at the same time both completely internal to the experience and culture of these women, and completely external, suspended in a temporary time-slot and in imaginary spaces. In the oral accounts, the relationship crops up as a central element of the war experience and as a sub-ject for many recollections; it is on the one hand escape, on the other a con-firmation of the women's own existence.

It is no coincidence that only at this point do the women's oral accounts reveal a recuperation and recollection of the war. In all other parts of the accounts this is entirely absent. While in the men's accounts, the experience of the war-front is revisited with a certain level of immediate identification, and often even with a reserved form of pride and nostalgia',[38] the women's accounts express a total rejection. Forced to endure the entire weight of the war, yet at the same time excluded from those 'heroic' aspects worth re-evoking, the women respond by denying them:

> I tell him: 'Drop it: you're boring, by now we are all tired of hearing the same stories over and over again.' But him? Never. Onward with Monte Grappa, the Neapolitans, the Germans, his colonels. I've heard about the war so many times it comes in one ear and goes out the other.[39]

And the women counter the four-year war with one that lasts a lifetime: with the fact that 'the war was out there, but here we had to eat every day'.[40]

For when the war was over and the men had come back home, apart from a few wives whose husbands returned seriously disabled, or went off abroad for work, the women had to retreat to their earlier confines, and forget most of the wider responsibility they had briefly borne. A venthole had been opened, which could not be wholly closed; and a good many wives continued to exercise their new-found expertise in dealing with state officials, now on behalf of their husbands. But, within the community, old roles were resumed, and the women forced back into traditional peasant silence, leaving the men to monopolize the claim to war honours. Yet the fight to feed the family had to continue without respite in the new circumstances. And the weight of that still fell primarily on the women: a seemingly timeless, immutable labour – a fate without history – moulding their consciousness of both past and present.

Notes

1 This is a research project on which I am working together with Lucetta Scaraffia. We are using the biographies of Piedmontese peasant women, born around the turn of the century, all married with children, and all from the same social stratum, and the biographies of Turinese working-class women. Altogether, we have carried out forty interviews.

   The peasant witnesses all belong to families of small or very small farmers. Some of them had short experiences as domestic servants in the city before marrying; a very few of them worked for some time in small industries; and others migrated as young girls to France for seasonal work. All of them married farmers and spent most of their lifetime in the country, where some of them still work, although now very old. On the whole their response to being interviewed was positive, as was their interest in a research project on women's conditions in the past. In fact, several of them told us that they saw this as a chance to re-evaluate their own life experience and communicate it to the outside world.

2 N. Revelli, *Il Mondo dei vinti,* Turin, 1977; E. Forcella and A. Monticone, *Plotone di esecuzione: i processi della prima guerra mondiale,* Bari, 1968.

3 See R. De Felice, 'Ordine pubblico e orientamento delle masse populari italiane nella prima meta del 1917, in *Rivista storica del socialismo,* VI, 20, 1963.

4 Among contributions to the study of consciousness and psychology, see especially, A Besançon, *Storia e psicanalisi,* Naples, 1975; and for women's consciousness., U. Prokop, *Realtà e desiderio L'ambivalenza femminile,* Milan, 1978.

5 Revelli, *Il mondo dei vinti.*

6 See A. Bravo and L. Scaraffia, 'Ruolo femminile e identità nelle contadine delle Langhe: un'ipotesi di storia orale', in *Rivista di storia contemporanea*, 1, 1979.

7 Oral account of Nina Rinaldi (b. 1893).

8 Oral account of Luisa Nebbia (b.1901).

9 Oral account of Maria Civalleri (b.1900).

10 Oral account of Nina Rinaldi.

11 Oral account of Maria Chiavarino (b.1894).

12 Oral account of Nina Rinaldi.

13 Oral account of Domenica Bertaina (b.1901).

14 Oral account of Maria Bernardino, (b.1893).

15 Oral account of Rita (b. 1902). In 1917, the worsening of living conditions in the region was such that there was a protest demonstration with insults, rocks, and vegetables thrown against the 'carabinieri', with the workers hidden in a tannery, the railroad station, and the grain warehouse: see Forcella and Monticone, *Plotone di esecuzione*, op. cit., pp. 124-6. This event does not often appear in the oral accounts, perhaps because it occurred in a nearby village and not in that of the women interviewed.

16 Oral account of Spirita Arneodo (b. 1891).

17 Oral account of Maria Bonetti (b. 1903).

18 See the correspondence of the soldier Sabino Traversa with his wife in A. Bandand 'Problemi e aspetti della participazione dei contadini delle Langhe alla prima guerra mondiale', University of Turin, 1979, unpublished dissertation supervised by Anna Bravo.

19 Oral account of Spirita Arneodo.

20 Oral account of Spirita Arneodo.

21 Oral account of Maria Domini (b. 1896).

22 Oral account of Spirita Arneodo.

23 Oral account of Spirita Arneodo.

24 Oral account of Lucia Cravero (b. 1892).

25 Oral account of Carolina Arneodo (b. 1902).

26 Oral account of Angiolina Boschis (b. 1893).

27 Oral account of Maria Cagnasso (b. 1893).

28 Oral account of Maria Chiavarino.

29 Oral account of Lucia Cravero.

30 Oral account of Nina Rinaldi.

31 On the phenomenon of desertion, see Revelli, *Il mondo dei vinti*, II, Le Langhe and Introduction.

32 Oral account of Nina Rinaldi.

33 Oral account of Maria Domini.

34 Oral account of Nina Rinaldi.

35 See Revelli, *Il Mondo dei vinti*, II, Le Langhe.

36 ibid; and N. Gallerano, '*Il Mondo dei vinti*', in *Rivista di storia contemporanea*, 4, 1978.

37 Oral acount of Nina Rinaldi.

38 M. Isenghi, 'Valori populari e valori "ufficiali" nella mentalità del soldato fra le due guerre mondiali', in *Quaderni storici*, 38, 1978, 704.

39 Oral account of Luisa Nebbia.

40 Oral account of Angiolina Boschis.

CHAPTER 6

Demobilization and Labour

RICHARD BESSEL

. . . Even in the best of circumstances, safeguarding the employment of the German work-force during the post-war transition would not have appeared easy. However, Germany was in the midst of a political revolution fuelled by labour unrest and the consequence of the privations, government bungling, and injustices of the War. Thus when peace broke out in November 1918, resurrecting a well-functioning peacetime labour-market appeared virtually impossible. Yet, in the event, the re-employment of the veterans of the First World War comprised the great success story of the economic demobilization.[1] By the beginning of December 1918 a fair amount of optimism about the transitional labour-market was being expressed in government circles,[2] and after some considerable difficulties in early 1919 were past, that optimism generally proved justified. This is to assert neither that unemployment presented no problem in 1918–1919 nor that the labour market had not been profoundly disrupted by the post-war transition. The transition was far from smooth, conditions were chaotic, and the changes massive and sudden. Yet the problem was largely solved, at least for the short term.

Why did this remarkable and unexpected success come about? There were a number of reasons. First, the re-employment of Germany's ex-soldiers was made possible by the shunting of many hundreds of thousands of other people – in the main, women and foreign labourers – out of their wartime jobs and, in many cases, out of the German labour-market entirely. Second, the widespread assumption that the soldiers would get 'their' old jobs back after the conflict acted as a self-fulfilling prophecy, since few employers contemplated anything other than welcoming back their former workers. Third, government policy – in general the acceptance that in a revolutionary situation political considerations took precedence over economic considerations, and in particular the financing of public-works projects[3] and maintaining contracts with private firms in order to preserve jobs – kept positions open. Fourth, there was a substantial increase in employment in the public sector: the administrative staff in Reich ministries was roughly 45 per cent greater in 1920 than it had been in 1914, and the number of civil servants in the Prussian administration nearly doubled; the personnel of the German postal administration was more than one-quarter greater in 1919 than it had been before the War, and the number employed on the railways was two-thirds higher (with an increase of over 200,000 between 1918 and 1919).[4] Fifth, the reduction of the working day, at a time of continuing inflation which allowed employers to raise prices to cover for increased labour-costs, increased the need for workers. Sixth, many employers were willing to take on ex-soldiers even where there was no immediate economic justification, because they wanted a reliable labour-force at their disposal in order to meet an expected post-war upsurge in consumer demand. Seventh, in so far as they were not severely crippled, ex-soldiers formed the most desirable group of potential employees – male, in the prime of life – and the section of the labour force which normally experiences the lowest unemployment. Finally, it needs to be remembered that, although German unemployment was far below that in other industrial countries after the War, it remained generally above pre-war levels for most of the 1919–24 period (with the exception of the period from the autumn of 1921 until the winter of 1922), and it was pre-war conditions rather than joblessness elsewhere in Europe which formed the basis of comparison. Furthermore, during 1919–21 periods of unemployment lasted on average one and a half times as long as they had before the War[5] . . .

. . . Although the post-war surge in unemployment proved temporary, the demobilization crisis had lasting consequences for the regulation of the German labour-market.[6] The post-war emergency was met with initiatives of far-reaching significance. First and foremost there was the question of what to do with the unemployed themselves. The problems which followed in the wake of the Armistice appeared to demand government action. The prospect of millions of embittered soldiers coming home to unemployment caused the German state hastily to put into place a system of support for those without work. No sooner had the new Reich Office for Economic Demobilization come into being than it issued a decree requiring local authorities to provide unemployment relief (for which the Reich bore half the cost, the federal states one-third, and local councils one-sixth).[7] While this was not a fully-fledged system of unemployment insurance – something which did not come into being until 1927 and collapsed soon after under the financial pressures of the Depression – it marked a major turning-point.

Providing payments to the unemployed in order to prevent a further radicalization of German workers was not enough, however. More direct intervention was deemed necessary, and during January 1919 the government published a series of decrees governing the hiring and dismissal of employees.[8] The terms of these decrees reflected generally accepted notions of how the labour market should be ordered – for example, that women not dependent upon their incomes should be dismissed in order to make way for men, and that people from outside a community should make way for local residents. Nevertheless, during early 1919 the regulations governing dismissals were often evaded.[9] These were followed at the end of March by a new decree governing 'the release of employment positions during the period of the economic demobilization', which was the most important piece of legislation delineating the powers and responsibilities of the local Demobilization Committees.[10] This marked a major new incursion of the state into the workings of the labour market. No longer was hiring and firing the sole prerogative of the employer; the state determined the order in which groups of employees were to be dismissed; and Demobilization Committees (which included representatives of employee interests, i.e. trade-union functionaries) were enabled to intervene extensively in matters of employment . . .

. . . These developments took place against the background of a tremendous increase in trade-union membership. Such an increase occurred in all major industrial countries after the First World War, and was lent extra force in Germany by industrialists' recognition of trade unions as collective-bargaining partners in the Stinnes–Legien Agreement of November 1918. During the War, the number of trade unionists in Germany had fallen precipitously, as male workers were called to the colours and many of those who replaced them (in particular, women) viewed their industrial employment as a temporary affair and did not bother to join unions. The socialist Free Trade Union Federation, which could count over 2.5 million members in 1913, saw the combined membership of its affiliated unions sink to less than one million in 1915 and 1916; the Catholic trade-unions and the liberal Hirsch–Duncker Associations also experienced steep declines in membership.[11] Although membership recovered somewhat in 1917 and 1918, at the War's end it still lay substantially below the pre-war figures (in the case of the socialist trade-unions, more than 40 per cent below). This changed suddenly after November 1918, as the trade unions were flooded with new members. By the end of 1918, the Free Trade Unions registered a total membership nearly twice that recorded three months previously and already in excess of the pre-war figure; by the end of March 1919 membership stood at nearly twice the pre-war total . . .

. . . The wartime fall and post-war rise in trade-union membership was paralleled by a wartime reduction and post-war expansion of union bureaucracies. During the War the decline in membership and the conscripting of many union activists into the army had led to a substantial dismantling of trade-union bureaucracies and a sharp reduction in the number of functionaries on trade-union payrolls. After the Armistice, however, not only were these processes reversed, but also the political and legal changes caused by the revolution and demobilization created a host of new tasks for union officials. Not only did they now have to represent the interests of many times more members and involve themselves in many more wage negotiations; they also had to sit on local Demobilisation Committees, committees to oversee the distribution of food, industrial tribunals, job-counselling centres and the like, and were far more likely to hold elected positions in local and regional legislatures.[12] Their representative duties in the public sphere expanded enormously as the interest-group politics which characterized the Weimar Republic took shape in the aftermath of the War . . .

. . . The huge upsurge in trade-union organization which accompanied the demobilization was a reflection of the relaxation of the old authoritarian system and the patterns of discipline and deference which it had sustained. When that system collapsed and Germans from all social groups rushed to join interest organizations, millions of people with only a tenuous commitment to the labour movement flocked to the trade unions. However, when the political and economic climate changed in the early and mid-1920s, millions of these new members left again. The hyperinflation (during which prices rose so quickly that the idea of negotiating and maintaining incomes through collective bargaining became absurd)[13], mass unemployment, and the reimposition of longer shifts and a longer working-day in many industries, combined to cut the ground from under the trade unions.[14] The end of the demobilization period coincided with the end of the extraordinary period of explosive trade-union growth . . .

. . . How can one explain the apparent and uncharacteristic masochism of German employers, who seem to have been willing to pay wages to workers they did not require? No doubt many employers were genuinely motivated by feelings of patriotism and a belief that Germany in general, and they in particular, owed a debt to those who had risked life and limb for the Fatherland. However, noble motives were seasoned with self-interest. Employers' testimonials to state authorities of their concern for their former employees and of their patriotic conduct were also used to frame cases for preferential treatment when it came to the handing-out of state contracts or the distribution of scarce raw materials. A fairly typical example was that of the Hirsch Copper and Brass Factory near Eberswalde, north-east of Berlin. The factory had employed roughly 1,800 workers before the War, and during the conflict this figure had risen to about 3,000. In February 1919, however, the number was back down to 1,845, while production had slumped to two-fifths of what it had been in August and September 1918 due to the ending of war contracts. Writing to the Regierungspräsident in Potsdam in his capacity as Demobilization Commissar, the firms' directors pointed out that 'immediately after the outbreak of the revolution we gave work to all the soldiers returning from the battlefield and the garrisons who presented themselves to us' and that even after having had to increase wages in January 'we would always attempt to keep the number of workers in future at the same level as we had had before the War'. However, 'unfortunately' they now had to contemplate the partial closure of the factory if new orders were not forthcoming 'immediately'. The letter closed with a plea that, 'in the interest of the maintenance of our factory and in the interest of avoiding the dismissal of workers, which with the current condition of the factory could number many hundreds, we ask you to recognize our present emergency' and help with securing contracts.[15] Desperate factory directors presented desperate state officials with the spectre of yet greater unemployment if sufficient contracts were not pushed their way during the transition from war to peace.

This was not the only element of self-interest which induced employers to take on workers they did not really need. Another was the threat of state intervention: the explicit threat embedded in the demobilization legislation, in particular the decree of 4 January 1919, which stipulated that factories with twenty or more workers were required 'to hire those workers who at the outbreak of the War had been employed in the factory as industrial workers';[16] and the implicit threat that state controls might be extended further if existing measures proved insufficient to deal with the emergency.[17] In addition, not too far in the background lurked the spectre of something even worse: a revolution which might do away altogether with private ownership. On 13 November 1918 the Association of German Employer Organizations (Vereinigung der Deutschen Arbeitgeberverbände) urged its members 'to employ people in the coming weeks, even if it is necessary to introduce double shifts of four hours each'. The Association went on to recommend that people be put to work doing something, even if 'they must tear it down again tomorrow; but they must be employed'.[18] As Ewald Hilger, speaking for Germany's iron and steel industrialists on 14 November 1918, declared: 'It is not a question of money now . . . right now we must see that we survive the chaos.'[19]

These worries enabled employers to swallow temporarily the introduction of the eight-hour day, agreed by representatives of German industry and trade-union leaders and written into the Stinnes–Legien Agreement of 15 November 1918.[20] Although the reduction in the working day without a corresponding reduction in wages raised industry's costs considerably, it was a price worth paying, if only to strengthen the hand of moderate trade-unionists and deflect the new government or a more radical working-class movement from taking direct control of factories. It also greatly increased the need for labour. With the shorter working day (often leading to the introduction of an additional, shorter shift), employers needed to maintain the size of their work-forces even as output slumped and many had to take on additional workers to maintain production.[21] Thus many employers, like the city electricity works in Dortmund, were able to rehire returning soldiers without having to dismiss all those people taken on during the War.[22] In other cases, where coal shortages forced employers to occupy workers with maintenance tasks and emergency works, acceptance of the eight-hour day proved a convenient way to link a necessary concession to labour to temporary economic imperatives.[23] Thus the most significant achievement of the labour movement in 1918, and the main concession of the employers in the face of the revolutionary threat, greatly facilitated the reabsorption into the civilian labour-market of the millions of men leaving military service.

Worried employers had many of their fears confirmed by the waves of industrial unrest which accompanied the political upheaval of 1918 and 1919.[24] With the collapse of the old order and the advent of democratic government, and with employers much more vulnerable than before to pressure, strike action became widespread. In 1919 more than seven times as many strikes took place as in 1918 and, perhaps more important, affected more than thirty times as many factories. Only a small proportion of these strikes ended with a victory for the employers.[25] This meant not only that strikes were more frequent and their outcomes more likely to reflect the new muscle of the workers, but also that they affected large numbers of smaller firms which hitherto had avoided industrial conflict.

Serious though they were, strikes and other overt expressions of worker militancy formed but the tip of the iceberg. After being compelled to make sacrifice upon sacrifice during the War, few Germans remained keen to exert themselves at the work-bench after the old order had been swept away. In the immediate aftermath of the military collapse and during the revolutionary upheaval, virtually the whole of the German economy was affected by an unwillingness of people to work hard . . .

. . . Women proved no easier than men to channel into jobs deemed necessary and suitable by the state authorities. In his discussion of the demobilization in Bavaria, Kurt Königsberger described the attempt 'to channel the weaker sex on to paths which are beneficial to the economy' – particularly the attempt to induce women who had worked in the armaments industry to accept positions in domestic service once again – as 'a labour of Hercules'.[26] During the demobilization period, unemployment among women was significantly higher than amongst men.[27] What is more, levels of female unemployment were probably understated in the available data, because the authorities tended not to consider home workers, mostly women, eligible for support and were more restrictive about granting women unemployment relief.[28] Nevertheless, the expectations of the demobilization authorities that unemployed women could easily be placed in agricultural work or in domestic service were frequently disappointed. Despite the high unemployment during 1919, positions for women in domestic service, in cleaning, and on the land often remained unfilled.[29] For example, from Danzig, where thousands of women had been drawn to the city for wartime work and were dismissed soon after the Armistice, it was reported in February 1919 that 'many were alienated from their former occupations by high wages usually for a short working day, and when the dismissals began at the end of 1918 many showed little inclination to return to their homes (*Heimat*) and to accept positions in service either on the land or in the towns, even though there is a great shortage of domestic servants'. The report concluded that 'the consequences of [women's] factory work will make themselves felt in this regard for a long time yet'.[30]

This last prediction seems to have come true. Many women remained quite resistant to being shunted into service after their experiences during the War. In June 1919 the Danzig labour exchange reported that 1,730 women were unemployed in the city, and in August the number had risen to 2,155, despite the continuing demand for female domestic servants and agricultural labour in the surrounding region.[31] Attempts to retrain women factory-workers, with day and evening vocational courses which concentrated on 'domestic subjects' and were designed to channel women into domestic employment, failed to induce large numbers of women to seek positions in service.[32] The wartime experience of relatively better-paid employment – and, no doubt for many, the prospect of marriage at the War's end – had changed the ideas of many women about the sorts of work they were willing to accept.

It would be mistaken, however, to assume that all the post-war unemployed were without work because they refused the jobs on offer. Some groups found it quite difficult to find employment. The labour exchange in Ludwigshafen, for example, reported at the end of 1919 (when unemployment was a fraction of its February peak and when women had largely been removed from the relief rolls) that there had been little success in placing some categories of workers: 'mainly clerical staff, commercial employees, artisans, war-wounded, disabled and older people for whom in any case it is difficult to find positions'.[33] The most serious unemployment problems and the most bitter competition over the jobs which were available arose among clerical staff. Providing appropriate work for ex-soldiers who had previously had white-collar jobs, and expected to occupy similar positions after leaving military service, often proved difficult.[34] In Bavaria, Kurt Königsberger described the employment prospects of commercial employees of both sexes as 'quite bleak';[35] and in his dissertation on the regulation of the post-war labour-market Joseph Müller observed that, while the re-employment of workers returning from military service caused few difficulties, cases involving white-collar staff frequently required arbitration by the demobilization authorities.[36] Thus office work, which had been a largely male preserve before the War, formed the area where continued working by women stirred the greatest resentment;[37] and the Deutschnationaler Handlungsgehilfen-Verband (DHV) in particular made strident demands that women be removed from their jobs to make way for men.[38] Although the militantly anti-feminist and conservative ideology of the DHV made its campaign against the employment of women in offices predictable, the intensity of the protests also stemmed from the fact that the job prospects for white-collar staff generally were much less rosy than for workers seeking jobs on the factory floor . . .

. . . One of the main reasons why a reconstitution of traditional roles at work and within households could occur was that the demobilization was accompanied by a short-lived but substantial rise in real wages. Of course, for a period characterized by shortages, black-marketeering, and tremendous upheavals on the labour market it is extremely difficult to calculate real wages with any degree of precision. Nevertheless, it has been suggested that, as a result of substantial wage-increases granted against the backdrop of the revolutionary threat, during 1919 and 1920 real wages in Germany rose to within 10 per cent of their pre-war levels – a process which Gerald Feldman has described as 'bribery through wage concessions'.[39] Although they complained bitterly about it, employers preferred to concede higher wages to a militant work-force than to close down their businesses or lose their property altogether. The spectre of left-wing uprisings in Germany's cities, the rapid spread of the Workers' and Soldiers' Councils (which supported workers' wage-demands),[40] and the mushrooming of trade-union membership led employers to accept reductions in the working day and wage rises as the lesser of evils. This meant that for a short time, during the demobilization period, it was possible for the man to function economically as 'head of household' – to provide for a family on his income alone. Thus, paradoxically, the pressures of labour militancy and political revolution helped bring about a reconstitution of traditional roles in the labour market and within the family, by allowing men to reoccupy the position of economic head of household and thus allowing many women (who in any case were being pressured to leave paid employment) to return to the home.

The general reduction in the numbers of unemployed during the early 1920s reflected the continuation of a process which became apparent during 1919: a return to 'normal' conditions made possible in large measure by the abnormality of galloping inflation. Nevertheless, the reduction of unemployment was not uninterrupted, and this posed problems for one particular group of war veterans: prisoners of war. After having fallen fairly steadily from early 1919, unemployment rose again during 1920 due to a short-lived appreciation of the Mark on foreign exchanges (and to the detrimental effects this had upon German exports), and then due to a renewed coal-shortage towards the end of the year.[41] This rise in unemployment occurred not long after the bulk of the German prisoners of war had returned from Allied captivity, and at a time when the Germans had to reduce the Reichswehr to 100,000 men as stipulated in the Versailles Treaty. During 1919 there had been understandable worry in government circles about what would happen, as Wilhelm Groener put it in mid-August, 'if we were to receive 800,000 men thrown on to the labour market at a single stroke'.[42] Although in fact the number of prisoners who arrived by mid-1920 was closer to 600,000,[43] their return contributed to the increase in unemployment during 1920.[44] The former prisoners themselves expressed concern that their delayed homecoming put them at a disadvantage on the labour market.[45]

The short-term upturn in unemployment in 1920, together with the return of the prisoners and the reduction in the size of the Reichswehr, led to renewed pressure for the removal of women and young people from jobs which were regarded as rightly belonging to the men.[46] Indeed, 1920 saw something of a repetition, on a smaller scale, of the developments which had accompanied the military demobilization of 1918 and 1919. The re-employment of the prisoners of war was guided by much the same considerations as had framed the reabsorption of the men who had left military service immediately after the War: agreement by employers that it was their patriotic duty to re-employ the returning men, legislation stipulating that these men had a right to their old jobs, general willingness to comply voluntarily with these guide-lines rather than provoke additional state intervention in the labour market, and a conviction that the solution to the problem involved a 'normalization' of the German labour-market, in the sense that priority for jobs was given to male breadwinners. Despite some initial difficulty, many returned prisoners were able to go back to their pre-war jobs (as the ex-soldiers had done after the Armistice) and most appear to have found work fairly quickly.[47]

The return of German prisoners of war was followed soon afterwards by an inflationary boom in which joblessness was replaced by labour shortages. Against this background, the activity and responsibility of local Demobilization Committees to intervene in the labour market was reduced in 1920, and at the end of March 1921 they were disbanded altogether.[48] With the coming of full employment, therefore, most of the remaining demobilization machinery was dismantled. Skilled workers were in particularly short supply; overtime working became commonplace; women and young people, who had been chased out of the factories and offices with such vigour in 1919 and 1920, were recruited once again; renewed employment opportunities allowed people who had previously emigrated into the mining areas to return to their home regions; and, even in former centres of high unemployment such as Saxony, by September 1921 people were 'working double shifts and overtime'.[49] As the Pomeranian Labour Office in Stettin noted when surveying developments during 1921, 'the well-known conditions on the foreign exchanges, the collapse of the Mark and resulting foreign attempts to buy things up' in Germany had led to a 'powerful increase in production' and 'created the appearance of an economic boom'.[50] Low unemployment, labour shortages, and the return of women to employment continued to characterize the German economy through most of 1922, until the accelerating depreciation of the German currency began to undermine rather than stimulate economic activity.[51] As long as the cracks in the German economy and the huge costs resulting from the War could be papered over with billions of Marks, the appearance of an economic boom could be maintained and the threat of mass unemployment pushed into the background.

Although a combination of the easy availability of jobs and the reduction in real wages due to inflation[52] drew many women back to paid employment in the early 1920s, they did not necessarily return to the sorts of work which they had taken up during the War – in heavy industry, for example. Instead they tended to return to what had traditionally been considered work suitable for women: in the textile and clothing industries, in food processing, cleaning, and laundry work. Some, however, were unable to take up their former types of work because their health was no longer up to it – often seen as a result of wartime work in the munitions factories. Many married women remained at home and worked from there, 'in order to devote themselves to family and domesticity'; this, so it was reported from Berlin for the year 1921, was 'true as well for the recently married, who had initially worked for a short time but then, either at the request of their husbands or compelled by the demobilization decrees, had to give up their jobs.[53]

The changing position of women in the German labour-market after the War illustrates particularly clearly the underlying drive for a 'normalization' of economic and social relationships. First, the relatively high unemployment led to the removal of women from jobs not generally considered to be appropriate for them. Then, the full employment of the inflationary boom years of 1921 and 1922 saw the return of many women to paid employment, but largely to sectors which were regarded as suitable for them and which paralleled the types of work they were expected to do in the home: cooking, cleaning, sewing. The gender-specific organization of the labour market, which to a considerable extent had been eroded during the second half of the War, was quickly reinstituted; and the fact that women were drawn back into paid employment during the early 1920s not only did not counteract this process but actually reinforced it.[54] Indeed, with the increased demand for labour in the early 1920s the *patterns* of women's employment came to resemble more closely those of the pre-war period, although the *number* of women working outside the home once again reached that of spring and summer 1918.[55]

The reversal of wartime changes and reassertion of conventional values emerges as a major theme permeating the history of labour during the demobilization. Employment was the central concern in the post-war transition, and not just in a quantitative sense. The concern was not just to provide jobs for all those thrown on to the German labour-market after the War, but also to ensure that people were in the kinds of jobs considered appropriate to them. The reconstitution of a peacetime labour-market involved not just economic but also social engineering. In both regards the Germans were, in the short term at least, surprisingly successful – far more successful than most people had thought possible in November 1918.

While the qualitative restructuring of the German labour-market between 1918 and 1922 may be characterized, at least in part, as a process of normalization and the reassertion of conventional social values, it did not coincide with economic normalization. Indeed, it proved possible to return so many social relationships to 'normal' after the First World War because of a highly *abnormal* economic situation: an inflationary boom which ended in a hyperinflation that brought hardship and mass unemployment in its wake. In the summer of 1923, as inflation galloped ahead, joblessness began to rise steeply, and after the German currency was stabilized in late 1923 unemployment reached a level far higher than that which had caused such alarm in early 1919. By the end of 1923 more than a quarter of German trade-unionists were without jobs, and the numbers of jobless remained high throughout 1924. The advent of high, structural, and long-term unemployment facilitated the rolling-back of revolutionary gains. This economic shock was delayed (in comparison, for example, with events in Britain and the United States)[56] by the inflation of the early 1920s, and its coming during the stabilization crisis of 1923–4 marked the final and real transition of the German labour-market to 'normal' peacetime conditions. Employers were pleased to see the final dismantling of demobolization legislation which had often functioned to protect workers from arbitrary dismissal, as hundreds of thousands of workers were sacrificed on the altar of economic necessity and lost their jobs, and the strength of the trade unions was dealt a major blow.[57] The stabilization, which constituted the belated triumph of economic considerations over political ones, marked the end of the demobilization; with the arrival of high unemployment, labour was finally put back firmly in its place.

On one level, the demobilization of the German labour-market after the

First World War had been amazingly successful. The millions of returning soldiers were reintegrated swiftly into the post-war economy, and unemployment, although a serious problem in early 1919, remained within bounds and rapidly diminished thereafter. Emergency works-projects and legislation regulating the labour market functioned reasonably well, given the chaotic circumstances prevailing in Germany during the months after the Armistice; women were shunted back into occupations regarded as fitting; and gradually the widespread disinclination to work and erosion of work discipline were reversed. However, the successful demobilization of labour in Germany rested upon an inflationary economy, which itself could not be sustained indefinitely and which in effect postponed the inevitable post-war depression until 1923–4. Indeed, the demobilization of labour – particularly the need to stimulate the economy so as to provide employment for the millions of returning soldiers and former employees of war industries – contributed greatly to the German post-war inflation. The political and economic dangers inherent in the demobilization probably left Germany's new rulers no other option in 1919, but the solution they found was necessarily temporary. Seen from a longer-term perspective, the attempt to reconstitute a stable peace-time economy which could provide work for all Germans was a failure. When the demobilization period formally came to an end on 31 March 1924, the labour movement was in retreat, real wages were substantially below pre-war levels, and unemployment was at dizzying heights . . .

Notes

1 For a general discussion of the post-war labour-market and unemployment problem, see also Richard Bessel, 'Unemployment and Demobilisation in Germany after the First World War', in Richard J. Evans and Dick Geary (eds.), *The German Unemployed: Experiences and Consequences of Mass Unemployment from the Weimar Republic to the Third Reich* (London and Sydney, 1987), 23–43.

2 A good example of this is a report circulated in early Dec. by the Bavarian Ministry of Military Affairs, which summarized information gathered at the end of Oct. from factories with 200 or more employees. In the report the Ministry concluded that 'one can expect with some certainty' that male workers already in Bavaria during the war would find employment, as would most of the workers returning from military service. The problem of finding work, so it was felt, would be limited essentially to women who had taken up jobs during the war. See BHSTA, Abt. IV mkr 14413. Ministerium jür milit. Angelegenheiten to all Regierungsprasidenten, Munich, 4 Dec. 1918.

3 Emergency works-projects designed to soak up unemployment during the demobilization period probably employed between 300,000 and 400,000 people altogether. See Müller, 'Die Regelung des Arbeitsmarktes', 79. It should also be noted that deferred maintenance during the War had left local government with a great deal of work to be done repairing the infrastructure.

4 See Andreas Kunz, *Civil Servants and the Politics of Inflation in Germany, 1914–1924* (Berlin and New York, 1986), 36–44. Part of the reason for the increase in public-sector employment, particularly among contractual employees, was the demobilization itself. According to Kunz (pp. 48–9), 'demobilisation *tasks* as well

as demobilisation *policy* favored the increased use of contractual employees in the German public sector after the First World War'.

5 On this point, see Robert Scholz, 'Lohn und Beschäftigung als Indikatoren für die soziale Lage der Arbeiterschaft in der Inflation', in Gerald D. Feldman, Carl-Ludwig Holtfrerich, Gerhard A. Ritter, and Peter-Christian Witt (eds.), *Die Anpassung an die Inflation* (Berlin and New York, 1986), 288–90.

6 See Preller, *Sozialpolitik in der Weimarer Republik*, 226–37, 290–1; Müller, 'Die Regelung des Arbeitsmarktes', 21–35.

7 *Reichsgesetzblatt*, 1918, no. 153, 1305–8: 'Verordnung über Erwerbslosenfürsorge. Vom 13. November 1918'. See also Anselm Faust, 'Von der Fürsorge zur Arbeitsmarktpolitik: Die Errichtung der Arbeitslosenversicherung', in Werner Abelshauser (ed.), *Die Weimarer Republik als Wohlfahrtsstaat: Zum Verhältnis von Wirtschafts- und Sozialpolitik in der Industriegesellschaft* (Stuttgart, 1987), 263; Merith Niehuss, 'From Welfare Provision to Social Insurance: The Unemployed in Augsburg 1918–27', in Evans and Geary (eds.), *The German Unemployed*, esp. 44–5.

8 For workers, *Reichsgesetzblatt*, 1919, no. 3, 8–13: 'Verordnung über die Einstellung, Entlassung und Entlohnung gewerblicher Arbeiter während der Zeit der wirtschaftlichen Demobilmachung. Vom 4. Januar 1919'; for invalids, ibid., no. 6, 28–30: 'Verordnung über Beschäftigung Schwerbeschädigter. Vom 9. Januar 1919'; for white-collar employees, ibid., no. 18, 100–6: 'Verordnung über die Einstellung, Entlassung und Entlohnung der Angestellten während der Zeit der wirtschaftlichen Demobilmachung. Vom 24. Januar 1919'.

9 This lay behind the tightening of enforcement provisions in the Decree on the Release of Employment Positions during the Period of the Economic Demobilization of 28 Mar. 1919. See Gunther Mai, 'Arbeitsmarktregulierung oder Sozialpolitik? Die personnelle Demobilmachung in Deutschland 1918 bis 1920/24', in Gerald D. Feldman, Carl-Ludwig Holtfrerich, Gerhard A. Ritter, and Peter-Christian Witt (eds.), *Die Anpassung an die Inflation* (Berlin and New York, 1986), 218.

10 *Reichsgesetzblatt*, 1919, no. 71, 355–9: 'Verordnung über die Freimachung von Arbeitsstellen während der Zeit der wirtschaftlichen Demobilmachung. Vom 28. März 1919'.

11 See Dietmar Petzina, Werner Abelshauser, and Anselm Faust, *Sozialgeschichtliches Arbeitsbuch*, iii: *Materialien zur Statistik des Deutschen Reiches 1914–1945* (Munich, 1978), 111.

12 For a good description of this on a local level, in Ludwigshafen, see Schiffmann, *Von der Revolution zum Neunstundentag*, 141–3.

13 Michael Schneider also makes this point, in *Die Christlichen Gewerkschaften*, 449–50. For an excellent description of the collapse of collective bargaining during the hyperinflation, see Kunz, *Civil Servants and the Politics of Inflation*, 362.

14 For a good coroncise discussion of this undermining of the trade unions in 1923–4, see William L. Patch, *Christian Trade Unions in the Weimar Republic 1918–1933: The Failure of 'Corporate Pluralism'* (New Haven, Conn., and London, 1985), 87–90.

15 BLHA, Rep. 2A, Reg, Potsdam I SW, no. 796, fo. 150: Hirsch-, Kupfer- und Messingwerke to Regierungspräsident als Demobilmachungskommissar, Messingwerk, 15 Feb. 1919.

16 *Reichsgesetzblatt*, 1919, 8–13: 'Verordnung über die Einstellung, Entlassung und Entlohnung gewerblicher Arbeiter während der Zeit der Demobilmachung. Vom 4. Januar 1919.'

17 Richard Bessel, 'State and Society in Germany in the Aftermath of the First World

War', in W. R. Lee and Eve Rosenhaft (eds.), *The State and Social Change in Germany, 1880-1980* (Oxford, Munich and New York, 1990), 209-10.

18 Quoted in H.-J. Bieber, *Gewerkschaften in Krieg und Revolution*, 610.

19 Quoted ibid.

20 For discussion of the negotiations culminating in, and the significance of, the Stinnes-Legien Agreement, see Gerald D. Feldman, 'The Origins of the Stinnes-Legien Agreement: A Documentation', *Internationale wissenschaftliche Korrespondenz zur Geschichte der deutschen Arbeiterbewegung*, 19/20 (Dec. 1972), 45-103; H.-J. Bierber, *Gewerkschaften in Krieg und Revolution*, 595-619.

21 See e.g. WWA, K1, no. 171: Westfälisches Verbands-Elektrizitätswerk to Handelskammer zu Dortmund, Dortmund, 13 Dec. 1918.

22 Ibid.: Städtisches Elektrizitätswerk to Handelskammer, Dortmund, 20 Dec. 1918.

23 This was true of the giant BASF chemicals works. Although the French occupying authorities in the Palatinate (where the BASF factories were located) initially refused to enforce the demobilization decrees, the management of BASF introduced the eight-hour day at the beginning of Dec. 1918 – largely because coal shortages meant that longer shifts were unnecessary. Other industrial employers in the Palatinate, however, used the French attitude as an excuse not to accept the eight-hour day until the spring of 1919. See Schiffmann, *Von der Revolution zum Neunstundentag*, 100-1, 164-5.

24 For accounts of the major strike-waves, in the Upper Silesian industrial region and among Ruhr miners, see esp. H.-J. Bieber, *Gewerkschaften in Krieg und Revolution*, 637-84.

25 In 1919 only 584 of the 3,682 recorded strikes ended in clear victory for the employers. See *Statistisches Jahrbuch für das Deutsche Reich 1934* (Berlin, 1934), 321.

26 Königsberger, 'Die wirtschaftliche Demobilmachung in Bayern', 213.

27 See the tables of male and female unemployment between 1919 and 1924 in Bessel, 'Unemployment and Demobilisation', 35.

28 GStAM, Rep. 120, BB, Abt. VII, Fach 1, No. 3o, Band 5, fos. 197-203: 'Eingabe des Berufsverbandes der Katholischen Metallarbeiterinnen (Abteilung Grubenarbeiterinnen) und der Berufsorganisation der Textilarbeiterinnen (Heimarbeiterinnen) im Verbande Katholischer Vereine erwerbstätiger Frauen und Mädchen Deutschlands', Kattowitz, 22 July 1920; Helgard Kramer, 'Frankfurt's Working Women: Scapegoats or Winners of the Great Depression?', in Evans and Geary (eds.), *The German Unemployed*, 115; Hagemann, *Frauenalltag und Männerpolitik*, 435. This had, in fact, been codified in the Decree on Unemployment Relief of 13 Nov. 1918, which stipulated that 'female persons are to be supported only if they depend upon employment for their livelihood', and that 'persons whose previous breadwinners return and are capable of working are to receive no unemployment relief'. See *Reichsgesetzblatt*, 1918, no. 153, 1305-8. These clauses were retained in the Reich Decree on Unemployment Relief of 16 Apr. 1919. See *Reichsgesetzblatt*, 1919, no. 89, 418.

29 BAP, RMwD, no. 18/1, fos. 154-5: Landwirtschaftsamt to Reichsamt für wirtschaftliche Demobilmachung, Karlsruhe, 11 Jan. 1919; ibid., fos. 195-8: Kriegsamtstelle to Demobilmachungsamt, Münster, 18 Jan. 1919; ibid. fos. 276-7: Kriegsamtstelle to Reichsamt für wirtschaftliche Demobilmachung, Magdeburg, 1 Feb 1919; ibid. fos. 297-301: Kriegsamtstelle to the Reichsamt für wirtschaftliche Demobilmachung, Breslau, 8 Feb. 1919; GStAM, Rep. 120, BB VII 1, 17, Bd. 13, 424-5: Reichsministerium für wirtschaftliche Demobilmachung 'Vermittlung von Hausangestellten', Berlin, 22 Mar. 1919. See also Bessel, 'Unemployment and Demobilisation', 33.

30 GStAB, Rep. 180, no. 15913: 'Bericht über den Arbeitsmarkt in Danzig während des Krieges', Danzig, 17 Feb. 1919. See also Bessel, ' "Eine nicht allzu große Beunruhigung des Arbeitsmarktes" ', 223.

31 GStAB, Rep. 180, no. 14430, fo. 245: Zentralauskunftstelle für Arbeitsnachweis to Regierungspräsident, Danzig, 7 June 1919; ibid., fo. 384: Zentralauskunftstelle für Arbeitsnachweis to Regierungspräsident, Danzig, 23 Aug. 1919.

32 See Müller, 'Die Regelung des Arbeitsmarktes', 82-4.

33 StdALu, no. 6670: Städtisches Arbeitsamt, report for 1919. For more discussion of this report, see Bessel, 'Unemployment and Demobilisation', 36-7.

34 See e.g. GLAK, 456/E.V. 6, Bund 112: Ministerium für soziale Fürsorge, 'Arbeitsbeschaffung für kaufmännische und technische Angestellten', Karlsruhe, 8 Jan. 1919. In late Jan. labour exchanges in Pomerania reported 634 men and 245 women applying for office work, while not a single post was on offer. See APS, Oberpräsidium von Pommern, no. 3952: Zentralauskunftstelle Stettin, 'Wochenbericht über den Arbeitsmarkt der Provinz Pommern', Stettin, 25 Jan. 1919. See also Mai, 'Arbeitsmarktregulierung oder Sozialpolitik?' 223-4.

35 Königsberger, 'Die wirtschaftliche Demobilmachung in Bayern', 213.

36 Müller, 'Die Regelung des Arbeitsmarktes', 53.

37 In Dresden, one meeting held by a women's white-collar union to protest against proposals to sack female employees was broken up by male clerks in early 1919. See Feldman, 'Saxony, the Reich, and the Problem of Unemployment', 112. In Cologne, a local 'committee for the representation of the interests of unemployed commercial employees' demanded that women be removed from white-collar jobs, arguing that this was 'not just a purely economic but also a moral demand, because the man is first of all the founder and provider of the family and the women should take care of domestic affairs and educate the children'; 'eminent physicians and hospital statistics demonstrate sufficiently that – with few exceptions – women's employment in trade and industry, as in all male occupations, is associated with serious health-risks and leads to demoralization and deterioration of the race'. See GStAM, Rep. 120, BB, Abt. VII, Fach 1, no. 3o, Band 5, fos. 73-5: Ausschuß zur Vertretung der Interessen der stellenlosen Handlungsgehilfen to Demobilmachungs-Kommissar, Cologne, 10 Aug. 1919.

38 e.g. APP, Rejencja w Pile, no. 1485: Deutschnationaler Handlungsgehilfen-Verband to Demobilmachungskommissar zu Marienwerder, Hamburg, 12 Nov. 1919. See also Stefan Bajohr, *Die Hälfte der Fabrik: Geschichte der Frauenarbeit in Deutschland 1914 bis 1945* (Marburg, 1979), 163; Bessel, " 'Eine nicht allzu große Beunruhigung des Arbeitsmarktes" ', 220-1.

39 Feldman, 'Socio-Economic Structures', 163. See also the tables of real weekly wages for railway workers, printers, and Ruhr coal miners in Carl-Ludwig Holtfrerich, *The German Inflation 1914-1923: Causes and Effects in International Perspective* (Berlin and New York, 1986), 233.

40 See e.g. GStAM, Rep. 120, BB, Abt. VII, Fach 1, no. 3o, Band 2, fos. 35-6: Regierungspräsident to Minister für Handel und Gewerbe, Marienwerder, 18 Nov. 1918.

41 See Wunderlich, *Die Bekämpfung der Arbeitslosigkeit*, 2-3.

42 BA/MA, RW1/W 01-2/5, fos. 1-2: 'Besprechung am 18. August 1919 in Kolberg'.

43 800,000 was the figure used in government discussions of the prisoners of war during 1919. See Hagen Schulze (ed.), *Akten der Reichskanzlei. Weimarer Republik. Das Kabinett Scheidemann. 13. Februar bis 20. Juni 1919* (Boppard/Rhein, 1971), 25: 'Vortrag des Generals v. Hammerstein vor dem Reichskabinett über die Arbeit der Waffenstillstandskommission in Spa, 4. März 1919, 10 Uhr in Weimar, Schloß'. In fact, by Aug. 1920 about 600,000 prisoners had returned to

Germany. The first to come home were those in British and American hands, in Sept. and Oct. 1919; those in French captivity followed between late Jan. and late Mar. 1920; and the return from Russia began in May 1920. See StAB, 3-M.2.h.2/N, 130: 'Denkschrift über Abwicklung des Krieges', Berlin, 26 Oct. 1920.

44 See BLHA, Rep. 30 Berlin C. Polizeipräsidium Berlin/Tit. 47, no. 1959, fos. 121-81: Oberregierungs- und Gewerberat Hartmann, 'Jahresbericht für das Jahr 1920. Aufsichtsbezirk Berlin'.

45 See e.g. the outline of demands presented by the 'Reichsvereinigung ehemaliger Kriegsgefangener' in BAP, RMdI, no. 13090/9, fos. 24-5: Reichszentrale für Kriegs-u. Zivilgefangene to Reichsministerium des Innern, Berlin, 14 Oct. 1920.

46 e.g. on the labour market in Berlin: BLHA, Rep. 30 Berlin C, Polizeipräsidium Berlin/Tit. 47, no. 1959, fos. 121-81: Oberregierungs- und Gewerberat Hartmann, 'Jahresbericht für das Jahr 1920. Aufsichtsbezirk Berlin'.

47 e.g. see the list of former prisoners of war in Wunstdorf, in the Regierungsbezirk Hanover, showing the dates of their release from captivity and of their return to work (which generally occurred a few weeks later, in late 1919 or early 1920), in NHStA, Hann. 174, Neustadt/Rbg., no. 3011. See also the reports from the first half of 1920 of the trade-union functionary who headed the army's job-counselling centre in Nürnberg, in BHStA, Abt. IV, MKr 14414. Although he reported difficulty in finding work for returned prisoners in Jan. and Feb., in mid-May he was able to conclude that 'the task of bringing men dismissed from the army, occupants of the garrisons and returned prisoners of war back into economic activity' was completed. Ibid., Arbeitsbeschaffungsstelle, Gewerkschaftsfunktionär Baierlein to Abwicklungsamt fr. III.b.A.K. Nürnberg, Nürnberg, 19 May 1920.

48 See Mai, 'Arbeitsmarktregulierung oder Sozialpolitik?' 228-30. The remaining functions of the local Demobilization Committees were handed over to the labour exchanges or to the regional Demobilization Commissars.

49 SHAD, Gesandtschaft Berlin, no. 692: Reichswirtschaftsminister to Reichspräsident, Berlin, 21 Oct. 1921.

50 PLA, Rep. 38 Loitz, no. 1382, fos. 166-9: 'Verwaltungsbericht des Pommerschen Landes arbeitsamt und des Provinzialberufsamts für das Jahr 1921'.

51 See BLHA, Rep. 30 Berlin C, Polizeipräsidium Berlin/Tit. 47, no. 1959, fos. 361-401: Regierungs- und Gewerberat Wenzel, 'Jahresbericht für das Jahr 1922'. The most direct effect of the inflation upon women's employment came with the recruitment in 1922 of an additional 1,500 women to work in printing factories producing banknotes.

52 See the tables showing the changes in real wages in Holtfrerich, *The German Inflation*, 233-4. For a yet more negative view of wage levels during the inflation, see Scholz, 'Zur sozialen Lage der Arbeiterschaft in der Inflation'.

53 BLHA, Rep. 30 Berlin C, Polizeipräsidium Berlin/Tit. 47, no. 1959, fos. 235-311.

54 Rouette, 'Die Erwerbslosenfürsorge für Frauen in Berlin', 9.

55 Friedrich Hesse, *Die deutsche Wirtschaftslage von 1914 bis 1923: Krieg, Geldblähe und Wechsellagen* (Jena, 1938), 480.

56 On points of international comparison, see Bessel, 'Unemployment and Demobilisation', 28.

57 See Gerald D. Feldman and Irmgard Steinisch, 'Die Weimarer Republik zwischen Sozialund Wirtschaftsstaat: Die Entscheidung gegen den Achtstundentag', in *Archiv für Sozialgeschichte*, 18 (1978). See also Mai, 'Arbeitsmarktregulierung oder Sozialpolitik?', 233-4.

CHAPTER 7

Recasting Bourgeois Europe

CHARLES MAIER

From bourgeois to corporatist Europe

In an era of upheaval, it is continuity and stability that need explanation. The premise of this study is that European social hierarchies in the twentieth century have proved strikingly tenacious when men often expected otherwise. Violence is not always a midwife of history: despite world wars and domestic conflict much of Europe's institutional and class structure has showed itself tough and durable; the forces of continuity and conservatism have held their own. Real changes have certainly taken place – growing enrichment, loosening family structures, broader educational opportunities. But these have occurred more as a product of the last quarter century's stability than of prior social turmoil, and they have not dispossessed the privileged groups. The Fiats and Renaults of the workers may now push to the campgrounds of the Riviera, but the Mercedes and Jaguars still convey their masters to Cap d'Antibes or Santa Margherita. Industrialists now, as after World War I can still lament the intrusion of labor unions upon their prerogatives; the respectable press can still denounce public service strikes; Ruhr managers command awe in Germany; the nation-state persists. This is not to claim that the relative social stability of the last quarter century may not finally disintegrate under new pressures. But it is to call attention to the persistence of social hegemonies that a half century ago seemed precarious if not doomed.

This study examines a critical period in the disciplining of change, in the survival and adaptation of political and economic elites, and in the twentieth-century capitalist order they dominated. The years after World War I are especially instructive, because security was apparently wrested from profound disorder and turbulence. If in the turmoil of 1918–19 a new European world seemed to be in birth by the late 1920s much of the pre-war order appeared to have been substantially restored. Both perspectives were skewed: the transformations of 1918 had been in good part superficial, and so was the stability of the 1920s. None the less, despite the limits of the restoration, the decade rewarded conservative efforts with striking success.

The process by which this occurred is the subject of this study. In retrospect, it is easy to note that the forces actively pressing for major social or political changes constituted a minority, and a badly divided one at that. But this response is not very revealing; it discourages investigation of how so great a degree of hierarchical social ordering was preserved when mass parties, 'total war', and economic dislocation made some social leveling inevitable. And if the weakness and divisions of the attackers are well known, the strategies of social and political defense remain unexplored. Political and economic institutions served as the outworks of a fortress – so Tocqueville had described them while waiting for the assault on private property he feared as the revolution of 1848 approached.[1] How in the decade after 1917 were the fortifications challenged? How were they defended? The strategy and the ultimate stakes were not always apparent. Partisans of order and partisans of change, besieged and besiegers, too often served as Tolstoyan commanders, mapping delusory tactics for misconceived battles. Noisy clashes were not always significant ones. The spectacular conflicts of the era were not always the important ones in shaking or re-establishing the structures of power. For every March on Rome, Kapp Putsch, or general strike, there were equally determinative disputes over factory council prerogatives, taxes, coal prices, and iron tariffs. These were quieter but still decisive struggles.

In the wake of World War I, these confrontations formed part of an overarching development. That long and grueling combat imposed parallel social and political strains upon the states of Europe, and for years after dictated a common rhythm of radicalism and reaction. All Western nations experienced new restiveness on the left after the Russian Revolutions of 1917 and continuing radical turmoil from the 1918 Armistice through the spring of 1919. The 'forces of order' had to make their peace either with political overturn, as in Germany, or, at the least, new attacks on capitalism. Yet, by 1920–1 they had recovered the upper hand and pushed the 'forces of movement' on to the defensive. By 1922–3 a new wave of nationalist, sometimes authoritarian, remedies replaced the earlier surge of leftist efforts. Right-wing schemes, however, could not durably settle the economic and social dislocations the war had left. By the mid-1920s each country had to find a new and precarious equilibrium, based less on the revival of traditional ideological prescriptions than upon new interest-group compromises or new forms of coercion. Despite their many differences, France, Germany and Italy all participated in this post-war political cycle.

This common tidal flow of politics virtually calls for comparative examination. In a more general work, post-World War I developments could be set in an even wider context of conservative reaction or liberal crisis. Other countries, Austria and Spain, and from some perspectives Britain and the United States, might also have been included. [*Recasting Bourgeois Europe*] sacrifices a broader range through space and time for intensive examination of three countries during one critical decade.

The three countries, moreover, do form a coherent unit for political and social analysis, despite the fact that Italy ended up under fascism, the German Republic as of the mid-1920s remained vulnerable to authoritarian pressures, while France maintained parliamentary institutions until its military defeat in 1940. Despite major differences, the three nations all had traditions of sharp ideological dispute and fragmentation, concepts of liberalism and labels for class distinction that set them apart from Britain or the United States. France, Italy and Germany certainly do not provide the only matrix for comparison, but they do offer a logical one.

In the last analysis, there can be no *a priori* validity or lack of validity in historical comparison. The researcher can group together any range of phenomena under some common rubric. The issue is whether the exercise suggests relationships that would otherwise remain unilluminated. Some comparative approaches are more fruitful than others. Comparative history remains superficial if it merely plucks out elites in different societies – or working-class organizations, or party systems, or revolutionary disturbances. Flower arranging is not botany. A bouquet of historic parallels provides little knowledge about society unless we dissect and analyze the component parts. What is important to learn is what functions were served by supposedly comparable historical phenomena in establishing and contesting power and values. Organized parties, for instance, were critical in Germany but less so in Italy and France, so to follow parties alone would distort historical perspective. Issues deemed vital at one moment often lose the symbolic importance with which they were originally charged. Nationalization of the French railroads was bitterly contested in 1920, yet it meant little when it was finally accomplished in 1937. Issues and associations, therefore, must be scrutinized not according to their external form, but according to the changing roles they played in revealing the stress lines of European society. For this reason, comparative analysis starts here, from the disputes wherein the basic distributions of power were contested or at least exposed.

The analytical description needed here is complicated because what the contestants themselves described as the stakes of conflict was often misleading. The defenders envisioned their struggle in terms of the clashes they knew from before the war. They entered the interwar years with an inherited imagery of social and political conflict. Borrowing their terminology, this study uses the term *bourgeois* to denote the arrangements which conservatives felt they were defending. In many instances the imagery of bourgeois defense was inadequate for understanding the new institutional realities that were emerging. To describe these new realities we cannot borrow from the terminology of the era, but must impose our own unifying concept. I have chosen the notion of corporatism. Each of these terms oversimplifies – distorting, on the one hand, conservative aspirations, and, on the other, the emerging institutional reality. Taken together, however, they force us to keep in mind the tension between aspiration and achievement.

What conservatives naturally aimed at was a stability and status associated with pre-war Europe. 'Bourgeois' was the most general term of orientation they invoked; they employed it as a shorthand for all they felt was threatened by war, mass politics and economic difficulty – in short, as the common denominator of social anxiety and political defense. For an observer suddenly transplanted from Restoration France or Germany before 1848, the conservative connotations of 'bourgeois Europe' might have been startling. In those earlier eras the bourgeoisie had spearheaded the liberalization of economy and politics against the prescriptive claims of dynasties and agrarian traditionalists. But during the course of the nineteenth century, bourgeois spokesmen achieved the civil rights and, at least partially, the access to power they desired. Increasingly, in Western Europe they formed long-term associations with the old elite. Universities, government bureaucracies, boards of directors and marriage beds could not produce a complete fusion of classes, but they did offer new chances to combine the assets of land, capital, public service and education.

Bourgeois reformers, moreover, had always had potential enemies to the left: democrats, artisans, spokesmen for working-class grievances. Except in periods of crisis, cooperation with these volatile forces was short-lived, even during the era of bourgeois reform. From the advent of mass suffrage in the 1860s and after, the left became even more threatening, especially as it advocated major changes in property relationships. Under this pressure, too, members of the old elites perceived the same dangers as did bourgeois leaders. Tory radicalism, or the effort to outflank bourgeois elites with working-class alliances, yielded meager results and was never popular for very long among conservative constituencies. By the twentieth century most of the old elites had formed a conservative cartel with bourgeois political representatives. They identified the same enemies and defended the same prerogatives. As the most preoccupying enemy, social democrats set the terms of attack for the defenders of the social order as well as for themselves. More consistently than any other group, the socialists challenged existing property and power relationships as the foundation of a bourgeois society that rested upon economic exploitation, sacrificed democracy to elitism, and created suicidal international conflicts to preserve its internal structure. Under the pressure of growing social-democratic strength, both sides focused upon bourgeois society as the ultimate stake of political and economic conflict.

Yet in what sense was 'bourgeois' a meaningful class category by 1918; or had it already been bled of all sociological precision? In the mid-1920s, Croce, for one, complained of the careless usage that 'bourgeois' was receiving as a historical term.[2] He argued that it had really come to mean little more than modern and secular. Similar reservations could be made of its widespread use by social commentators. But its broad use also suggests that 'bourgeois' really did evoke the basic social divisions of a market economy and industrial social order. Frequent recourse to the term revealed a nagging preoccupation with inequality and class antagonism. Conservatives liked to claim that class conflict as Marxists portrayed it was merely conjured up by agitators and demagogues. And yet they devoted major efforts to shoring up the very institutions that anchored class domination in the eyes of the left: they extolled the nation-state, fretted about nationalization of coal mines or railroads, praised property and entrepreneurship. As men of the 1920s employed the term, 'bourgeois' invoked fundamental questions of social hierarchy and power. It remained the code word for a matrix of relationships defined in opposition to what socialists suggested as alternatives.[3] For the elites of the 1920s, bourgeois Europe was both elegiac and compelling: the image of an *ancien régime* that was still salvageable and whose rescue became the broadest common purpose of post-war politics.

This is not to claim that bourgeois defense was the stake of all political conflict in the 1920s. Disputes between Catholics and anti-clerical liberals remained deep enough to influence party organization in each country and to cut across the issues of social defense. Italian fascists or German right-radicals would also have rejected any claim that they sought to strengthen bourgeois Europe, for they fundamentally despised its parliamentary institutions. Even before the war a 'new' European right had moved beyond the conservatism of agrarian, business and bureaucratic elites to embrace a strident chauvinism, anti-Semitism and antiparliamentarism. This new right comprised distressed farmers, retired officers, intellectuals and university youth, clerical employees and hard-pressed small businessmen and shopkeepers. Yet ironically, this rag-tag right-radical constituency could also contribute to the defense of bourgeois Europe. By the 1920s both the old and new right were attacking Marxist socialism (and communism) as an evil incubated by liberal democracy. The gains of socialism testified to a bourgeois failure of nerve; they made counteraction urgent and sanctioned a violent assault on liberalism itself. Thus, even as the radical right rhetorically lashed out against the parasites of finance or corrupt party politics, it moved with violence against the major organized opposition to bourgeois institutions. Disillusioned liberals, traditionalist conservatives, nationalists, and new right-radicals converged in their hostility to socialism and the democracy that permitted it to thrive.[4]

Nonetheless, [this chapter] focuses neither on the old nor the new right *per se,* but upon the process of stabilizing institutions under attack. It must, in fact, explore positions that were never considered to be on the right at all, in the militant sense usually given to that word. The right incorporated only one of two possible approaches to protecting the social order. While the right accepted a clear clash of ideologies and aimed at repressing changes, moderate and democratic leaders dreaded Armageddon and hoped to disarm the attackers by reformist initiatives. Both strategies come under study here in so far as both envisaged a social order according to bourgeois criteria. To reconsolidate that social order was the overriding aim of conservative thought and action after 1918. It was the essential effort for the old right, often catalytic for the emergence of the radical new right, and a preoccupation as well for many progressives not on the right at all. To anticipate our conclusions, it was an effort that was largely successful, even if the victory required significant institutional transformation.

For there was no simple restoration. While Europeans sought stability in the image of a pre-war bourgeois society, they were creating new institutional arrangements and distributions of power. What began to evolve was a political economy that I have chosen to call corporatist.[5] This involved the displacement of power from elected representatives or a career bureaucracy to the major organized forces of European society and economy, sometimes bargaining directly among themselves, sometimes exerting influence through a weakened parliament, and occasionally seeking advantages through new executive authority. In each case corporatism meant the growth of private power and the twilight of sovereignty.

Most conspicuously, this evolution toward corporatism involved a decay of parliamentary influence. Already effaced during World War I, parliaments proved incapable of recovering a decisive position of power. Even in Germany, where the Reichstag had always been subordinate, the Weimar Republic's parliament proved a reflection and not a source of effective power. In part, parliamentary incapacity was a consequence of the harsher political tasks imposed by the 1920s. Not the fruits of growth but the costs of war had to be distributed: parliaments faced dilemmas of economic reallocation and relative deprivation that strained older party alignments and precluded coherent majorities. Ultimately, the weakening of parliaments also meant the undermining of older notions of a common good and a traditionally conceived citizenry of free individuals.[6]

In the liberal polity, decisions demanded periodic ratification by a supposedly atomized electorate. The new corporatism, however, sought consensus less through the occasional approval of a mass public than through continued bargaining among organized interests. Consequently, policy depended less upon the aggregation of individual preferences than upon averting or overcoming the vetoes that interest groups could impose at the center. Consensus became hostage to the cooperation of each major interest. If industry, agriculture, labor, or in some cases the military, resisted government policy, they could make its costs unacceptable.

The leverage that each major interest could exert had further institutional consequences. It tended to dissolve the old line between parliament and the marketplace – between state and society – that continental liberals had claimed to defend. The political veto power of an interest group came to depend upon its strength in the economic arena. Conversely, viability in the marketplace required a voice in determining the political ground rules for economic competition, such as tariffs and taxes or the rights of collective bargaining.[7]

Consequently, too, the locus of policy-making changed. Parliamentary assemblies grew too unwieldy for the continuing brokerage of interests. Bargaining moved outside the chamber to unofficial party or coalition caucuses, and to government ministries that tended to identify with major economic groupings, such as the Weimar Republic's Ministry of Labor.

Even the modalities of exerting influence altered. The liberal polity had always sanctioned discreet compacts between powerful individuals and ministers or parliamentary delegates. Influence was also transmitted less directly but just as pervasively in the clubs, lodges, schools, and regiments that formed the social milieu of the government elites. But in the emerging corporatist system, new social elements had to be consulted, above all labor leaders who had earlier been outside the system. Domestic policy no longer emerged intact from the foyers of the ruling class, no longer represented just the shared premises of the era's 'best and the brightest'. Policy formation required formal confrontation in offices and ministries between old social antagonists. Political stability demanded a more bureaucratic and centralized bargaining. If Marx, in short, dictated the preoccupations of bourgeois society, Weber discerned its emerging structures of power.

It would be wrong to exaggerate the suddenness of this transformation, which began before World War I and is really still underway. Labor and tariff disputes spurred the organization of modern pressure groups in the late nineteenth century. Cartelization further signaled the consolidation of economic power. Observers of the same era noted the growing affiliation of political parties with economic interest groups; and they discussed how party competition was changing from a clubby and whiggish rivalry into a professional mobilization of opinion through electoral machines. These developments quietly altered the nature of representative government.[8]

But they did not create a corporatist polity. Two further significant developments emerged only with the massive economic mobilization of World War I. The first was the integration of organized labor into a bargaining system supervised by the state. This accreditation of labor also had been underway, but the urgency of war production accelerated the process. Adding labor to the interest groups bargaining around the table suggested that a new division between those producer groups which could organize effectively and the fragmented components of the middle classes might become more politically significant than the older class cleavage between bourgeois and worker.

A second decisive impulse was the wartime erosion of the distinction between private and public sectors. As the state claimed important new powers to control prices, the movement of labor, and the allocation of raw materials, it turned over this new regulatory authority to delegates of business, labor, or agriculture, not merely through informal consultation but also through official supervisory boards and committees. A new commonwealth that dissolved the old distinction between state and economy seemed at hand; and some of its beneficiaries looked forward to extending wartime organization as the basis, in Rathenau's phrase, of a 'new economy'.

Advocates for this parceling out of sovereignty spoke out from different points along the political spectrum. Men of the left, right, and center noted the new tendencies at the turn of the century: the growing web of interest groups and cartels, the obsolescence of the market economy, the interpenetration of government and industry. But they hoped to rationalize and order what they saw taking place as an unplanned evolution before 1914 and as an emergency response during the war. Rather than just a new centralization of interest-group bargaining, they wanted to leave brokerage behind entirely and create a planned and harmonious productive system based upon technological or moral imperatives. On the moderate left, guild socialists, Marxist revisionists, and some democratic liberals envisioned a gradual dissolution of central state authority and the growth of works councils and industrial self-government. Their premise was that if normally antagonistic groups, such as the workers and entrepreneurs of a given industry, could be seated at the same table and hammer out common policy, the result must be impartial enough to guarantee the public interest as a whole. Their concept of decentralization sometimes borrowed from French and Italian syndicalism, but the syndicalists envisaged a more radical elimination of the entrepreneurs.

There were also spokesmen for an older corporatism on the right, represented by writers from La Tour du Pin in the 1870s to Othmar Spann a half-century later. These theorists felt that they could undo the social ravages of an atomistic liberalism by creating an estatist representation. This vision differed in an important respect from the new corporatism that was actually emerging, because it envisioned not merely a *de facto* representation of economic forces, but a society of legal orders. As on the left, the corporatism invoked by conservatives was designed to secure a social harmony that transcended mere pressure-group bargaining. The new corporatism, however, did not eliminate class transactions but merely centralized them.

Finally, a technocratic vision of a new industrial order emerged from the ranks of professional engineers and progressive businessmen. American enthusiasts joined Europeans in blueprinting the future industrial commonwealth. Herbert Hoover's crusade for an orderly community of abundance and Walther Rathenau's more mystical revery of a postcompetitive industrial order both drew on the promises of technology and organization. Both men envisaged moving beyond an often wasteful *laissez-faire* economy, subject to cycles of boom and bust and to overproduction in some sectors and shortages in others. Horizontal association among producers would eliminate wasteful competition. Vertical association between industry and labor would ultimately rest upon technological determination of how to share the rewards of productivity.[9]

Each of these groups rejected the Manchesterite, bourgeois state, but their final visions remained different. Socialist and syndicalist theorists, who eschewed the term 'corporative' because of its reactionary overtones, hoped to move beyond state authority to a less coercive and more egalitarian economy. Corporatists of the right, however, sought to recreate earlier hierarchies. The old ladders of subordination and domination, deference and largesse, reflected an ethical universal ordering that liberalism and the commercial spirit had shattered. Technocratic spokesmen denied class objectives in favor of a new efficiency, enhanced productivity, and a society of abundance.

History was to play tricks on each group; for the new corporatism encouraged restriction of output as much as abundance, and it led neither to radical liberation nor to recovery of an estatist social order. Instead it brought enhanced control for the very elites that had come to prominence under parliamentary auspices. Nor could any far-seeing statesman oversee the transformation: there was no Bismarck for the bourgeoisie as there had been for the Junkers. Rather, corporatist stability arose out of new pressures and false starts: as noted, wartime demands upon industry and labor for massive industrial production with a minimum of conflict; the accompanying wartime inflation, which permitted big business and the unions to reward themselves jointly – or at least to lose less than the other, less organized sectors of the economy; thereafter, the failure of liberal parliamentary leaders to solve post-war economic and social problems by traditional coalition compromises; finally, the terms of American economic intervention and of stabilization in the mid-1920s. It was this sequence of events that helped to consolidate the new relationships between private and public power, the development of which is presented below.

It is not claimed here that the trend was uniform throughout Europe. By the mid-1920s the thrust toward corporatism was clear in Germany, emerging under authoritarian auspices in Italy, but only embryonic in France. Corporatist trends in the Weimar Republic could build upon estatist patterns of authority and economic organization that had survived the nineteenth century in Germany. In Italy the traditional elites were more isolated and less protected by guild-like economic organization or by vigorous local self-government. A corporatist defense could not emerge from the fragmented pattern of business groupings and antiquated bourgeois parties. It had to be imposed by political coercion. In France, corporatist developments were even more retarded. Estatist patterns had been pulverized by prerevolutionary and postrevolutionary regimes, while a gentler pace of industrialization than Germany's lessened the scope and impact of powerful pressure groups. Less buffeted by radicalism, too, the French could preserve a bourgeois society through the parliamentary institutions of the Third Republic. Yet even in France the incapacities of the parliamentary regime pointed the way toward corporatist development.

The notion of corporatism is applied to all three countries, in any case, not as a simple description but rather as an ideal type. As such, it helps us to make sense of French tendencies as well as German ones and to forecast the structure of stability throughout Europe. The decade after World War I was a decisive era in this regrouping of conservative forces. The legacy of war precluded any simple return to the model of the liberal polity; and the role of the United States – a society marked by a new cooperation of government and business in the wake of wartime mobilization – helped advance the transformation in Europe.[10] The Depression, World War II, and subsequent American aid in reconstruction would thrust the evolution of corporatism even further along. After 1945, it would no longer be necessary or even comforting for conservatives to imagine the restoration of a bourgeois society as the endpoint of their efforts. The corporatist structure that was emerging in the 1920s as the instrument of social reconsolidation became a goal in its own right by the end of World War II. To re-establish the given hierarchies in western Europe by the late 1940s, it was sufficient to assure the independence of private industry and interest groups. Conservative goals were less Utopian than they were after 1918, less fraught with nostalgia for a deferential and stable bourgeois order. After 1945 bourgeois Europe neither existed nor ceased to exist: an ideological construct, it faded from concern. Stratification, inequality and corporatist power remained, but few had sought to abolish them.

Bourgeois society, considered in retrospect, amounted to a conservative Utopia.[11] It incorporated a collection of images, ideas and memories about desirable ranking in a tensely divided industrial Europe. As a Utopia it spurred conservative, and ultimately corporatist strategies, once simple restoration proved beyond reach. These corporatist arrangements not only helped re-entrench pre-war elites, but also rewarded labor leadership and injured the less organized middle classes. The history of stabilization after World War I thus involved, not a political freeze or simple reaction, but a decade of capitalist restructuring and renovation. The tension between bourgeois Utopia and corporatist outcome – part of history's constant dialectic between men's intentions and their collective realization – provides the interpretive structure for what was a key era of conservative transformation.

Notes

1 *The Recollections of Alexis de Tocqueville,* trans. Alexander Teixera de Mattos, J. P. Mayer (ed.), Cleveland and New York, 1959, p. 10.

2 Benedetto Croce, 'Di un equivoco concetto storico: la "Borghesia" ', *Atti della Academia di Scienze Morali e Politiche della Società Reale di Napoli,* LI, 1927; reprinted in *Etica e politica,* Bari, 1967, p. 275. Although valid as a crossnational designation, the term 'bourgeois' still suggested different qualities from country to country: 'civic' in Germany, a ruling elite in Italy, and refined, perhaps smug upper-middle-class leisure in France.

3 For the generation of class division: cf. Stanislaw Ossowski, *Class Structure in the Social Consciousness,* trans. Sheila Patterson, London, 1963, pp. 72–3, 133; Ralf Dahrendorf, *Class and Class Conflict in Industrial Society,* Stanford, Calif., 1959, pp. 162–79, 201–5; useful surveys of the literature are in T. B. Bottomore, *Elites in Society,* Baltimore, Md, 1966, and *Classes in Modern Society,* New York, 1968. Cf. also the essays in André Béteille (ed.) *Social Inequality,* Baltimore, Md, 1969.

4 For an introduction to concepts of the right: Hans Rogger and Eugen Weber (eds), *The European Right,* Berkeley and Los Angeles, 1965; René Rémond, *The Right Wing in France from 1815 to de Gaulle,* trans. James M. Laux, Philadelphia, 1966; Ernst Nolte, *Three Faces of Fascism,* trans. Leila Vennewitz, New York, 1966, pp. 29ff, 429ff; Armin Mohler, *Die konservative Revolution in Deutschland, 1918-1932,* Stuttgart, 1950; Karl Mannheim, 'Das konservative Denken. Soziologische Beiträge zum Werden des politisch-historischen Denkens in Deutschland', *Archiv für Sozialwissenschaft und Sozialpolitik,* 57, 1 and 2 1927, 68–142, 470–95.

5 Like an emergency paper currency, the concept of a 'corporatist' Europe is assigned a given value for internal use within the argumentation of this book. I make no claim that the term has a universal value. In fact, it is chosen hesitantly

since it generally suggests 'estatist' or a society of legally defined 'orders'. Political scientists might prefer 'pluralist-', but this notion usually suggests a free competition among social forces. And while I have resorted to the term 'corporative pluralism' elsewhere it is inappropriate to deal with fascist Italy as pluralist. The Germans have tried 'organized capitalism', but I wish to emphasize the political more than economic transition; hence 'corporatist' as a provsional description of social bargaining under fascism and democratic conditions alike. On the general theme see my own and others' essays in Heinrich August Winkler (ed.) *Organisierter Kapitalismus, Voraussetzungen und Anfänge*, Göttingen, 1974. For discussions of analogous developments within the United States, cf. Grant McConnell, *Private Power and American Democracy*, New York, 1966; Theodore J. Lowi, *The End of Liberalism: Ideology, Policy, and the Crisis of Public Authority*, New York, 1969. Samuel Beer, *British Politics in the Collectivist Age*, New York, 1967, also introduces comparable concepts.

6 On this problem: Brian M. Barry, *Political Argument*, London, 1965, pp. 187-291; 'The Public Interest', *Proceedings of the Aristotelian Society*, suppl. vol. 38, 1964, pp. 1-18. Cf. Jürgen Habermas, *Strukturwandel der Öffentlichkeit*, Neuwied, 1965, for the loss of the idea of the public in liberal society.

7 Cf. Rudolf Hilferding's analysis of 'organized capitalism' as it developed between 1915 and 1927, esp. 'Probleme der Zeit, *Die Gesellschaft*, 1, 1924, 1-13; 'Die Aufgaben der Sozialdemokratie in der Republik', Sozialdemokratischer Parteitag 1927 in Kiel, *Protokoll*, Berlin, 1927, pp. 166-170; also Wilfried Gottschalch, *Strukturveränderungen der Gesellschaft und politisches Handeln in der Lehre von Rudolf Hilferding*, Berlin, 1962, pp. 190-3, 207; and Heinrich August Winkler, 'Einleitende Bermerkungen zu Hilferdings Theorie des Organisierten Kapitalismus', Winkler (ed.) *Organisierter Kapitalismus*, pp. 9-18.

8 Michael Ostrogorsky, *La Démocratie et l'organisation des partis politiques*, 2 vols, Paris, 1903; Max Weber, 'Politics as a Vocation', and 'Class, Status, Party', in Hans Gerth and C. Wright Mills (eds), *From Max Weber*, New York, 1958, pp. 99-112, 194-5; Robert Michels, *Political Parties, A Social Study of the Oligarchical Tendencies of Modern Democracy*, trans. Eden and Cedar Paul, New York, 1915; Vilfredo Pareto, *Les Systèmes socialistes* [1902]; Geneva, 1965. On interest-group development: Hans-Jürgen Puhle, 'Parlament, Parteien und Interessenverbände 1890-1914', in Michael Sturmer (ed.) *Das kaiserliche Deutschland*, Dusseldorf, 1970, pp. 340-77; Thomas Nipperdey, 'Interessenverbände und Parteien in Deutschland vor dem Ersten Weltkrieg', now in Hans-Ulrich Wehler (ed.) *Moderne deutsche Sozialgeschichte*, Cologne-Berlin, 1970, pp. 369-78; Heinrich A. Winkler, *Pluralismus oder Protektionismus. Verfassungspolitische Probleme des Verbandswesens im deutschen Kaiserreich*, Wiesbaden, 1972; Etienne Villey, *L'organisation professionnelle des employeurs dans l'industrie française*, Paris, 1923; Mario Abrate, *La lotta sindacale nella industralizzazione in Italia 1906-1926*, Turin, 1967, pp. 31-61.

9 For corporatism on the right: Ralph Bowen, *German Theories of the Corporative State: With Special Reference to the Period 1870-1919*, New York, 1947; Matthew Elbow, *French Corporative Theory, 1789-1948*, New York, 1953; Herman Lebovics, *Social Conservatism and the Middle Classes in Germany, 1914-1933*, Princeton, NJ, 1969, pp. 109-38; on the left, cf. M. Beer, *A History of British Socialism* [1919] 2 vols, London, 1953, II, pp. 363-72; G. D. H. Cole, *Self-Government in Industry*, London, 1917.

10 For diverse perspectives on trends in the United States: Gabriel Kolko, *Railroads*

and Regulation, 1877-1916, Princeton, NJ, 1965 and *The Triumph of Conservatism: A Reinterpretation of American History, 1900-1916,* New York, 1963; Robert Wiebe, *Businessmen and Reform, A Study of the Progressive Movement,* Cambridge, Mass., 1962; Wiebe, *The Search for Order, 1877-1920,* New York, 1967; Paul A. C. Koistinen, 'The "Industrial-Military Complex" in Historical Perspective: World War I, *Business History Review*, XLI, 4, 1967, 378-403; Ellis W. Hawley, *The New Deal and the Problem of Monopoly,* Princeton, NJ, 1966, 8-13, 36-42; and Hawley's essay in *Herbert Hoover and the Crisis of American Capitalism,* Cambridge, Mass., 1973.

11 Cf. Karl Mannheim, *Ideology and Utopia,* London, 1960, pp. 206-11.

CHAPTER 8

Hitler's Foreign Policy

NORMAN RICH

The very fact that the original volume for which this essay was prepared was intended to mark the twenty-fifth anniversary of the publication of A. J. P. Taylor's *The Origins of the Second World War* attests to the impact of the book on historical thinking and its importance for all subsequent considerations of the subject. One may disagree with those admirers of Taylor who regard him as England's greatest living historian, but there can be no argument that he is one of the most provocative and controversial. And in none of his many works did he set forth more provocative ideas than in that book [. . .]

It is a brilliant book, filled with astute observations and insights, with challenges to conventional wisdom in almost every line. It is also a very readable book, in part because it is so controversial, for it constantly prods the assumptions of its readers, stirring up annoyance, argument – and upon occasion, admiration. It has compelled every student of the Nazi era to re-examine his or her own views about the subject, and over the years some of the ideas once considered controversial have become part of the conventional wisdom.

Taylor professes to be unhappy with his acceptance into the realm of conventional wisdom. In his memoirs he observes that *Origins* 'despite its defects, has now become the new orthodoxy, much to my alarm'. He denies, however, that his book has the qualities I have described above and which most of his colleagues have attributed to it. 'Where others see it as original and provocative, I find it simply a careful scholarly work, surprising only to those who had never been faced with the truth before'.[1] Taylor's work may be scholarly, but it is not careful, and much of it remains surprising to other historians, many of them as scholarly as Taylor and considerably more careful, who have arrived at very different interpretations of the 'truth'. For, contrary to what Taylor may think, much of *Origins* has not become part of the new orthodoxy, and the parts of the book which continue to be most vigorously contested are those which aroused most controversy in the first place, namely his theories about the subject of the present essay, Hitler's foreign policy.

In *Origins,* Taylor challenges the interpretation of other historians who based their views about Hitler's foreign policy, at least in part, on documents presented in evidence at the Nuremberg trials. He points out, quite correctly, that these documents were 'loaded' and he maintains, without bothering to prove his point, that scholars who relied on them had found it impossible to escape from the load with which they were charged.[2] Taylor's method of escaping from that load was to ignore these documents altogether, and at the same time he cavalierly disregarded a great deal of other evidence which did not happen to fit with his own theories. Every historian, of course, is compelled to be selective in his use of evidence. The great weakness of Taylor's book, especially his treatment of Hitler's foreign policy, is the perverse nature of his selectivity and his deliberate rejection of much of the thoroughly reliable evidence on which the theories of many of his colleagues are based. An even graver weakness is that Taylor's own theories are frequently inconsistent and contradictory.

He rejects the Nazi claim that the formation of a Hitler government in January 1933 was a seizure of power, but he challenges the views of other historians as to why and how Hitler came to power:

> Whatever ingenious speculators, liberal or Marxist, might say, Hitler was not made Chancellor because he would help the German capitalists to destroy the trade unions, nor because he would give the German generals a great army, still less a great war. . . . He was not expected to carry through revolutionary changes in either home or foreign affairs. On the contrary the conservative politicians . . . who recommended him to Hindenburg kept the key posts for themselves and expected Hitler to be a tame figurehead.

These expectations were confounded, Taylor says, for Hitler proved to be the most radical of revolutionaries. He made himself all-powerful dictator, destroyed political freedom and the rule of law, transformed German economics and finance, abolished the individual German states, and made Germany for the first time a united country.

In one sphere alone, Taylor says, Hitler changed nothing. 'His foreign policy was that of his predecessors, of the professional diplomats at the foreign ministry, and indeed of virtually all Germans. Hitler, too, wanted to free Germany from the restrictions of the [Versailles] peace treaty; to restore a great German army; and then to make Germany the greatest power in Europe from her natural weight.' The only difference between Hitler and 'virtually all Germans' were occasional differences in emphasis. Two paragraphs later, however, Taylor informs us that Hitler's foreign policy did in fact differ from that of at least some of his predecessors, for Hitler did not attempt to revive the 'world policy' which Germany had pursued before 1914, he made no plans for a great German battle fleet, he did not parade a grievance about lost colonies except to embarrass the British, and he was not at all interested in the Middle East. Taylor concludes that 'the primary purpose of his policy, if not the only one' was expansion into eastern Europe.

With that Taylor is saying that the differences between Hitler's foreign policy and that of his predecessors were in fact far more significant than mere matters of emphasis. He then goes on to describe precisely that quality which distinguished Hitler most radically not only from his predecessors but also from all other ordinary statesmen. 'The unique quality in Hitler was the gift of translating commonplace thoughts into action. . . . The driving force in him was a terrifying literalism.' There was nothing new about denunciations of democracy; it took Hitler to create a totalitarian dictatorship. There was nothing new about anti-Semitism; it took Hitler to push anti-Semitism to the gas chambers:

> It was the same with foreign policy. Not many Germans really cared passionately and persistently whether Germany again dominated Europe. But they talked as if they did. Hitler took them at their word. He made the Germans live up to their professions, or down to them – much to their regret.

More careful scholars may deplore Taylor's tendency to assume a knowledge of what 'not many Germans' cared for, and with what intensity, and his own frequent inconsistencies on that subject, but many historians share his views about the importance of Hitler's terrifying literalism and many had drawn attention to this quality long before the appearance of *Origins*. Taylor, however, always unwilling to be thought in agreement with generally accepted opinions, pours scorn on colleagues who have purported to discover in Hitler's writings and policy statements an exposition of the ideas which he proposed to translate into action. *Mein Kampf,* Hitler's table talk, the records of his top-secret conferences with his senior aides and officers in which he described his future plans in minute detail – all these revelations of Hitler's thinking are dismissed by Taylor as irrelevant flights of fancy, not to be taken seriously as indications of his true intentions. Writers of great authority, Taylor says, have seen in Hitler a system-maker who from the first deliberately prepared a great war that would make him master of the world. Taylor rejects such theories with some contempt. In his opinion, statesmen are too absorbed by events to follow a preconceived plan; such plans are in reality the creation of historians, and the systems attributed to Hitler are really those of Trevor-Roper, Elizabeth Wiskemann, and Alan Bullock. Taylor concludes that Hitler did indeed create systems, but these were no more than day-dreams concocted in his spare time.

Taylor attributes much of the success of Hitler's foreign policy to his very lack of preconceptions and prejudices, and cites as examples his willingness to conclude a non-aggression pact with Poland and his disregard of German nationalist sentiment in conceding the South Tyrol to Mussolini to secure Italian friendship. Apart from that, Taylor attributes Hitler's success primarily to his ability to play a waiting game, to take advantage of the offers and opportunities presented to him by his adversaries. Even then Taylor is not sure whether this technique was at first either conscious or deliberate. 'The greatest masters of statecraft are those who do not know what they are doing,' he says, thereby suggesting that Hitler was both a great master of statecraft and that he did not know what he was doing.[3] Yet Taylor has already stated, on the preceding page, that the primary purpose of Hitler's foreign policy was expansion into eastern Europe, and only a few pages later he says that the mainspring of Hitler's immediate policy had been the destruction of the Versailles treaty, although once this objective had been attained he was at a loss as to what to do next. As for any long-range plans, Taylor considers it 'doubtful whether he had any'.[4]

Taylor's inconsistencies continue. Although he states (p. 72) that the primary purpose of Hitler's policy was eastward expansion (which for Hitler meant the acquisition of living space or *Lebensraum),* he then denies (p. 105) that Hitler's desire for *Lebensraum* or economic motives in general were a cause of the Second World War. *Lebensraum* did not drive Germany to war, he says. Rather war, or a warlike policy, produced the demand for *Lebensraum.* Hitler and Mussolini were not driven by economic motives. Like most statesmen, they had an appetite for successes. They differed from others only in that their appetite was greater and that they fed it by more unscrupulous means. *Lebensraum* in its crudest sense meant a demand for empty space where Germans could settle but, Taylor argues, Germany was not over-populated in comparison with most European countries and there was no empty space in Europe. 'When Hitler lamented: 'If only we had a Ukraine . . .', he seemed to suppose that there were no Ukrainians. Did he propose to exploit, or to exterminate them? Apparently he never considered the question one way or the other.'[5]

These statements glaringly expose the disastrous consequences of Taylor's refusal to acknowledge the significance of those sources in which Hitler set forth his ideological preconceptions and revealed his long-range plans based upon them. For Hitler *had* considered the question of what to do about the Ukrainians; he *did* propose to exploit or exterminate them – and all other non-Aryan peoples in eastern Europe besides. These plans were set forth in detail in *Mein Kampf,* and Hitler continued to expound them in almost identical terms in subsequent policy statements before and during the war. In rejecting the evidence of such policy statements, Taylor misses the absolutely fundamental point of Hitler's foreign policy – the nature of the literalism which he proposed to translate into practice.

Taylor recognizes that when Germany actually conquered the Ukraine in 1941, Hitler and his henchmen tried both methods, exploitation and extermination, but he comments that neither method brought them any economic advantages.[6] Here again Taylor completely misses the point. Hitler was not primarily concerned with any immediate economic advantage – in 1941 he still thought Russia could be conquered within weeks, and when it became obvious that this would not be possible it was too late to reverse his policies even if he wanted to do so, which he did not. The primary purpose of Hitler's

foreign policy and his fundamental aim in the Second World War was the realization of his long-range plan for the acquisition of *Lebensraum* in eastern
Europe which was to ensure the security and well-being of the German
people for all time. As he specifically declared in *Mein Kampf* and subsequent policy statements, this conquest of territory should not include the
conquest of people and the absorption of non-Aryans into the Germanic
empire, for such absorption would dilute the purity of Germanic blood and
thereby weaken the Germanic peoples. It was for this reason that the
non-Aryans would have to be eliminated. This was the policy Hitler and his
henchmen actually introduced in Russia after 1941, a policy which, as Taylor
correctly says, brought them no economic advantage. On the contrary, the
economic consequences of that policy, not to mention the moral, political
and military consequences, were disastrous and contributed significantly to
Germany's ultimate defeat. This policy, like the extermination of the Jews,
cannot be equated with that of other statesmen with a mere appetite for
success. It was the policy of a fanatic idealogue who ignored sober calculations of national interest in order to put his manic ideas into practice.

Taylor's belief that Hitler was simply a political opportunist without
long-range purposes remains a central theme of his chronicle and analysis of
the actual course of Hitler's foreign policy, in which he continues to present
us with inconsistencies and contradictions. In his discussion of the annexation of Austria, for example, Taylor concedes that Hitler 'certainly meant to
establish control over Austria', but he believes that the way in which this
came about was for him a tiresome accident, 'an interruption of his long-term
policy' (whereby Taylor seems to admit that there was in fact a long-term
policy). At the same time he dismisses as a myth the theory that Hitler's
seizure of Austria was a deliberate plot, devised long in advance:

> By the *Anschluss* – or rather by the way in which it was accomplished –
> Hitler took the first step in the policy which was to brand him as the
> greatest of war criminals. Yet he took this step unintentionally. Indeed
> he did not know that he had taken it.[7]

Taylor is absolutely correct in saying that the *way* the *Anschluss* took place
was to a large extent accidental and improvised, and that it was not carried
out in accordance with a strategy prepared long in advance. In the *Anschluss*
crisis, Hitler's hand was forced by the actions of others and he took the final
step of actually incorporating Austria into the Reich only when the events of
the *Anschluss* convinced him he could afford to do so. But to say that he took
this step unintentionally, or did not know he had taken it, is nonsense. On the
first page of *Mein Kampf* and in numerous subsequent policy statements,
Hitler declared that the incorporation of Austria into the Reich was the primary immediate objective of his policy, and the documentary evidence leaves
no doubt whatever that the annexation of Austria was indeed a deliberate
plot, prepared long in advance, and that it was conceived as the first step in
the domination of eastern Europe.

In his analysis of the *Anschluss* and all other episodes in Hitler's foreign policy, Taylor challenges the theory that Hitler was operating according to a carefully prepared blueprint and timetable. Taylor's emphasis on the accidental and improvised quality in Hitler's actual execution of his policies is valid, but in tilting against the blueprint or timetable theories he seems to be setting up straw men in order to knock them down. It is true that some historians have written about blueprints and timetables, but even the most extreme champions of blueprint-timetable theories never suggested that Hitler had precisely conceived plans for every step of his expansionist policy and a precise timetable for carrying them out. Obviously he had to improvise, to take into account the constant fluctuations in the political scene, and to adjust to the moves of his opponents. All the blueprint-timetables people were saying was that Hitler had precisely defined war aims, primarily the conquest of *Lebensraum* in eastern Europe, that he had detailed plans for carrying them out, and that there was an uncanny consistency between the ideas expressed in his pre-war policy statements and the policies he actually put into effect.

When *Origins* was first published, much of the critical wrath directed against the book (and in certain quarters, much of the critical approval it received) was aroused by the belief that Taylor was defending Hitler. Nothing could have been further from the truth. In saying that in foreign policy alone Hitler changed nothing, that his foreign policy was that of his predecessors 'and indeed of virtually all Germans', he is not defending Hitler. Instead he is equating Hitler with 'virtually all Germans', as he makes clear in a later edition of *Origins*:

> Most of all, [Hitler] was the creation of German history and of the German present. He would have counted for nothing without the support and cooperation of the German people. . . . Hitler was a sounding-board for the German nation. Thousands, many hundred thousand, Germans carried out his evil orders without qualm or question.

And he concludes: 'In international affairs there was nothing wrong with Hitler except that he was a German.' [8]

With that Taylor reverts to the line adopted in his wartime book, *The Course of German History,* which some of his admirers have excused as a regrettable wartime polemic but which Taylor himself stoutly defended in a new preface to that book when it was republished in 1962, the year after the publication of *Origins*. In this preface he explains that his book had proved unacceptable to its original sponsors because it failed to show that Hitler was a bit of bad luck in German history and that all Germans, apart from a few wicked men, were bubbling over with enthusiasm for democracy, Christianity, or some other noble cause which would turn them into acceptable allies once we had liberated them from their tyrants. Not so, says Taylor. The entire course of German history:

> shows that it was no more a mistake for the German people to end up with Hitler than it is an accident when a river flows into the sea. . . .

Nothing, it seems to me, has happened since [i.e. between 1945 and 1962] to disturb the conclusions at which I then arrived.

According to Taylor, the 70–80 million Germans have always feared the Slavs, and this fear underlay the Germans' plans for their conquest and extermination. 'No German of political consequence thought of accepting the Slavs as equals and living at peace with them' – and Taylor believes the Germans have not changed in this respect.[9] The Third Reich, he writes in *The Course of German History,* represented the deepest wishes of the German people. 'Every German desired the achievement which only total war could give. By no other means could the Reich be held together. It had been made by conquest and for conquest; if it ever gave up its career of conquest it would dissolve.' In contrast to the Germans there were the Slavic peoples 'with their deep sense of equality, their love of freedom, and their devotion to humanity', under whose auspices, Taylor believes, conditions in eastern Europe have improved immensely since the dark days of German and Magyar domination.[10]

Taylor continued to adhere to this interpretation of Germany and the Germans. In a discussion of the German problem as it emerged from the First World War, he writes that there has been an almost universal misunderstanding about the nature of that problem, 'a misunderstanding perhaps even shared by Hitler'. The Germans desired equality with the victor states, they wanted to cast off restrictions on their national sovereignty imposed by the Versailles treaty, and many non-Germans sympathized with what they regarded as these perfectly legitimate aspirations. But the inevitable consequences of fulfilling those German desires, Taylor says, was that Germany would become the dominant state in Europe. And what this would have meant for Europe can be seen from the German plans for the rearrangement of Europe if they had won the First World War, plans exposed in detail in 1961 and after in the publications of the German historian Fritz Fischer and his school:

> It was a Europe indistinguishable from Hitler's empire at its greatest extent, including even a Poland and a Ukraine cleared of their native inhabitants. Hitler was treading, rather cautiously, in Bethmann's footsteps. There was nothing new or unusual in his aims or outlook.[11]

Taylor thus endorses the most extreme interpretations of Fischer and his followers who, with virtually unrestricted access to German archival records following Germany's defeat in the Second World War, put together a monumental collection of policy statements and speculations about German diplomatic and military goals drawn up by German leaders from every walk of life before and during the First World War.

Taylor and the more extreme representatives of the Fischer school may be right in assuming that a German government victorious in the First World War would have behaved exactly as Hitler did in the Second World War, or worse. The only record we have of a German government's actual treatment of Slavs, however, is that of Prusso-German rule over those segments of Poland taken by Prussia in the eighteenth-century partitions of Poland, at which time, it will be recalled, Slavic Russia took the lion's share. The Prusso-German treatment of the Poles has often been criticized, and with good reason, but during the entire period of German rule over the Poles there was never any suggestion of an attempt to exterminate them. What the Germans were trying to do was to Germanize them, and with notable lack of success.[12] It was Hitler, and only Hitler, who attempted to rectify what he regarded as this mistaken policy of Germanization through extermination – and not at all cautiously, either.

In the years since the Second World War, the United States seems to have replaced Germany as Taylor's principal political bugbear, and although he is not uncritical of the Soviet Union, he has complacently accepted that state's assumption of the role of protector and spokesman of the Slavic peoples and all other nationalities of Eastern Europe. 'I had not the slightest illusion about the tyranny and brutality of Stalin's regime,' Taylor writes in his memoirs:

> But I had been convinced throughout the nineteen thirties that Soviet predominance in eastern Europe was the only alternative to Germany's and I preferred the Soviet one. Moreover I believed that East European states, even when under Soviet control, would be preferable to what they had been between the wars, as has proved to be the case. Hence Soviet ascendency of eastern Europe had no perils for me.'

Taylor defends the communist takeover in Czechoslovakia and the Russian suppression of the Hungarian revolution. 'Better a Communist regime supported by Soviet Russia . . . than an anti-Communist regime led by Cardinal Mindszenty. Hence my conscience was not troubled by the Soviet intervention.' Taylor's conscience was similarly untroubled when it was learned that the British art historian Anthony Blunt had spied for the Russians, and he successfully opposed Blunt's expulsion from the British Academy.[13] In notable contrast to this attitude towards the Russians, Taylor has condemned almost every act of American foreign policy. At the time of the Korean war, Taylor, who claims to have been a staunch opponent of appeasement in the 1930s, declared appeasement to be 'the noblest word in the diplomat's language'[14] 'Even now,' he wrote in 1956, 'which of us on the Left could say, hand on heart, that in a conflict between the United States and the Soviet Union our individual sympathies would be with the United States?'[15]

Such comments aroused consternation among many Americans and their British friends, and they were clearly intended to do so. For in his most recent books, as in *Origins* and indeed all his works, Taylor continues to play the role of gadfly, often striking out wildly and unfairly but often telling us unpalatable truths which other commentators lack the imagination to perceive or the audacity to express. In this essay I have not been sparing of my criticism of Taylor. I find many of his ideas ridiculous and his prejudices downright shameful for a historian, and I am irritated by his persistent efforts to surprise and confound his readers. Yet he has always been and he remains one of the most stimulating and readable of historians, whose great contribution is not his own scholarship but his challenges to the values and assumptions of his audience. In response to critics of *Origins* who accused him, quite mistakenly, of failing to condemn Hitler's criminality with sufficient vigor, Taylor confessed that he himself could not get it out of his head that Hitler was an indescribably wicked man:

> But this is because I belonged to his generation. He was as wicked as he could be. But he was only a beginner. The rulers of the United States and of Soviet Russia are now cheerfully contemplating a hideous death for seventy million people or perhaps a hundred and fifty million people in the first week of the next war. What has Hitler to show in comparison with this? I think we had better leave Hitler's immorality alone as long as we go clanking around with nuclear weapons.[16]

[. . .] The publication of *The Origins of the Second World War* aroused enormous furor in the historical profession and provoked a reconsideration of the policies of all the major powers involved. So far as Hitler's foreign policy was concerned, the principal historical debate set off by Taylor's book was whether, as the Nuremberg prosecution and numerous historians maintained, his policy was dedicated to the achievement of long-range objectives, his strategy and tactics worked out long in advance; or whether, as Taylor contended, Hitler was an opportunist and improviser who took advantage of the accidental shifts in the international situation and the mistakes of his opponents. Taylor says that this debate is now sterile, but in stirring it up in the first place he compelled many historians to revise or modify their views and to recognize how much of Hitler's foreign policy was in fact improvised and opportunistic. Moreover, although the debate as originally formulated may be sterile, it remains central to controversies over Hitler's policies in general, despite changes in the terminology employed, differences in emphasis, and the introduction of new varieties of evidence.

Because of the sheer amount of historical literature dealing with Hitler's foreign policy that has been produced during the past quarter-century, it is manifestly impossible to provide an adequate evaluation of the individual works representing the various schools of thought on the subject in the scope of a brief essay – a mere list of such works would fill a substantial volume. I have therefore confined myself to a short survey of what appear to me to be the principal lines of interpretation and controversy.[17]

Let me dispose at once of the small group of writers who seek to defend Hitler, who represent him as a man of peace who sought only justice and equality for Germany, as the hapless victim of the implacable hostility of Germany's enemies and of Bolshevik-Jewish-capitalist conspiracies. Taylor describes one of these apologies as a 'perfectly plausible book', which it is not.[18] Moreover, all such works are characterized by flagrant misrepresentations or outright falsifications of the evidence and do not deserve to be considered in a discussion of serious historical scholarship.

Apart from the old and neo-Nazis, those writers bearing the heaviest and most obvious ideological burden are the members of the Soviet and East European school of thought, which has been joined by a number of Marxists and other left-wing intellectuals in the west. This group represents Hitler, Nazism and fascism in general as the products and instruments of capitalist-imperialist society, and the Second World War as a western-capitalist conspiracy to destroy the Soviet Union. From this school we hear nothing about the Anglo-French guarantees to Poland in 1939 or the Hitler–Stalin pact, but much about appeasement which is generally interpreted as a diplomatic maneuver to direct Nazi aggression against Russia. Proceeding from these assumptions, the members of this school have no trouble finding and interpreting evidence which proves their case.

Theoretically akin to the East Europeans and their adherents, but on the whole far more honest in their use of evidence and imaginative in the questions they raise, are the members of what might be called the 'fundamental forces' school of thought. These scholars regard Hitler and the Nazi movement as the products of fundamental forces in German political, economic and social life, and of the institutions, modes of thought and behavioral patterns developed in the course of the German historical experience. In their basic assumptions, the members of this school are thus in general agreement with Taylor, especially his *Course of German History,* but they have gone far beyond his simplistic explanations and generalizations. In their own search for explanations of the Hitler phenomenon, they have produced many profound and original studies of German life and society, and altogether they have enormously enriched our understanding of German history and institutions. There is nevertheless a certain uniformity and even sterility about their work. In proceeding from the assumption that Hitlerism was a product of fundamental forces in German history, they tend to search for and focus on those aspects of the German past which can be interpreted as being precursors of the Nazi movement. In the process they frequently ignore the contemporary circumstances in which those policies were conceived and conducted, or fail to take adequate account of the differences in values and attitudes of earlier epochs. And because their research is dedicated to discovering those qualities in German life that produced Hitler, the lines of their research as well as their conclusions are to a large extent predetermined.

Inseparable from the 'fundamental forces' school, but requiring special mention because of its importance in contemporary German historiography, is the 'continuity' school of German history. The members of this group differ from the 'fundamental forces' scholars in their special emphasis on the consistency in the aims and methods of German leaders, and in their efforts to demonstrate that the policies of Hitler were a continuation of policies already pursued or planned by the rulers of Austria, Prussia, Imperial Germany, and Weimar. They too are thus in basic agreement with the Taylor thesis about German history, and in their research they have discovered an enormous quantity of evidence to substantiate that thesis. But, as in the case of the 'fundamental forces' school, the results of that research are to a large extent predetermined, and as one recent critic has commented, 'with the exercise of a little ingenuity almost anything can be fitted into this concept'.[19]

To be fair to the 'fundamental forces-continuity' historians, they do not all share the view that the Germans are invested with a particularly heavy dose of original sin. A number of them stress the importance of the peculiar nature of the German historical experience, the devastating effects of the Thirty Years' War, and the more lasting effects of the treaties of Westphalia ending that war, which sanctioned permanent French and Swedish interference in German affairs and for over two centuries halted German national development. Others have drawn attention to the importance of geographical factors, the position of the Germans in central Europe between the French in the west and the Slavs in the east, the Germans' lack of readily defensible or even definable frontiers and their consequent emphasis on the need for a strong army.

Opposed to both the 'fundamental forces' and 'continuity' schools are historians who refuse to accept the theory that Hitler was an inevitable product of German history or that his policies were simply the continuation of policies of earlier German leaders. Instead they regard him as a unique phenomenon in the German historical experience, and his regime and its bestial policies as a disastrous deviation from the main lines of German history. Members of this 'discontinuity' school are of course unable to deny the existence of continuity, for all history is a continuous process, but they contend that both Hitler's domestic and foreign policies represented departures from previous German political and diplomatic traditions. This was particularly true of his foreign policy which, unlike all previous German foreign policies, was consciously based on racist ideology, conducted with revolutionary methods and dedicated to the realization of unlimited aims. 'Discontinuity' historians concede that other German leaders and many ordinary Germans were anti-Semitic (as were the leaders and peoples of many other nations), but they insist that only Hitler advocated and actually attempted to carry out the total extermination of the Jews; other German leaders may have desired the acquisition of additional territories in Europe or overseas, but only Hitler conducted a war of conquest which involved the removal or extermination of the indigenous population.

Members of the 'discontinuity' school, with their interpretation of Hitler as a unique phenomenon in German history, have been accused of attempting to exonerate the German people as a whole from blame for the Nazi experience, and the arguments of some of them are certainly intended to achieve this purpose. Whatever their motives, the members of the 'discontinuity' school cannot avoid dealing with the question of how the German people as a whole accepted Hitler, how so many Germans were able to condone his bestial policies, and how so many were willing to put these policies into effect. Their attempts at explanation often bring them close to the 'fundamental forces' school, but with notable differences in emphasis. Whereas the 'fundamental forces' historians regard the Nazi experience as the inevitable product of the German past, their opponents contend that it required the demonic genius of a Hitler to mobilize all the most depraved features of German thought and behavior, that his propaganda successfully deceived the German people about his true intentions (as it deceived foreign governments with far better access to information), and that his totalitarian government successfully repressed all movements of dissent.

Into the controversies among the 'fundamental forces', 'continuity' and 'discontinuity' schools fits the debate over the primacy of foreign politics versus the primacy of domestic politics. Is a country's foreign policy based in large measure on foreign political considerations and conducted quasi-independently of domestic affairs? Or is foreign policy conducted primarily in response to domestic problems and pressures? In dealing with Hitler's foreign policy, scholars who argue in favor of the primacy of foreign policy believe that his domestic program was designed to serve the purposes of his foreign policy; whereas their opponents believe his foreign policy was the product of domestic necessities.

Closely linked with this debate, and more specifically related to the Third Reich, is the controversy between what have been called the 'functionalists' and the 'intentionalists' (terms which seem to me only to add confusion to the argument). The 'functionalists' agree fundamentally with the primacy of domestic politics viewpoint. They contend that Nazi foreign policy was far more the outcome (function) of domestic dynamisms and crises within Hitler's Germany than the result of rational planning, that it was the result of the frantic but completely uncoordinated activity of competing power groups which produced a progressive radicalization of their measures. The 'functionalists' emphasize the polycentric nature of the Nazi government and argue that Hitler, far from being an all-powerful dictator and decision-maker, was on the contrary a weak leader who pursued radical programs to ward off the rivalry of his associates and to escape from the realities of his own weakness. The 'intentionalists', on the other hand, believe that Hitler himself made the major foreign policy decisions of the Nazi state, that he pursued politically intelligible goals, and that the best way to understand the foreign policy of the Third Reich is to understand the personality of Hitler and his ideology.

In their theoretical conceptions at any rate, the 'fundamental forces' school and the 'functionalist' historians deny the importance of the personal qualities of Hitler, and in effect they are saying that if Hitler had not appeared on the German political scene, his place would have been filled by a Müller or a Schmidt. Their arguments are ingenious and they have contributed much to our understanding of the internal dynamics of the Third Reich, but they have obviously not convinced most scholars dealing with the Nazi question, if one is to judge by the volume of research devoted to the background, personality and ideas of Hitler, or by the central position Hitler continues to occupy in virtually all studies of the Nazi state.

What is surprising, in view of the controversy aroused by Taylor's book and the immense amount of research devoted to the Nazi question since its publication, is how little the fundamental lines of interpretation and argument have in fact changed, and to what extent historians are still at a loss to explain the Nazi phenomenon. This situation may be observed in numerous works that have been published analyzing or reviewing interpretations of the Nazi question.[20] The most recent of these is by the German scholar Eberhard Jäckel. His *Hitler in History* summarizes the results of the latest research and comes to conclusions with which I agree on the whole and which I would like to use as a vehicle for conveying my own views.[21]

Jäckel makes the same point as Taylor that Hitler was not the pawn of big business, the Junkers, the army, or other established vested interests in Germany. Representatives of these interests recommended his appointment to Hindenburg in order to make use of the popular support he enjoyed, confident that they could control and manipulate him. Instead Hitler used the power conferred upon him to establish his totalitarian state. Those vested interests that did not seem a threat to his authority and which co-operated with his policies were absorbed into his political and social system, but he disregarded them completely in making all major policy decisions.[22]

It is over the question of Hitler's policies and their implementation that Jäckel, and I believe most historians who have worked through the evidence, would disagree with one of Taylor's most provocative points, namely that Hitler did not know what he was doing and merely took advantage of the opportunities presented to him by his opponents (although as mentioned earlier, Taylor himself is not altogether consistent on this point). Jäckel, who has written one of the most authoritative books on Hitler's ideology, says about this question: 'Perhaps never in history did a ruler write down before he came to power what he was to do afterwards as precisely as did Adolf Hitler. Hitler set himself two goals: a war of conquest and the elimination of the Jews.' Jackel goes on to review Hitler's war plans, the fundamental points of which he had already formulated in the 1920s, and comments:[23]

> Without knowing his war plans we cannot evaluate how he prepared for, initiated and conducted the war . . . Hitler's ultimate goal was the establishment of a greater Germany than had ever existed before in history. The way to this greater Germany was a war of conquest fought mainly at the expense of Soviet Russia. It was in the east of the European continent that the German nation was to gain living space *(Lebensraum)* for generations to come. This expansion would in turn provide the foundation for Germany's renewed position as a world power. Militarily the war would be easy because Germany would be opposed only by a disorganized country of Jewish Bolsheviks and incompetent Slavs.

Before launching his war of conquest in the east, however, Hitler had to meet certain fundamental preconditions. The first was the consolidation of his authority in Germany and rearmament. The second was to put an end to the possibility of a stab in the back in the west while Germany was at war in the east, for a successful attack on the Rhine-Ruhr industrial areas would deal a mortal blow to Germany's ability to wage war of any kind. France was the only power capable of striking such a blow: France, therefore, had to be eliminated as a military power before Germany could launch its campaign in the east. To counter the power of France, Hitler hoped to win alliances with Britain, which was to be offered German support to retain its global empire, and with Italy, which was to be offered supremacy in the Mediterranean and assurances of continued control over the South Tyrol, despite that region's large German population. Hitler gained his alliance with Italy but by 1937 he had despaired of winning an alliance with Britain, although at least until 1941 he continued to hope that such an alliance might yet be possible. 'Even a cursory glance at the diplomatic and military history of the Third Reich demonstrates that this program served as an outline of those German policies that were defined by Hitler himself,' Jäckel says, 'and there is ample documentary evidence to prove that he always kept this outline in mind. It was, of course, not a timetable or even a detailed prospectus, but a definite and structured list of objectives, priorities and conditions.'[24]

Jäckel believes that the controversy between the 'functionalists' and the 'intentionalists' is based on a profound misunderstanding on both sides. 'There is abundant evidence', he says, 'that all major decisions in the Third Reich were made by Hitler, and there is equally abundant evidence that the regime was largely anarchic and can thus be described as a polycracy. The misunderstanding is to suppose that the two observations are contradictory and that only one of them can be true.' Jäckel himself sees no contradiction here. 'The monocrat comes to power on a polycratic basis, supported by conflicting groups that paralyze each other, and he maintains his power by ruling polycratically – that is, by playing the conflicting groups against each other. It is precisely this method that permits him to make the major decisions alone.'[25] The ideas, too, were Hitler's. 'He undoubtedly developed a program of his own, individually and alone', Jäckel says, but he goes on to observe that 'his program must have coincided with the deeper tendencies and ambitions of his country and of his time. We may not be able to explain this, and yet we have to recognize it. Was he an author or an executor, a producer or a product?'[26]

In dealing with this question, Jäckel confesses his inability to provide definite answers, and refuses to take refuge in simplistic explanations. 'What the fact-bound researcher can state and perhaps explain is only that the governments of the Weimar Republic did not seriously prepare for war, whereas Hitler did.'[27] He points out that both the Japanese and Italians preceded the Germans in going to war for imperial reasons in the 1930s, and he might have added that the Poles and Hungarians were happy to join Hitler in the final spoliation of Czechoslovakia in 1939, that the Russians joined in the spoliation of Poland later in that same year and that they went on to take over the Baltic states, Northern Bukovina (at the expense of Romania) and to go to war against Finland. He might have added further that so-called democratic societies have not been altogether pacific in the past, that Britain and France, having acquired the world's largest overseas empires, were hardly in a moral position to point a finger of guilt at peoples (or regimes) which attempted to acquire similar empires, that the Soviet Union continues to control with an iron hand the multitude of national minorities conquered by the regimes of the tsars, and that the United States policy of westward expansion, in the course of which the white man ruthlessly thrust aside the 'inferior' indigenous population, served as the model for Hitler's entire concept of *Lebensraum*.

Jäckel makes no attempt to exonerate the Germans. He stresses that they supported Hitler and carried out his criminal orders, and that their support and obedience was voluntary and not the result of terror and repression. Yet he believes 'this pessimistic view cannot and should not lead to a blanket moral condemnation of the Germans living at that time, for they were as a whole no worse and no better than the generations before and after them. But they were subjected to ordeals and to temptations that others escaped.' Again Jäckel attempts to avoid facile explanations. He is obviously uncomfortable with many of the schools of historical thought discussed earlier in this essay, especially attempts to explain the origins of National Socialism through polemical allusions to one's own political or ideological adversaries. 'Such biased efforts are not only unscholarly but in most cases thoroughly contemptible.' Jäckel believes it is vital to remember that the vast majority of Germans were denied the kind of information that ordinarily builds the foundation of public opinion and that, although we now know that Hitler intended to implement the program presented in such detail in *Mein Kampf*, it is 'beyond doubt that the Germans did not grant him power in order to implement that program'.[28]

But then Jäkel plunges into a simplistic explanation of his own and seems to fall squarely into the 'fundamental forces' school of thought. Hitler's foreign policy followed a rigid plan, he says, but that plan 'was not wholly incongruent with general developments and its realization was therefore ensured'. Later imperialistic territorial conquest was presaged in the development of Germany, just as it was in the development of Japan and Italy. 'Thus Hitler, notwithstanding his own great personal responsibility in shaping events, was no more than the executor of a longstanding tendency.'[29]

Here I part company with Jäckel, with whose views I am in almost complete agreement up to this point. All events, of course, are conditioned by the past, but to say that Hitler was no more than the executor of a longstanding tendency, thereby implying that the man and his policies were an inevitable product of German history, seems to me to place a dangerous emphasis on the principle of historical determinism and suggests that there is nothing an individual or nation can do to escape the fate dictated by its heritage.[30] To me there is something profoundly unhistorical about the fundamental forces' school of thought for, by concentrating on problems that apparently foreshadow future development, the historian may neglect or underestimate the importance of other aspects of a nation's past that may have been far more significant in an earlier age, or at least appeared so to perceptive contemporary observers. Such an approach in effect denies the importance of human beings in history, the role of thinkers, artists, leaders in a people's development, nor does it make sufficient allowance for the many accidents which befall a people (plagues, famines, foreign conquest) which are not necessarily the product of their heritage.

For the study of German history, the inevitability thesis has had the unfortunate result of requiring an emphasis on those features of the German past which seem to have produced the Third Reich and which made Germany different from, and by implication inferior to, more modern, moral and democratic societies. Such an attitude has led to a certain smugness if not to outright racism on the part of many non-Germans (vide Taylor), and to an exaggerated moral self-flagellation on the part of the Germans themselves. It has also contributed to a curiously myopic quality in many works on German history, which by focusing exclusively and obsessively on the problems of Germany and the Germans tend to ignore comparable problems in other societies and fail to take sufficient account of the terrifying universality of the German historical experience. If German history has anything to teach, it is that the veneer of civilization in all societies is perilously thin, and that the qualities we most admire in western societies are in no way guaranteed by western traditions, institutions or national character, but must be safeguarded by eternal vigilance.

Notes

1 A. J. P. Taylor, *A Personal History*, New York, 1983, p. 235.

2 A. J. P. Taylor, *The Origins of the Second World War*, first published in 1961. My references are to the American paperback Premier edition, Greenwich, Conn., 1963, p. 19.

3 ibid., pp. 69-73.

4 ibid., p. 107.

5 ibid., p. 105.

6 ibid., p. 105.

7 ibid., p. 146.

8 Foreword to a new edition of the *Origins*, 'Second thoughts'; Penguin paperback edition, Harmondsworth, 1964, pp. 26-7.

9 A. J. P. Taylor, *The Course of German History*, first published in 1945. My references are to the American paperback Capricorn edition, New York, 1962, pp. 7-8.

10 *Course of German History*, pp. 213-14, 222.

11 A. J. P. Taylor, 'War origins again', reprinted from *Past and Present* (April 1965) in E. M. Robertson (ed.) *The Origins of the Second World War: Historical Interpretations*, London, 1971, pp. 139-40. Bethmann was German chancellor at the beginning of the First World War.

12 Taylor takes it for granted that Habsburg rule was German, but the Habsburgs made no efforts comparable to those of Prussia to Germanize the Slavs, and Hitler certainly never regarded their policies as a model for his own.

13 *Personal History*, pp. 181, 214, 270-1.

14 ibid., p. 182.

15 *New Statesman*, 52, 1956, 523-4, quoted by John W. Boyer, 'A. J. P. Taylor and the art of modern history', *Journal of Modern History*, 49, March 1977, 56.

16 'War origins again', p. 138.

17 All references to schools of thought must be qualified by observing that there

are sharp differences of opinion among scholars who adopt the same general approach to historical problems. For a more detailed survey-analysis of major historical interpretations, see the recent intelligent and level-headed study by John Hiden and John Farquharson, *Explaining Hitler's Germany. Historians and the Third Reich*, Totowa, NJ, 1983.

18 'War origins again', p. 138.

19 Hiden and Farquharson, *Explaining Hitler's Germany*, p. 56.

20 The French scholar Pierre Ayçoberry, for example, concludes: 'One cannot say for certain whether the Third Reich was a radical departure from, or a continuation of preceding regimes. The question remains open, like a gaping hole in the historical consciousness. We still have not settled with the past.' (*The Nazi Question. An Essay on the Interpretations. of National Socialism 1922-1975*), New York, 1981, p. 225.) Anthony Adamthwaite, writing in 1984, takes a parallel line. Many interesting questions remain unanswered he says, 'but in the last analysis Hitler and Nazism can be understood, interpreted, or used as each generation wishes' ('War origins again', *Journal of Modern History*, 56, March 1984, 114).

21 Eberhard Jäckel, *Hitler in History*, Hanover, NH, 1984. My own interpretations may be found in 'Die Deutsche Frage und der nationalsozialistische Imperialismus: Rückblick und Ausblick', in Josef Becker and Andreas Hillgruber (eds), *Die Deutsche Frage im 19. und 20. Jahrhundert*, Munich, 1983, pp. 373-92, and in the introductions and conclusions to my two volumes, *Hitler's War Aims*. vol. 1, *Ideology, the Nazi State and the Course of Expansion*; vol. 2, *The Establishment of the New Order*, New York, 1973-4.

22 Jäckel, *Hitler in History*, ch. 1.

23 ibid., pp. 23-5.

24 ibid., pp. 25-6.

25 ibid., p. 30.

26 ibid., p. 43.

27 ibid., p. 40.

28 ibid., pp. 90, 94, 96.

29 ibid., p. 104.

30 In an earlier draft of his book, which his publisher kindly sent me for purposes of writing this review article, Jäckel had emphasized the quality of inevitability more specifically. In this draft version he wrote that the realization of Hitler's foreign policy plan was ensured because it 'derived from and conformed to' general developments, and that Hitler 'was no more than the executor of the inevitable' (rather than merely the executor of a long-standing tendency).

CHAPTER 9

Hitler's War and the German Economy: A Reinterpretation[1]

R. J. OVERY

When the Allied intelligence services at the end of the Second World War examined the performance of the German war economy a paradox was uncovered. Instead of operating at full throttle, the German economy appeared to have been only partially mobilized for war until 1942, despite the fact that Germany had embarked on a programme of European conquest in 1939 for which it was assumed by the Allies that large military and economic resources were necessary. The traditional explanation that this prompted was that the German economy, encumbered with the apparatus of Nazism, performed its tasks inefficiently.[2] This view laid the foundation for an interpretation based on the concept of the *Blitzkrieg*.[3] According to this explanation the German economy was mobilized at a low level because Hitler had intended it to be that way, partly to complement the military concept of the 'lightning war'; partly to take account of the peculiar administrative and political circumstances of the Nazi state; but primarily because he wanted to reduce the burden of war on the German people and thus remove the prospect of an internal upheaval. It was to be 'a system of waging war without reducing civilian consumer standards'.[4] According to these arguments the fear of an internal crisis reached a peak in 1939 and made necessary the launching of the first of those short wars for which the German economy had been specially prepared.[5] This was rearmament in 'width' rather than 'depth'; war in short bursts rather than total war'.

Although the military concept of the *Blitzkrieg* has been critically re-examined, the idea of the *Blitzkrieg* economy, and the reasons for it, still remain an orthodoxy. The purpose of this article is twofold: first, to carry out the same critical examination of the concept of *Blitzkrieg* economics to show that in most respects the concept does not fit with the actual facts of German economic life between 1936 and 1942; second, to suggest an alternative interpretation based on a reassessment of Hitler's intentions and the response of the German economy to the demands of war in 1939. It will be argued below that Hitler's plans were large in scale, not limited, and were intended for a major war of conquest to be fought considerably later than 1939. The fact that the large armament failed to materialize was not due to any *Blitzkrieg* conception, but to the fact that economic preparations were out of step with the course of foreign policy; a dislocation that was exacerbated after 1939 by a combination of poor planning, structural constraints within German industry, and weaknesses in the process of constructing and communicating policy. The intention was large-scale mobilization. Hitler's object, in the long run, was European conquest and world hegemony.[6]

I

If the idea of the *Blitzkrieg* economy is to work, it must be shown that Hitler, strongly influenced by short-term economic and political considerations, conceived of, planned and launched a war based on this economic policy in the late summer of 1939.[7] Yet all the evidence – or rather lack of it – suggests that short-term economic and social considerations played only the smallest part in Hitler's foreign policy calculations. If anything, it was the part that he deliberately chose to ignore, since those who understood the intelligence available tried without success, throughout the year leading to war, to demonstrate that the Allies were economically stronger than the Axis and that German economic preparations were inadequate.[8] The reason for this situation is clear enough. Hitler did not think in narrow 'economic' or 'social' terms. He was happy for the economy to perform the political tasks which he set it to do: the creation of employment before 1937, and preparation for war thereafter. But he left Schacht and big business to achieve the first, and, unwisely, expected Goering to achieve the second. His concerns were not primarily with the day-to-day problems of economics, living standards and social peace, as were those of his contemporaries, but with questions of race and foreign policy. What economic views he had were placed in the context of his broader military or social ambitions in a general and uncritical way. Of plans for a *Blitzkrieg* economy before 1939 there is little sign. Hitler provided no detailed analysis of how such an economy might work, no systematic intervention in economic affairs, no plan to switch abruptly from consumer goods to arms and back again, whether in response to raw material shortages or to the monthly reports of his internal security police. Economic questions, when considered at all, were all subsumed into his great plans for the future; the plans for *Lebensraum* and the plan to wage a 'life and death struggle' for the survival of the race.[9]

Indeed the tenor of all Hitler's statements before the outbreak of war pointed towards, not *Blitzkrieg,* but its exact opposite, the prospect of a massive and long-term war of the continents from which Germany would emerge either victorious or destroyed[10] and towards which he believed himself to be progressively restructuring the German economy. For this struggle he announced in May 1939 that 'the government must be prepared for a war of ten to fifteen years' duration' during which the requirements of the army in particular would become a 'bottomless pit'.[11] Most important of all, the lesson he drew from the First World War was not that the hardships of total mobilization should be avoided but, on the contrary, the belief that 'the unrestricted use of all resources is essential'.[12] To the leaders of the Armed Forces to whom Hitler delivered this lecture, the sentiments were unrealistic to say the least. But for the historian it is almost the only evidence available on what Hitler's long-term intentions for the economy were; and it is hardly the language of *Blitzkrieg*. Any review of the projects that Hitler had authorized under the Four-Year Plan and German rearmament confirms this wider intention. The naval programme, the enormous fortifications designed to be completed only in the 1950s, the synthetic oil and rubber programmes, the steel programme of the Reichswerke 'Hermann Goering' were large and expensive projects, launched with Hitler's blessing, but designed for completion only in the long term. Such projects had already begun well before 1939, diverting resources of labour, raw materials and machinery from the consumer sector to the sectors necessary for large-scale war.[13] If it is argued that Hitler's intention had been a limited war fought in 1939 together with the safeguarding of domestic living standards, such preparations did not make sense. But that is not what Hitler intended. Hitler wanted a healthy and expanding economy so that he could convert it to the giant task of European and Asian conquest.

Some of the confusion over Hitler's intentions has been fuelled by his own uncertainty about how an economy worked. He expected much more to be delivered than was actually possible, and had only a very hazy idea of economic time-scale. He wanted a high level of preparation for war and at the same time wanted *Autobahnen* and the *Volkswagen* for the purposes of completing the material structure of the *Volksgemeinschaft* [People's community].[14] He wanted massive building programmes on an unprecedented scale. Speer calculated the cost of 25 milliard marks.[15] Significantly the buildings were scheduled for completion by 1950 to coincide with the achievement of total victory, suggesting that Hitler had already seen his coming war as a long-term struggle of heroic proportions.[16] These many ambitions betrayed Hitler's inability to see the economy as a whole, to grasp that cars and tanks could not be produced at the same time, that fortifications vied for resources with the rebuilding of Berlin. It is this inability that has been mistaken for a positive desire to restrict military production in favour of the civilian sector. This was not so. It was a result of Hitler's curiously compartmentalized view of German affairs which persuaded him that each aim was possible simultaneously. His petulant reaction to all advice during the war to restrict his 'peace-time' projects demonstrated the confusion of his economic thinking.[17]

But, it will be objected, how can the outbreak of war in 1939 be accounted for if not in terms of a short war designed to suit the special economic and social crisis of 1939? Put another way, can it be explained in terms of the large-scale total war-effort which Hitler's plans clearly did express? The answer to both questions lies in the particular circumstances of the Polish crisis. It is necessary to digress a little to examine this explanation because it is on Hitler's intention that so much of the argument rests. The first point to make is that Hitler did not expect a European war to break out in 1939. Of course there was an element of risk as in any act of aggression. But all the evidence shows that from 1938 onwards, and increasingly after March 1939, Hitler had persuaded himself that the western Allies would not take action over Poland and, by implication, over further German action in the east.[18] As late as August 1939 Hitler expressed his conviction to Ciano 'that the conflict will be localized' and that it was 'out of the question that this struggle can begin war'.[19] The head of Hitler's military planning staff was allowed to take leave during August, and even to have it extended until the 18th, so confident were the armed forces that a general crisis would not develop over the Danzig question.[20] When news of the pact with Stalin arrived, Hitler was finally, and it could be argued, sensibly, convinced that the West would not attack.[21] Any hesitation before the invasion of Poland was caused by Italy's panic and the prospect of a second Munich, but on no account did the outbreak of a general war seem any more likely to Hitler in August 1939 than in September 1938 – if anything less so. Indeed, all the intelligence available to the Germans of Allied rearmament and strength confirmed that neither Britain nor France was in a position to risk war with the Axis powers.[22] The general war for which Hitler was preparing was not supposed to break out in 1939, and even when it did, would, according to Hitler, peter out as the Western powers grew tired of their gesture.[23] He did not shirk the war when it came, not because he had any *Blitzkrieg* economic plan prepared, but for the quite different reason that he believed in the long run that the economic and moral resources of the Reich, when stretched to their utmost, would prove greater than those available to the Allies.[24] In other words, even when general war broke out against his expectations in 1939 Hitler immediately thought in terms of the large-scale contest which had coloured so much of his thinking beforehand.

The second point to emphasize is the long-term nature of Hitler's imperial ambitions. The fact that the Polish question led to general war prematurely in 1939 obscured the character of the imperialism, which was designed in two complementary stages.[25] The first was to create a military-economic core for the new German empire comprising Germany, Austria, Czechoslovakia and parts of Poland, to be achieved without a general war. This core was to be protected by fortifications to east and west and was to provide the resources of the autarkic economy.[26] The achievement of this first stage was to be guaranteed by neutralizing the threat of intervention by concessions to one or other potential enemy, Britain in 1938, Russia in 1939. The second stage involved using this large economic region as the base for launching war against the major powers. It was for this racial struggle that the German economy was to be prepared. Much of the evidence from the pre-war period shows the extent to which Hitler's view of foreign policy was coloured by such irrational biological and geo-political perspectives. France, Russia,

Britain and even the United States were the main enemies, a conviction that wavered only with the tactics of diplomacy.[27] This interpretation of Hitler's economic and military ambitions, which required a large rearmament and a continuing militarization of German society, accords much more satisfactorily with the evidence of war preparations, most of which pointed to a war to be fought in the mid-1940s or later. The first stage of the build-up of the Luftwaffe was not to be completed until 1942, and it was to be prepared for a long war only by 1947 or 1950.[28] The naval programme was due for completion only by the mid-1940s.[29] The plans for refurbishing the Reichsbahn laid down in 1939 were to reach fruition in 1944.[30] Hitler himself authorized Keitel to inform the armed forces that they should concentrate on training and internal development until at least 1944 or 1945.[31] And the impression that was given to the Italian leadership throughout 1938 and 1939 was that the war with the major powers, the larger and inevitable conflict, would be postponed until 1942 at the earliest.[32]

Finally, it must be remembered that German strategy was very much dictated by Hitler's personal and fantastic perspectives on world affairs, so different from those of his contemporaries abroad. The *Blitzkrieg* strategy suggests a degree of economic and political realism, and of careful calculation, which the evidence of Hitler's activities does not confirm. Throughout 1938 and 1939 he became more and more preoccupied with the fulfilment of a German destiny to which he alone claimed the insight, and for which he was quite prepared for the German people to bear the severest consequences. 'War does not frighten me', Hitler told Dahlerus. 'If privation lies ahead of the German people, I shall be the first to starve and set my people a good example. It will spur them to superhuman efforts'.[33] When he told his generals in 1939 that he was the first man since Charlemagne to hold ultimate power in his own hand 'and would know how to use it in a struggle for Germany',[34] he was stating his firmly held belief that the destiny of Germany lay in his hands alone. Hence the reasons which Hitler himself gave for the attack on Poland; that he was growing old and could afford to wait no longer to create the new German empire; and that what counted in foreign policy was will. Lacking the will to restrain Hitler before 1939, the western nations had forfeited their claim to the status of great powers and would not fight.[35]

The fact that Hitler's wider intentions failed to produce the large-scale armament that he wanted was not because he lowered his sights and chose *Blitzkrieg,* but because of the premature outbreak of a general war in 1939 and the difficulties experienced thereafter in mobilizing an economy starved of strategic guidelines and a satisfactory wartime administration.

II

The *Blitzkrieg* economy is just as elusive in the wider context of German war preparations. The restructuring of the economy implied by the Four-Year Plan, and the acceleration of Hitler's diplomacy after 1937, showed what the ultimate purposes of the regime were. If Hitler's precise intentions were not always clear, or were not always taken seriously by the business or military elites, there could be no doubt that the restructuring was taking place.[36] It was a necessary step in preparing for large-scale war and German hegemony. In fact it was precisely because this was a long-term goal that exact details were lacking. The reorientation of the economy was bound to be a lengthy and clumsy process. The absence of precise economic planning confirmed that the intention was not to wage a short, carefully calculated war in the near future, but a big war at a later date.

It was Hitler's intention that Goering should co-ordinate the efforts to prepare the economy as a whole, using Party agencies and leaders where possible to carry the programme out. Goering's view of the economy was, like Hitler's, concerned with its role in the future conquest of Europe and world war. Like Hitler, he assumed that the scale of preparation should involve the whole economy. His task within the Four-Year Plan was to reorient the total economy to war purposes. That Goering was unsuccessful in doing so by 1939 was an indication not only that he was an inappropriate choice as plenipotentiary, but also that he expected to have much more time to complete his task.[37] Working on a wide range of uncompleted projects, Goering was among the foremost of those who argued against risking war in 1939 and who accepted Hitler's assurances that the crisis in August would be localized.[38] Goering worked on the assumption that any war would be a general and large-scale conflict; hence his anxiety to prevent war until Germany was fully prepared. To the *Gauleiter* in 1938 he spoke of the 'new war' of 'great proportions' to come.[39] To industry in October 1938 he stressed that 'the economy must be completely converted'.[40] A year later he warned industry that 'Today's war is a total war, whose end no one can even approximately foretell'.[41] In December 1939 he wrote to all Reich authorities telling them to 'direct all energies to a lengthy war'.[42] In all this he was merely echoing Hitler's own intention, even though the timing of war had misfired. The picture he presented to the German economy at large, if at times unspecified or unrealistic, was of a future and large-scale conflict for which the complete transformation of the economic structure was required.[43]

The same contingency was prepared for by the armed forces, which were compelled to perform their functions in partial ignorance of the exact nature of Hitler's long-term intentions. The lack of precise information reflected Hitler's own secretiveness and administrative methods. To Halder, the Army Chief-of-Staff, he remarked: 'my true intentions you will never know. Even those in my closest circle who feel quite sure they know my intentions will not know about them'.[44] In this light the armed forces geared preparations to a wide number of major contingencies which they regarded as reasonable. It was widely agreed that all such contingencies required preparations for a total war economy, and the army developed during the 1930s the theory of the *Wehrwirtschaft* – the defence-based economy – to cope with the requirement.[45] General Thomas, head of the army economic office, planned economic mobilization as though any war might mean total war, hoping to avoid the mistakes of 1914. Preparations for this 'armament in depth' existed throughout the 1930s and continued after the outbreak of war in 1939, co-inciding with Hitler's view of future warfare.[46]

Thomas himself complained after the war that such preparations had been much less successful than he had expected. Part of the reason for this lay with the administrative confusion surrounding rearmament, what Thomas called 'the war of all against all'.[47] But a major explanation lay in the general unwill-ingness of much of German industry to cooperate in preparing for total war, the more so as many industrialists regarded a general war as unthinkable in 1939. Industry was faced in 1939 with the prospect of rising trade and a con-sumer boom based on the continued modernization of the German economy. Instructions from Goering and Thomas were circumvented or ignored.[48] The whole structure of controls and *Wehrwirtschaft* [war economy] preparations was sabotaged by the unwillingness of many industrialists, happy enough to take rearmament orders, to follow the logic through to actual war. The prob-lems with which private industry and banking were concerned were those of markets (including the newly won areas of central Europe) investment, and money supply.[49] This was not, of course, true of all industrialists. The large state sector developed after 1936 was designed to provide the Nazis with war materials which private industry might have been reluctant to provide. There were also sympathizers in private firms, whose board-rooms were penetrated by the Nazis, who were willing to co-operate in the economic restructuring. But the increasing tension between these elements and the rest of the econ-omy, symbolized by the clash over the *Reichswerke* and the *Volkswagen,* placed limits on the pace and extent of the Nazi war-economic programme.[50] The emergence of just such a division showed clearly that the *Blitzkrieg* solu-tion of a small arms sector and protected consumer output was not the option that the Nazis had chosen. The purposes of Nazism and the purposes of German capitalism no longer coincided, as they had appeared to do in 1933. The resistance of business was caused by the crude attempt to force the whole economy after 1936 along the path towards the successful prose-cution of a major 'racial struggle'.

III

In the light of this interpretation of Nazi intentions, it is not surprising to find that in most important respects the *Blitzkrieg* economy does not fit with the actual circumstances of German economic life during the period in question. The first problem is the sheer scale of Nazi rearmament. If it is looked at from a pre-war perspective, military expenditure in Germany up to 1940 was very large, much greater than that of any other power, with perhaps the exception of the Soviet Union, and much greater as a proportion of GNP than that of any power.[51] In May 1939 General Thomas boasted that in the following twelve months German rearmament would have almost reached the levels of the First World War.[52] Far from avoiding the total commitment of the previous conflict, the German economy was on the brink of exceeding it. It will be argued later that Hitler did not get value for money, but to contrast German 'limited' mobilization with the 'total' mobilization of the Allies is, before 1941, historically misleading.[53]

More important, however, is the fact that economic mobilization was intended to continue at a high and rising rate. Where the *Blitzkrieg* economy represented the peak of a short-term armaments effort to be used up in a short campaign, the German economy in 1939 was already operating at a high level of military production and was designed to reach even higher levels in the future. Nearly all the plans indicate this. The Navy's 'Z-Plan' required a huge industrial effort which had only just begun when the Polish crisis arose.[54] Such a programme was essential to waging the larger, long-term conflict that Hitler had in mind. Moreover Hitler gave priority to the 'Z-Plan' over every other service programme, even over exports, something which made no sense at all in terms of a *Blitzkrieg* economy.[55] Demands for the air force followed the same course. Germany already possessed a large force of modern aircraft by 1939, if smaller than those of the Allies together.[56] In addition to this, Hitler demanded a five-fold increase in air strength late in 1938, a request that would have needed an annual production of 20,000 aircraft in peacetime and 30,000–40,000 in wartime.[57] Although German aircraft production planners scaled these plans down substantially during 1939, they were almost exactly the sort of plans that Britain was laying down at the same time for 'total' mobilization.[58] Even the Luftwaffe itself, less ambitious than Hitler, planned a much larger output of aircraft than it in fact got from 1939 onwards. The last peacetime programme for the Luftwaffe planned an output of 14,000 aircraft a year by 1941, nearly three times the output for 1938.[59] The *Wehrmacht* mobilization plans for the air force expected production to rise to over 20,000 aircraft in the first full year of war: actual production was 10,247.[60] All this suggests that Hitler wanted a huge increase in the proportion of the economy devoted to military purposes, even if war had not broken out in 1939.

To carry out such an expansion the Nazi leadership began from 1937–8 onwards to build up a large state-owned and state-operated industrial structure designed to speed up the reorientation of the economy for war. In aircraft production most new investment came from the state and much of it was concentrated in building large-scale production units.[61] In 1938 Goering demanded the construction of three giant aeroengine works capable of producing 1,000 engines a month each, to be followed by plans for a 10,000-a-year bomber factory.[62] In iron and steel Goering pioneered the extraction of low-grade iron-ore, but was also able to use the *Reichswerke* as a convenient cover for large-scale expansion of state involvement in industry, taking over control of Rheinmetall Borsig, almost the whole of the Austrian and Czech iron and machinery industry, and slices of the Thyssen empire.[63] The purpose, as Goering privately admitted, was to construct an industrial empire sensitive to the demands of Hitler's imperialism and on the largest scale .[64] The investments involved were very substantial. The hydrogenation plant at Brüx alone cost 250 million marks, more than all government investment in the aircraft industry in 1939/40.[65] Moreover, the investments were largely long term, making very little sense if the object were to design a *Blitzkrieg* economy. In fact the very scale of all these projects proved to be a drain on productive potential in the early years of war, thus explaining part of the paradox between Hitler's large-scale planning and expenditure and the poor return in the shape of finished armaments. Hitler's intention had been to create this necessary industrial substructure before developing the super-structure of armaments production. War in 1939 interrupted the programme and threw industrial planning into confusion.

The industrial evidence is unhelpful to the *Blitzkrieg* as well. The con-version of industry was planned comprehensively by the armed forces under Thomas, who worked on the 'total war' contingency.[66] The new Volkswagen complex, for example, which Hitler, with his fragmented view of the econ-omy had detailed as a peacetime project, was assigned to the Luftwaffe in the event of war. While its conversion was hopelessly planned, as with so much of the effort to convert, the intention to do so was certainly there.[67] The plan was to draw on the civilian industries to make up for the inadequate pro-vision of factory capacity and to close down inessential consumer produc-tion. In February 1940 Goering made it clear that such capacity had to be found 'to a much greater extent in the idle factories, even if in one way or another this does not correspond to all wishes'.[68] The head of the air indus-try economic group instructed air firms in October 1939 to take over any spare capacity in those sectors that were being closed down or were on short-time.[69] So rapid and wide-ranging was this conversion that the Four-Year Plan Office estimated that the proportion of the work-force employed for military purposes had risen from 20 per cent in 1939 to 60 per cent by early 1941.[70]

Not surprisingly, this led to reductions in civilian goods production. That this did not happen is a crucial part of the *Blitzkrieg* economy. 'There can be little doubt', wrote Professor Milward, 'that the impact of war on the German people over these years was very small'.[71] Consumer spending and civilian output, it is argued, were maintained in the face of the demands of war, while the military budget rose sharply only after the end of the *Blitzkrieg* in 1942. The facts show otherwise. Looking at the German economy as a whole, mili-tary spending rose at a consistent rate between 1938/9 and 1943/4. There was no abrupt change in 1942, nor any halt in expenditure in 1940 and 1941, as Table 10.1 shows.

In fact the greatest percentage increases in military expenditure were in the years 1939 to 1941. This pattern confirms the fact that German rearma-ment and war expenditure followed a relatively smooth course of expansion over the period with none of the implied discontinuities of the *Blitzkrieg* economy. As a proportion of National Income and GNP the figures also com-pare favourably with the performance of the Allied economies.[72] Since mili-tary expenditure grew at a faster rate than the German economy as a whole this could only have been at the expense of civilian consumption.

And so in fact it was. Car production, for example, hungry for raw materi-als and labour, was dramatically cut back from a peak of 276,592 in 1938 to a

Table 10.1 Military expenditure, state expenditure, and national income in Germany, 1938/9–43/4 (mrd. RM, current prices)

Year	Military expenditure	State expenditure	National income
1938/9	17.2	39.4	98
1939/40	38.0	58.0	109
1940/1	55.9	80.0	120
1941/2	72.3	100.5*	125
1942/3	86.2	124.0*	134
1943/4	99.4	130.0*	130

Source: W. Boelcke, 'Kriegsfinanzierung im internationalen Vergleich' in Forstmeier Volkmann, *Kriegs-wirtschaft und Rüstung*, pp. 55–6: Klein, *Germany's Preparations*, pp. 256–8.
Note: * based on revenue from occupied Europe and the Reich.

mere 67,561 in 1940 and to 35,195 in 1941. The military took 42 per cent of the total in 1940, and 77 per cent in 1941.[73] It is the same story for the construction industry. The number of housing units completed fell from 303,000 in 1938 to 117,000 in 1940, and to 80,000 in 1941; again with many of the latter for military use. The volume of construction as a whole fell from 12.8 milliard marks in 1939 to 8.3 milliard in 1940 and to 6.9 milliard in 1941.[74] These were the important areas from which resources could be released into the military economy. Goods whose survival is supposed to demonstrate the maintenance of consumer spending were either those which would be expected to increase under war conditions (such as basic foodstuffs, the output of which increased enormously in Britain as well during the war)[75] or those whose production was divided between military and civilian use, a division disguised by the gross figures. In fact it was the high quality of the equipment that the *Wehrmacht* demanded for its members that swallowed up much of the consumer goods production as well as the increased output of food.[76] For the ordinary civilian consumer much less was available than before the war. By 1943 the armed forces took 44 per cent of all textile production, 43 per cent of all leather goods, and 40 per cent of all paper produced.[77] Of course Hitler kept a propaganda eye on domestic living standards, and the conquest of Europe allowed greater flexibility than might otherwise have been possible, but many of the concessions made were, literally, cosmetic.[78]

The result of this diversion to military purposes was widespread and increasingly comprehensive rationing, some of it before 1939.[79] The Four-Year Plan Office itself openly admitted the need to cut back on consumption. In a speech early in 1941 State Secretary Neumann acknowledged that:

> not only almost all articles of daily use but also practically all other goods have become increasingly scarce in recent years – even prior to the outbreak of war . . . a higher standard of living is the ultimate goal, not the immediate object of the Four Year Plan. Whatever was available by way

of labour, materials and machines had to be invested in the production of military-economic importance according to an explicit Führer order. . . . The fact that consumer interests had to be put second is regrettable but cannot be helped.[80]

Civilian production as a whole was severely cut back from the outbreak of war, while the bulk of surviving consumer goods production was diverted to the armed forces. The problem facing the German economy was not the release of resources but the ineffective use to which they were then put.

The final question concerns the degree of 'flexibility' in the German economy; the extent to which, under the terms of the *Blitzkrieg* economy, production could be switched within weeks from one weapons group to another or back to civilian production, as strategy dictated.[81] While it is true that priority changed, as would be expected, under the circumstances of war, in practice little substantial shift between weapons groups occurred during the period. The air force, for example, found it impossible to increase production significantly after the Fall of France while enjoying a production priority, but was able to expand output to new levels when the priority was removed and returned to the army.[82] In practice, the production for all the services expanded more or less continuously over the whole period 1939-41, for it was difficult to disrupt production programmes at short notice, and the services jealously guarded their own economic spheres of influence.[83] The same is true of the switch from arms to the civilian economy. Hitler certainly explored the idea of running down arms production in 1940 and again in 1941, not in response to any *Blitzkrieg* conception or preparation, but in reaction to the extraordinary degree of success that his relatively underarmed but well-run forces were able to achieve. But it must be stressed that Hitler did no more than explore the possibility. Success did not blind the Nazi leadership to the fact that enemies remained undefeated, and expenditure on weapons, like overall military expenditure, rose steadily and continuously over the whole period, helped by the expansion of output in the dependent territories in central Europe (see Table 10.2).

Table 10.2   Expenditure on selected weapons in Germany, 1939-41

Weapon	1939*	1940 (1941/2 prices, million marks)	1941
aircraft	1,040.0	4,141.2	4,452.0
ships	41.2	474.0	1,293.6
armour	8.4	171.6	384.0
weapons	180.0	676.8	903.6
explosive	17.6	223.2	338.4
traction vehicles	30.8	154.8	228.0

Source: calculated from Wagenfür, *Deutsche Industrie*, p. 29.
Note: * September-December.

The problem which Hitler faced was not the degree of commitment from what was, after all, a large and heavily industrialized economy, but the fact that, despite such a commitment, the output of finished weapons failed to match the extent of revenue and resources devoted to arms production. This made necessary a significant change in the level of productivity in 1941–2, rather than in the level of aggregate resources.

IV

Why was there such a gap between what Hitler wanted and what was actually produced? The immediate explanation is that the war broke out before the economy could be satisfactorily converted. Both the military and economic leadership were caught in the middle of restructuring the economy, and were compelled to divert energies to the needs of war before the economy was prepared for it. But that is not the whole answer. There were structural problems in the German economy that were not satisfactorily solved by 1939. There were also difficulties that arose from the very nature of German rearmament. This had started late in terms of a war to be fought in 1939, only reaching significant levels by 1937–8. There was little time to build up the plant and resources Hitler's plans warranted.[84] Not only was the question of time crucial, but also there was the fact that so much of the money was spent on refurnishing Germany with a military infrastructure (airfields, barracks, etc.) which had been destroyed or prohibited under the terms of the Versailles Treaty. This was an expensive business made more so by the fact that German weapons were also expensive. The insistence on very high standards of workmanship, and the preference for small-scale over large-scale mass-production contributed to this. So too did the cost-plus system of contracts, which gave no incentive to reduce prices and actually encouraged firms to produce inefficient methods and a high-priced end product.[85] The 50 milliard marks spent on rearmament by 1939 could have been expected, as Hitler no doubt wished, to yield more in terms of military goods than was in fact the case.[86] This situation continued into the war. In 1940 Germany spent an estimated $6 billion on weapons, while Britain spent $3.5 billion. Yet Britain produced over 50 per cent more aircraft, 100 per cent more vehicles and almost as many tanks as Germany in 1940.[87] If German armaments had been less well made and more efficiently produced and paid for, the number of weapons available in 1940 would have been considerably greater.

Another answer lay in Hitler's limited access to accurate information on the performance of the economy. This was partly a product of his style of government. But during the war it was as much a product of self-delusion and misinformation. Having spent large sums on rearmament with the most modern weapons Hitler failed to ensure that they were produced in quantity. He accepted new developments uncritically. He found it difficult to accept the long time-scale involved in developing a weapon or in distinguishing between weapons that were mere prototypes and those that were battle-ready.[88] This element of self-delusion was complemented by a good deal of poor or misleading intelligence. This was very much a product of the regime. Subordinates in the hierarchy hesitated to take initiatives on the economy and preferred to provide only that information which would present an optimistic impression of their achievements.[89] The information that finally reached Hitler was often partial and unrealistic, reflecting the intelligence that it was believed Hitler wanted to hear. Hence Hitler's reproaches to Goering over the failure of aircraft production later in the war; and hence Hitler's bitterness that the range of advanced weapons shown to him in 1939 as virtually ready for combat had failed in every case to materialize by 1942.[90] Hence, too, the persistent underestimation of enemy economic strength provided by German intelligence from 1939 to the invasion of Russia.[91]

One of the main culprits in this process of misrepresentation was Goering. His eagerness to enlarge his political empire through the economy, and his anxiety to present to Hitler the most optimistic picture of his achievement with war production, obscured much of the true state of preparations. Goering was then able to shelter behind the German victories until the poor performance of the economy became more obvious in the course of 1941, after which he was gradually excluded from its direction.[92] Before then, he had taken up all his tasks in the economy with much political enthusiasm, little economic or technical understanding and exceedingly poor relations with sections of heavy industry, the Reichsbank, and the Finance Ministry.[93] He insisted on treating his office as if he were personally responsible for preparing the future war economy, demanding that other agencies should be fused with his to increase the centralization of the economy under his direction.[94] Yet the civilian and military economic leadership did not want to work under Goering, and was able to circumvent his jurisdiction whenever possible. Goering himself was unequal to the tasks of organization that Hitler had set him. The result was that, during the crucial years of build-up towards war and in the early years of conflict, the military economy was not directed in a co-ordinated way.[95] Up to 1938 under Schacht, and after 1942 under Speer, the performance of the German economy came up to expectations. Between those dates came what Speer later saw as an era of 'incompetence, arrogance and egotism'.[96]

The main characteristics of the 'era of incompetence' were the ineffective way in which the resources released for war were taken up, and the general inefficiency and confusion of the military economy. Not that German industry, particularly large-scale industry, was uncompetitive commercially. The problem lay in adopting the same practices in the armament factories. Not only was this slow to happen, but those commercial firms brought into war-work also became infected by the incompetence and inflexibility of the system. One obvious explanation for ineffective mobilization was that industry was caught by surprise by the actual outbreak of war in 1939, and had to divert resources from long-term military projects and from civilian life without a competent central authority for the economy. When war broke out, industry was unprepared for the scale of demands and was anxious, like much of the military leadership, that the war should be over as soon as possible. Moreover, the firms often expressed a marked hostility to a high level of government intervention or military interference and failed to co-operate in achieving high levels of arms output in the way that American or British businessmen did.[97] It is perhaps not surprising that in a situation where not even Hitler's closest subordinates could guess his intentions, business in Germany was unable to comprehend the scope of what was happening in 1940 and 1941, and to prepare accordingly. Moreover, German business was anxious not to lose the prospect of rising profits and expanding trade which had been held out at the end of the 1930s, and the first years of war saw a continuation of the silent struggle over the nature and destination of the German economy.[98] Too much energy was used up in combating excessive state interference on the one hand and in competing for contracts and influence abroad on the other. This, combined with the incomplete nature of preparations for a war in 1939 and the lack of a competent war economic administration, substantially reduced the level of war goods that Hitler had wanted.

There was also the question of industrial constraints. This was not simply a result of a lack of central planning, jurisdictional confusion, and poor co-ordination, or of a shortage of raw materials, the lack of which has been much exaggerated. There were problems within the armaments industry itself. There was too great a reliance on skilled labour in areas of manufacture where increasing automation might have been expected. The reluctance of the work-force to accept dilution during the 1930s and the early years of war brought many difficulties in introducing mass-production methods and made labour more of a problem than was necessary.[99] So, too, did the conservatism of management faced with the requirements of making the transition from small-scale to large-scale manufacture. This was less of a problem with established firms, such as Krupps. But many of the firms that grew large on government orders in the 1930s were small firms faced with all the strains of making the transition to a different style of management at a vital stage in German war preparations.[100] Only when industrialists from the large commercial firms were brought in to run the war economy in 1942 were some of these difficulties overcome.[101]

One final problem, industry could do very little about: the exceptional degree of control exercised over armaments firms by the armed forces. In the absence of a strong civilian economic administration this was perhaps inevitable. But the tight military control over contracts, product selection, and production methods stifled industrial initiatives.[102] The most damaging problem was the extent to which minor technical demands from the armed forces at the front held up the introduction of mass-production methods and encouraged only short and expensive production runs.[103] When the more successful commercial firms were drafted into war production, their productive performance was similarly blighted by contact with the poor planning of the military production authorities.[104] When Todt, Speer and Milch revolutionized production in 1941 and 1942 they did so not by a massive redirecting of resources but simply by using existing resources better. The aircraft industry in 1942 produced 40 per cent more aircraft than in 1941 with only 5 per cent more labour and substantially less aluminium.[105] What produced the low level of mobilization was not a lack of resources but the problem of coping with a premature war in an economy lacking effective central control, dominated by military requirements, and guided by an impulsive strategist whose understanding of the economy was deliberately obscured. Under these circumstances it was possible to produce just enough for the early German campaigns, but not enough for Hitler's 'big war'; not enough, that is, to defeat Britain in 1940 or Russia in 1941.

V

The first conclusion to draw from this interpretation of the German war economy is the inappropriateness of applying a *Blitzkrieg* conception. In terms of economic planning, industrial conversion, consumer goods production, civilian consumption, and strategic 'flexibility', the model breaks down. The ideas that Germany deliberately sought to restrict the economic costs of war, and that German civilian consumption levels were maintained intact over the early war period while the military economy had its resources skilfully switched from one weapon group to another, fit with neither the general strategic picture nor with the details of economic life in Germany between 1939 and 1941.

Hitler's intention was to prepare for a long and total war, using all Germany's resources to achieve a final victory. This perspective explains the nature of the autarkic and rearmament programmes initiated from 1936 onwards, many of them quite redundant for the purposes of a limited and conventional 'short war'. The evidence shows that Hitler expected such a confrontation in the mid-1940s, after an initial period of consolidation in central Europe achieved without a general war, and protected by a series of diplomatic *coups* of which the Nazi-Soviet Pact was the most important. It was this initial stage of preparing a large economic and military bloc in central Europe that backfired in 1939 into a more general war, against Hitler's expectations. That is why the German economy appeared to be prepared for a limited war. It was caught halfway towards the transformation planned by Hitler, with a military base capable of achieving the limited first stage but not the second, more general, one.

It is clear that Hitler, faced with the fact of war in 1939, changed his mind about the time-scale involved in his imperialism, accelerating the move towards the 'big' war which found him in conflict with Britain, Russia and the United States by the end of 1941. That he did so was in part because he believed that the economic time-scale could be speeded up and conversion to the needs of the larger war achieved in the early 1940s instead of later. This expectation was in turn derived from misinformation or lack of information on how the economy was developing. This failure of communication was crucial. It was compounded of Goering's anxiety that the achievements of the Four-Year Plan should be presented in as favourable a light as possible, and

Hitler's own predilection for secretiveness and fragmented administration. The failure was helped, too, by Hitler's own poor understanding of production and finance, which led him to expect that military goods could be produced much more quickly and cheaply than was in fact possible. Goering's remark that Hitler was interested only in how many bombers there were, and not in how many engines each had, was symptomatic of this approach.[106]

Most important of all in persuading Hitler that the 'big' war was possible was the remarkable military success enjoyed between September 1939 and June 1940 against enemies whose combined material strength was more than equal to that of Germany. This success was not produced by a *Blitzkrieg* economy. The victories were due, first and foremost, to the staff work, leadership and fighting qualities of the German forces, together with the weaknesses, poor leadership and wrong intelligence on the part of the Allies. Hitler's belief that the 'big' war could now be won still required a huge economic effort based on the large-scale plans laid down, but not yet completed, between 1936 and 1939. It is true that the extent of the military victories, which surprised Hitler as well as the generals, tempted him at times to question the need for a greater economic effort and to rely more on military prowess. But these second thoughts were very much *post hoc*, reflecting the changing circumstances of war, and were not pre-planned; nor, it must be emphasized, did Hitler ever hold back the continued expansion of the arms economy over the whole of the period 1939 to 1942. Moreover, such second thoughts were soon dispelled by the failures against Britain in 1940 and Russia in 1941, which showed the limit of German military potential and the extent to which the German armed forces were underarmed. As it turned out, the German forces were able to perform remarkably in the face of massive material superiority throughout the war. That they were comparatively under-armed was the result of the fact that the German economy could not be converted satisfactorily in 1939–41 to the needs of a large-scale war.

This failure to convert satisfactorily, to adjust to the 'big' war when asked to do so, had many causes. At one level the failure was simply a result of the fact that the war broke out prematurely, while many of the preparations were of a long-term character. Hitler's own uncertainty and impulsive strategy created uncertainty among business leaders and economic planners. The economy was caught between peaceful economic recovery and the programme of war preparations laid down since 1936. This lack of appropriate planning was made more acute by the lack of a satisfactory central economic administration in war time. In the absence of central direction the military had a much greater say in economic affairs, concentrating on matters (such as tactical suitability) that concerned the front line, and not on questions of large-scale industrial production and distribution. When this was added to a reluctance on the part of much of industry to convert for war, and the rapid and unpredictable shifts in strategy, the economy failed to rise to the challenge of a large-scale war as it did in Britain, the United States and Russia. The failure to solve the problem of arms production (disguised by the very good use to which the *Wehrmacht* put what weapons it had) was caused not by a preference for consumer-goods production over armaments, nor by *Blitz-krieg* campaigns deliberately based on a small military economy, but by the fact that Hitler's larger war arrived before preparations for it were complete. The low level of mobilization was not intentional but was a product of this contradiction between economic and diplomatic reality.

Notes

1 I would like to thank Mr B. Bond, Dr W. Deist, Dr Z. Steiner and Professor A. Teichova for advice in the preparation of this article.

2 B. H. Klein, 'Germany's preparation for war; a re-examination', *American Economic Review*, XXXVIII, 1948, pp. 56-77; Klein, *Germany's Economic Preparations for War*, Harvard, Mass., 1959.

3 A. S. Milward, 'Der Einfluss ökonomischer und nicht-Ökonomischer Faktoren auf die Strategie des Blitzkriegs', in F. Forstmeier and H. E. Volkmann (eds), *Wirtschaft und Rüstung am Vorabend des Zweiten Weltkrieges*, Düsseldorf, 1975, pp. 189-201; A. S. Milward, 'The end of the Blitzkrieg, *Economic History Review*, 2nd ser., XVI, 1963/4, 499-518; Milward, *The German Economy at War,* 1965; Milward, 'Hitlers Konzept des Blitzkrieges', in A. Hillgruber (ed.) *Probleme des Zweiten Welkrieges*, Köln, 1967, pp. 19-40.

4 A. S. Milward, 'Could Sweden have stopped the Second World War?', *Scandinavian Economic History Review*, XV, 1967, p. 135.

5 On the question of the internal crisis see T. W. Mason, 'Innere Krise und Angriffskrieg', in Forstmeier and Volkmann, *Wirtschaft und Rüstung*, pp. 158-88; Mason, 'Labour in the Third Reich', *Past & Present*, 33, 1966, pp. 112-41; Mason, 'Some origins of the Second World War', *P. & P.* 23, 1964, pp. 67-87; E. Hennig, 'Industrie, Aufrüstung und Kriegsvorbereitung im deutschen Faschismus', in *Gesellschaft: Beiträge zur Marxschen Theorie 5*, Frankfurt, 1975, pp. 68-148.

6 For criticism of the military *Blitzkrieg* conception see: W. Deist *et al., Das Deutsche Reich und der Zweite Weltkrieg*, I, *Ursachen und Voraussetzungen der deutschen Kriegspolitik*, Stuttgart, 1979; L. Herbst, 'Die Krise des nationalsozialistischen Regimes am Vorabend des Zweiten Weltkrieges und die forcierte Aufrüstung', *Vierteljahresbefte für Zeitgeschichte*, XXVI, 1978, pp. 347-92; J. Dülffer, *Weimar, Hitler und die Marine*, Düsseldorf, 1973; and J. Thies, *Architekt der Weltherrschaft. Die Endziele Hitlers*, Düsseldorf, 1976.

7 T. W. Mason, *Sozialpolitik im Dritten Reich*, Opladen, 1977, pp. 305-10; Milward, *German Economy*, pp. 8-14.

8 International Military Tribunal, *Trial of the Major War Criminals* (hereafter IMT), Nuremberg, 1947-9, XXXVI, pp. 493-7, Doc. 419-EC, Finance Minister to Hitler, 1 September 1938; W. Warlimont, *Inside Hitler's Headquarters,* 1964, p. 24; on General Thomas's efforts to convince Hitler of Germany's poor economic position see H.B. Gisevius, *To the Bitter End*, 1948, pp. 355-7; B. A. Carroll, *Design for Total War,* The Hague, 1968, p. 178.

9 *Nazi Conspiracy and Aggression* (hereafter NCA), Washington, 1946, VII, pp. 847, 850-1; Doc. L-79 report of a conference with Hitler, 23 May 1939. For a general discussion see E. Jäckel, *Hitler's Weltanschauung*, Wesleyan UP, 1972, pp. 27-46; K. Hildebrand, *The Foreign Policy of the Third Reich*, 1973, pp. 91-104; A. Kuhn, *Hitlers aussenpolitisches Programm*, Stuttgart 1970, pp. 96-140.

10 A. Speer, *Inside the Third Reich*, 1970, p. 166. Speer recorded Hitler's statement

to his generals that 'if the war were not won, that would mean that Germany had not stood the test of strength; in that case she would deserve to be and would be doomed'; H. Rauschning, *Hitler Speaks*, 1939, p. 125, 'even if we could not conquer then, we should drag half the world into destruction with us, and leave no-one to triumph over Germany'; also pp. 126-8.

11 NCA, VII, pp. 851-3, Doc. L-79. This conviction is echoed in M. Muggeridge (ed.) *Ciano's Diplomatic Papers*, 1948, p. 284, 'Conversation with the Reich Foreign Minister, 6-7 May 1939', when Ribbentrop assured Ciano that 'preparations are being made to carry on a war of several years' duration'.

12 NCA, VII, p. 851.

13 W. Birkenfeld, *Der synthetische Trebstoff, 1933-1943*, Göttingen, 1963, pp. 112-40; M. Riedel, *Eisen und Kohle für das Dritte Reich*, Göttingen, 1973, pp. 155-232; D. Petzina, *Autarkiepolitik im Dritten Reich*, Stuttgart, 1968; Düffer, *Hitler und die Marine*, p. 498; Thies, *Architekt*, pp. 151-2, 186-7.

14 R. J. Overy, 'Transportation and rearmament in the Third Reich', *Historical Journal*, XVI, 1973, pp. 389-409.

15 Speer, *Inside the Reich, p.* 176; J. Dülffer, J. Henke and J. Thies (eds) *Hitlers Städte. Baupolitik im Dritten Reich*, Köln, 1978.

16 J. Thies, 'Hitler's European building programme', *Journal of Contemporary History*, XIII, 1978, pp. 423-4; Speer, *Inside the Reich*, p. 174.

17 On the Autobahnen in wartime see K. Lärmer, 'Autobahnenbau und Staatsmonopolistischer Kapitalismus', in L. Zumpe (ed.) *Wirtschaft und Staat im Imperialismus*, Berlin, 1976, pp. 253-81; Speer, *Inside the Reich*, p. 176; Carroll, *Design*, pp. 171, 245. For more details of the economic cost of these projects see J. Dülffer, 'Der Beginn des Krieges 1939; Hitler, die innere Krise und das Mächtesystem', *Geschichte und Gesellschaft*, II, 1976, pp. 457-9.

18 L. E. Hill (ed.) *Die Weizsäcker-Papiere, 1933-1950*, Frankfurt, 1974, pp. 149, 153, 155-6; A. Bullock, 'Hitler and the Origins of the Second World War', *Proceedings of the British Academy*, LIII, 1967, pp. 280-1; E. M. Robertson, *Hitler's Pre-war Policy and Military Plans*, 1963, pp. 160-2; Hildebrand, *Foreign Policy*, pp. 84-90. According to Rauschning, *Hitler Speaks*, pp. 123-4, Hitler had already reached this conclusion in 1934.

19 *Ciano's Papers*, pp. 301-2, 'First Conversation with the Fuehrer, 12 Aug. 1939; p. 303, 'Second Conversation with the Fuehrer, 13 Aug. 1939'.

20 Nuremberg Trials, Case XI documents, Foreign Office Library (hereafter Case XI), Körner Defence Doc. Book IB, pp. 154-5.

21 Speer, *Inside the Reich*, pp. 161-2; W. Carr, *Arms, Autarky and Aggression*, 1972, p. 123; *Weizsäcker-Papiere*, pp. 159-60; J. Toland, *Adolf Hitler*, New York, 1976, p. 548.

22 E. Homze, *Arming the Luftwaffe*, Nebraska UP, 1976, pp. 244-5; W. Baumbach, *Broken Swastika* 1960, pp. 30-1; *Ciano's Papers*, p. 298, 'Conversation with the Reich Foreign Minister, 11 August, 1939'.

23 *Weizsäcker-Papiere*, p. 164.

24 NCA, VII, p. 854, Doc. L-79; according to B. Bahlerus, *The Last Attempt*, 1948, p. 163, Hitler told him: 'If the enemy can hold out for several years, I, with my power over the German people, can hold out one year longer'.

25 There is considerable debate on how many such 'stages' there were. Since there is general agreement that Hitler's policy involved some kind of primary imperialism to make possible the final war for wider dominion, I have concentrated on this broader strategic intention. It did not seem necessary to enter the discussion about

how many minor 'steps' each stage required. See M. Hauner, 'Did Hitler want a world dominion?', *Journal of Contemporary History*, XIII, 1978, 15-31; A. Hillgruber, *Hitlers Strategie. Politik und Kriegführung 1940-41*, Frankfurt, 1965; B. Stegemann, 'Hitlers Ziele im ersten Kriegsjahr 1939/40', *Militdräeschichtliche Mitteilungen*, XXII, 1980, 93-105.

26 Carr, *Arms*, pp. 72-80.

27 ibid. pp. 5-20; K. Hildebrand, 'La programme de Hitler et sa réalisation', *Revue d'histoire de la deuxième Guerre Mondiale*, XXI, 1971, pp. 7-36; F. Zipfel, 'Hitlers Konzept einer Neuordnung Europas', in D. Kurse (ed.) *Aus Theorie und Praxis des Geschichtswissenschaft*, Berlin, 1972, pp. 154-74; Rauschning, *Hitler Speaks*, pp. 126-37; A. Speer, *Spandau. The Secret Diaries*, 1976, p. 70, who recalls Hitler's remark: 'But I'll still have to lead the great clash with the U.S.A. If only I have time enough, there would be nothing finer for me than to stand at the head of my people in that decisive struggle as well'; Thies, *Architekt*, pp. 165-6, 187.

28 Bundesarchiv-Militärarchiv (hereafter BA-MA), RL3 234 'Industrielle Vorplanung bis 1.4.1945', 15 October 1940; IMT, XXXVII, Doc. 043-L 'Organisationstudie 1950' 2 May 1938; IMT, IX, p. 60, Milch cross-examination; R. J. Overy, 'The German pre-war aircraft production plans: Nov. 1936 - April 1939', *English Historical Review*, XC, 1975, pp. 779-83; Homze, *Arming*, pp. 242-50.

29 Hauner, 'World dominion', p. 27; Dülffer, 'Beginn des Krieges', pp. 467-8.

30 NCA, VI, p. 729, Doc. 3787-PS, Second Meeting of the Reich Defense Council, 10 July 1939.

31 Case XI, Körner Defence Doc. Book 1B, p. 140.

32 *Ciano's Papers*, p. 242, 'Conversation between the Duce and the Foreign Minister of the Reich, 28 October 1938'; *Documents on German Foreign Policy* (1956) Ser. D, VI, Doc. 211, 'Unsigned Memorandum, Discussion with Göring, 16 April 1939'.

33 Dahlerus, *Last Attempt*, p. 63: Hauner, 'World dominion', pp. 28-9.

34 Speer, *Inside the Reich*, p. 165.

35 Gisevius, *Bitter End*, pp. 361-2; Rauschning, *Hitler Speaks*, pp. 276-87, for a record of Hitler's increasing morbidity and isolation in 1939.

36 Case XI, Körner Defence Doc. Book 1B, p. 140, Fritsche Affidavit, 29.6.1948; pp. 155-6, Warlimont cross-examination; Gisevius, *Bitter End*, pp. 277-360; according to D. Orlow, *The History of the Nazi Party*, Newton Abbot, 1973, II, p. 263, the party itself had no indication that a general war might break out in 1939 and was taken by surprise.

37 W. Treue, 'Hitlers Denkschrift zum Vierjahresplan', *Vierteljahrshefte für Zeitgeschichte*, III, 1955, 184-210; D. Petzina, 'Vierjahresplan und Rüstungspolitik', in Forstmeier and Volkmann (eds) *Wirtschaft und Rüstung*, pp. 65-80.

38 R. Manvell and H. Fraenkel, *Göring*, pp. 154-65.

39 Case XI, Körner Defence Doc. Book 1B, p. 8, statement of Gauleiter Uiberreither, 27 February 1946; see also IMT, XXXVIII, p. 380, Doc. 140-R, Göring address to aircraft manufacturers, 8 July 1938, in which he called for the achievement of a long-term production of 'a colossal quantity' of aircraft.

40 IMT, XXVII, pp. 161-2, Doc. 1301-PS, 'Besprechung bei Göring, 14 Okt. 1938'.

41 Milch Documents (MD), Imperial War Museum, London, LXV, 7302-3, letter from General Brauchitsch, 6 May 1939.

42 MD, LXV, 7299, letter from Goering to Reich authorities, 7 December 1939.

43 Case XI, Prosecution Doc. Book 112, Doc. NI-090, minutes of meeting of iron industry and Four-Year Plan Office, 17 March 1937; Doc. NI-084, minutes of meeting held by Göring, 16 June 1937; Doc, NI-8590, Report from Loeb to Göring, 30

October 1937, 'Results of work done during the first year of the Four-Year Plan'; *Documents on German Foreign Policy*, Ser. D, IV p. 260, Doc. 211.

44 Case XI, Körner Defence Doc. Book 1B, p. 81, Halder cross-examination. See also Gisevius, *Bitter End*, p. 353; R. J. Overy, 'Hitler and air strategy', *Journal of Contemporary History*, XV, 1980, 407-8; W. Carr, *Hitler: A Study in Personality and Politics*, 1978, pp. 41-5.

45 W. Warlimont, *Inside Hitler's Headquarters*, 1964, pp. 17-23.

46 Carroll, *Design for War*, pp. 192-212.

47 Milward, *German Economy*, p. 23.

48 On the resistance of the car industry, see Overy, 'Transportation', pp. 404-5; on industry as a whole, see A. Schröter, J. Bach, 'Zur Planung der wehrwirtschaftlichen Mobilmachung durch den deutschen faschistischen Imperialismus vor dem Beginn des Zweiten Weltkrieges', *Jahrbuch für Wirtschaftsgeschichte*, Part 1, 1978, pp. 42-5. By May 1939 only 60 per cent of the mobilization plan could be accounted for by the existing industrial agreements.

49 Christie Papers, Churchill College, Cambridge; 180/125, letter from 'a senior German industrialist' to Christie, 7 July 1939; 'Memo by members of Big Business in Germany 1937, pp. 2-23; 'Rough notes of a recent conversation with a German industrialist, 1 June 1939'.

50 Riedel, *Kohle und Eisen*, pp. 167-78, on the Reichswerke; P. Kluke, 'Hitler und das Volkswagenprojekt', *Vierteljahreshefte für Zeitgeschichte*, VIII, 1960, pp. 376-9.

51 Carroll, *Design for War*, pp. 184-8.

52 IMT, XXXVI, p. 116, Doc. 028-EC, 'Vortrag gehalten vor General-major Thomas am 24 mai 1939 im Auswärtigen Amt'.

53 To some extent this is a statistical illusion. The percentage increase in British military expenditure was much greater than that of Germany in 1939-40 and 1940-1 because it was growing from a much smaller base. It is difficult, too, to compare like with like since the structure of state finances and the definition of military expenditure differed between the two countries.

54 M. Salewski, *Die deutsche Seekriegsleitung 1939-1945*, Frankfurt, 1970, I, pp. 58- 65.

55 ibid. 1, p. 59. The order was given on 29 January 1939 and was confirmed in May. See NCA, VII, p. 854.

56 French, British and Polish front-line air strength was marginally greater than German in quantity, though not in quality, in September 1939. See R. J. Overy, *The Air War, 1939-1945*, 1980, p. 23.

57 K-H. Völker, *Dokumente und Dokumentarfotos zur Geschichte der deutschen Luftwaffe*, Stuttgart, 1968, p. 211, 'Festlegung der Planungen zur Bergrösserung der Luftwaffe, 7.11.1938'; NCA, III, p. 901, Doc. 1301-PS, 'Conference at General Field Marshal Goering's, 14 October 1938'; R. Suchenwirth, *Historical Turning Points in the German Air Force War Effort*, New York, 1959, pp. 23-4.

58 M. M. Postan, *British War Production*, 1952, pp. 21, 66-8.

59 BA-MA RL3 159, 'Lieferprogramm Nr. 15, 1.9.1939'.

60 National Archives, Washington (NA) T 177, Roll 31, frame 3719681, 'Nachsuchubzahlen für Luftfahrtgerät, 1.4.1938'; MD, LXV, 7410-11, 'Vortragsunterlagen für den Vortrag vor dem Herrn Generalfeldmarschall, 13 Dez. 1938'.

61 For example the Heinkel works at Oranienberg, the Messerschmitt works at Wiener-Neustadt, and the large new investments in the Junkers aeroengine and aircraft factories. Details on state investment can be found in BA-MA RL3 46, Chart 1 'Investitionen; Zellenbau'; Chart 2, 'Investitionen; Motorenbau'.

62 MD, LXV, 7429 'Besprechung in Berlin, 29.11.1938'; LI, 451, letter from Milch to Göring on the Volkswagen factories, 21 September 1938.

63 K. Lachmann, 'The Hermann Göring Works', *Social Research*, VIII, 1941, pp. 35–8; on Austria see NA T 83, Roll 74, frames 3445159-77, I. G. Farben volkswirtschaftliche Abteilung, 'Konzernaufbau und Entwicklung der Reichswerke AG Hermann Göring, 19 October 1939; on Rheinmetall-Borsig see NA T 83, Roll 74, frames 3445356-60.

64 NA T 83, Roll 75, Frame 3445754, Pleiger to heads of firms in Reichswerke organization, 29 April 1942; frames 3445997-8, Göring to Gritzbach, 23 March 1942; T 83, Roll 74, frames 3445207-10, 'Gründung und Wachsen der Hermann Göring Werke 1937-1942'.

65 Speer Collection, Imperial War Museum, London, Reichswerke documents, FD 264/46 'HGW Konzern-Verzeichnis, 15.8.1944'. The Reichswerke alone cost 400 million marks, 93 per cent from state sources. Although many of the factories were set up outside the old Reich, much of the money had to be found from Reich sources.

66 Carroll, *Design for War*, pp. 162–4; NA T 177, Roll 3, frame 3684363, Thomas to heads of services 'betr. wehrwirtschaftliche Räumung, 29 Sept. 1939'; frame 3684308, Göring to all Reich authorities, 24 September 1939; B. Mueller–Hillebrand, *Die Blitzfeldzüge 1939-4*, Frankfurt, 1956, pp. 23–39 on the work of the army.

67 BA-MA RL3 20, letter from Göring to Ley, 15 Sept. 1939; MD LI, 451, letter from Milch to Göring, 21 September 1938. On the difficulties of establishing production there see BA-MA RL3 247, report of a meeting at Junkers, Dessau, 17 October 1939; Speer Collection FD 969/45, Bayersiche Motorenwerke 'Ablauf der Lieferungen seit Kriegsbeginn', p. 5: On Göring's determination to convert all or any firms see NCA III, pp. 901–4, Doc. 1301-PS.

68 MD LXV, 7285, report of a conference with Göring, 9 February 1940; T. Mason, *Arbeiterklasse und Volksgemeinschaft*, Opladen, 1975, p. 1044, Doc. 174, 'Rede Görings in dem Rheinmetall-Borsig-Werke, Berlin am 9 Sept. 1939', in which he said 'In as far as we don't have the production facilities they will be created through conversion, expansion and new construction'.

69 NA T 83, Roll 5, frame 3745418, letter from Admiral Lahs to all aircraft firms, 10 October 1939.

70 Case XI, Prosecution Doc. Book 112, p. 301, Doc. NID-13844, lecture given by State Secretary Neumann at the Verwaltungsakademie, 29 April 1941.

71 Milward, *German Economy*, p. 29.

72 Carroll, *Design for War*, pp. 264–5.

73 United States Strategic Bombing Survey (USSBS), Report 77 *German Motor Vehicles Industry Report*, p. 8.

74 Number of housing units from R. Wagenführ, *Die Deutsche Industrie im Kriege*, Berlin, 1963, pp. 37, 56; volume of construction from Klein, *German Preparations*, p. 105. By 1942, 80 per cent of all construction was for military or industrial purposes.

75 K.A. Murray, *Agriculture*, 1955, p. 375. British grain production increased from 4.6 million tons in 1939 to 8.2 in 1944; potatoes from 5.2 million tons in 1939 to 9.8 in 1943; vegetables from 2.3 million tons in 1939 to 3.4 in 1943. There seems little remarkable about the German economy, better endowed with agricultural potential than Britain, increasing its domestic food production, much of it destined for the well-fed armed forces. It should be noticed that in those areas where the

German agricultural economy was weakest – dairy products, fats, oils – production dropped sharply. Milk output fell by a third between 1938/9 and 1939/40; vegetable oils by the same amount.

76 Case XI, Prosecution Doc. Book 112, pp. 296-7, Neumann lecture; see the discussion in W. Williams, *Riddle of the Reich*, 1941, pp. 10-14.

77 Wagenführ, *Deutsche Industrie*, p. 174.

78 One feature of the 'survival' of consumer goods industries was Hitler's insistence that cosmetics, stockings, etc. should still be produced to keep up home morale. But cigarettes, for which there was a large domestic demand, were heavily restricted and of poor quality. In 1941 a heavy tax was placed on tobacco, and women were restricted to a ration half that of men (1½ cigarettes a day). See L. Lochner, *What about Germany?*, 1943, pp. 144-5.

79 M. Steinert, *Hitler's War and the Germans*, Ohio UP, 1977, pp. 53, 64-5, 92-3; Lochner, *What about Germany?*, pp. 142-5, who wrote that both before and after 1939 'the simplest articles of daily life were lacking . . . Things made of leather, rubber, metal, wool or cotton were almost non-existent'; NCA VI, p. 723, Doc. 3787-PS, 'Second Meeting of the Reich Defense Council, 10 July 1939', on the intention to take resources away from 'the vital industries which are of importance to the life of the people'.

80 Case XI, Prosecution Document Book 112, pp. 293-4, Doc. NID-13844, Neumann lecture.

81 Milward, *German Economy*, p. 32; Milward, 'Der Einfluss', p. 195.

82 R. J. Overy, 'German aircraft production, 1939-42', unpublished Ph.D. thesis, University of Cambridge, 1978, pp. 23-32.

83 Klein, *German Preparations*, p. 161; Carroll, *Design for War*, pp. 154-5; Warlimont, *Hitler's Headquarters*, pp. 8-9.

84 On rearmament totals see BA R2 21776-81, Reichsfinanzministerium, Abteilung I, 'Entwicklung der Ausgaben in den Rechnungsjahren 1934-9', 17 July 1939. Rearmament from 1933/4 to 1935/6 averaged 3.445 milliard marks per year, including the *Mefowechseln*.

85 On the cost of the fortifications, see Dülffer, 'Beginn des Krieges', p. 457. On German arms finance, see A. Schweitzer, 'Profits under Nazi Planning', *Quarterly Journal of Economics*, LXI, 1946, pp. 9-18.

86 Military expenditure had to cover investment in industry, military installations, airfields, as well as military mobilization preparations over the Rhineland crisis, the Anschluss and the Munich crisis.

87 Wagenführ, *Deutsche Industrie*, p. 34; R. J. Overy, 'Die Mobilisierung der britischen Wirtschaft während des Zweiten Weltkrieges', in F. Forstmeier and H. E. Volkmann (eds) *Kriegswirtschaft und Rüstung im Zweiten Weltkrieg*, Düsseldorf, 1977, p. 289.

88 Overy, 'Air Strategy', pp. 406, 415-16; F. H. Hinsley, *Hitler's Strategy*, Cambridge, 1951, pp. 1-4.

89 D. Kahn, *Hitler's Spies*, 1979, pp. 386-7; on the misrepresentation of the strength of the Luftwaffe, see D. Irving, *The Rise and Fall of the Luftwaffe*, 1973, pp. 65-8; R. Suchenwirth, *Command and Leadership in the German Air Force*, New York, 1969, pp. 75-81.

90 Irving, *Rise and Fall*, pp. 73-4, 155-6.

91 Homze, *Arming*, p. 244; W. Schwabedissen, *The Russian Air Force in the Eyes of German Commanders*, New York, 1960, pp. 48-51.

92 Speer, *Inside the Reich*, pp. 252-66.

93 A. E. Simpson, 'The struggle for control of the German economy, 1936-1937', *Journal of Modern History*, XXI, 1959, pp. 37-45; H. Schacht, 76 *Jahre meines Lebens*, Bad Wörishofen, 1953, pp. 461-74.

94 Case XI, Prosecution Doc. Book 112, pp. 283-8, Neumann lecture, MD LXV, 7299, letter from Göring to all Reich Authorities, 7 December 1939.

95 Carroll, *Design for War*, chs vii-viii.

96 Speer, *Diaries*, p. 63.

97 Overy, 'German aircraft production', pp. 170-88.

98 In particular the struggle over the whole question of state ownership. See Christie Papers, 180/1 25, 'Die deutsche Staatswirtschaft'. On the Reichswerke and state ownership see NA T 83, Roll 74, frames 3445207-10, 'Gründung und Wachsen der Hermann Göring Werke 1937-42'; Case XI, Prosecution Doc. Book 112, p. 149, Doc. NID-13797, Körner to Schwerin-Krosigk, 7 October 1940.

99 Overy, 'German aircraft production', pp. 159-61.

100 NA T 177, Roll 14, frames 3698887-916, General Bauer 'Rationalisierung der Luftwaffengerät-Fertigung, 1.6.1941'; Roll 12, frames 3695910-12, General Bauer 'Fertigungsvorbereitung, 1935'; Roll 3, frames 3684551-4, 'Klein- und Mittelbetrieb oder Grossbetrieb, GL Report, 24 April 1939.

101 For aircraft production this process began early in 1941 with the establishment of an *Industrierat*. See MD LIV, 1555; D. Eichholtz (ed.) *Anatomie des Krieges*, Berlin, 1969, p. 331, Doc. 161.

102 Schröter, Bach, 'Zur Planung der Mobilmachung', pp. 45-7; A. Bagel-Bohlan, *Hitlers industrielle Kriegsvorbereitung 1936 bis 1939*, Koblenz, 1975, pp. 137-8.

103 Overy, *Air War*, pp. 179-80.

104 Opel claimed for example that when the firm began military production output per man-hour dropped 40 per cent compared with peace-time output. See British Intelligence Objectives Sub-Committee, Final Report 537, p. 7. On the poor utilization of the car industry as a whole, see USSBS Report 77, pp. 5-11.

105 By contrast in 1941 some 50 per cent more labour was diverted to aircraft production but only a 5 per cent increase in aircraft output was achieved. See USSBS, European Report 4, Chart VI-11; USSBS, Report 20, *Light Metal Industry of Germany* (Part I), p. 17a; Irving, *Rise and Fall*, p. 167; Speer Collection, IWM/FDC9, Zentrale Planung, p. 789.

106 Overy, 'Hitler and air strategy', p. 407.

One Day in Józefów: Initiation to Mass Murder

CHRISTOPHER BROWNING

In mid-March of 1942, some 75 to 80 per cent of all victims of the Holocaust were still alive, while some 20 to 25 per cent had already perished. A mere eleven months later, in mid-February 1943, the situation was exactly the reverse. Some 75 to 80 per cent of all Holocaust victims were already dead, and a mere 20 to 25 per cent still clung to a precarious existence. At the core of the Holocaust was an intense eleven-month wave of mass murder. The center of gravity of this mass murder was Poland, where in March 1942, despite two and a half years of terrible hardship, deprivation, and persecution, every major Jewish community was still intact; eleven months later, only remnants of Polish Jewry survived in a few rump ghettos and labor camps. In short, the German attack on the Polish ghettos was not a gradual or incremental program stretched over a long period of time, but a veritable blitzkrieg, a massive offensive requiring the mobilization of large numbers of shock troops at the very period when the German war effort in Russia hung in the balance.

The first question I would like to pose, therefore, is what were the manpower sources the Germans tapped for their assault on Polish Jewry? Since the personnel of the death camps was quite minimal, the real question quite

This study is based entirely on the judicial records in the Staatsanwaltschaft Hamburg that resulted from two investigations of Reserve Police Battalion 101: 141 Js 1957/62 and 141 Js 128/65. German laws and regulations for the protection of privacy prohibit the revealing of names from such court records. Thus, with the exception of Major Trapp, who was tried, convicted, and executed in Poland after the war, I have chosen simply to refer to individuals generically by rank and unit rather than by pseudonyms.

simply is who were the ghetto-clearers? On close examination one discovers that the Nazi regime diverted almost nothing in terms of real military resources for this offensive against the ghettos. The local German authorities in Poland, above all SS and Police Leader (SSPF) Odilo Globocnik, were given the task but not the men to carry it out. They had to improvise by creating ad hoc 'private armies.' Co-ordination and guidance of the ghetto-clearing was provided by the staffs of the SSPF and commander of the security police in each district in Poland. Security Police and Gendarmerie in the branch offices in each district provided local expertise.[1] But the bulk of the manpower had to be recruited from two sources. The first source was the Ukrainians, Lithuanians, and Latvians recruited out of the prisoner of war camps and trained at the SS camp in Trawniki. A few hundred of these men, among them Ivan Demjanjuk, were then sent to the death camps of Operation Reinhard, where they outnumbered the German staff roughly 4 to 1. The majority, however, were organized into mobile units and became itinerant ghetto-clearers, traveling out from Trawniki to one ghetto after another and returning to their base camp between operations.[2]

The second major source of manpower for the ghetto-clearing operations was the numerous battalions of Order Police (*Ordnungspolizei*) stationed in the General Government. In 1936, when Himmler gained centralized control over all German police, the Secret State Police (Gestapo) and Criminal Police (Kripo) were consolidated under the Security Police Main Office of Reinhard Heydrich. The German equivalent of the city police (*Schutzpolizei*) and county sheriffs (*Gendarmerie*) were consolidated under the Order Police Main Office of Kurt Daluege. The Order Police were far more numerous than the more notorious Security Police and encompassed not only the regular policemen distributed among various urban and rural police stations in Germany, but also large battalion-size units, which were stationed in barracks and were given some military training. As with National Guard units in the United States, these battalions were organized regionally. As war approached in 1938–39, many young Germans volunteered for the Order Police in order to avoid being drafted into the regular army.

Beginning in September 1939, the Order Police battalions, each of approximately five hundred men, were rotated out from their home cities on tours of duty in the occupied territories. As the German empire expanded and the demand for occupation forces increased, the Order Police was vastly expanded by creating new reserve police battalions. The career police and prewar volunteers of the old battalions were distributed to become the non-commissioned officer cadres of these new reserve units, whose rank and file were now composed of civilian draftees considered too old by the Wehrmacht for frontline military service.

One such unit, Reserve Police Battalion 101 from Hamburg, was one of three police battalions stationed in the district of Lublin during the onslaught against the Polish ghettos. Because no fewer than 210 former members of this battalion were interrogated during more than a decade of judicial investigation and trials in the 1960s and early 1970s, we know a great deal about its composition. First let us examine the officer and noncommissioned officer (NCO) cadres.

The battalion was commanded by Major Wilhelm Trapp, a fifty-three-year-old career policeman who had risen through the ranks and was affectionately referred to by his men as 'Papa Trapp.' Though he had joined the Nazi Party in December 1932, he had never been taken into the SS or even given an SS-equivalent rank. He was clearly not considered SS material. His two captains, in contrast, were young men in their late twenties, both party members and SS officers. Even in their testimony twenty-five years later they made no attempt to conceal their contempt for their commander as both weak and unmilitary. Little is known about the first lieutenant who was Trapp's adjutant, for he died in the spring of 1943. In addition, however, the battalion had seven reserve lieutenants, that is men who were not career policeman but who, after they were drafted into the Order Police, had been selected to receive officer training because of their middle-class status, education, and success in civilian life. Their ages ranged from 33 to 48; five were party members, but none belonged to the SS. Of the 32 NCOs on whom we have information, 22 were party members but only seven were in the SS. They ranged in age from 27 to 40 years old; their average was 33½.

The vast majority of the rank and file had been born and reared in Hamburg and its environs. The Hamburg element was so dominant and the ethos of the battalion so provincial that contingents from nearby Wilhelmshaven and Schleswig-Holstein were considered outsiders. Over 60 per cent were of working-class background, but few of them were skilled laborers. The majority of them held typical Hamburg working-class jobs: dock workers and truck drivers were most numerous, but there were also many warehouse and construction workers, machine operators, seamen and waiters. About 35 per cent were lower-middle class, virtually all of whom were white-collar workers. Three-quarters of them were in sales of some sort; the other one-quarter performed various office jobs, both in the government and private sectors. The number of independent artisans, such as tailors and watch makers was small; and there were only three middle-class professionals – two druggists and one teacher. The average age of the men was 39; over half were between 37 and 42, the *Jahrgänge* most intensively drafted for police duty after September 1939.

The men of Reserve Police Battalion 101 were from the lower orders of German society. They had experienced neither social nor geographic mobility. Very few were economically independent. Except for apprenticeship or vocational training, virtually none had any education after leaving school at age 14 or 15. About 25 per cent were Nazi Party members in 1942, most having joined in 1937 or later. Though not questioned about their pre-1933 political affiliation during their interrogations, presumably many had been Communists, Socialists, and labor union members before 1933. By virtue of their age, of course, all went through their formative period in the pre-Nazi era. These were men who had known political standards and moral norms other than those of the Nazis. Most came from Hamburg, one of the least

Nazified cities in Germany, and the majority came from a social class that in its political culture had been anti-Nazi.

These men would not seem to have been a very promising group from which to recruit mass murderers of the Holocaust. Yet this unit was to be extraordinarily active both in clearing ghettos and in massacring Jews outright during the blitzkrieg against Polish Jewry. If these middle-aged reserve policemen became one major component of the murderers, the second question posed is how? Specifically, what happened when they were first assigned to kill Jews? What choices did they have, and how did they react?

Reserve Police Battalion 101 departed from Hamburg on June 20, 1942, and was initially stationed in the town of Bilgoraj, fifty miles south of Lublin. Around July 11 it received orders for its first major action, aimed against the approximately 1,800 Jews living in the village of Józefów, about twenty miles slightly south and to the east of Bilgoraj. In the General Government a seventeen-day stoppage of Jewish transports due to a shortage of rolling stock had just ended, but the only such trains that had been resumed were several per week from the district of Cracow to Belzec. The railway line to Sobibor was down, and that camp had become practically inaccessible. In short the Final Solution in the Lublin district had been paralyzed, and Globocnik was obviously anxious to resume the killing. But Józefów could not be a deportation action. Therefore the battalion was to select out the young male Jews in Józefów and send them to a work camp in Lublin. The remaining Jews – about 1,500 women, children, and elderly – were simply to be shot on the spot.

On July 12 Major Trapp summoned his officers and explained the next day's assignment. One officer, a reserve lieutenant in 1st company and owner of a family lumber business in Hamburg, approached the major's adjutant, indicated his inability to take part in such an action in which unarmed women and children were to be shot, and asked for a different assignment. He was given the task of accompanying the work Jews to Lublin.[3] The men were not as yet informed of their imminent assignment, though the 1st company captain at least confided to some of his men that the battalion had an 'extremely interesting task' (*hochinteressante Aufgabe*) the next day.[4]

Around 2 a.m. the men climbed aboard waiting trucks, and the battalion drove for about an hour and a half over an unpaved road to Józefów. Just as daylight was breaking, the men arrived at the village and assembled in a half-circle around Major Trapp, who proceeded to give a short speech. With choking voice and tears in his eyes, he visibly fought to control himself as he informed his men that they had received orders to perform a very unpleasant task. These orders were not to his liking, either, but they came from above. It might perhaps make their task easier, he told the men, if they remembered that in Germany bombs were falling on the women and children. Two witnesses claimed that Trapp also mentioned that the Jews of this village had supported the partisans. Another witness recalled Trapp's mentioning that the Jews had instigated the boycott against Germany.[5] Trapp then explained to the men that the Jews in the village of Józefów would have to be rounded up, whereupon the young males were to be selected out for labor and the others shot.

Trapp then made an extraordinary offer to his battalion: if any of the older men among them did not feel up to the task that lay before him, he could step out. Trapp paused, and after some moments, one man stepped forward. The captain of 3rd company, enraged that one of his men had broken ranks, began to berate the man. The major told the captain to hold his tongue. Then ten or twelve other men stepped forward as well. They turned in their rifles and were told to await a further assignment from the major.[6]

Trapp then summoned the company commanders and gave them their respective assignments. Two platoons of 3rd company were to surround the village; the men were explicitly ordered to shoot anyone trying to escape. The remaining men were to round up the Jews and take them to the market place. Those too sick or frail to walk to the market place, as well as infants and anyone offering resistance or attempting to hide, were to be shot on the spot. Thereafter, a few men of 1st company were to accompany the work Jews selected at the market place, while the rest were to proceed to the forest to form the firing squads. The Jews were to be loaded onto battalion trucks by 2nd company and shuttled from the market place to the forest.

Having given the company commanders their respective assignments, Trapp spent the rest of the day in town, mostly in a school room converted into his headquarters but also at the homes of the Polish mayor and the local priest. Witnesses who saw him at various times during the day described him as bitterly complaining about the orders he had been given and 'weeping like a child.' He nevertheless affirmed that 'orders were orders' and had to be carried out.[7] Not a single witness recalled seeing him at the shooting site, a fact that was not lost upon the men, who felt some anger about it.[8] Trapp's driver remembers him saying later, 'If this Jewish business is ever avenged on earth, then have mercy on us Germans.' (Wenn sich diese Judensache einmal auf Erden rächt, dann gnade uns Deutschen.)[9]

After the company commanders had relayed orders to the men, those assigned to the village broke up into small groups and began to comb the Jewish quarter. The air was soon filled with cries, and shots rang out. The market place filled rapidly with Jews, including mothers with infants. While the men of Reserve Police Battalion 101 were apparently willing to shoot those Jews too weak or sick to move, they still shied for the most part from shooting infants, despite their orders.[10] No officer intervened, though subsequently one officer warned his men that in the future they would have to be more energetic.[11]

As the roundup neared completion, the men of 1st company were withdrawn from the search and given a quick lesson in the gruesome task that awaited them by the battalion doctor and the company's first sergeant. The doctor traced the outline of a human figure on the ground and showed the men how to use a fixed bayonet placed between and just above the shoulder blades as a guide for aiming their carbines.[12] Several men now approached the 1st company captain and asked to be given a different assignment; he curtly refused.[13] Several others who approached the first sergeant rather than the captain fared better. They were given guard duty along the route from the village to the forest.[14]

The first sergeant organized his men into two groups of about thirty-five men, which was roughly equivalent to the number of Jews who could be loaded into each truck. In turn each squad met an arriving truck at the unloading point on the edge of the forest. The individual squad members paired off *face-to-face* with the individual Jews they were to shoot, and marched their victims into the forest. The first sergeant remained in the forest to supervise the shooting. The Jews were forced to lie face down in a row. The policemen stepped up behind them, and on a signal from the first sergeant fired their carbines at point-blank range into the necks of their victims. The first sergeant then moved a few yards deeper into the forest to supervise the next execution. So-called 'mercy shots' were given by a non-commissioned officer, as many of the men, some out of excitement and some intentionally, shot past their victims.[15] By mid-day alcohol had appeared from somewhere to 'refresh' the shooters.[16] Also around mid-day the first sergeant relieved the older men, after several had come to him and asked to be let out.[17] The other men of 1st company, however, continued shooting throughout the day.

Meanwhile the Jews in the market place were being guarded by the men of 2nd company, who loaded the victims onto the trucks. When the first salvo was heard from the woods, a terrible cry swept the market place, as the collected Jews now knew their fate.[18] Thereafter, however, a quiet – indeed 'unbelievable' – composure settled over the Jews, which the German policemen found equally unnerving. By mid-morning the officers in the market place became increasingly agitated. At the present rate, the executions would never be completed by nightfall. The 3rd company was called in from its outposts around the village to take over close guard of the market place. The men of 2nd company were informed that they too must now go to the woods to join the shooters.[19] At least one sergeant once again offered his men the opportunity to report if they did not feel up to it. No one took up his offer.[20] In another unit, one policeman confessed to his lieutenant that he was 'very weak' and could not shoot. He was released.[21]

In the forest 2nd company was divided into small groups of six to eight men rather than the larger squads of thirty-five as in 1st company. In the confusion of the small groups coming and going from the unloading point, several men managed to stay around the trucks looking busy and thus avoided shooting. One was noticed by his comrades, who swore at him for shirking, but he ignored them.[22] Among those who began shooting, some could not last long. One man shot an old woman on his first round, after which his nerves were finished and he could not continue.[23] Another discovered to his dismay that his second victim was a German Jew – a mother from Kassel with her daughter. He too then asked out.[24] This encounter with a German Jew was not exceptional. Several other men also remembered Hamburg and Bremen Jews in Józefów.[25] It was a grotesque irony that some of the men of

Reserve Police Battalion 101 had guarded the collection center in Hamburg, the confiscated freemason lodge house on the Moorweide next to the university library, from which the Hamburg Jews had been deported the previous fall. A few had even guarded the deportation transports to Lodz, Riga, and Minsk. These Hamburg policemen had now followed other Jews deported from northern Germany, in order to shoot them in southern Poland.

A third policeman was in such an agitated state that on his first shot he aimed too high. He shot off the top of the head of his victim, splattering brains into the face of his sergeant. His request to be relieved was granted.[26] One policeman made it to the fourth round, when his nerves gave way. He shot past his victim, then turned and ran deep into the forest and vomited. After several hours he returned to the trucks and rode back to the market place.[27]

As had happened with 1st company, bottles of vodka appeared at the unloading point and were passed around.[28] There was much demand, for among 2nd company, shooting instructions had been less explicit and initially bayonets had not been fixed as an aiming guide. The result was that many of the men did not give neck shots but fired directly into the heads of their victims at point-blank range. The victims' heads exploded, and in no time the policemen's uniforms were saturated with blood and splattered with brains and splinters of bone. When several officers noted that some of their men could no longer continue or had begun intentionally to fire past their victims, they excused them from the firing squads.[29]

Though a fairly significant number of men in Reserve Police Battalion 101 either did not shoot at all or started but could not continue shooting, most persevered to the end and lost all count of how many Jews they had killed that day. The forest was so filled with bodies that it became difficult to find places to make the Jews lie down. When the action was finally over at dusk, and some 1,500 Jews lay dead, the men climbed into their trucks and returned to Bilgoraj. Extra rations of alcohol were provided, and the men talked little, ate almost nothing, but drank a great deal. That night one of them awoke from a nightmare firing his gun into the ceiling of the barracks.[30]

Following the massacre at Józefów, Reserve Police Battalion 101 was transferred to the northern part of the Lublin district. The various platoons of the battalion were stationed in different towns but brought together for company-size actions. Each company was engaged in at least one more shooting action, but more often the Jews were driven from the ghettos onto trains bound for the extermination camp of Treblinka. Usually one police company worked in conjunction with a Trawniki unit for each action. The 'dirty work' – driving the Jews out of their dwellings with whips, clubs, and guns; shooting on the spot the frail, sick, elderly, and infants who could not march to the train station; and packing the train cars to the bursting point so that only with the greatest of effort could the doors even be closed – was usually left to the so-called 'Hiwis' (*Hilfswilligen* or 'volunteers') from Trawniki.

Once a ghetto had been entirely cleared, it was the responsibility of the men of Reserve Police Battalion 101 to keep the surrounding region '*judenfrei.*'

Through a network of Polish informers and frequent search patrols – casually referred to as *Judenjagden* or 'Jew hunts' – the policemen remorselessly tracked down those Jews who had evaded the roundups and fled to the forests. Any Jew found in these circumstances was simply shot on the spot. By the end of the year there was scarcely a Jew alive in the northern Lublin district, and Reserve Police Battalion 101 increasingly turned its attention from murdering Jews to combating partisans.

In looking at the half-year after Józefów, one sees that this massacre drew an important dividing line. Those men who stayed with the assignment and shot all day found the subsequent actions much easier to perform. Most of the men were bitter about what they had been asked to do at Józefów, and it became taboo even to speak of it. Even twenty-five years later they could not hide the horror of endlessly shooting Jews at point-blank range. In contrast, however, they spoke of surrounding ghettos and watching the Hiwis brutally drive the Jews onto the death trains with considerable detachment and a near-total absence of any sense of participation or responsibility. Such actions they routinely dismissed with a standard refrain: 'I was *only* in the police cordon there.' The shock treatment of Józefów had created an effective and desensitized unit of ghetto-clearers and, when the occasion required, outright murderers. After Józefów nothing else seemed so terrible. Heavy drinking also contributed to numbing the men's sensibilities. One non-drinking policeman noted that 'most of the other men drank so much solely because of the many shootings of Jews, for such a life was quite intolerable sober' (die meisten der anderen Kameraden lediglich auf Grund der vielen Judenerschiessungen soviel getrunken haben, da ein derartiges Leben nüchtern gar nicht zu ertragen war).[31]

Among those who either chose not to shoot at Józefów or proved 'too weak' to carry on and made no subsequent attempt to rectify this image of 'weakness,' a different trend developed. If they wished they were for the most part left alone and excluded from further killing actions, especially the frequent 'Jew hunts.' The consequences of their holding aloof from the mass murder were not grave. The reserve lieutenant of 1st company who had protested against being involved in the Józefów shooting and been allowed to accompany the work Jews to Lublin subsequently went to Major Trapp and declared that in the future he would not take part in any *Aktion* unless explicitly ordered. He made no attempt to hide his aversion to what the battalion was doing, and his attitude was known to almost everyone in the company.[32] He also wrote to Hamburg and requested that he be recalled from the General Government because he did not agree with the 'non-police' functions being performed by the battalion there. Major Trapp not only avoided any confrontation but protected him. Orders involving actions against the Jews were simply passed from battalion or company headquarters to his deputy. He was, in current terminology, 'left out of the loop.' In November 1942 he was recalled to Hamburg, made adjutant to the Police President of that city, and subsequently promoted![33]

The man who had first stepped out at Józefów was sent on almost every partisan action but not on the 'Jew hunts.' He suspected that this pattern resulted from his earlier behavior in Józefów.[34] Another man who had not joined the shooters at Józefów was given excessive tours of guard duty and other unpleasant assignments and was not promoted. But he was not assigned to the 'Jew hunts' and firing squads, because the officers wanted only 'men' with them and in their eyes he was 'no man.' Others who felt as he did received the same treatment, he said.[35] Such men could not, however, always protect themselves against officers out to get them. One man was assigned to a firing squad by a vengeful officer precisely because he had not yet been involved in a shooting.[36]

The experience of Reserve Police Battalion 101 poses disturbing questions to those concerned with the lessons and legacies of the Holocaust. Previous explanations for the behavior of the perpetrators, especially those at the lowest level who came face-to-face with the Jews they killed, seem inadequate. Above all the perpetrators themselves have constantly cited inescapable orders to account for their behavior. In Józefów, however, the men had the opportunity both before and during the shooting to withdraw. The battalion in general was under orders to kill the Jews of Józefów, but each individual man was not.

Special selection, indoctrination, and ideological motivation are equally unsatisfying as explanations. The men of Reserve Police Battalion 101 were certainly not a group carefully selected for their suitability as mass murderers, nor were they given special training and indoctrination for the task that awaited them. They were mainly apolitical, and even the officers were only partly hard-core Nazi. Major Trapp in particular made no secret of his disagreement with the battalion's orders, and by Nazi standards he displayed shameful weakness in the way he carried them out. Among the men who did the killing there was much bitterness about what they had been asked to do and sufficient discomfort that no one wished to talk about it thereafter. They certainly did not take pride in achieving some historic mission.

While many murderous contributions to the Final Solution – especially those of the desk murderers – can be explained as routinized, depersonalized, segmented, and incremental, thus vitiating any sense of personal responsibility, that was clearly not the case in Józefów, where the killers confronted the reality of their actions in the starkest way. Finally, the men of Reserve Police Battalion 101 were not from a generation that had been reared and educated solely under the Nazi regime and thus had no other political norms or standards by which to measure their behavior. They were older; many were married family men; and many came from a social and political background that would have exposed them to anti-Nazi sentiments before 1933.

What lessons, then, can one draw from the testimony given by the perpetrators of the massacre of the Jews in Józefów? Nothing is more elusive in this testimony than the consciousness of the men that morning of July 13, 1942, and above all their attitude toward Jews at the time. Most simply denied that they had had any choice. Faced with the testimony of others, they did not contest that Trapp had made the offer but repeatedly claimed that they had not heard that part of his speech or could not remember it. A few who admitted that they had been given the choice and yet failed to opt out were quite blunt. One said that he had not wanted to be considered a coward by his comrades.[37] Another – more aware of what truly required courage – said quite simply: 'I was cowardly.'[38] A few others also made the attempt to confront the question of choice but failed to find the words. It was a different time and place, as if they had been on another political planet, and the political vocabulary and values of the 1960s were helpless to explain the situation in which they had found themselves in 1942. As one man admitted, it was not until years later that he began to consider that what he had done had not been right. He had not given it a thought at the time.[39]

Several men who chose not to take part were more specific about their motives. One said that he accepted the possible disadvantages of his course of action 'because I was not a career policeman and also did not want to become one, but rather an independent skilled craftsman, and I had my business back home . . . thus it was of no consequence that my police career would not prosper' (denn ich war kein aktiver Polizist und wollte auch keiner werden, sondern selbstständiger Handwerksmeister und ich hatte zu Hause meinen Beittieb . . . deshalb macht es mir nichts aus, dass mein Karriere keinen Aufstieg haben würde).[40] The reserve lieutenant of 1st company placed a similar emphasis on the importance of economic independence when explaining why his situation was not analogous to that of the two SS captains on trial. 'I was somewhat older then and moreover a reserve officer, so it was not particularly important to me to be promoted or otherwise to advance, because I had my prosperous business back home. The company chiefs . . . on the other hand were young men and career policemen, who wanted to become something. Through my business experience, especially because it extended abroad, I had gained a better overview of things.' He alone then broached the most taboo subject of all: 'Moreover through my earlier business activities I already knew many Jews.' (Ich war damals etwas älter und ausserdem Reserveoffizier, mir kam es insbesondere nicht darauf an, befördert zu werden oder sonstwie weiterzukommen, denn ich hatte ja zuhause mein gutgehendes Geschäft. Die Kompaniechefs . . . dagegen waren junge Leute vom aktiven Dienst, die noch etwas werden wollten. Ich hatte durch meine kaufmännische Tätigkeit, die sich insbesondere auch auf das Ausland erstreckte, einen besseren Überlick über die Dinge. Ausserdem kannte ich schon durch meine geschäftliche Tätigkeit von frühen viele Juden.)[41]

Crushing conformity and blind, unthinking acceptance of the political norms of the time on the one hand, careerism on the other – these emerge as the factors that at least some of the men of Reserve Police Battalion 101 were able to discuss twenty-five years later. What remained virtually unexamined by the interrogators and unmentioned by the policemen was the role of anti-Semitism. Did they not speak of it because anti-Semitism had not been a motivating factor? Or were they unwilling and unable to confront this issue even after twenty-five years, because it had been all too important, all too pervasive? One is tempted to wonder if the silence speaks louder than words, but in the end – the silence is still silence, and the question remains unanswered.

Was the incident at Józefów typical? Certainly not. I know of no other case in which a commander so openly invited and sanctioned the nonparticipation of his men in a killing action. But in the end the most important fact is not that the experience of Reserve Police Battalion 101 was untypical, but rather that Trapp's extraordinary offer did not matter. Like any other unit, Reserve Police Battalion 101 killed the Jews they had been told to kill.

Notes

1 For ghetto-clearing in the various districts of the General Government, the following are the most important judicial sources. For Lublin: Staatsanwaltschaft Hamburg 147 Js 24/72 (indictment of Georg Michalson) and StA Wiesbaden 8 Js 1145/60 (indictment of Lothar Hoffmann and Hermann Worthoff); for Warsaw, StA Hamburg 147 Js 16/69 (indictment of Ludwig Hahn); for Cracow, Landgericht Kiel 2 Ks 6/63 (judgment against Martin Fellenz); for Radom, StA Hamburg 147 Js 38/65 (indictment of Hermann Weinrauch and Paul Fuchs); for Bialystok, StA Dortmund 45 Js 1/61 (indictment of Herbert Zimmermann and Wilhelm Altenloh), and *Documents Concerning the Destruction of Grodno*, ed. Serge Klarsfeld (Publications of the Beate Klarsfeld Foundation); for Galicia, LG Münster 5 Ks 4/65 (judgment against Hans Krüger), and LG Stuttgart Ks 5/65 (judgment against Rudolf Röder).

2 For the Trawniki units, see StA Hamburg 147 Js 43/69 (indictment of Karl Streibel).

3 StA Hamburg 141 Js 1957/62 gegen H. and W. u.a. (thereafter cited as HW), 820–21, 2437, 4414–15.

4 HW, 2091.

5 HW, 1952, 2039, 2655–56.

6 HW, 1953–54, 2041–42, 3298, 4576–77, 4589.

7 HW, 1852, 2182: StA Hamburg 141 Js 128/65 gegen G. u.a. (thereafter cited as G), 363, 383.

8 G, 645–52.

9 HW, 1741–43.

10 HW, 2618, 2717, 2742.

11 HW, 1947.

12 G, 504–14, 642, 647.

13 HW, 2092.

14 HW, 1648: G, 453.

15 G, 647.

16 G, 624, 659.

17 HW, 2093, 2236.

18 HW, 1686, 2659.

19 HW, 2717–18.

20 HW, 1640, 2505.

21 HW, 1336, 3542.

22 G, 168–69, 206–7.

23 G, 230.

24 HW, 2635.

25 HW, 1540, 2534, 2951, 4579.
26 G, 277.
27 HW, 2483.
28 HW, 2621, 2635, 2694.
29 HW, 1640, 2149, 2505, 2540, 2692, 2720.
30 HW, 2657.
31 HW, 2239.
32 HW, 2172, 2252, 3939; G, 582.
33 HW, 822-24, 2438-41, 4415.
34 HW, 4578.
35 G, 169-70.
36 G, 244.
37 HW, 2535.
38 HW, 4592.
39 HW, 1640, 2505, 4344.
40 G, 169-70.
41 HW, 2439-40.

CHAPTER 11

The Effects of World War II on French Society and Politics*

STANLEY HOFFMANN

The purpose of this [chapter] is to suggest a number of hypotheses concerning the impact of the war on the French body politic. Most of these hypotheses need further study and qualification; their author knows very well that as they are presented here, they might appear to be rather arbitrary and insufficiently demonstrated.

These suggestions must first of all be put into proper historical perspective, for what the war did was to bring to a climax a number of trends which had appeared in the last years of the Third Republic. It is the theme of this article that in the period 1934-44 a political and social system which had gradually emerged during the nineteenth century and which had flourished in the period 1878–1934, was actually liquidated; that from 1934 to 1940, this system, which I call the Republican synthesis, suffered severe shocks; that the events of 1940-4 turned these shocks into death-blows, for a return to the previous equilibrium has been made impossible; and that many of the political, economic and social forces which have carried post-war France increasingly farther from the pre-war pattern have their origins in the war years. What the next equilibrium will be like is hard to say, and France still seems far away from any. But it is in 1934 that movement began in earnest, and by 1946, when a political 'restoration' did in fact take place, the departures from the previous equilibrium were already considerable.

Before we examine the impact of the war years in detail, we must first summarize broadly the main characteristics of the Republican synthesis which serves as our baseline, and second, describe briefly the process which, between 1934 and 1940, led to the subsequent destruction of this synthesis.

I

The equilibrium which France had painfully attained before 1934 can be analyzed as follows: the basis was a certain kind of social and economic balance, which will be referred to here as the 'stalemate society' – a term chosen in order to suggest not a *static* society (for there was considerable social mobility and economic change) but a society in which social mobility and economic evolution toward a more industrialized order were accepted only within sharp limits and along well-defined channels. Economic change was welcome only if new factors (such as industrial techniques) were fitted into pre-existing frameworks, so that the traditional way of life was affected only slowly. Social mobility presented some very special features; a remark of Goblot sums them all up: class barriers could be crossed but not destroyed;[1] when one jumped over such a barrier, one had to leave one's previous way of thinking and living behind, and accept (for oneself and one's family) the values and attitudes one found on the other side of the fence. This society was mainly characterized by three features.

1 A form of economic *équilibre* [equilibrium] which thwarted or diluted industrialization and ensured the predominance of a bourgeoisie composed essentially of *indépendants* (non-wage-earners), backed by huge peasant reserves. This system was maintained in various ways. Its first bulwark was the structure of society itself, in which two passageways for entrance into the bourgeoisie were kept open: the line of wealth, passing through the petite-bourgeoisie of artisans and shopkeepers; the line of prestige, which passed through the civil service; those two *antichambres* were protected by state policy. So was the peasant reservoir (through tariff and tax legislation), by contrast with the proletarian swamp. A second bulwark was to be found in the values of society: the bourgeoisie was the model for and the matrix of the rest of society.[2] It emphasized values largely acceptable by all groups in France – values of stability, harmony, permanence, rather than competition, which means both mobility and elimination. It stressed values and attitudes which were dissolvers of class solidarities, so that society would appear like a collection of individuals psychologically alike, of whom the bourgeois would seem like a perfect average. Among those values and attitudes two were particularly significant: the resistance to the machine age and the emphasis on moderation and equilibrium: France was thus presented and seen as a spiritual as well as physical hexagon.

2 A broad consensus on the maintenance of this kind of economic system. This agreement left out – indeed it pushed out – the industrial proletariat, relegated to a social ghetto. The consensus which included the bourgeoisie, its two preserves and its reserves, was perpetuated through a tight and somewhat cramped solidarity between these varied elements: in business, social considerations prevailed over economic ones,[3] and the celebrated 'freezing' of the capitalist spirit in France proved to be a prerequisite for the conciliation of the interests of the various groups included in the consensus.[4] As result, there were severe tensions between the workers and those groups, and there developed a tradition of non-cooperation (a

clumsy expression, but a more accurate one than 'revolutionary tradition')
among labor unions.
3 Its individualism: it was a society in which interests were barely organized.
Pressure groups were more effective on a local than on a regional or
national scale. Neither business nor peasant nor middle-class organizations
had a large membership or a solid structure. The only exceptions were on
the one hand the Church, on the other (but only by comparison with other
economic interest groups) the labor unions.

The genius of the Third Republic had been to devise an institutional set-up
most effectively adapted to such a society. In conformity with the desire of
the 'consensus groups' the role of the state was strictly limited. Economic
intervention was justified only when it served to preserve the economic equilibrium described, either through legislation or through piecemeal administrative interventions. Otherwise the state's function was an ideological one:
it was a state wedded to the social status quo; it was neither industrial (à la
Saint-Simon) nor reformist, but politically doctrinaire and economically beleaguered.

Its organization was such that an effective executive, clear-cut economic or
social alternatives and a strong party system simply could not emerge. Parliament was supreme but immobile: its supremacy, under the French doctrine
of delegated national sovereignty, freed it from any mass pressures from
below; its role was deliberative rather than representative. Law was the product of a compromise between opinions, rather than the result of a weighing
of forces. Parties, thanks largely to the electoral system, were primarily parliamentary collections of 'fief-holders'; their function was to occupy power
rather than to govern. Political life was close to the model of a pure game of
parliamentary politics, i.e. the government of the nation by a Parliament
which dictated policy-making, put the life of cabinets constantly at stake, and
knew no effective institutional restraints on its powers. This game, which
was being played in isolation from the nation-at-large by a self-perpetuating
political class, saw to it that the fundamental equilibrium of society would not
be changed by the state.

This system rested in turn on the rosy hypothesis of an outside world distant enough to allow the French to care primarily about their private affairs.
Pride in the universality of French values combined with a pleasant sense of
superiority or distance to keep the number of people concerned with
France's demographic decline or economic retardation small. After World
War I, victory plus new alliances plastered the cracks opened by the shock of
invasion. Indeed, World War I – the one war which has not led to a change of
regime – froze French society in many ways. (There are of course areas in
which the opposite happened, i.e. forces of change or discontent were
turned loose, which finally became hurricanes in the 1930s.)

The challenge of the 1930s, by contrast with previous challenges such as
World War I, the Dreyfus case, or Boulangism, undermined all the foun-
dations of the Republican synthesis.

First, the equilibrium of society was shattered by the depression and by the financial policies of the Conservative governments of 1932–6 (the policy of deflation, with its 'mystique' of the sanctity of contracts and its stubborn faith in tax cuts and balanced budgets symbolized beautifully the nature and beliefs of the stalemate society). Not only did workers' grievances and the issue of social reform reach the highest danger level since 1848, but also the workers found allies among the 'consensus groups', in their protest against the situation as it had become during the depression: in particular among peasants, civil servants, small businessmen and shopkeepers. The fact that those allies wanted a return to the *status quo ante,* not a jump to the Grand Soir [literally, Great Evening, in the sense of Grand Chinese], was something else again.

Second, the institutions proved of course too weak to weather such a storm. At a time when executive action was needed, the deep divisions within Parliament condemned cabinets to shorter lives than ever before, and to immobility or incoherence during their brief existence. The impotence of Parliament itself was underlined by the abdication of its legislative powers through decree-laws. The ordinary weaknesses of a multi-party system were aggravated by the splits which appeared within some of the major parties.

Finally, the outside world, whose pressure had been strong, though ignored, ever since Versailles, simply could not be explained away anymore. In a world of motion, indeed revolution (Stalin, Mussolini, Hitler, Scandinavian experiments in socialism, Roosevelt's experiment in muscular liberalism), France and England began to appear, even to the most musty readers of the *Revue des Deux Mondes,* like big logs of dead wood.

II

I want to turn now to the process of destruction of the Republican synthesis. The main feature, in the period 1934–40, was the victory of centrifugal forces everywhere. Until then, the Republic had functioned neatly: most of France's political *and* social forces joined in a broad consensus; the rest (i.e. the political Extreme Right and the proletarian Extreme Left) was kept in its ghettos, and stayed there. Now, suddenly, confusion and flux replaced the tiny, if cramped, order of Alain's *République Radicale.*

Why? Because in a period of major trouble the citizens, and especially those who feel the pinch of a depression, rediscover the function and importance of politics. Such a rediscovery occurred all over the world, and it affected parliamentary government all over the continent of Europe; but we are concerned here only with the way in which it stirred up France. Robert de Jouvenel's famous sentence (politics in France was a luxury, not the condition of men's lives) was true only as long as the bases of the system were not threatened. Now, the return to politics of previously indifferent groups can mean two completely different things. It can mean that the existing political system will be *reactivated* because the discontents have found easy access to power through the political parties and pressure groups available.

But when those parties do not fulfill their task and when the pressure groups are able only to increase the weaknesses of the state by milking it at the expense of the common good, the political system will be in danger of *collapse.*

The latter situation is the one which obtained in France. Existing political parties simply did not adjust to the new issues: they locked themselves in the traditional Republican fortress, instead of rebuilding it. A look at their program in 1936 shows the extent of sclerosis on both sides of the political fence. The left prevented constitutional reform, a prerequisite of political reconstruction, and, instead of building a positive alliance for the solution of the new problems enumerated above, it threw together a negative one against the forces which attacked the regime for its incapacity to solve those problems. Anti-Ligues [the Ligues were right-wing organizations] feelings were merely put in the place of former anticlericalism: 1935 was 1899 revisited; the economic program of the Popular Front baptised with the new slogan of 'purchasing power theory' the old practice of promising benefits to a huge quantity of groups.

Consequently people, groups, reviews, etc., who 'came from' the Republican parties originally, and found that they could not get their views across within those parties, became dissenters and started to float away. In the middle of the ocean, they found all those men, movements, journals, etc., of the Right, who had never had much faith in the Republic anyhow and had either attacked it all along from their past ghetto, or made it clear that their support was conditional upon the preservation of the kind of society the regime now seemed unable to save. These people became, on the whole, outspoken enemies. Thus the regular institutions looked more like a façade, with real life – suddenly turned most turbulent – somewhere else.

The Right-wing enemies were a highly interesting mass of people. They felt almost permanently deprived of real access to political power: *la République* was, on the whole, the Left. As long as political power did not matter because the dominance of the middle classes was secure, this insufficient access was not a major nuisance: the fact that left-wing parties were better organized than rightist parliamentary clans, that labor unions were more real than business or peasant groups, was of minor importance as long as the conservatives' Bastilles in society (civil service, industry and banks, the professions, the salons) still stood. With those positions threatened by economic chaos and political 'disorder' (1936), access to power had to be reopened. And such access was to be sought in anti-Republican ways rather than through the organization of new, but Republican, parties and pressure groups, for a variety of reasons, of which the most important was that such an effort would have gone against the grain – for it supposed a total change of heart among people who had supported (or tolerated) the Republic only because the regime required no big organizational work or apparatus from groups which wanted to dominate society *qua* élites, not *qua* political parties or *qua* special interests.[5] Anti-parliamentarism came infinitely more naturally – as had been shown by so many historical precedents.

How did the process of destruction unfold? The participants in the revolt against, or dissent from, the Republican system belonged to many categories, which I cannot enumerate in detail here. On the one hand, there were dissidents from existing political parties, such as the three men, who, ironically enough, were the first to speak of a Popular Front, only to be kept away or to turn away from it later: Doriot (ex-Communist), Déat (neo-Socialist) and Bergery (ex-Radical); Tardieu switched also from being one of the main statesmen of the regime to being one of the chief publicists against it. Those dissidents rubbed elbows with various political figures which had turned anti-parliamentary before 1934: the Maurrassiens, the Jeunesses Patriotes of Taittinger. One can put into the same category, or into a neighboring one, the newspapers which came more and more to support the themes of anti-Republicanism and played such a crucial role in bringing to France the climate of Vichy before Vichy.[6]

On the other hand, the 1930s were marked by the 'politization' of various groups of men who, in happier days, would not have dreamed of singing the *garstig Lied* [awful song] of politics: large quantities of intellectuals, after a period in which intellectuals had been singularly non-political – hence the mushrooming of new reviews and sects with grandiloquent programs and spiritualist verbiage; equally surprising numbers of engineers, especially from the École Polytechnique (cf. the X-Crise movement), where the old Saint-Simonian tradition of illuminism-cum-technology flourished again; students, who built up impressive-sounding youth movements (at a time when the parties also reactivated or created youth sections); veterans' associations, who substituted the jargon of national overhaul for the vocabulary of special financial complaints (the Croix de Feu are of course the biggest example); union leaders and businessmen who turned from their previous attitudes of non-cooperation or of no comment on politics, to studies of general reform and examples from other countries *(Syndicats; Les Nouveaux Cahiers . . .).*

Coming from so many different milieux, counting so many people whose sudden discovery of public affairs had gone to their heads like extra-fine champagne, these groups amounted more to a maelstrom of confused anger than to a coherent onslaught on the Republican synthesis. Indeed, if there is one characteristic of these movements in the period under consideration, it is the bitterness of their own divisions. At first, their quarrels were not more than yelps of dissent among dissenters, although, of course, French yelps can be a mighty strain on any ear. Indeed, after a few months in 1933–4, when all these people fraternized in astonishment at their common feelings and slogans, they immediately began to excommunicate each other and to raise nuances to the dignity of abysses once again. Later, once the regime was abolished, or had rather fainted into the trap the Germans, plus Laval, had opened, the disputes among the former critics of the regime led to a quasi-civil war between Vichy and the Resistance, both being composed essentially of the discontents of the 1930s.

Nevertheless they had common grievances against the Republican synthesis and since these themes announce post-war France, it is important to list them. They all express a revolt against the kind of society and state which was described above.

The most superficial common theme was the critique of French parliamentarism. The most interesting example is probably Tardieu's set of volumes composed between 1934 and 1936. Tardieu's remark that if one wants to be heard by the country it is best not to be a parliamentarian is significant enough. Practically all the dissenters from the Republic argued in favor of a stronger State, one less dependent on the whims of the representatives and less submissive to the individual pressures of the voters on the parliamentarians.

A deeper theme is an attack, not so much on the stalemate society as such, but on its individualistic form. This meant two things.

[First], an attack on the neglect of groups in French 'official' thought and public law. The proliferation of youth movements, the concern for new formulas of organization and representation of interests, the rediscovery of man-as-a-social-being in contemporary 'public philosophy', under the loftily vague name of *personnalisme* (*ésprit, l'ordre nouveau* – [spirit, new order]) were the various aspects of this revival of group thinking, opposed to the doctrine of Alain or of the Jacobin state.

[Second], an attack on French capitalism. Here of course ambiguity was supreme, and misunderstandings were most juicy, for some of those attackers wanted (at least they thought so) to overthrow the private-enterprise economy, whereas others criticized French capitalism only because it had not succeeded in freezing the stalemate society once and for all. Thus the former argued for greater socialization of the economy, for more state intervention and planning. But the latter still feared state dabbling more than anything except communism (but that was about the same in their eyes); therefore, they merely wanted France's economic forces to organize solidly at last, and to coordinate their policies among themselves, in order precisely to prevent the state from using the present lack of organization as a pretext for 'étatisme'. What all nevertheless agreed upon, was that present disorganized (i.e. neither state- nor self-regulated) capitalism was rotten; for it wasted national resources through the excesses of competition (Doriot), it demoralized the nation through its materialism (La Rocque), it encouraged uprooted adventurers and nomadic speculators (Bardoux, *L'Ordre nouveau*)[7], it crushed '*les petits*' and benefited only '*les gros*' (*Frontisme*), it built new 'feudal orders' in France (veterans' movements). There is marvelous irony in the spectacle of so many people denouncing in the fiasco of French 1934–5 capitalism the discomfiture of '*l'économie libérale*', if one remembers how little free competition and indeed how much self-regulation there was in this most restrictive economy. But it was well-concealed self-regulation, and what the partisans of 'organized professions' wanted was officially proclaimed and sanctioned self-regulation, giving to business groups powers snatched away from the state, or from unions. The 'plan du 9 juillet' (1934) shows in its text and in its list of signatories a fine case of generalized but significant confusion.

In both these attacks, all the groups involved addressed themselves primarily to the French middle classes. This was as true of La Rocque or Doriot as it was of men like Déat, Bergery, Izard, or Belin.

Another theme, which went perhaps even deeper, was a universal lament about the moral climate of France. This was the generation of *péguysme* (poor Péguy!), on whom Mounier had just written a book, and the epoch of activism: Sorel, Proudhon, were the patron saints of many of the new reviews. Malraux was of course a shining hero-witness of the revolt against the climate of mediocrity and immobility. The examples given by other countries were constantly displayed, discussed, and sometimes even studied (cf. the meetings at Pontigny).

The ways in which all these groups participated in the demise of the Republican synthesis and pushed France out of the drydock in which it had been waiting for permanently postponed repairs are far too complicated to be described in detail, but two points are of major interest.

First, the confusing mass of dissenters ultimately split into two blocs (heterogeneous, to be sure). On the one hand, all the people who ended on the side of Vichy, or rather those whom de Gaulle calls 'les amants inconsolables de la défaite et de la collaboration' [the inconsolable lovers of defeat and collaboration]: the Murrassiens – hermetically sealed counter-revolutionaries; the Fascists of occupied Paris (literary types, like Drieu, or gangsters, like Doriot's pals) and of Vichy France (muddleheaded activists like Darnand or schemers like Benoist-Méchin), the much bigger groups of disgruntled conservatives, shaking sheep with wolves' voices, like La Rocque, Pétain's Légionnaires and so many of his civil servants, business or peasant leaders; pacifists whose left-wing origins had been erased by their prolonged fight against communism and for appeasement, like Belin and many of Déat's friends. On the other hand, all those dissenters from the Third Republic who nevertheless hated defeat and Nazism more than a French form of democracy and who became the leaven in the more political Resistance organizations, where they met thousands of intellectuals, journalists, doctors, lawyers, military men, and so on, many of whom had had no previous political activity. Those future '*Résistants*' dissenters belonged largely to two groups: a relatively tight one, the Christian Democrats, whose *personnalisme* was politically liberal, not authoritarian, and whose pluralism was democratic, not élitist; a much more loose group, the former *planistes* from business or from the unions.[8] It was only later in the Resistance that the members of the parties of the Third Republic (and, of course, not all of them) joined those former dissenters, gradually submerged them, and turned the Resistance into a second coming of the Popular Front.

Second, if one looks at the direction taken by France after 1934, starting from the equilibrium described in the beginning, one can distinguish, with some exaggeration, two phases. First there was, under Vichy, a movement of contraction: the triumph for a few years of a reactionaries' delirium, which broke with the 'individualistic' society of the Third Republic in order to establish a *société communautaire* whose organized and self-regulating groups were even more Malthusian in economic practice, and more dominated by the anti-industrial, anti-urban ideal than the Republic had ever been. Then, after 1944, movement went in the opposite direction: economic expansion, a loosening up of society instead of the tight and petrified moral order of Vichy.

III

We now have to establish a balance sheet of the effects which the process we have just sketchily described brought about during World War II. The central fact is that the two movements – constriction and renovation – converged on a number of very important points. This strange dialectic can be explained without any recourse to the invisible hand of history: the participants in the two revolutions of Vichy and the Resistance had some common (if often negative) ideas, and since many of Vichy's dreams were beyond realization – 'ce qui est exagéré ne compte pas' [that which is exaggerated does not count] – many of Vichy's reforms inevitably turned into directions Vichy neither expected nor desired, or even produced effects contrary to those which the authors of these reforms had hoped to obtain.

If we look at changes in society at the end of the war, we see both major innovations and a few sharp limits. As for the innovations, the most significant is largely due to Vichy's impact. A number of groups in society emerged from pre-war chaos or confusion with the kind of organization which made of them possible levers for economic and social change. Alain's individualistic society has indeed been left behind. Vichy's motives in setting up these bodies were mixed: corporatist ideology (the 'restitution' to organized groups in society of powers which the Republican state had supposedly usurped) was strengthened by the need to set up bodies which could administer the restrictions forced upon the French economy by defeat and occupation. Furthermore, some of Vichy's authorities wanted to prevent the Germans from controlling the French economy, as they could otherwise have done, either by benefiting from its lack of organization or by setting up a German-directed organization.[9] The result was, in business, the creation of 'organization committees' which became the mold of the post-war Conseil National du Patronat Français.[10] Vichy's Peasant Corporation provided first its structure for the Confédération Générale Agricole instituted at the Liberation in reaction against the Corporation's ideology and leaders, and later many of its former key men for the Fédération Nationale des Syndicats d'Exploitants Agricoles which grew out of the ill-starred CGA. The leaders which the Resistance teams had put in charge of the CGA were gradually ousted as the peasants moved politically back toward the right, and the 'men of Vichy' were returned to the jobs from which M. Tanguy-Prigent, the Socialist Minister of Agriculture of 1945, had expelled them.[11] Embryonic organizations of *cadres* created within the Labor Charter of Vichy have flourished, since. The professions' orders (lawyers, doctors, etc.), established between 1940 and 1944, have been preserved and consolidated.

Continuity here has been most striking. In spite of their revulsion against Vichy corporatism, the Resistance movements did not propose a return to pre-war 'individualism'. The shortages of the Liberation made a continuation of the Vichy-created bodies inevitable anyhow (under different names). But, more significantly, the programs of the main Resistance movements and parties contained, in addition to ritual attacks on *féodalités économiques* [feudal economics] and 'corporative dictatorship' a plea for a new economic system in which the economy would be directed by the state after consultation with the representatives of economic interests.[12] The pluralism advocated by the MRP in particular contributed to remove any tinge of illegitimacy from the organized groups which had survived the Vichy period. Vichy certainly did not create these bodies for purposes of industrialization, economic modernization, or education toward a less fragmented society. But after having been the transmission belts for Vichy's philistine propaganda or for the German war machine, such institutions could serve as the relays of the Monnet plan.[13] Indeed, the sense of shame or embarrassment which many of the leaders of business felt after the Liberation, at a time when the business community was widely accused of having collaborated wholesale with the Germans, probably contributed to making these men almost eager to prove their patriotism by cooperating with the new regime for economic reconstruction and expansion.

A second phenomenon was also initiated by Vichy. The business and peasant organizations set up in these years were put under the direction of men far less reluctant to break away from economic Malthusianism than the spokesmen for 'organized' business and farmers before the war – the Gignoux or the CGPF [Confederation of Businessmen] or the Pesquidoux of the Société des Agriculteurs. In the business committees, delegates of big business, not of small enterprises, were put in charge; furthermore, these men were managers rather than owners. Indeed, spokesmen for small business and representatives of certain traditional, patriarchal family enterprises expressed considerable hostility toward the Committees;[14] they realized that in these bodies men with bolder ideas, who were far from scared by the thought of planning and of economic cooperation with the government, were entrusted with more means of action than the leading businessmen had ever had in France's predominantly non-organized economy before the war. The solidarity between small and large business – the latter protecting the former, the former accepting in return the leadership of the latter in trade associations – was severely tried by the circumstances of 1940–4; under German pressure, but with less resistance from some of the Committee's leaders than from some of Vichy's officials, measures of concentration of enterprises were put into effect.[15]

In the Peasant Corporation, the men in control were neither small peasants representing the more backward areas of rural France, nor big old-fashioned landowners – members of the aristocracy whose farms were really in the hands of tenants – but commercially minded men more concerned with markets and remuneration than with status, or rather, aware of the fact that the traditional *économie familiale* of French peasants could be preserved best through technical improvements, professional education, the regrouping of excessively divided lands, extended credit facilities, and a better organization of markets.[16]

Thus the more dynamic elements of the economy were given effective positions, instead of remaining dispersed or submerged. The ideas of groups such as the *Jeunes Patrons* or the pre-war *Nouveaux Cahiers* received, in these institutions, a kind of official blessing they had never had before. Needless to say, these men were still primarily interested in obtaining advantages for their respective groups; as the post-war record of continued milking of the state by pressure groups shows, an old history of state intervention designed to preserve the status quo and to give privileges to all had not ended by 1945.[17] Nevertheless, one major change of outlook had taken place: the 'new men' had a less parochial and less compartmentalized view of the economic problems of their profession and of the nation than their predecessors. Here as in other areas, one of the paradoxical results of a period which saw France divided into more administrative zones and separate realms than at any time since the Revolution – in part because of the restrictions on, and later the breakdown of, communications – was to inject a greater awareness of the nation-wide scope of economic problems. Consequently, the need for attacking these problems at least from within the framework of a whole profession, rather than through reliance on individual and local pressures, also became understood. The physical fragmentation of 1940–4 dealt a heavy blow to the economic and social fragmentation of pre-war France.

This became apparent in another way as well. Because of the defeat and later in reaction against Vichy there occurred a kind of rediscovery of France and of the French by the French. Common sufferings did a great deal to submerge, if not to close, some of the fissures which the social fabric of France had suffered before the war. This rediscovery took many forms. One of the most paradoxical at first sight was the celebration of Péguy by Vichy as well as by the Resistance; but wasn't Péguy a symbol of love for *la France charnelle* [physical France] independently of political ideologies or philosophical abstractions? It is important to remember that after the orgy of self-lacerations and doubts which had marked the 1930s, both the Resistance forces and the non-Fascist elements of Vichy fostered what I would call a nationalist revival. Much of it may have been Boy-Scoutish, but it was Boy-Scoutism nationalized. The kind of civic education, the *veillées* [evenings] at which Barrès or Péguy were read, the cult of Joan of Arc, which Vichy's youth camps and youth movements offered to their members, the intense, generous and somewhat confused social nationalism of the École des Cadres at Uriage,[18] pointed in the same direction as the Jacobin nationalism of much of the Resistance. Finally, when Vichy became a shrunken, isolated and Fascist-dominated little clique, common opposition to the occupants and the collaborators brought together people and groups who had remained separated both in pre-war France and in the period of Vichy which preceded Laval's return to power. The collaborators played in 1944–5 the sad but useful role of scapegoats, and the shrillest of their enemies were often men who had first put their faith in Pétain and shared in Vichy's integral nationalism of 1940-1. The myth which the Resistance men gladly endorsed – that almost all of France was *résistante* in 1944 – contributed to healing some of the wounds which the clash between Vichy's forces and the Resistance had opened. If Vichy was a well-localized cancer, and the rest of the body of France was healthy, then a reunion in nationalism was possible for all except the black sheep. The extraordinary nationalist fervor of the Communists in the Resistance and Liberation days[19] was far more than a tactical shift. It constituted in many cases a genuine emotional wave of relief after (or should I say expiation for) the somber period 1939–41, when Communist opposition to the war had pushed the Party's members and sympathizers outside of the national community – or out of the Party. The executions of collaborators in the summer and fall of the Liberation were examples of ritual murders far more than evidence of civil war.

Another aspect of this rediscovery of France as a community was the growth of Catholic influence. Again, both political forces contributed to it. Most of the youth organizations created by Vichy were fiascos almost from the start, in the sense that they never succeeded either in attracting the bulk of the nation's youth, or in bringing their members to endorse Vichy's brand of ideology.[20] But Catholic action groups and Catholic youth movements benefited greatly from the encouragements received during the war years: Vichy-created movements, in search *of cadres,* turned to men obligingly placed at their disposal by Catholic movements. The Catholic Association of French Youth thus became a link between the movements operating in France during the Vichy period, and post-war French youth organizations.[21] The role of Catholics in the Resistance needs hardly to be stressed: whereas the Catholic element in the making of France had been more and more minimized by official political leaders, textbook writers, and Sorbonne representatives of the pre-war Republic, the Resistance movements reversed the trend. 'Celui qui croyait au ciel, celui qui n'y croyait pas' [He who believes in heaven, he who does not believe]: Aragon's famous poem testifies to the reconciliation which had taken place thanks to Christian Democracy.

This reconciliation took on more concrete aspects as well. Just as economic groups were encouraged to organize, other associations were launched in order to bring the French closer together: roving companies of young comedians, groups of young music lovers were supposed to bring art back to non-Parisians and to shake the French out of their individualism.[22] The emphasis so heavily put on youth and on the family by Vichy was intended to contribute to the rebirth of a sense of community. The Resistance did nothing to reverse the movement – were not its organizations dominated by young men who acceded to responsibilities which French youth had been deprived of since the days of the Revolution? As for the emphasis on the importance of family life, the Christian-Democrats saw to it that it would not disappear with the Vichy regime.

The revival of community was obviously far from complete or final, and it is impossible to measure the degree of community in a nation. But I would maintain that it has been much higher after 1944 than in the 1930s, despite the return of the Communists into their ghetto, and such phenomena as Poujadism; the tone of public arguments has been much milder; the hysteria so characteristic of debates in the 1930s has been limited to lunatic fringes. France as a *political* community may have been almost as pathetic after 1946 as before 1939. But there are other levels or forms of community as well, and those, which had been badly damaged in the 1930s, were in much better shape after the Liberation.

However, two obvious limitations must be mentioned:

[First], relations between workers and other social groups were not permanently improved. Indeed, they did not improve at all under Vichy, where the policy practiced both by the state and by business organizations was one of reaction and repression. The legislation which the Popular Front had made in order to bring classes closer together had failed almost completely.[23] The bitter denunciations of business attitudes toward labor in most Resistance platforms indicate how deep this fissure had become. The bad memories left, on the workers' side, by the Labor Charter and the rump unions sponsored by Vichy or by Paris collaborators, and, on the management side, by the reforms of the Liberation, were going to doom legislative attempts such as the Comités d'Entreprises (needless to say, Communist domination of the labor movement contributed to the failure). Nationalization has not noticeably contributed to the 'reintegration of the proletariat into the nation' which the Resistance wanted to achieve and which Socialists saw as one of the main advantages of public ownership. What Michel Crozier calls 'l'horreur du face à face' [the horrors of meeting face-to-face][24] has remained a basic obstacle.

[Second], one group has emerged from World War II both split and largely alienated from the rest of the national community: the army. The breach between elements which remained faithful to Pétain and those which followed De Gaulle was never completely repaired. If the Vichy armed forces found themselves increasingly unpopular in a country which was at first put under quasi-military control by a defeated army and navy, the Gaullist military leaders, who fought outside of France (and often against other Frenchmen) found it difficult to adjust to the political and moral climate of France after the war ended. Their dream of a France *pure et dure* had been cruelly shattered, and the famous clash of December 1945 between the Constituent Assembly and General de Gaulle indicated that in the new regime, once De Gaulle was eliminated, the army would not have a *'place de choix'*. In a way, both the misuse of its armed forces by Vichy, and the predominantly civilian character of the Resistance contributed to discredit the army, despite De Gaulle's attempts at an *amalgame* between Resistance, Free French, and formerly Vichyite forces.[25]

The changes on the political front have been more contradictory than those in society, but many nevertheless deserve to be discussed.

The following innovations have drastically transformed the political system as it had developed before:

[First], power fell into the hands of the previous 'minorities' – of those groups of men who, for one reason or another, did not belong to, or had become separated from, *'la République des Camarades'*. The fall of France was the 'divine surprise' of many of the dissenters or enemies whom we have mentioned before; metropolitan France became the battlefield between the factions into which those groups split – corporatists against *belinistes,* pro-Pétain Christian-Democrats against Maurrassiens, and of course Fascists against conservatives or technocrats – or against other Fascists. Those dissenters who either refused to support Vichy or abandoned Vichy after a few months of hesitation (as did many Catholics, who were first taken in by institutions such as the Uriage school or youth camps)[26] became, as we know, the backbone of the early Resistance. One of the paradoxes of the restoration of 1945-6 is that although it brought back many of the parties discredited in 1940, and political institutions close to those which had collapsed on 10 July, the political personnel of the Third Republic never succeeded in coming back in toto. Of course there was Queuille and Schuman; but the latter had hardly been a star before the war: he had belonged to a party which never fitted the system of the Third Republic. Neither these two men, nor Herriot – more a monument now than a leader – ever gave its tone to the Fourth Republic. In the old parties which re-emerged, purges liquidated many of the pre-war leaders. Thus in the Socialist Party, new men like Mollet, Daniel Mayer, and the syndicalists (Lacoste, Pineau) took over from the generation of Blum and Paul Faure.

[Second], a second and major change was the acceptance of an interventionist state – at last. Vichy's philosophy was, to start with, diametrically opposed to it; Vichy's dream was the 'absolute but limited' state, so dear to counter-revolutionaries ever since Bonald. But despite its theory of decentralization and of corporations running the economy under a distant and discreet check from the state, Petain's regime was unable to practice what it preached. In the business organizations Vichy set up, civil servants and managers learned to run the show together. Here, Bichelonne's influence was considerable. One of his associates calls him the father of professional statistics in France;[27] his all-encompassing activity as minister of industry marked a break with the past tradition of a civil service whose interventions in economic affairs were largely limited to measures protecting vested interests, defending them against competition but never challenging their privately decided policies. Bichelonne's selection of the bosses of the business committees contributed mightily to replacement of those businessmen for whom the state could only be either an enemy or a servant with managers for whom the state could be a guide. Thus Bichelonne's administration initiated practices of cooperation which the Monnet Plan later institutionalized.

Indeed, on the other side of the political fence, the need for a more active state had become one of the main planks of Resistance platforms: planning by the state, nationalization, by public investments, 'economic and social democracy', state control over cartels, prices or capital movements, all these suggestions showed that the revulsion against the lopsided 'economic liberalism' of pre-war times had become irresistible. The measures taken in 1944-6 in order to put these proposals into effect are well known. None of the 'conquests of the Liberation' has been seriously threatened since; the attacks against 'dirigisme' by Radicals and Conservatives were successful only when they were aimed at price controls and at those measures of intervention into the affairs of rural France which the peasant organizations had not requested themselves.

[Third], a change in public issues resulted. Already before 1939, a subtle shift had occurred. On the one hand the key ideological issue of the Third Republic had begun to fade away, for official hostility to the Church had weakened ever since the Popular Front.[28] Except for the years 1945-51, private schools have received help from the state since 1941. [. . .]

On the other hand, the state began to promote measures of income redistribution which went far beyond what the theory of the stalemate society allowed, or showed concern for social welfare on a scale unknown before. The *politique de la famille* [politics of the family] has been followed by every regime since Daladier's decrees of July 1939. Vichy gave tremendous publicity to its main contribution to social insurances: the old age pensions for retired workers. Resistance platforms emphasized the need for extending protection against social risks, and the social security system of the Liberation was built by a man who had been one of the main drafters of the law of August 1940 setting up Vichy's business committees.[29] The participation of workers' delegates in at least some of the activities of the firm became the subject of various laws, from the Popular Front's shop stewards to Vichy's *comités sociaux* and the Liberation's *comités d'entreprises*. Thus, economic and social issues tended to replace the old ideological ones, and this shift contributed to the 'nationalization' of opinion and issues which proportional representation accelerated. The fragmentation of the political scene into 'fiefs' and local issues began to fade just as economic fragmentation did. [. . .]

A few words should be said about the changes in the French image of France in the world; this is a subject which is very difficult to treat, for there is little evidence to back one's statements, and which deserves much further study.

On the one hand, the need to readjust France to a changed world was felt by many, both in Vichy and in the Resistance; even though the battle between those two groups of forces was fought largely because of their different views of the world and of France's role, there were again at least two points on which the antagonism was far from complete.

The need to put an end to the alarming economic retardation of France in order to restore or preserve France's position in the world was understood by a large number of the dissenters from the Third Republic. Many of the civil servants who joined in Resistance movements, or even served throughout in the Vichy regime, were in close touch with the formidable German war economy and came to realize how strong the link between industrial organization and political power was.[30] Many of the business leaders and engineers of Vichy were also thrown into contact - often collaboration - with Germany's extraordinary dynamism; they negotiated with German business leaders and officials, and many of them visited German plants and business offices. As a consequence, these men became far more aware of the need for organization, concentration, higher productivity, an improved statistical equipment, better industrial relations and more cooperation between the business community and the state. In the last period of the war and in the months which followed its end, the contact with America's own war machine, industrial economy and bureaucratic efficiency provided the same groups of Frenchmen with another compelling display of the prerequisites of influence in the modern world.

Civil servants and businessmen had also realized – often under duress – during the occupation the amount of interdependence of Western European economies and the possibilities of cooperation across borders. This point, like the preceding one, had been made by small cliques of 'dissenters' before the war: the men of *Les Nouveaux Cahiers* or X-Crise, Déat and his *planiste*s. Now it became a matter of daily life. Second, within a different context, post-war European unity became also a theme of many Resistance movements, who were either looking forward to a European holy alliance of the peoples against trusts and munition makers, or dreaming of a powerful Europe playing once again a major role in world affairs. Despite this more ideological or political approach, Resistance 'European' feelings buttressed the practical concern of the more technocratic Vichyites; indeed it is thanks to such Resistance dreams that the idea of European unity survived its exploitation by Nazi propaganda. Third, General de Gaulle also looked forward to a European political force playing its own part in world affairs.[31] Of course, the officials and businessmen of Vichy thought primarily in terms of Franco-German cooperation, whereas the Resistance and De Gaulle thought in terms of the links forged between the victims of Germany by Nazi domination. But the two conceptions were not mutually exclusive. After the war, when the Fourth Republic decided to scrap its policy of revenge and to replace it with a Franco-German partnership, although the new approach met with numerous protectionist objections from French businessmen, it did not encounter much opposition (outside of the Communist Party) to its basic idea of the need for reconciliation and cooperation between the two former enemies. Many Resistance platforms and De Gaulle himself had mentioned such a need for after the war and denazification. In a way, Laval's statement that, whatever the result of the war, France and Germany would remain neighbors and would therefore have to find a *modus vivendi* was more universally understood than one realized at first, and the contacts which had been established between 'élites' of the two countries during the occupation period, especially in the business world, were probably far from wasted. Within the *Festung Europa* [Fortress Europe] which waited for its liberation from the outside, occupied peoples and temporary masters discovered that they might be enemies, but that they also had a lot in common, which distinguished them from the outsiders.

The separation between Nazi-dominated Europe and the outside world however had some far less constructive effects, which were probably more important at least in the immediate post-war period.

The main factor here could be described as follows: at the same time as many Frenchmen came to understand that a deep economic transformation was needed in order to preserve France's importance in the world, the trauma of the war years blinded them to changes which made France's restoration to the status of a world power highly problematic, even in case of domestic economic overhaul. They overlooked the forces which were turning into an obsolescent delusion the old French image of a world responsive to the universality of French values and the vision of a map in which French colors would occupy almost as much space as England's. Here again, many elements contributed to the same result – Vichy's fantasy of neutral France mediating in the war;[32] the lack of concern for foreign affairs displayed by the Resistance; the inevitable reaction of bitter and almost desperate pride which the humiliation of submission to the occupant was bound to provoke; the tremendous effort by De Gaulle in 1944–5 to restore French self-respect by emphasizing France's contribution to the Allied victory; the huge quantities of war prisoners who spent the war *hors jeu* in German camps. On the colonial front in particular, the curtain which cut off France from the world outside of Europe prevented both the Vichy élites and the future leaders of the Fourth Republic who were in the metropolitan Resistance from realizing how deep the revolt against a simple restoration of pre-war colonial rule, or even against half-hearted liberal measures, had become in the former Empire.

The force which, because of its very humiliations, internal splits and traditions, was least likely to adjust to the change in the international position of France was of course the army. Those elements which remained on the side of Vichy were both submitted to, and willing partners in, constant xenophobic propaganda; those elements which joined De Gaulle or re-entered the war after the Giraud detour, primarily wanted to erase the memory of the defeat of 1940 and to restore France to an uncontested position of eminence. Many of the post-war aspects of *le malaise de l'armée* – the tendency to see a plot against France behind every incident, the readiness to see defeatism in every concession – have their roots in World War II.

IV

By way of a summary and instead of a conclusion, here are a few paradoxes for our meditation.

First, the Resistance and Vichy, which fought one another so bloodily, cooperated in many ways without wanting or knowing it, and thus carried the nation to the threshold of a new social order. It can be said that the two groups which gained most from the war years were business and the Catholic Church – a far cry from the France of 1936. Vichy brought into existence social institutions which could become the channels for state action, and gave a considerable boost to the descendants of the Saint-Simoniens, men who were willing to serve as agents of the Count's old dream – organization, production, industrialism. The Resistance brought to power teams of engineers, civil servants and politicians determined to use these agents and these channels for economic and consequently for social change. Had those teams not arrived, it is quite possible that the social institutions erected by Vichy would have withered away just as the consortiums of World War I had vanished after 1919. But without readily available transmission belts and without the shock of discovery produced on French economic élites by sudden and brutal contact with foreign economies, post-war planning might have failed. The transformation of the French economy and society since 1952 is due to the combination of the wills of a statist De Gaulle – and a Saint-Simonien Monnet – who used instruments prepared by Vichy and strengthened them by adding quite a few of their own (nationalizations, the Planning Commission, a reform of the civil service, etc.). The meekness of the *patronat* [business owners], unwilling to oppose the government of the Liberation, and the big production drive of the Communists in 1944–7 which contrasted with labor's pre-war attitude, both contributed to the initial success of the movement. The process is far from completed, and no transformation of French political life has resulted from it so far. But World War II had on French society effects opposite from those of World War I.

Second, the continuity between Vichy and its successor, which we have noted when we mentioned the economy, family protection, the 'rediscovery of youth and the revival of Catholicism, appears also, in more ironic fashion, in a number of failures. The hope of reconciling the workers and the employers has not been fulfilled. Neither the paternalistic solutions of the Vichy Labor Charter nor the social measures of the Liberation have succeeded in overcoming a long tradition of mutual suspicion. In the future, perhaps new attitudes among businessmen concerned with 'human relations', and the increasing hierarchy and specialization within the working class – all resulting from economic change – might gradually overcome old antagonisms. Both Vichy and the Resistance movements emphasized the need to preserve, in agriculture, the traditional family units; their post-war decline has been spectacular, and no amount of protection from the state has been able to suspend it. Indeed, mechanization of the farms has often contributed to this process, for it increases the financial difficulties of farmers whose products sell at prices which remain at a lower level than the cost of the machines, as well as the plight of peasants whose land is too small for efficient production. Both regimes have failed to preserve the morale, the unity and the strength of the army. Finally, both have failed to stabilize the French political system. The new society of France still awaits a political synthesis comparable to the early Third Republic; all it presently has is a respite.

Third, both regimes provide us with choice examples of serendipity. Vichy, which wanted to coax the French back to the land and back to rule by traditional notables, consolidated instead the business community and demonstrated conclusively that the elites of 'static' France could not provide leadership any more. Vichy also wanted to restore old provincial customs and dialects and peculiarities – instead of which it put into motion powerful forces of further economic and social unification. The Resistance, which wanted to purify French political life and was prone to proclaim the death of the bourgeoisie, ended as a political fiasco, but was the lever of an economic modernization which has certainly not meant the demise of the bourgeoisie. Indeed, those of the dissenters from the Third Republic who turned against it because they wanted to save the stalemate society which the Republic seemed unable to defend, an order based on the preponderance of the middle classes, could remark today that French society is still dominated by these classes. The proportion of industrial workers has barely increased.

However, French society is no longer the same. The division between proletarians and *indépendants* has been largely replaced by a less original hierarchy of functional groups in which many of the workers partake of middle-class characteristics and in which managers, *cadres* and employees are increasingly numerous. The village is less important as an economic unit; the family is a less tightly closed one; the attitude toward savings and credit has been reversed; there is less distance between ranks and statuses in society; businessmen, peasants and shopkeepers alike are more dependent on the national economy than on a mere segment of it; the economy is far more planned (or at least *concertée* [organized]), and the market is at last seen as growing instead of frozen. In other words, a more dynamic society has replaced the tight stalemate society of the past. Between 1934 and today, the transition from *la France bourgeoise* to *la France des classes moyennes*, from the *Revue des Deux Mondes* to *Réalités* has been crossed.

The double consensus on which the Third Republic had lived (with increasing discomfort) has consequently been transformed. The political consensus included all the groups which accepted the tenets of the Revolution; it left out only the Extreme Right, and it had its center of gravity on the left. But this formula has been affected by the division and deterioration of the left after the Liberation, as well as by the quasi-liquidation of the Extreme Right. Hence the weight has shifted to the right, and the relevance of the old issues has diminished. The social consensus encompassed all the groups which accepted the stalemate society; it excluded only the proletariat, and had its center of gravity on the conservative side, but this formula has been affected by industrialization, which tends to reintegrate the working class into the enterprises and the nation, and to make the business community less economically and socially conservative. [. . .]

Notes

1 Edmond Goblot, *La barrière et le niveau*, (Paris 1925), p. 6.
2 See Sartre's definition of the bourgeois: 'le moyen terme élevé à la toutepuissance', [the middle way raised to omnipotence] in 'Qu'est-ce que la littérature', *Situations*, II, Paris, 1948, p. 157.
3 See the analyses by David Landes and John Sawyer in E. Earle (ed.) *Modern France*, Princeton, NJ, 1950, and Jesse R. Pitts, 'The Bourgeois Family and French Economic Retardation', Harvard Ph.D. thesis, unpublished, 1957.
4 For instance: within the business world, between big firms and small firms thus

protected against cut-throat competition; in the relations between the business world and the landed notables, both groups indulging in joint investments in land . . . or in protectionism; in the relations between business and the civil servants, with highly developed practices of *connubium, convivium,* and 'pantouflage'.

5 See for further elaboration, my article 'Aspects du Régime de Vichy', *Revue française de science politique,* January–March, 1956, pp. 44–69.

6 See C. Micaud, *The French Right and Nazi Germany,* Durham, 1943.

7 See his book, *L'Ordre nouveau face au communisme et au racisme,* Paris, 1939.

8 Cf. the Resistance movements *Libération-Sud* and especially the *OCM.*

9 See on this point René Belin's statement in *La vie de la France sous l'occupation,* Paris, 1957, I, 145.

10 See Henry Ehrmann, *Organized Business in France,* Princeton, NJ, 1957, chs II–III.

11 See Adolphe Pointier's embattled testimony in *La vie de la France sous l'occupation,* I, 275 ff, and H. Mendras and J. Fauvet (eds) *Les paysans et la politique,* Paris, 1958, *passim.*

12 See for instance the famous program of the Conseil National de la Résistance in B. Mirkine-Guetzévitch and H. Michel (eds) *Les Idées politiques et sociales de la Résistance,* Paris, 1954, pp. 215 ff. [Reprinted, in translation in *War, Peace and Social Change: Documents 2,* Milton Keynes, 1989.]

13 Continuity is well demonstrated by the case of Aimé Lepercq, who was the head of one of Vichy's main business committees (coal mines) and later De Gaulle's Finance Minister.

14 See for instance Belin's reference to a letter of M. de Peyerimhoff, the head of the Comité des Houillères, *La Vie de la France,* I, 150. Pierre Nicolle's book, *Cinquante mois d'armistice,* Paris, 1947, is a perfect record of all the campaigns waged by small business against Vichy's Business Committees.

15 See *La Vie de la France,* vol. I, pp. 14ff.

16 See the interesting collection of *Syndicats Paysans,* for 1940–2 (the paper of Jacques Leroy-Ladurie and Louis Salleron).

17 See for instance the story of such measures in post-war France in Warren C. Baum's rather one-sided book, *The French Economy and the State,* Princeton, NJ, 1958.

18 See the study of the School by Janine Bourdin, in the *Revue française de science politique,* IX, 4, Sept.–Dec. 1959.

19 Remember Aragon's poems ('mon parti m'a rendu les couleurs de la France . . .') [Reprinted in translation in *War, Peace and Social Change: Documents 2,* Milton Keynes, 1989]

20 The most edifying story is that of the movement of *Les Compagnons de France:* see issue 27 (1943) of *Métier de Chef,* which tells most of it.

21 See *Positions d'ACJF, 7 ans d'histoire au service de la jeunesse de France,* Paris, 1946.

22 The artistic association *Jeune France,* sponsored by Vichy, became a breeding ground for numerous talents that were to become famous in post-war France. The *Jeunesses Musicals Françaises* dates from the war years also.

23 See Val R. Lorwin, *The French Labor Movement,* Cambridge, 1954, pp. 78–9.

24 In his article, 'La France, terre de commandement' in *Esprit,* December 1957, pp. 779–97.

25 On these points, there are many interesting remarks, in vol. III of De Gaulle's Memoirs, *Le Salut,* Paris, 1959.

26 The very swift evolution of *Esprit* in the latter half of 1940 is particularly interesting; so is that of the Uriage school, whose last class joined the Maquis.

27 See M. de Calan's testimony in *La Vie de la France*, I, 31ff.

28 See for instance the article by Father Renaud in *Revue des Deux Mondes* of 1 June 1939.

29 On Pierre Laroque's role in August 1940, see Belin in *La Vie de la France*, I, 146.

30 The testimonies in *La Vie de la France*, vol. I, show how extensive the contacts between French civil servants in charge of the economy, and their German civilian or military counterparts had been.

31 See *Le Salut*, pp. 221ff.

32 See for instance Thierry-Maulnier, *La France, la guerre et la paix*, Paris, 1942.

* This article was presented as a paper in April, 1960 at the meeting of the Society for French Historical Studies in Rochester.

CHAPTER **12**

The 'Levelling of Class'

PENNY SUMMERFIELD

Many historians subscribe to the idea that the Second World War was a 'leveller of classes'. Above all, Arthur Marwick depicted the war as a time when the gulf between classes narrowed. He attributed the change to the opportunities for participation in areas of work, politics and social life usually reserved for members of a single class which arose as a result of the labour shortage and political pressure associated with the war.[1]

This interpretation is influenced by the earlier writings of Stanislas Andrzejewski[2] and of R. M. Titmuss, who wrote, 'Mass war, involving a high proportion of the total population tends to a levelling in social class differences'.[3] Marwick argued that the 'relative changes' were greatest for the 'working class', which experienced a significant reduction in class differences *vis-à-vis* the 'middle class', even though the position of the 'upper class' was not much altered. He supported his argument with evidence of changes in the political position of the working class due to such things as the participation of trade union leaders and Labour politicians in government and with examples of new working-class self-images in wartime. Though indicative of change, however, this evidence does not represent a complete substantiation of the contention that a 'levelling of class' specifically benefiting the working class was achieved during the war. Discussion of the issue requires, first and foremost, clarification of the concept 'class'.

The definition of 'class' is itself a contentious issue.[4] But an omission from Marwick's account which is common ground in other discussions of class is a serious attempt to grapple with class as an economic relationship, whether in terms of income, occupation or ownership of capital. There is, of course, more to class than 'stratification' according to these criteria, notably 'consciousness of the nature and distribution of power in society' and 'sensations of collective identity of interest among individuals' which give rise to class consciousness and political and industrial organization and action.[5] A full investigation of 'the levelling of class' in the Second World War would embrace changes in both social stratification and class consciousness and activity, and if the hypothesis that wartime participation led to 'levelling' is right, one would expect to find both a reduction in the degree of stratification and a weakening of the political identity of separate social classes.

My intention here is to address only the first part of the hypothesis. This does not mean that I attribute exclusive importance to 'objective' economic indicators of class rather than to 'subjective' experiential ones relating to perception, consciousness and political expression, but it seemed important to tackle the issue of economic stratification in order to redress the balance of previous writing, and the matter became so complex and intriguing that I decided to devote this chapter to it.

The question of changes in social stratification before, during and after the war has been discussed, particularly in the 1950s and 1960s, by historians and sociologists interested in the course of social change during the twentieth century. They can be divided into three camps: those who believed that levelling took place in the Second World War and was permanent; those who argued that by some criteria levelling can be seen to have taken place but that it was not necessarily permanent; and those who concluded that no levelling took place at all.

D. C. Marsh's book *The Changing Social Structure of England and Wales* presents a case for permanent levelling over the period in which the Second World War occurred. Writing in 1958, Marsh concluded from his survey of income data based on tax returns that 'the gap between the very rich and the very poor is much smaller than it was even thirty years ago, and in money terms the inequalities in the distribution of income are less marked'.[6] Two and a half times as many incomes came within the tax ranges in 1950 as in 1920, embracing half the adult population, compared with about a quarter in 1919–20. A larger proportion came into the higher range of incomes over £500 (8 per cent compared with 2 per cent), and a smaller number declared themselves to be in the highest tax bracket, of incomes over £20,000. As far as accumulated wealth was concerned, in both 1930 and 1950 the vast majority of estates assessed for death duties were in the lower ranges, under £5,000, and only a small number were in the highest ranges over £100,000. The main change was in the range between these two figures, in which more than twice the number of estates were left in 1950 compared with 1930.[7] This apparent evidence of expansion of numbers in the middle income brackets and improvement in the position of those at the bottom gave rise to both optimism and alarm in the late 1940s and 1950s. The optimism was voiced by those who saw the war and, particularly, post-war reconstruction as ushering in a period of rising affluence and social stability.[8] The alarm was expressed by those such as Roy Lewis and Angus Maude who feared that the lowest income groups were making gains at the expense of 'the middle classes', whose drive and initiative were being fatally weakened as a result.[9]

In fact, of course, analyses of money incomes based on tax returns have well-known imperfections. Tax returns tell us nothing about the incomes of those below taxable levels, who constituted half of income-earners even in 1950, and, as many critics have pointed out, returns may not be accurate and will almost certainly not reflect 'hidden' income such as occupational perquisites most likely to benefit the higher-income earners.[10] Further, tax returns are taken to represent individually earned and consumed incomes, and it is rare for any attempt to be made to assess how many individuals in fact contributed to and lived on each income: wives (whether earning or not) and dependants such as children are invisible. Finally, the usefulness of tax returns for comparisons of income over time is severely limited by the changing value of money. G. D. H. Cole argued in 1955 that the fact that the value of money diminished in the period 1930 to 1950 by a factor of between two and three, while tax thresholds remained the same, 'accounts for a large part of the increase in the total number of incomes over £250, and also for a large part of the shift from lower to higher income grades'.[11] Thus Marsh's failure to take account of *real* incomes greatly exaggerates the 'levelling up' of incomes over the period of the war.

Work on income changes by Dudley Seers in the late 1940s came to more qualified conclusions. Seers made a crude division of income-earners into 'working-class', i.e. all wage-earners and non-manual workers with salaries of less than £250 per annum, and 'middle-class', i.e. all other salaried non-manual employees, and then used technically complex methods of attaching correct weightings to class-specific indices of pay and prices in order to assess changes in the real incomes of these two classes.[12] Seers claimed that after the war (1947) wages took up a larger proportion of the national income than salaries, which, coupled with the faster rise in the middle-class than in the working-class cost-of-living index, meant that the gap between the real net incomes of the two classes had narrowed. Comparing aggregates, Seers concluded that the real net incomes of the working class had risen by over 9 per cent, and those of the middle class had fallen by 7 per cent, between 1938 and 1947.[13] As far as causes were concerned, Seers explained the improved working-class share partly as a result of the rise in the national product during the war, and partly as a result of fiscal changes, including subsidies, which gave the working class 59 per cent of post-tax incomes in 1947 compared with 55 per cent in 1938. This led Seers to point out that the wartime redistribution of income could be 'largely reversed by fiscal means (e.g. by lowering the standard rate of income tax, reducing food subsidies, etc.)'. He suggested that such changes were already beginning with tax changes in 1947, the reduction of subsidies and the government policy of 'wage stabilization'.[14]

The upshot of Seers's arguments was that the future of the wartime redistribution of income was dependent on State action, a conclusion at which others arrived by different routes. For example, after observing that higher income groups retained less of their income than they had pre-war, G. D. H. Cole argued in 1955 that 'the effect of taxation on the distribution of real incomes has clearly been very substantial',[15] and later writers such as Westergaard and Resler noted that the more progressive direct taxation of the 1940s indeed reduced the share of top and middle incomes in the post-tax total between 1938 and 1949, while government controls over the cost of necessities – notably food, housing and fuel – during the war 'favoured those on low and moderate incomes'. These authors argued that the removal of controls after the war led to disproportionate increases in the price of these necessities, and that the reduction of the share of the richest 20 per cent in post-tax income was slight after 1949: 'The effect of this reversal of trends is to sharpen the contrast between the equalising tendencies of the decade of war and post-war "social reconstruction", and the stability or accentuation of income inequality from around 1950.'[16]

Thus the conclusion of these authors, led by Seers, on the subject of the levelling of class in the Second World War, differed from that of Marsh. The examination of real, post-tax incomes produced a more convincing case for levelling during the war than that which Marsh presented, but the stress on fiscal policy suggested that wartime levelling was not permanent, but was being reversed in the 1950s by government action. On the other hand, two aspects of this body of work may have led to overstatement of the degree of levelling during the war. First, the data used were aggregates rather than *per capita* incomes. The relative growth of the group earning either wages or salaries under £250, compared to that earning larger salaries, may have been important in pushing up the proportion of national income going to wages as opposed to salaries.[17] Second, this division of the recipients of income into wage – and salary-earners, manual and non-manual workers, members of the working and of the middle classes, is arbitrary and may have obscured both overlap between the two groups and stratification within them. We shall return to these points later in the discussion of levelling.

Of course, levelling of earned income is not all there is to levelling of social strata, let alone of social classes. Several authors have seen the situation with regard to property as ultimately more decisive. Thus T. B. Bottomore wrote, 'the inequality of incomes depends very largely upon the unequal distribution of property through inheritance, and not primarily upon the differences in earned income'.[18] For the class position of wage-earners to change, then, does not require simply enlargement of earnings, but the kind of consistent saving which would allow them to acquire and pass on property. 'Levelling', by this argument, is meaningful only if it is seen as a change in the distribution of property owners in society.

Most authors agree that the belief held by some public figures, particularly Liberal spokesmen, in the 1930s, that there was a widespread distribution of small savings and property in the working class, was erroneous.[19] However, the shift from high levels of unemployment and underemployment in the 1930s to full employment, overtime work and rising wage rates during the war caused some investigators to ask whether this situation was transformed between 1939 and 1945. Notably, Charles Madge, a sociologist, undertook to discover the truth about working-class accumulation during the war. He expected to find widespread and extensive working-class saving caused by the pressure, on the one hand, of improved earnings coupled with a limited supply of consumer goods due to shortages and rationing, and, on the other, of the official wartime campaign to promote savings as a counter to inflation. He therefore thought he would find a process of 'levelling up' within the social structure as more members of relatively low-income groups joined the ranks of small property holders.[20]

Madge reported that 'a great campaign' had been launched since 1939, to persuade people to save in three principal ways, through Trustee Saving Banks, by buying National Savings Certificates through the Post Office and through Savings Groups, which were usually based in the work-place, where a fixed deduction from the member's pay was made each week. The government had spent £834,100 on this campaign by June 1941. Madge found that the campaign had been successful in increasing the number of savers. There was considerable regional variation, but in the towns which Madge looked at, between 10 per cent and 30 per cent more families were saving by the new methods in 1942 than had been before the war, and they included those usually outside 'the orbit of national savings, such as 'families at low income levels and secondary earners'. This wartime saving was in addition to traditional methods of working-class saving, such as contributions to industrial assurance, pension funds, trade union subscriptions and voluntary health insurance, which Madge said were 'relatively unaffected by the war', and which would not lead to a change in the class position of the saver.[21]

Nevertheless, although there was an absolute increase in the number of working-class savers, Madge concluded from his survey of a large sample of households in Glasgow, Leeds and Bristol that the new savers represented a tiny proportion of the working class as a whole. Madge concluded that 'a large proportion of wage-earners' savings are due to a small proportion of wage-earners'; to be precise, among Leeds wage-earners 31 per cent of national saving came from 3 per cent of families. Forty-four per cent of families had no savings at all, and the majority of the rest (38 per cent of the total) saved less than 5s a week. The median weekly amount saved was 3s 4d, while the most popular single figure was 1s.[22]

Madge found that patterns of saving were in some respects not surprising. National saving behaved as a luxury – that is the proportion saved rose rapidly as income increased, whereas the proportion saved in the form of insurance behaved as a necessity, decreasing slightly as income rose. But beyond this the relation between income and saving was less straightforward. Madge did not look simply at the income of the 'chief wage-earner' of a household, but took account of the entire income and outgoings of each housekeeping unit, from which he calculated its 'excess income', that is the money beyond that necessary to satisfy its basic needs in terms of housing, food, fuel and clothing. He found, at both low and high levels of 'excess income', only a weak relation between excess income and national saving; for example, just seven out of seventy-one Leeds families with excess incomes below £1 5s did 57 per cent of the saving at this level. 'Heavy' saving of over 13s a week, likely to lead to significant capital accumulation on average began with a gross family income of more than £6 10s, but even here 'not all the heavy savers have so much as £2 10s in excess income. Neither are all those who have £2 10s excess income heavy savers'.[23] Even in this subgroup, savers were a minority. Madge commented, 'National saving is much more strongly concentrated than insurance saving, mainly because saving, apart from for a definite security purpose, is a new thing for the majority of wage-earners'.[24] He concluded (in 1943) that this meant that even 'if real incomes continue to rise and there is a progressive redistribution of incomes, the wage-earning class will not advance as a class towards middle-class standards'.[25] Rather, the small group of *'rentier* proletarians', whose growth the war had stimulated, would continue the process of accumulation and try to assimilate with the middle class. Madge thought that the principal methods of doing this were by acquiring property or a small business (such as a shop), or investing in education for children with a view to their joining the ranks of the black-coated or professional salariat.

Even within the minority group of savers, however, such upward social mobility was not the universally held objective. The interviews conducted in the course of his inquiry led Madge to conclude that most savers were motivated first by the fact that large consumables (like furniture or motor cycles) were not available in wartime but might be afterwards, and second by the not unconnected 'fear that present earning capacity may not last'.[26] Many of Madge's respondents expected and dreaded a post-war slump, but their desire to 'put something by' to meet such an emergency did not represent an urge to change their class position, nor did the amounts they typically saved warrant such as a result.

Madge thought that wartime unpredictabilities themselves encouraged 'mild hoarding', but questioning in Glasgow suggested that not more than a quarter of manual and black-coated workers kept reserves at home, typically behind the clock or in a jar on the mantlepiece, and the amounts put by were usually under £2. Madge was adamant that the apparently numerous 'suitcases full of ancient crumpled notes' deposited by workers in the Glasgow Savings Bank when the town was blitzed were 'exceptional'.[27] In this context it is worth noting that Madge's own methodology would tend to exaggerate rather than diminish the proportion of savers in his samples. He based his findings on budgets voluntarily kept by his respondents, and, as Seers pointed out, 'only the more literate and more careful would keep budgets, and there is reason to expect a correlation between ability to keep budgets and care in arranging outlay'.[28] The fact that only a tiny proportion of these budget-keepers were amassing war savings which might permanently alter their class position is therefore the more remarkable.

Madge's investigation of working-class patterns of saving and spending tends to make Seers's presentation of the improved aggregate share of the working class in national income as a form of 'levelling' look somewhat misleading. Madge showed that, as far as working-class experience was concerned, its rising share of the national income did not signify a trend towards economic equivalence in terms of property ownership. Indeed, the achievement of social mobility through the accumulation of savings appeared extremely limited. In addition, Madge's work emphasized that there were many divisions within the class of manual workers. It is relevant to our discussion to consider whether a 'levelling' process occurred as between these different groups within the working class during the war, or whether pre-war subgroups continued to exist and new ones were created.

Looking first at the overall picture, the numbers of those in paid employment rose during the war, from 19,473,000 in 1938 to a peak of 22,285,000 in 1943, composed of 15,032,000 men and 7,253,000 women (compared with 14,476,000 men and 4,997,000 women in 1938).[29] This expansion of the labour force obviously meant an improvement in living standards for the nearly 3 million people who in 1938 had been outside paid employment (e.g. housewives, schoolchildren and those unemployed). Average earnings rose, according to official figures, by 80 per cent (from 53s 3d in October 1938 to 96s 1d in July 1945).[30] On the other hand, hours worked also went up – from an average of 46.5 per week in 1938 to 50 in 1943, falling to 47.4 in July 1945 – and so too did the cost of living. The official figure for the rise in the working-class cost of living index was 31 per cent between 1939 and 1945,[31] although Seers criticizes this for underweighting some items of working-class expenditure, notably alcohol and tobacco, and put the increase between 1938 and 1947 at 61–62 per cent.[32] Either way, these averages suggest that full employment made manual workers better off than they had been pre-war.

However, they are no more than averages. Earnings during the war varied greatly between men and women, and between different industries, as they had done before it. If there was any 'levelling' of the differences between men and women it was very moderate. Women's average weekly earnings in manual work were 47 per cent of those of men in 1938 and 52 per cent in 1945.[33] As this suggests, few women received equal pay with men, in spite of the 'dilution agreements' which were supposed to guarantee women on 'mens work' the full male rate after a certain length of time. Both private employers and government ministries were loath to give women '100 per cent' and exploited clauses in the agreements stating that, to qualify, women must do the work 'without additional supervision or assistance'.[34] However, by far the most important means by which the gender differential was maintained was the classification of work as either 'men's' or 'women's'. Employers endeavoured to place any jobs women did in the 'women's work' category, where lower wage rates applied, and the trade unions pressed for as much work as possible to be labelled 'men's work', in which case it would be paid at men's rates and the women doing it would be regarded as temporary.[35] According to the official historian, in September 1942 three-quarters of women in munitions 'came under the women's schedule as performing women's work.[36] This did not only mean that the economic position of male and female wage-earners remained sharply differentiated; it also meant that there could be wide differences in what women earned within a single factory, according to whether they were paid at men's or women's rates .[37] Age made a difference, too. The average earnings of girls under 18 were the lowest of any group throughout the war. In addition, women's earnings in different industries diverged increasingly. In 1938 women's average weekly earnings in six industrial groups were within 3s 3d of each other, the lowest being textiles at 31s 9d and the highest, transport, at 34s 11d. By 1945 the differential was 26s, with women transport workers' average earnings standing at 81s 7d and clothing workers' at 55s 7d.[38]

To some extent this is accounted for by differences in union bargaining power in the different industries, since women's hourly pay, bonuses and piece rates were mostly fixed at a proportion of those of men. Like women, male workers in textiles, clothing and food, drink and tobacco received lower earnings than workers in other industries in 1938, and the differential widened during the war. However, the top male earners in 1945 were in metals, engineering and shipbuilding. Their average earnings of 133s exceeded those of male workers in chemicals by 10s 2d and in transport by 20s 2d. In contrast, the earnings of women transport workers exceeded those of women engineering workers by 12s 6d. The tendency among employers to confine women to 'women's work' in engineering and metals, together with divisions in policy towards women between the unions involved (notably the craft and the general unions), may go some way to explaining why, in contrast to the situation for men, engineering and metals were not the industries in which women's average earnings were greatest by the end of the war.

Far from industrial workers' earnings levelling during the war, differentials widened. To put a figure on this in the case of men, the gap between the highest and the lowest average earnings had been 12s in 1938 whereas in 1945 it was 28s 5d[39] (over twice the amount Madge thought necessary for significant saving). Further, within the 'best paying' industries – engineering and metals – earnings varied very greatly, and union efforts to maintain differentials were, if anything, more successful than counter-pressures to reduce them.

Earnings varied not only between grades and skill categories of men, but also between districts, mainly owing to factors like local union strength, the level of organization among employers, the degree of technological change in the particular branch of the industry and the position with regard to labour supply.[40] For example, earnings in Midland aircraft and engineering factories were relatively high before the war, and in the context of labour shortage arising during rearmament and the rapid expansion of production during the first years of the war, unions succeeded in pushing them up higher.[41] Much engineering work was organized as piece work, the rates for which were settled job by job. Some skilled craftsmen on time rates, such as tool-room workers, were given guarantees that their earnings would not be allowed to fall below those of the most productive piece workers. In addition, in both the engineering and the aircraft industries, there was a system of bonus payments. Before the war these bonuses were typically 25–30 per cent of time rates; by spring 1940 they had risen to 40–50 per cent in the north-west region, while in the Midlands they were as much as 100 per cent and by 1942 one Coventry motor factory was reported to be paying an average bonus of 324 per cent, with a top figure of 581 per cent. Not suprisingly, Coventry engineering workers rejected the employers' offer to fix the bonus at 100 per cent![42]

The particularly high earnings of men in the Midland engineering and air-craft factories gave rise to national concern. It came not so much from employers, whose anxiety to limit the size of their wage bills was less press-ing in wartime because they could pass on their labour costs to the govern-ment, but more from various government departments dealing with the control of labour. For example, the Ministry of Labour was concerned about the difficulties of transferring skilled men from the Midlands to new factories in other districts where rates were lower, the Ministry of Supply was worried about the impact of high engineering wages in private firms on the expec-tations of its workers in Royal Ordnance Factories, and the Select Committee on National Expenditure was worried about the negative effects on pro-ductivity of very high earnings.[43] Its suggestion that £12 to £15 a week con-stituted a threshold beyond which a man lost interest in increasing his efficiency underlines the great divergence of earnings among manual workers in wartime.[44] Expressed in shillings, these sums are 240*s* and 300*s*, compared with average male earnings in engineering in 1941 of 112*s* 2*d*, average female earnings in engineering of 48*s* 1*d*, average male earnings throughout manufacturing of 99*s* 5*d* and equivalent female earnings of 43*s* 11*d*.[45]

Whether this small minority of men with exceptionally high wartime earn-ings should be regarded as having 'levelled up,' to the middle class is another matter. Most of the social surveys of the 1940s used an income of £250 a year, or £5 (i.e. 100*s*) a week as the approximate dividing line between the work-ing and middle classes, by which criterion such men would qualify as 'middle-class'. However, Madge believed that skilled men earning spectacularly large amounts in new industries tended not to be regular savers, but enjoyed the 'windfall' while it lasted, especially if they came from a background of unem-ployment in the 1930s.[46] They therefore did not, in general, accumulate capi-tal which could have assisted their assimilation into the middle class.

Further, in the debate of the 1950s and 1960s on the class position of manual workers with high incomes, numerous sociologists argued against seeing working-class affluence alone as sufficient to close the gap between classes. For example, W. G. Runciman pointed out that the conditions under which a manual worker earned a relatively high income differed sharply from those of a non-manual worker at the same level of income, in terms of the overtime and piece-work components, the meals, furnishings and sanitation available in the workplace, rights to holidays and pensions, chances of pro-motion and the degree of security in the employment.[47]

It would be fascinating to draw up a balance sheet of these aspects of manual and non-manual work in wartime. In the absence of the kind of research which would permit such precision, it can be said that there was improvement in some of these areas for some manual workers, while some non-manual workers, evacuated to temporary office accommodation, for example, may have been worse off than pre-war. Most obviously, the number of work-place canteens expanded from about 1,500 pre-war to 11,800 in 1944 under a requirement in the Essential Work Order, and the Ministry of

Labour also urged employers to improve lavatory facilities and to employ a works doctor or nurse. The occurrence of change was patchy, however. For example, the increase in the number of work-places with canteens by over 10,000 must be set against the total of 67,400 undertakings covered by Essential Work Orders in 1944, and against the fact that in no industry did more than half the workers use the canteens. Married women workers in particular missed out because of the tendency to use the lunch hour for shopping.[48]

Any improvements in work-place conditions need to be seen in the context of the increasing organization of manual work on a piece-work basis (which brought with it greater pressure), the long hours expected and infrequent holidays.[49] The chances of promotion for a male manual worker (e.g. from machinist to setter, setter to chargehand and so to overseer, foreman and manager) may have been slightly greater in wartime, with the expansion of work-forces and introduction of new processes, though the same may have been true for salaried workers (moving, for example, from clerical to administrative or managerial grades). But security of employment for manual workers lasted for only as long as the war effort required a particular type of production, as the transfers and lay-offs from engineering and Royal Ordnance Factories in 1944–5 demonstrated.[50]

Thus I am arguing here that widening differentials in wartime both caused the working class to become more heterogeneous, and did not automatically lead to the 'levelling up' of the best-paid manual workers.

Undoubtedly government departments would have liked there to have been a levelling of income among manual workers, and pressed for it when they could, as in the case of the Royal Ordnance Factories, where the Ministry of Supply did achieve some degree of standardization between districts, if not between grades of worker. The upward movement of earnings stabilized in the Midlands during the war, though not because of government intervention. Rather, the explanation lies in the fact that the pace of technological change slowed somewhat, so there was no longer a constant process of fixing new prices, and communist shop stewards tended to work against disruption in the shops after the entry of Russia to the war in June 1941, while in other districts growing militancy and a mounting propensity to strike in 1943–4 may have made earnings less stable.[51]

But differentials between grades of workers and between districts continued throughout the war and after it. The official historian wrote, 'In June 1953 weekly earnings in the Coventry district averaged more than 43s 0d above those in any other district even though hours worked there were comparatively short'.[52] In other branches of the munition industries the regional pattern of differentials was different; for instance, in shipbuilding, earnings were particularly high in London and Southampton, and the best-paying Royal Ordnance Factories (ROFs) were in London and South Wales. Although greater geographical uniformity was achieved in these industries than in the case of the motor and aircraft branches of engineering, differences remained between the earnings of time and piece workers (particularly between those of machine setters on time rates and dilutees on piece rates in ROFs), between the rates of adults and apprentices, and between those of men and women, and frequently caused contention.[53]

To sum up, the division of industries into 'essential' and 'non-essential' and the combination in the former of labour shortage, 'dilution', the premium on 'skill', and growing union strength, coupled with the government's fear of strikes, in the context of major local differences dating from before the war, ensured that the war had the opposite effect on manual workers' earnings to 'levelling'.

Another aspect of the distribution of income within the working class is its allocation between and within households. It is possible that the overall rise in working-class earnings during the war led to 'levelling' in this respect. Madge's data on working-class spending patterns provide a basis for discussion of this question.

Commenting on expenditure trends since 1904, Madge wrote, 'The most striking change in the pattern of demand is the great decline in the proportion allotted to food, and the corresponding increase in the proportion allotted to "other items" '.[54] The war accelerated, though it obviously had not initiated, this trend. 'Other items', which were mainly 'non-essentials' like alcohol, tobacco and entertainment, rose from 30 per cent of working-class budgets in 1938 to 34 per cent in 1942, and the proportion spent on food fell by 3 per cent (from 40 per cent to 37 per cent),[55] even though (in spite of relatively heavy subsidies, price control and rationing) food had risen by 22 per cent in the working-class cost-of-living index between 1939 and 1941.[56]

Authors of social surveys agree that a major factor explaining the declining proportion of working-class expenditure on food was the reduction in family size during the twentieth century. The war made a special contribution to this, with particularly low birth-rates 1939–41, though during 1942–5 there was something of a recovery.[57]

However, there were of course wide variations in family size, as there had been pre-war. In wartime, as before, an increase in the number of children heralded the decline of the family's standard of living, a point graphically illustrated by the finding of the Wartime Social Survey in 1942 that the heaviest users of credit facilities were families with three or more children under 14.[58] It follows that the majority of three-child families (75 per cent) had no National Savings.[59] Madge observed that working-class families with five or six non-earning children were almost invariably in relative poverty, regardless of the skill status of the main wage-earner. He wrote, 'If one arranges a random sample of wage-earning families in order of effective wealth, skilled, well-paid workers with children will come lower down than unskilled, low-paid workers without any children'.[60]

A survey of 'The British Household' in 1947 found that in fact a higher proportion of households of the middle-income group of 'better-paid unskilled operatives', 'lower-paid skilled operatives' and 'lower-paid clerical workers', with a basic weekly wage rate of £4 to £5 10s, had children under 15 than any other income group. Twenty-four per cent had two or more children, compared with 15 per cent in the group of lower-paid unskilled operatives immediately below them and 20 per cent in the group of better-paid skilled and clerical workers, and lower paid managerial and professional workers, above them. The households of the middle group were also more over-crowded than those of the other groups: 33 per cent had more than one person per habitable room, compared with 24 per cent in the group below, 17 per cent in the group above, and 4 per cent in the top income group.[61] The larger than average family size of the middle group, then, limited the potential for 'levelling up' offered by its improved wartime earnings.

The uneven distribution of income per head of the working-class popu-lation due to family size was further intensified by uneven distribution within families. Madge noticed that wage-earning husbands quite frequently did not share the rise in their incomes with their wives and children. In none of the seven towns he looked at did a majority of husbands hand over all their weekly earnings to their wives, and in most only a small proportion (under 15 per cent) did so. The dominant pattern was for husbands to give wives a fixed sum as a result of an 'actual or implicit bargain . . . driven at intervals', and in some towns, notably Glasgow, a majority of husbands kept their wives in the dark about the wartime increase in their earnings. It was here that Madge 'came across evidence of revolt against the whole system' of housekeeping 'allowances'.[62] Madge wrote, 'fortunately the deceptions occurred mainly at the higher income levels', meaning by the word 'fortunately' that actual undernourishment of wives and children due to the husband's contribution of too low a figure to meet the rising cost of living was limited to a minority.[63] But his findings nevertheless suggest that in the majority of families in Glas-gow, and possibly elsewhere, the husband neither declared his income accu-rately nor passed on a rising proportion of his rising earnings to his wife.[64] Thus, far from there being any 'levelling' in the household distribution of income, the economic gulf between husbands and wives actually widened.

The households in which the wife was most likely to share the benefit of her husband's wartime earnings were those in which incomes were pooled and then distributed according to need. Though nowhere universal, Madge found that this pattern was most prevalent in Leeds and Blackburn, where 24 per cent and 49 per cent of families pooled their incomes. The benefits to wives and children are reflected in the proportions of family income allocated to housekeeping and husband's pocket money, which were 65 per cent and 17 per cent in Leeds, in contrast to 58 per cent and 27 per cent in Glasgow, where only 14 per cent of families pooled their earnings.[65]

The extent of pooling appears to have been a very local matter, only partly determined by the degree to which it was customary for women, including wives, to do paid work. Madge noticed that in Bradford only 15 per cent of families pooled their incomes, in contrast to the high figure of 49 per cent in Blackburn, even though there was a high female participation rate in both towns. In spite of the rising numbers of married women in war work (43 per cent of women workers were married in 1943, compared with 16 per cent in 1931),[66] Madge did not observe an increase in the habit of pooling, and was emphatic that the wife's economic position remained highly inequitable.[67]

Having said this, there is no doubt that women's earnings made a significant contribution to family incomes in wartime. It could be that the rising share of total personal allocated income going to the lower income groups in the 1940s, which Seers depicted, was a result less of 'redistribution' (which, as we have seen, was how it was interpreted) than of the greater extent of paid employment among the wives of lower-income than higher-income husbands during and after the war. It would, of course, be difficult to determine this accurately.[68]

The idea of extensive social mixing among women workers, much vaunted in wartime propaganda, is a confusing factor when considering which class benefited more from women's work. It is usually suggested that women from upper and middle-class families took wartime jobs beneath their social status for the duration.[69] The Wartime Social Survey report *Women at Work* contains evidence that 28 per cent of women who had worked pre-war in the white-collar category 'professional, administrative and clerical' took manual jobs of various types. However, they formed no more than 7½ per cent of the total number of women manual workers of all types of the sample, and the report commented that most of these ex-white-collar women had been clerks,[70] whose class position was in any case somewhat intermediate, especially after a decade in which opportunities for the daughters of manual workers to obtain their first job in white-collar work had increased rapidly.[71] This evidence, plus information on the educational backgrounds of women factory workers, strongly suggests that social mixing among women war workers, and the social levelling implied by it, has been exaggerated.[72]

The most compelling evidence against social mixing, however, is the attempt by the Wartime Social Survey to classify women workers in wartime industries by the income of the 'chief wage-earner' in the woman's household, which revealed that a higher proportion of women war workers were in households in which the 'chief wage-earner' received up to £5 a week than the proportion of such households in the population as a whole (87 per cent, compared with 75 per cent). The WSS concluded that 'Women in the higher income groups have gone into other forms of National Service and that the group from which the greatest proportion of working women has been drawn is that of the semi-skilled and skilled workers with wage rates of £3 12s 0d to £5 0s 0d'.[73] In view of the evidence which we have already reviewed about the large family size of precisely this middle group and its tendency towards financial shortfall, it makes good sense that wives and daughters from such households filled the factories in greater proportion than they occurred in the community at large.

The WSS evidence also lends substance to the view that women's wartime paid employment contributed more to the increase in the share of the working class in national income than to that of the middle class. The forms of National Service chosen by the majority of women whose husbands or fathers were in the middle-class income groups were either relatively low-paying, as in the case of the women's auxiliary services and the Women's

Land Army, or entirely voluntary, like the Red Cross and the Women's Voluntary Service. Participation of this sort in the war effort would have added little to middle-class aggregate income, and thus would have assisted 'levelling' – ironically, in view of the resentment which middle-class women's preference for exemption from paid work and for involvement in voluntary work provoked among some working women, who saw it as a sign of 'inequality of sacrifice'.[74]

However, it is difficult to assess the extent of working-class women's contribution, either in terms of the financial effects on individual families, or in terms of the proportion of families affected in each working class income group, given the invisibility in survey data of working women's earnings.[75] One can only return to the WSS statement that the majority of working women came from homes classified as belonging to the middle-income bracket of the working class, and official evidence that the overall average earnings of women workers were 64s in 1944.

Whether the addition of this average sum to the budget of working-class homes either did no more than pull a family out of debt or succeeded in pushing it into the narrow ranks of upwardly mobile savers must have depended on how many mouths there were to feed in the household, the extent of additional expenditure on nurseries, laundries and other facilities for the domestic work which the wife was no longer doing unpaid, and the proportion of the couple's joint income which they chose to spend on those 'other items' to which, as we have seen, the working class had been devoting an increasing proportion of its expenditure since 1904, a trend which the war intensified.

Madge repeatedly stated that, after they had given their wives an allowance or paid for their board and lodging if they were single, men spent the surplus of their increased wartime earnings on such 'non-essential' items of consumption. Though critical when such spending was at the expense of the well-being of wives and children, he was mainly concerned to show that alcohol and tobacco were more important to the vast majority of working men than were savings: 'National savings is . . . considered more of a luxury than tobacco and alcohol in that, when there are more mouths to feed, it is the former and not the latter which are dispensed with.'[76]

Women were, of course, not immune to these pleasures, and many started smoking cigarettes for the first time during the war, but Madge said that 'the great bulk of the spending on tobacco and alcohol is contributed by husbands and other male earners'.[77] In contrast, 'most of the spending on 'Entertainment – comes from female earners'. Madge thought the reasons for increased spending on these items were primarily social and narcotic, though he hinted that for men there was an element of compensation for 'giving up' the bulk of their income for housekeeping.[78] One may add that, for both men and women, beer, cigarettes and cinemas offered some solace in the face of the immeasurably discomforting aspects of war: the blackout, bombardment, long hours of work, the difficulties of travel and the anxiety of separation.

Such reasons for spending a rising proportion of income on 'non-essentials' evidently outweighed the relatively rapid rise in cost. The price of tobacco doubled between 1939 and 1942, and the price of beer went up steeply, unchecked by the government (and underweighted in the government's calculation of the working-class cost-of-living index) because of its value as a source of revenue.[79]

Of course, the working class was not alone in its consumption of tobacco and alcohol, nor in its need for consolation. But according to Seers it devoted a larger proportion of its total expenditure to these things than did the population as a whole: 5 per cent on tobacco and 7 per cent on alcohol, compared with a global figure of just over 4 per cent on each. A more direct comparison with middle-class spending shows that nearly half working-class expenditure on 'other items' went on drink and tobacco, compared with under a fifth of middle-class expenditure.[80] It is almost irresistible to conclude (with Madge) that most male members of the working class were drinking and smoking their wartime 'excess incomes' rather than using them as a means by which to 'level up' socially, because for the majority such a shift in class position had very little meaning.[81]

We have established, I hope, that there was a great deal of variety in the economic circumstances of working-class families during the war. Whether both husband and wife were earning, the occupations and industries in which they worked, the region in which they lived, the number of dependants and the method by which income was allocated in the household were important determinants of the capacity of a family to generate 'excess income'. But, even when all these circumstances were favourable, spending rather than accumulation was the norm, even (or especially) in the face of wartime shortages.

Individuals living outside family households tended to be particularly disadvantaged, in economic terms. Pensioners had been a relatively poor subgroup before the war which, because of its dependence upon a fixed income at a time of rising cost of living, became worse off during the war, in spite of a patchily applied Exchequer supplement to old age pensions on a 'household needs' basis after January 1940.[82] Nevertheless, Madge showed that 'single' pensioners were falling into heavier debt during the war than those living in 'mixed pensioner families'.[83]

The same contrast occurred in the economic circumstances of servicemen's wives. A private soldier's wife with two children received a total allowance of 32s in 1939, which rose to 33s in 1940, 38s in 1941 and 43s in 1942.[84] But Madge discovered a sharp contrast in standard of living between the 20 per cent of service wives in his sample with no children, living with their parents and working, who were saving heavily (to the tune of 27s a week), and the 20 per cent of service wives at the other extreme, who did not live with other adults, were not doing paid work and had children to support, who were falling heavily into debt (to the tune of 15s 6d per week).[85]

A large proportion of service wives were dependent on credit buying (nearly 53 per cent compared with 38 per cent of a sample of working-class women), though it is not surprising that the Wartime Social Survey found that they were the main group to which shopkeepers were reluctant to give credit and landlords loath to let rooms.[86] Nor is it surprising that servicemen's wives were keen to find paid work and were often given priority for places in wartime nurseries.[87] As 'the new poor' of the war, whose plight was caused by their husbands' service in defence of the country, they commanded considerable sympathy from members of the public who did not stand in a direct financial relationship with them. Public pressure resulted in a 'rise' to an allowance of 60s for the service wife with two children.[88] Though an improvement, this was still below the woman's average wage of 64s.

Servicemen and women themselves (whatever their class) were, of course, a relatively low-paid group. They had little chance of amassing savings during their period in the forces, even though part of a pay rise in January 1942 took the form of a post-war credit of 6d a day.[89] Madge would not have considered this a high saving. It represented 3s 6d a week, and about £9 a year. However, there were opportunities in the forces for men and women to 'level up' in non-financial ways, for instance raising their status by becoming non–commissioned or commissioned officers, and acquiring skills ranging from clerical and administrative to technical, which may have opened up new job prospects in the postwar world. The financially disadvantaged position of the private soldier also applied to the officer, who received more pay and allowances but was still at an income level well below a middling white-collar salary. There was much complaint in 1941–2 that officers' pay was so inadequate that it needed supplementing with a private income simply to cover mess bills, uniform and other essentials.[90] Officers' wives received larger allowances than privates', but their incomes were still relatively low in the wartime context.[91] Much the same stratification must have existed where officers' wives were concerned as Madge depicted for servicemen's wives, the best-off being those without children who were living with relatives, and the worst-off those struggling to make ends meet on their own with children.

Servicemen of all ranks and their wives may have experienced quite considerable 'levelling', in the sense of sharing a similar economic position, depressed in comparison to their civilian pre-war peers. Ironically the service hierarchy, which was apparently maintained as energetically among service wives as within the services themselves, countered with sharp status differentiation this economic levelling.

Up to this point in the discussion the 'middle class' has been largely neglected, because interest has focused on the question of whether the rise in the working-class share of the national income meant for that class (or a substantial part of it) a process of permanent 'levelling up', either as between the working class and the middle class or within the ranks of the working class. It has not been possible to be definitive, but the suggestion here is that permanent levelling up affected only a tiny group of self-denying savers, and that the war may have increased differentials between groups of workers and between husbands and wives, rather than diminishing them. It is now time to examine the other side of the coin of Seers's findings on the working-class aggregate income. Did the relative fall in the middle-class share of national income mean that the middle class (defined as non-manual workers with an income over £250 p.a.) experienced permanent 'levelling down'?

To recap, Seers wrote that between 1938 and 1947 the salary bill had 'risen by only just over fifty per cent, compared with a near doubling of most other forms of income'. When taxes and the cost of living were taken into account, this meant that 'the real net incomes of the working class had risen over nine per cent, and those of the middle class had fallen over seven per cent'.[92] Seers stated that outside these aggregates there were wide differences in the income position of different groups within the middle class, but though he presented evidence about differences in the middle-class cost of living he omitted evidence about income differences.

Guy Routh, however, looked at trends in average earnings in the various occupational classes used in the census, over a longer period than that of the war itself. He found that 'the only really big changes' between 1910 and 1960 were the declining differentials of three occupational classes – professionals, clerks and foremen – between 1935 and 1955. The income of all three groups had been 'levelled down' towards the average for men and women in all occupational classes, although the extent of the fall varied and in some cases the differential was still extensive. For instance, 'higher professionals' enjoyed incomes nearly three times the average, even though this represented a fall of 26 per cent compared with their position in 1935–6. The relative drop had been particularly severe for men and women in the 'lower professional' group, though clerks of both sexes were the non-manual group with the lowest earnings. The occupational group 'managers and administrators', in contrast, improved its position.[93] Thus, as in the working class, so in the middle class, the picture was not one of overall levelling, but of differing fortunes for different groups.

Of course, it may be misleading to look at change over the period 1935–55, since by then the effects of war may have been overtaken by subsequent developments. But Routh provided some details on the relative movement of average manual earnings and the salaries of various classes of civil servants, which show the period 1938–40 to have marked the beginning of the fall of non-manual pay in relation to manual earnings and 1944 to have marked its nadir.[94]

Undoubtedly, the shortage of manual labour in the munition industries and the improved leverage of the trade unions immediately before and during the war had much to do with the overall narrowing of differentials between non-manual and manual occupations. However, Routh stated that changes in the averages of occupational groups were only partly caused by changes in the pay of individual occupations, and were also caused 'by changes in the numbers occupied in occupations at different levels of pay'.[95] Elsewhere he suggested that the apparent reduction in the average pay of the non-manual industrial employee population in 1938–40 'could have been brought about by the substitution of female for male labour'.[96] In other words, because of the influx of women at low rates of pay, and the outflow of men, the earnings averages of various non-manual occupational groups were depressed. Routh unfortunately did not subject this suggestion to careful scrutiny, and the necessary research is a larger project than can be undertaken here. It is made particularly difficult by the absence of an occupational census for the war. However, using the rather unsatisfactory Industrial Classification some suggestions can be made.

Workers in national government can be taken as primarily 'non-manual'. The wartime influx of women into this group was extreme. The total in 1945 was 1,214 per cent what it was in 1939, whereas the number of men was 174 per cent of the 1939 figure, making the proportion of women rise from 14 to 54 per cent of the total number of workers in national government. By comparison, the total number of insured women in industry in 1945 was 128 per cent of the number in 1939, and the proportion rose from 28 to 39 per cent.[97]

It does look possible, then, as Routh suggested, that the extensive substitution for men in white-collar work of women, employed by custom in different grades from men and at lower rates of pay, made a significant contribution to the reduction of the differential between civil service non-manual salaries and average manual earnings.

Earlier, however, we suggested that the wartime earnings of women in manual work may have made a significant contribution to aggregate working-class income, even though women's average manual earnings were only just over half those of men. Why did the increased number of white-collar women not augment middle-class earnings in the same way? The issue hinges on where low-paid non-manual workers, especially women, are placed in terms of class. Routh simply compared all civil service salary-earners with wage-earners, but Seers took as his criterion for membership of the middle class 1938–47 non-manual workers with incomes of £250 or above. This would disqualify numerous male clerks, whose average pay in 1938 was £192 p.a. (rising to approximately £224 in 1942), almost all women clerks, whose average was £99 (rising to approximately £115), and many women in the lower professions, whose average was £211 (rising to approximately £246).[98] By his own declaration Seers cannot have included the salaries of low-paid white-collar workers, particularly those of the numerous women entering this section during the war, in his estimate of the middle-class share of national income, but subsumed them in aggregate 'working-class' income.[99] In Seers's work, then, the wartime influx of women to white-collar work assisted the levelling up of the working class, whereas in Routh's work the low salaries of such women contributed to the levelling down of the salariat.

All this points to the difficulty of using income and occupational criteria of 'class', as well as to the particular problem of locating white-collar women workers in the class structure.[100] It also supports the idea of the growth of a 'cross-class' group of low salary-earners and better-paid manual workers, which George Orwell described as an 'intermediate stratum at which the older class distinctions are beginning to break down,'[101] and which excited both him and G. D. H. Cole, who thought it would swell the ranks of Labour voters.[102] However, harmonious assimilation within the 'intermediate class' after the war was not guaranteed, notably when it came to housing. Referring to the feelings of manual and low-paid non-manual groups, a Middlesbrough planner wrote in 1948, 'there is a good deal of evidence that mixing of social classes and other groups . . . creates social friction', and he recommended separate housing provision.[103]

Let us look, finally and very briefly, at the extent to which the middle class was accumulating savings during the war. Though unfortunately we do not have details of middle-class patterns of saving of the kind Madge collected from the working class, both he and Seers made some suggestive comments.

They both argued that during the war the middle class (or, as Madge emphasized, its wealthier sections) saved money which would normally have been spent on 'other items, notably motor cars, education and domestic help.[104] Certainly expenditure on large 'luxury' items dried up during the war. For example, that on 'cars and motor cycles' fell from £152 million in 1938 to nil in 1943.[105] In addition Seers noted that shortages, subsidies and rationing meant that the goods which members of the middle class bought during the war were cheaper than the sort of things they had bought pre-war. Further, they stood to benefit from the 'undistributed profits' of wartime, which enforced the saving of dividends and increased the value of shares.[106]

Madge viewed wealthier middle-class families as 'pertinacious savers' by dint of both their 'high excess incomes' and their 'outlook and upbringing', and attributed to them the bulk of the money raised by National Savings and the sale of Defence Bonds.[107] If indeed they were saving heavily in wartime, they would have increased the property differential between themselves and other middle-class as well as working-class groups. In a 'hidden', or at any rate individualized and private way, then, the narrowing of income differentials such as those of 'higher professionals' may have been offset by wartime savings, and the improvement in the position of 'managers and administrators' may have been even greater than it appeared. This is ironic in that levelling of consumption during the war was a major component of the popular impression of the 'levelling of class'.[108]

What can we conclude from this review of surveys and accounts pertinent to the issue of the 'levelling of class'? I should like to end by drawing together three main points.

First, permanent 'levelling up' of the working class, as depicted by both defenders of middle-class status and advocates of a 'classless' society in the 1940s and 1950s, is thrown in doubt by the absence of any guarantee of the permanence of relatively enlarged working-class incomes and by the beginnings in the late 1940s of the reversal of fiscal policies which had favoured the working class during the war.

Second, on the other hand, there were certainly wartime changes in social stratification, and there is no doubt that some groups of manual workers improved their pay position markedly, relative both to other groups of manual workers and to some groups of salaried workers. In addition, it seems that working-class women undertook paid work to a greater extent (and at higher levels of pay) than women of the middle class, apart from those in the latter group who entered low-salary white-collar jobs, whose class position is one of the unresolved problems of stratification theory. All the same, there were wide variations in the income levels of different working-class groups – for example, aircraft workers and servicemen's wives – and little sign of any 'levelling' within the working-class household. Likewise, some middle-class groups, such as 'managers and administrators', fared better than others, such as 'professionals'.

Third, evidence of differences in saving patterns within and between classes suggests that when class is seen in relation to property, rather than income, the war gave rise to very little movement out of the working class via accumulation, and it may even have encouraged the widening of property differentials, both within the middle class and between it and the working class.

Finally, it must be emphasized that much of the above is, of necessity in view of the available data, tentative. It is intended as an antidote to a focus entirely upon images and attitudes, and indeed has at some points suggested that popular contemporary ideas of the way levelling would be achieved in wartime (e.g. by drawing women of all classes into paid industrial work and by establishing equality of consumption) may have been quite mistaken, in terms of underlying economic tendencies conducive to levelling, as opposed to appearances of equality. This chapter, then, is offered as a challenge to previous interpretations and it is hoped that it will both provoke debate and stimulate further research.

Notes

1 Arthur Marwick, *Class, Image and Reality in Britain, France and the U.S.A. since 1930*, London, Collins, 1980, ch. 11.
2 Stanislas Andrzejewski, *Military Organisation and Society*, London, Routledge, 1954.
3 R. M. Titmuss, 'War and social policy', in *Essays on 'The Welfare State'*, London, Allen & Unwin, 1963, p. 86.
4 For a stimulating discussion of the way recent historians have used 'class' see R. S. Neale, *Class in English History, 1680–1850*, Oxford, Blackwell, 1981.
5 Neal, *Class*, p. 132.
6 D. C. Marsh, *The Changing Social Structure of England and Wales, 1871–1951*, London, Routledge, 1958, p. 220.
7 Marsh, *Changing Social Structure*, pp. 218 and 223.
8 See discussion in J. Westergaard and H. Resler, *Class in a Capitalist Society: a Study of Contemporary Britain*, London, Heinemann, 1975, p. 32.
9 Roy Lewis and Angus Maude, *The English Middle Classes*, London, Phoenix House, 1949. See also discussion in W. G. Runciman, *Relative Deprivation and Social Justice: a Study of Attitudes to Social Inequality in Twentieth-century England*, Harmondsworth, Penguin, 1972, p. 94.
10 See for example, Richard M. Titmuss, *Income Distribution and Social Change: A Study in Criticism*, London, Allen & Unwin, 1962, chs 3 and 8.
11 G. D. H. Cole, *Studies in Class Structure*, London, Routledge, 1955, p. 75. Cole's reservations are supported in A. H. Halsey (ed.) *Trends in British Society since*

1900: a Guide to the Changing Social Structure of Britain, London, Macmillan, 1972, p. 75.

12 Dudley Seers, *Changes in the Cost-of-living and the Distribution of Income since 1938*, Oxford University Institute of Statistics, Oxford, Blackwell, 1949, pp. 5 and 8. Westergaard and Resler refer to Seers's work as 'probably the most comprehensive examination of the 1940s shift' in incomes, *Class*, p. 55.

13 Seers, *Changes*, p. 65.

14 ibid.

15 Cole, *Studies*, p. 76. See also Halsey, *Trends*, table 3.15, p. 95.

16 Westegaard and Resler, *Class*, pp. 54-5, and tables 1 and 2, pp. 39-40. T. B. Bottomore also believed this to be so. See *Classes in Modern Society*, London, Allen & Unwin, 1965, p. 34: 'between 1939 and 1949 redistribution may have transferred some ten per cent of the national income from property owners to wage earners; but . . . since 1949 there has again been growing inequality'.

17 Seers is explicit on how he arrived at figures for the total wage and salary bills (see *Changes*, pp. 59-65), but surprisingly silent on the issue of the calculation of the size of the two groups. In the absence of an occupational census for the war period, and in view of the presentation of all employment data using industrial classifications, it seems that there is no obvious way in which it could be done.

18 Bottomore, *Classes*, p. 16.

19 See discussion in Runciman, *Relative Deprivation*, p. 90, and John Hilton, *Rich Man, Poor Man*, London, Allen & Unwin, 1944, pp. 60 and 68-9. He found that 70 per cent of savings in Post Office accounts were under £25, and 90 per cent of those earning less than £200 rented their accommodation.

20 Charles Madge, *War-time Patterns of Saving and Spending*, National Institute of Economic and Social Research Occasional Papers, IV, Cambridge University Press, 1943, pp. 1, 4, 7, 9.

21 Madge, *War-time Patterns*, pp. 41-9.

22 ibid., pp. 1 and 50.

23 ibid., p. 69.

24 ibid., p. 67.

25 ibid., p. 82.

26 ibid., p. 73.

27 ibid., pp. 47-8.

28 Seers, *Changes*, p. 6.

29 Central Statistical Office, *Statistical Digest of the War*, London, HMSO, 1951, table 9, p. 8.

30 Central Statistical Office, *Digest*, table 187, p. 204.

31 ibid., table 188, p. 204, and table 190, p. 205.

32 Seers, *Changes*, pp. 22-3.

33 Penny Summerfield, *Women Workers in the Second World War: Production and Patriarchy in Conflict*, London, Croom Helm, 1984, p. 200.

34 The official historian wrote that the practice was 'that the 100 per cent concession should be limited to individual cases', P. Inman, *Labour in the Munition Industries*, London, HMSO, 1957, p. 357.

35 Summerfield, *Women Workers*, ch. 7.

36 Inman, *Labour*, p. 354.

37 Summerfield, *Women Workers*, p. 170.

38 Central Statistical Office, *Digest*, table 189, p. 205.

39 ibid.

40 Richard Croucher, 'Communist politics and shop stewards in engineering, 1935-46', unpublished Ph.D. thesis, University of Warwick, 1978, ch. 1.

41 Inman, *Labour*, pp. 319-20.

42 ibid., pp. 320-5.

43 ibid., pp. 323, 338, 355.

44 Select Committee on National Expenditure, *Fifteenth Report*, Session 1940-1, section 7.

45 Central Statistical Office, *Digest*, pp. 204-5.

46 Madge, *War-time Patterns*, p. 15. See also W. K. Hancock and M. M. Gowing, *British War Economy*, London, HMSO, 1949, p. 330, who corroborate this.

47 Runciman, *Relative Deprivation*, pp. 98-100.

48 Summerfield, *Women Workers*, pp. 19, 100-1.

49 Inman, *Labour*, pp. 396-7; PRO, Lab. 10/281, 'Causes of Industrial Unrest, 1943'.

50 Richard Croucher, *Engineers at War, 1939-1945*, London, Merlin, 1982, pp. 297-9; Summerfield, *Women Workers*, pp. 160-1.

51 Croucher, *Engineers*, ch. 3, particularly p. 168.

52 Inman, *Labour*, p. 327, n. 2.

53 ibid., pp. 329-30, 340-6, 334; Croucher, *Engineers*, pp. 197-244; Summerfield, *Women Workers*, ch. 7.

54 Madge, *War-time Patterns*, p. 70.

55 ibid., table XLIV, p. 70.

56 Central Statistical Office, *Digest*, table 190, p. 205. On food subsidies, etc., see Hancock and Cowing, *War Economy*, pp. 167, 333-4, 501-2. Clothes consumed more of working-class expenditure in 1942 than 1938, not surprisingly in view of their steep rise in the working-class cost-of-living index (92 per cent in 1939-42), though clothes rationing (1941) and the Utility clothing scheme (1942) brought clothes' prices down thereafter. There was a small decline in the proportion spent on rent, probably due to rent control under the Rent and Mortgage Interest Restrictions Act, 1939, which held rents to an (official) rise of only 1 per cent in 1939-42. See Hancock and Gowing, *War Economy*, pp. 502-3 and 166.

57 Central Statistical Office, *Digest*, table 7, p. 5.

58 Central Office of Information, Wartime Social Survey, Report no. 23, New Series, 42, *Credit Buying*, July, 1942.

59 Madge, *War-time Patterns*, p. 62.

60 ibid., p. 16.

61 Central Office of Information, Social Survey, *The British Household*, by P. G. Gray, based on an inquiry carried out in 1947 (1949), table 5, p. 7, and table 33, p. 24.

62 Madge, *War-time Patterns*, p. 54.

63 ibid., p. 53.

64 ibid., pp. 53, 58-9.

65 ibid., table XXVIII, p. 54.

66 Central Office of Information, Wartime Social Survey, *Women at Work*, by Geoffrey Thomas, June 1944, p. 1; Census of England and Wales, 1931, *Occupational Tables*, 1, 1934.

67 Madge, *War-time Patterns*, p. 55.

68 As Westergaard and Resler point out when making a similar point, *Class*, p. 41.

69 Summerfield, *Women Workers*, pp. 55-7.

70 Central Office of Information, Wartime Social Survey, *Women at Work*, table 14, p. 9.

71 E. Gamarnikow *et al., Gender, Class and Work*, London, Heinemann, 1983, ch. 5, 'Trends in female social mobility', by Geoff Payne, Judy Payne and Tony Chapman.

72 Ninety-four per cent of women on assembly and unskilled repetitive work and 96 per cent of machinists and hand-tool operators had received no secondary education, compared with a total of 80 per cent of the age group who had received such education in 1938. Central Office of Information, Wartime Social Survey, *Women at Work*, p. 6; Board of Education, *Report of the Consultative Committee on Secondary Education*, London, HMSO, 1938, table 1, p. 88.

73 Central Office of Information, Wartime Social Survey, *Women at Work*, p. 7. The actual proportions given were as follows:

Weekly wage of chief wage-earner	%
Up to £3 12s	29
£3 12s–£5	58
£5–£10	11
Over £10	3 (as in original)

74 Ian McLaine, *Ministry of Morale: Home Front Morale and the Ministry of Information in World War II*, London, Allen & Unwin, 1979, pp. 176–7. Middle-class women showed a preference for the Women's Royal Naval Service and the Women's Auxiliary Air Force rather than the Auxiliary Territorial Service, where the gulf between working-class privates and upper-class officers was thought to present a problem for recruitment. See PRO, Lab. 26/63, Women's Services (Welfare and Amenities) Committee, 'Recruiting of Womanpower', and Central Office of Information, Wartime Social Survey, *An Investigation of the Attitudes of Women, the General Public and A. T. S. Personnel to the Auxiliary Territorial Service*, October 1941.

75 The convention (followed by the Wartime Social Survey) was (and remained) to classify families by the income of the 'chief' wage earner, defined as male. Even Madge, who did attempt to assess complete family incomes, did not record the separate contribution made by wives, and actually blurred it in his breakdown of Glasgow family incomes into husbands, 62 per cent; 'other earners over twenty-one', 26 per cent; and juvenile earners, 12 per cent. Madge, *War-time Patterns*, p. 53.

76 ibid., p. 62.

77 ibid., p. 32. A comparison of the spending of a male and female lodger-earner in Leeds showed that the man spent 8s 6d on tobacco, compared with the woman's 2s 6d, 5s 1d on alcohol compared with 3d, and 2s 8d on entertainment, compared with 2s 3d. See table XII, p. 33.

78 ibid., p. 73.

79 ibid.; Seers, *Changes*, p. 23; Hancock and Gowing, *War Economy*, pp. 170, 327, 330.

80 Seers, *Changes*, pp. 22 and 8.

81 See especially appendix 11 of Madge's book, in which many negative working-class opinions about saving are quoted, e.g. a man whose family generated a considerable 'excess income' but who drank and smoked more than the average, said, 'the average man, if he does himself and his family justice, has nothing to save', and a riveter said, 'some people will starve their weans to put money in the bank'.

82 Hancock and Gowing, *War Economy*, p. 169.

83 Madge, *War-time Patterns*, p. 40.

84 Hancock and Gowing, *War Economy*, p. 169, n 5; R. M. Titmuss, *Problems of Social Policy*, London, HMSO, 1950, p. 162.

85 Madge, *War-time Patterns*, pp. 17 and 39.

86 Central Office of Information, Wartime Social Survey, *Credit Buying*, p. 3. Middlesbrough service wives reciprocated the negativity of landlords by being 'the group most dissatisfied' with their social environment. See Central Office of Information, Social Survey, *Middlesbrough: A Social Survey*, 1948, Part IV, p. 4.

87 Titmuss, *Problems*, p. 414, n. 2; Summerfield, *Women Workers*, pp. 83–4.

88 Hancock and Gowing, *War Economy*, pp. 505–6.

89 ibid., pp. 325, 340, n. 4. p. 505. It was alleged by the government that a private's total pay and allowances, including payments in kind and income tax relief, were close to average industrial earnings, but this argument was apparently rather unconvincing to privates themselves.

90 Mass-Observation Archive, Topic Collection: Armed Forces, box 4, file E. Cuttings from *Sunday Express*, 13 April 1941, and other newspapers. An officer's pay at this time was said to be £3 17s per week, whereas a male clerk's pay (relatively low down on the salary scale) was about £4 15s.

91 The differential provoked adverse comment. For example, a 'teacher and house-wife' wrote in her diary in September 1942, 'I can't see why a soldier's child should have 1s 0d per week increase, but an officer's 1s 0d per day'. Mass–Observation Archive, Topic Collection: Armed Forces, box 4, file E.

92 Seers, *Changes*, pp. 62 and 65.

93 Guy Routh, *Occupation and Pay in Great Britain, 1906-1960*, Cambridge University Press, 1965, p. 106, and table 48, p. 107. Men in the lower professions earned 115 per cent of the average in 1955/56, a fall of 40 per cent since 1935/36, and women in this group earned 82 per cent, a fall of 37 per cent. Male clerks earned 98 per cent of the average, a fall of 18 per cent, and women clerks earned 60 per cent, a fall of 2 per cent. Male managers improved their position by 3 per cent, earning 279 per cent of average earnings, female managers earned 151 per cent, an improvement of 45 per cent.

94 Routh, *Occupation and Pay*, p. 124. Manual earnings increased by 30 per cent in 1938–40, whereas the increase for all employees was 14 per cent, and by 1944 manual earnings stood at 182 per cent of the 1938 level, compared with an average of 117 per cent for white-collar civil servants.

95 ibid., p. 106.

96 ibid., p. 125, n. 1.

97 Ministry of Labour and National Service, *Tables Relating to Employment and Unemployment in Great Britain, 1939, 1945 and 1946*, London, HMSO, 1947, pp. 4–5. In another relatively 'white-collar' industrial category, 'commerce, banking, insurance and finance', the number of men had actually fallen by 1945 to 38 per cent of the 1939 number, whereas the number of women rose to 149 per cent of what it had been, changing the proportion of women from 31 per cent to 63 per cent.

98 Routh, *Occupation and Pay*, pp. 104 and 124.

99 Seers, *Changes*, p. 64.

100 The first jobs of around 35 per cent of the daughters of working-class fathers entering the Scottish labour market between 1939 and 1945 were non-manual. See Gamarnikow, *Gender*, pp. 65–6, especially fig. 5.1. Other authors in the same collection suggest that a high proportion of women in low-paid non-manual work marry men in manual occupations. If this was occurring in the 1930s and 1940s

it would again have caused the group of women white-collar workers to straddle the conventional class boundaries. See Gamarnikow, *Gender*, p. 60.

101 George Orwell, 'England, your England', 1941, quoted by Runciman, *Relative Deprivation*, p. 130.

102 Cole, *Studies*, p. 77.

103 Central Office of Information, Social Survey, *Middlesbrough*, Part IV, p. 3. See also H. Orlans, *Stevenage: a Sociological Study of a New Town*, London, Greenwood, 1971, pp. 160-3.

104 Madge, *War-time Patterns*, p. 74; Seers, *Changes*, pp. 41-2.

105 Halsey, *Trends*, table 3.5, p. 87.

106 Seers, *Changes*, pp. 41, 59.

107 Madge, *War-time Patterns*, pp. 74, 50. Both the National Savings scheme and the sale of Defence Bonds were introduced as a form of government borrowing in November 1939. See Hancock and Gowing, *War Economy*, p. 171.

108 McLaine, *Ministry of Morale*, pp. 177-8. 'Home Intelligence' reported in 1941-2 that apparent 'unfairness' in the distribution of consumer goods due to the greater purchasing power of better-off groups 'seemed to rankle increasingly', but McLaine comments, 'As long as the government appeared to be doing its best to impose the burdens of war equally upon all sections of the community, expressions of discontent did not threaten to coalesce into a serious danger to morale and national unity'.

CHAPTER **1 3**

'Barbarossa': The Soviet Response, 1941

MARK HARRISON

The war in Russia

On 22 June 1941, Hitler's war against the USSR began. It was fought mainly on Soviet territory, with tens of millions of soldiers, and hundreds of thousands of aircraft, tanks, and guns on each side. It was the greatest land war of all time.

If the Second World War was to directly cause the premature deaths of 50–60 million people, then three-fifths of them would die on the eastern front. Official estimates of Soviet national losses, once given as 'more than 20 million', are now put at 26–27 million (one in 7 of the pre-war population).[1] With total wartime deaths among Soviet regular forces now officially fixed at 8,668,400,[2] it is clear that civilians made up the majority of the Soviet war dead, caught in military crossfire, killed by bombing, by blockade, or by hunger and dying as partisans, hostages, and slaves. In the worst period, the winter of 1941, more Leningraders starved to death every month than the total of British civilians killed by German bombs in the entire war; the million premature deaths in this one city comfortably exceeded the combined military and civilian casualties (killed and died of wounds) of the British Empire and Dominions and of the United States. As far as military losses are concerned, the great majority of the German dead also fell on the eastern front – 5,600,000, compared with 750,000 on other fronts between June 1941 and the war's end.[3]

The unique scale and intensity of the war in Russia was already apparent in its opening phase. 'Barbarossa' itself was the war's biggest single land operation. The Soviet defenders faced the full frontline combat strength of the Wehrmacht.[4] The clash devastated the personnel of both the opposing armies. By December 1941 the Russians had cost the Wehrmacht 750,000 casualties, the German dead totalling nearly 200,000 (by contrast, in the whole of the western campaign in 1940, the Wehrmacht had lost some 156,000 men, including 30,000 dead).[5] Even so, the German losses were dwarfed by the 1,750,000 dead of the Soviet regular forces up to the end of the year.[6] The latter figure does not apparently include the millions taken prisoner in 1941 but remaining alive at the end of the year, most of whom died later in captivity.

These six months were of profound significance. At first the Wehrmacht continued along its trail of victories. By mid-autumn Kiev was taken, Leningrad was besieged, and Moscow was directly threatened. But in the end neither Leningrad nor Moscow fell. On the Leningrad front the war of manoeuvre degenerated into a siege war of attrition. In the long and bloody battle of Moscow, which began in September and lasted until the spring thaw of 1942, Hitler's hopes of a lightning victory were decisively blocked. For the first time, if temporarily, Germany had lost the strategic initiative.

During 1942, Hitler would struggle to regain it. For the Soviet side, in 1942 things would get still worse. German forces advanced across the south to Stalingrad [Volgograd] and the edge of the Caucasian oilfields. The German campaign ended with the Soviet encirclement of German forces at Stalingrad in the winter of 1942. The last big German offensive in the east, against the Kursk salient in July 1943, ended in further defeat. The rest of the war was the story of the slow, still costly, but now inevitable expulsion of German forces from Soviet territory, and the advance of Soviet troops into the heart of Europe in pursuit.

Soviet war preparations

The Soviet ability to deny victory to Germany in 1941 was rooted in pre-war preparations. High military spending and continual preparation for war were already ingrained in Soviet military-economic policy in the 1930s. This contrasted with a background of low military spending in most other European countries where, after the First World War, it was believed that Great Wars had become prohibitively costly.[7]

Soviet readiness to maintain high military spending in peacetime went back to 1918, when Bolshevik leaders had learnt the propensity of powerful imperialist adversaries to take advantage of any moment of weakness, and to intervene against the Russian revolution by force. They had learnt then to put more trust in munitions than in paper treaties or diplomacy. Soviet policy prepared continually for war. At the same time, this was not preparation for any particular war, forecast or planned for any specific time and place, but insurance against the possibility of war in general. Soviet military and economic planners did not set their sights on some particular operation to be launched on a set date, but instead aimed to build up an all-round, generalized military power ready for war at some point in the indefinite future.

This pattern of rearmament suffered from two main drawbacks. First, it was enormously costly. It required diversion from the civilian economy both of millions of young men who could otherwise have been available for work, and also of just those industrial commodities in which the USSR was poorest: refined fuels, rare metals and high-quality alloys, precision engineering, scientific knowledge, and technical expertise. Rearmament cut deeply into the civilian economy and living standards.

The other drawback lay in the possibility of miscalculation. Because the Soviet rearmament pattern aimed at some future war, it was never ready for war in the present. Changing forecasts and expectations meant that military plans were always under revision. The armed forces were always in the midst of re-equipment and reorganization. Military products already in mass production were always on the verge of obsolescence; defence industries were always halfway through retraining and retooling.

At the same time, the Soviet pattern carried important advantages. Germany's strategy was a gamble, staking everything on the possibility of immediate victory. If Soviet resistance could deny victory to the aggressor in the short run, and turn the lightning war that the aggressor expected to win into a protracted struggle; if the Soviets could finally bring to bear their entire national resources upon the struggle – then the aggressor would have lost the advantage. Germany would have entered the war with limited military stocks and low rates of defence output, expecting to win without major loss or need of replacement of weapons on any significant scale. If this expectation were frustrated, Germany's position would be relatively weak; it would be Germany's turn to mobilize frantically, to be forced to sacrifice the civilian economy to the needs of the Army. Conscious of the fragility of the Nazi regime, Hitler was determined to avoid this outcome.[8]

Soviet rearmament proceeded in the 1930s in two main waves. The first accompanied the First Five Year Plan. By the end of it the Soviet Union was already producing a full range of modern weapons; Soviet defence output had reached a high plateau, considerably exceeding the level of output of any other European power. But in the mid-1930s Soviet rearmament lost its head start, in terms of both quantity of forces and quality of weapons produced. From 1937, Soviet defence output and force levels began to multiply again; in 1939 conscription was reintroduced.

The Soviet rearmament of the last years before the war was impressive on its volume and scope. Defence output and Red Army force levels doubled and trebled. By 1940 there were more than 4 million Soviet citizens in uniform (6 per cent of the working population); every month, Soviet industry was producing 230 tanks, 700 military aircraft, 4,000 guns and mortars, more than 100,000 rifles, and more than a million shells.

At the same time, this activity won far less immediate military security for the Soviet Union than might have been expected. One reason is that the Soviet concept of combining massive expansion with modernization resulted in wide differences of quality. Of the millions of soldiers, few were properly trained or experienced in combat. Most were operating large numbers of obsolete weapons according to outmoded tactical guidelines; a minority were in process of learning to operate modernized weapons in relatively small quantities, using new, poorly absorbed military doctrines.

There were further reasons for poor results, which stemmed from domestic politics. In the Great Purge of 1937–8 the Red Army command had been almost wiped out. The experienced core of general and field officers had been replaced by an immature, ill-educated cohort whose members were typically either drilled in Stalinist dogmas, or cowed by Stalinist threats. Those advocating a flexible response to external aggression, including the inevitability of giving ground to the invader and the necessity of defence in depth, had been accused of conspiring with Nazi leaders to hand over territory, and executed or imprisoned.

In military doctrine, the concept of the operation in depth was replaced by a rigid insistence on frontier defence: invading forces must be met on the Soviet border and repulsed by an immediate Soviet counteroffensive; then the war must be carried in to enemy territory. Thus Stalin, like Hitler, was preparing his country for a short war, an offensive one. By massing Soviet forces on Soviet frontiers and giving the appearance of an offensive deployment, Stalin hoped to deter German aggression. In practice, the bluff worked badly; it calmed Soviet fears and stimulated Stalin's own complacency, while German observers were not impressed.

The atmosphere of repression inevitably influenced the content of military-economic plans drawn up in the pre-war years. Plans for boosting ammunition production in the event of war contained no realistic assessment of combat needs because they assumed a short war ending in a victorious offensive. In factories and cities contingency plans were drawn up for war production in the event of war, but the most obvious preparations for a defensive campaign were neglected. Specialized defence factories were concentrated in vulnerable territories to the south and west. There was talk of dispersing capacity into the interior regions, but nothing was done; it was always cheaper to expand output where production was already concentrated. Nothing was done to prepare vital industrial assets for defence against air attack, or for possible evacuation, since the idea that an invader might penetrate Soviet territory had become treasonous.[9]

Everyone in positions of responsibility believed that there would always be time to make good any oversights.

The shock of war

The war was a shattering blow to an unprepared population, and to a political leadership that had successfully deceived itself. Stalin himself was not immediately paralysed, and his recently published engagement diary shows that in the first days of the war he was constantly involved in conferences with military leaders and economic administrators.[10] By 28 June, however, the endless succession of stunning setbacks temporarily broke his will; depressed and demoralized, he retreated to a country residence near Moscow. Molotov had to break the news to the Soviet population on the radio. When senior Politburo members came to see Stalin, to propose formation of a war cabinet, his reaction (first anxiety, then relief) implied that he thought they had come to arrest him.[11] Later, facing the failure of frontal defence in October 1941, Stalin tried to buy peace from Hitler in return for the Baltic, Belorussia, Moldavia, and part of the Ukraine.[12]

The formal administrative system did not collapse, but its effectiveness was gravely weakened. Rules and planning procedures became irrelevant. While the Wehrmacht cut away Soviet territory, including the country's most important military-industrial centres, economic planners went on turning out factory plans and coordinating supplies. But the factories and supplies only existed on paper. Meanwhile, Army requirements for new supplies of munitions and soldiers just to replace early losses hugely exceeded plans. The gap between needs and resources could not be bridged by any paper plan, and swiftly grew to unbearable dimensions.

What happened now was that informal leadership took over and carried out the essential tasks of war mobilization. In the economy, the most important measures were a crash programme to evacuate the big munitions factories in the war zones to the remote interior of the country, and the all-out conversion of civilian industry to war production. The evacuation, carried out without any planning beforehand, was an act of inspired improvisation in which the key roles fell to individual leaders – Kaganovich, Kosygin, Shvernik. Other individual leaders – Beriya, Malenkov, Malyshev, Mikoyan, Molotov, Voznesensky – armed with unlimited personal responsibility, took on key tasks of industrial mobilization and conversion.[13] All this was carried on regardless of economic plans and attempts at high level coordination, which were irrelevant to the needs of the situation.

Of course individual leaders did not do everything themselves, and their efforts would have been utterly useless if they had not been joined by a common current of mobilization from below. There was initiative from below, both in the evacuation of economic assets, especially farm stocks, and in the conversion of factories to war production (which followed pre-war plans drawn up in factories, municipalities, and industrial branch administration). Initiative from below did not mean that there was no organization, but the point was that people did these things without first waiting for instructions from the Kremlin.

Soviet political authority remained in civilians hands. This is reflected in composition of Stalin's war cabinet, the GKO (State Committee of Defence), formed on 30 June, which included only one soldier, Marshal Voroshilov; Stalin himself took on the role of Supreme Commander-in-Chief. The Army itself was fully occupied with fighting the Germans, and had neither time nor resources to divert to matters of home or foreign policy.

This does not mean that civil-military relations would remain unchanged. At the outset, Stalin exercised untrammelled personal influence over grand strategy and detail of military policy and appointments. This was a result of the lack of professional autonomy of military leaders, and among the institutions ensuring this were the savage Red Army purge of 1937–8, which created an atmosphere of terror, and resulted in wholesale replacement of the officer corps; and the colossal numerical expansion during 1938–40, which further lowered the average professional standards of army officers. However, the setbacks of 1941 (and more would come in the following spring) rendered embarrassingly visible Stalin's defects as a military commander in wrong strategic dispositions and in an incapacity to organize defence in depth. After a while, professional soldiers would begin to wrest back some control over military operations and planning. Stalin would learn to act less like a dictator, and more like an arbitrator between conflicting professional standpoints. In 1941, however, this remained in the future. For the time being, Stalin would deflect potential criticism by executing the generals responsible for frontier defence.

Stalin never ceded any military influence over grand strategy or diplomacy. Additionally, even in the planning and conduct of military operations, Stalinism left an indelible stamp, for example in the lack of previous calculation of casualties, and in the reckless pursuit of arbitrary objectives despite huge military and civilian losses, from start to finish of the war.[14]

Economic requirements

The key to victory in the Second World War was munitions of all kinds; aircraft, tanks, ships, guns, and shells. In the end, the Allies won the war because they were able to produce munitions in vastly greater quantity than Germany and Japan.

The Soviet Union's contribution to Allied munitions was ultimately very substantial – at least as much as that of the United Kingdom, and as much as half that of the United States. Soviet war production would exceed Germany's total by as much as two-thirds.[15] The quantities involved were fantastic. During the war, Soviet production alone would amount to 100,000 tanks, 130,000 aircraft, 800,000 field guns and mortars, and up to half a billion artillery shells, 1,400,000 machine-guns, 6,000,000 machine-pistols and 12,000,000 rifles. (However, the Soviet Union produced hardly any warships, jeeps, or military trucks.)

In 1941 these quantities were still unimaginable. No-one expected a war of these dimensions. The Germans did not expect it because they planned to win their wars quickly and without major losses. Even now, the Allies knew that to beat the Germans would take time and resources, but they did not understand how much. After the failure of the German *Blitzkrieg* the Allies succeeded in committing increasing resources to the war. But as yet they did not understand that Germany, although stalemated and under increasing pressure, was far from exhausted. On the contrary, German leaders had only begun to tap the available resources. From the Soviet invasion to July 1944, Germany's war production would treble. This burst of effort would be too late. Nonetheless it meant that the Allies, too, would be forced to devote absolutely undreamt-of resources to their own war production.

Still, the most important factor underlying the future war of production was already clearly visible in 1941. This was the unprecedented expenditure of combat equipment. A Red Army gun would last 18 weeks in the field. The average life of a Soviet combat aircraft was 3 months, and that of a Soviet tank was barely longer. At the worst, in a typical week of the winter of 1941, the Soviet frontline forces would be losing one-sixth of their aircraft, one-seventh of their guns and mortars, and one-tenth of their armoured equipment.[16]

There were special reasons that heightened the demands of the eastern front. One was the relatively intense character of the fighting. Much more than the British and the Americans, the Russians were faced with a war of national extermination. They carried on fighting under conditions in which soldiers of other nations might have given ground; and their losses were correspondingly heavy.

Another reason was the profound disadvantage of the Soviet soldier when it came to handling the equipment of modern war. Soviet pilots and tank or gun crews lacked the training and combat experience of the Wehrmacht, especially in the early stages. The threshing of Red Army personnel, first by Stalin in 1937–8, and then by Hitler in 1941–2, ensured this. By 1942 the typical Soviet soldier was very young and green, as likely to write off his brand new Il-2 on the airfield as under enemy fire. The Luftwaffe rated the Soviet air forces much lower than their British and American counterparts, and 'used Russia as a school for inexperienced pilots. There they could build flying and fighting skills before being thrown into the cauldron of western air battles'.[17]

Conditioning everything was a third factor, the Stalinist reliance on harsh and wasteful military policies that set too little emphasis on the avoidance of losses. For example, Soviet home militia units, consisting largely of untrained industrial workers lacking qualified officers and proper weapons, were sent to the front to be slaughtered. Soviet tanks were also squandered.[18] When planning military operations, high officials generally did not take into account the possible human casualties, and also ignored the likely losses of equipment. Formed in the desperate days of 1941, reinforced by the low valuation that Stalinist ideology placed on the human 'cogs' that made up the military and economic machine, this habit would persist through the war into the period when there was no compelling need to spend resources so carelessly.

Soviet war industries thus faced a double task of daunting magnitude – not only to make good the initial heavy losses, under conditions that were far from ideal in the first place, but also to supply additional resources for the huge expansion of the armed forces that the war required.

Restructuring the economy

From 22 June 1941 a new acceleration of Soviet war production was remarked. In the first half of the year the monthly output of Soviet war factories had included 1,000 aircraft, 300 tanks, nearly 4,000 guns and mortars, and 175,000 rifles. In the second half of the year these rates rose to 3,300 aircraft, 800 tanks, 12,000 guns and mortars, and 270,000 rifles per month. More than 10 million shells, mines, and bombs were produced on a monthly basis. Even so, this was just the beginning. By the wartime peak in 1944, monthly Soviet output would stand at 3,400 aircraft and nearly 1,800 armoured fighting vehicles, 11,000 guns and mortars, 200,000 rifles, and 19 million shells, mines, and bombs.[19]

The great expansion was very costly. Neither the defence industries nor the civilian economy were ready for it. Different lines of war production were not coordinated with each other; for example, at first the output of guns raced ahead of shell production. In the autumn, the production of aircraft and armour fell behind because of the high proportion of factories being decommissioned and put on wheels for transfer from the battle zones to the interior regions.

Moreover, the expansion of war production was completely out of balance with what was happening elsewhere in the economy. While defence output climbed, everything else pointed to collapse. Between the first and second halves of 1941, supplies of coal and electric power fell by a third. Supplies of pig iron, crude steel, and rolled steel products were down by as much as one-half. The output of machine tools had fallen by two-fifths. The 1941 grain harvest was also down by two-fifths in comparison with 1940. And even these disastrous declines would look good in comparison with the further setbacks waiting round the corner in 1942.

The dreadful performance of the civilian economy was partly a measure of German success in capturing territory. Huge industrial complexes vital to the manufacture of modern weapons were lost or decommissioned. On the remaining territory, agricultural production was carried only with great difficulty; the main causes were the loss of the best agricultural land in the southern regions, the loss of horses and tractors, and the disappearance of young men from the agricultural workforce. But the downward spiral of the civilian economy was worsened further by the Soviet pursuit of war production at any price, which took away additional resources and intensified the disequilibrium between the growth of munitions and the collapse of everything else.

Moreover, the widening imbalance would also take its toll of munitions output. Without a minimum level of civilian output, there could be no war production. To be operated, defence factories needed metals, fuels, machinery, and electric power. They also needed workers, who could not live without food, clothing, and shelter. The civilian economy was also crucial because, as well as munitions, the Army needed huge quantities of food rations, petrol and aircraft fuel, transport services, and building materials – the means of military construction and operations.

While expanding defence output continued to be coupled with civilian economic collapse, there was still a danger that war production might at any moment grind to a halt. Munitions plants might simply run out of steel and power, or munitions workers might starve. In 1941–2 these things were clear and present dangers, all of the time to some degree, but especially in the winter months of 1941 and 1942.

To prove the point, in the winter of 1941 war production faltered. More than 2,200 aircraft were produced monthly in the third quarter, but barely more than 1,000 in the fourth. In December only 39 per cent of the aircraft programme was fulfilled, and only 24 per cent of the plan for aeroengines.

The monthly supply of medium T-34 and heavy KV tanks fell from 540 to 400. By the first ten days of January 1942, shell production had fallen to 20–30 per cent of the plan.[20] Measured by the gap between military needs and available supplies of war goods, this was the worst moment of the war, and it accompanied the nerve-racking, decisive stages of the battle of Moscow. Early in 1942 the meteoric rise of war production would be resumed; but to stabilize its foundations in the civilian economy would take further titanic efforts, and eventually considerable external economic support.

Labour, food

This was a war of production, and productive effort was limited chiefly by the availability of workers, hours, and intensity of work. The problem was that, when war broke out, several millions of additional soldiers and war workers were required almost overnight; on the other hand, the supply of workers not only did not increase, but was cut by many millions because of the loss of territory.

The pre-war industrial labour market was already under strain. It was also heavily regimented under emergency labour laws enacted in 1938 and 1940, which had brought increased hours of work and reduced freedom of movement from one job to another. The war brought with it a further proliferation of controls on workers. Steps were taken immediately to reduce normal leisure time and holiday and to increase hours of work, which, in industry, rose from 41 hours on average before 1940 and 48 hours thereafter to 54–55 hours in 1942.[21] Other measures were adopted, although with some delay, to ensure that the working population was mobilized to the maximum extent through universal liability to perform either military or civilian service.

A more complex issue was how to ensure that the right proportions were maintained between numbers of military personnel, of war workers delivering munitions, fuel, and other goods to the armed forces, and of civilian workers. At first there was chaos in the labour market, with different rival military and civilian agencies competing to recruit workers for different purposes. New, more centralized institutional controls were required to overcome this; they were worked out in the course of war mobilization, and it would take right through 1942 to get them right.[22]

These measures, undertaken from above, were met with a ready response from below. There was an immediate flow of volunteers for war work, including many hundreds of thousands of housewives, college and school students, and pensioners. The response from below extended to massive participation in organized programmes such as the emergency tasks of industrial evacuation and conversion, and the industrial movements of 'socialist emulation' – individuals and groups pledged to double and triple fulfilment of low peacetime work norms.[23] Lower-level responses were also represented by recruitment into war work from the rural economy, Russia's traditional labour reserve, which was not, however, inexhaustible when compared with wartime needs.

The disruption of the rural economy meant that, for most civilian households and consumers, life in wartime teetered on a precipice. Food became the central concern of household economics.[24] By November 1941, bread, cereals, meat, fish, fats, and sugar were rationed for almost half the population of the country (the only important foodstuff not to be rationed was potatoes). Most important was bread, which supplied 80–90 per cent of rationed calories and proteins.

Not everyone got the same: there was a pronounced differentiation by age and working status (roughly, in ascending order – adult dependants, children, office workers, industrial workers, war workers, coal-face workers). But no-one except soldiers and war workers in the most hazardous occupations got enough from rations to live. There was simply not enough to go round, and most people went hungry. In 1941, however, deaths from starvation were restricted to Leningrad.

If rations alone were not sufficient to sustain life, most supplemented their diet from unofficial sources (except for Leningraders, who lacked any surrounding farmlands). From the winter of 1941 these made up the difference between life and death. Big factories and urban households went in for sideline farming on a massive scale. Another unofficial means of survival was the declining trickle of peasant food surpluses sold in the unregulated urban food markets.

How did the collective farmer live under wartime conditions? Here is a 'blank space' in Soviet history that we can hardly begin to fill. Certainly, food output per farmworker was falling, while government needs rose. And this happened in a context where, even in peacetime, the attitude of authority to the consumer needs of the village was harsh and arbitrary.

What bread was to the urban worker, the potato became to the peasant. Everything else of importance – proteins, fats, and vitamins – came from milk (and, if neither potatoes, nor bread, nor milk, then from grass).[25]

Not all rural dwellers suffered equally. Food produce became fantastically scarce – but those with food surpluses, however small, could take them to market. In wartime many did so, and this contributed to the survival of the urban population. With rising free market prices, a few would become rouble millionaires. But the cash income from food sales on the free market would not contribute significantly to peasant living standards, since there was soon nothing else to be bought for cash.

National feeling

National feeling was of great importance to the Soviet war effort, but not in a simple way. What led Russians and Uzbeks, Ukrainians, Armenians, and Azeris, to join in waging war against Germany? Was it in defence of 'their' Soviet state, out of loyalty to Soviet institutions and traditions, embodied in a Soviet culture and guided by Soviet leaders? How did ethnic affiliation blend with wartime participation in Soviet political structures? These are questions which have evoked doubt and speculation, and not much else.

It is fairly certain, though, that national feeling did not always point in one direction. This would be demonstrated clearly in 1941. For significant elements of the Soviet ethnic groups most directly confronted by war and German occupation threw in their lot with the invader, and one factor in this may have been a mistaken sense of national feeling, a belief that the Nazis offered some better route to national salvation than the Bolsheviks.[26] The basis for such a belief was soon weakened by experience of German treatment of Soviet prisoners of war and of occupation policies, but it would still be possible for Vlasov's Russian Liberation Movement to find popular support in the occupied territories as late as 1943.[27]

As far as the war effort in the interior of the country was concerned, national feeling was certainly a factor. It was all the more important for the supply of resources to the war economy, because compulsion alone did not prove effective. Wartime experience in the construction industry would show that military-style organization without attention to worker morale would not give good results.[28] Nor could monetary incentives be as effective in wartime, given the extent to which market allocation of consumer goods had been displaced – partly by official rationing, partly by barter, which tended to drive out cash on the free market.[29] (However, privileged access to rationed goods could evidently be a powerful incentive to participate in war work and to perform reliably at work.)

There was an important relationship between food and morale. In the USSR, as in other warring nations, the wartime food shortage gave rise to 'food crimes'. Illicit activity included diversion of state stocks to the black market for resale at high prices; and trade in ration coupons, which could be forced, or stolen from the authorities, or procured by deceit or by theft from individuals.[30] All food crimes imposed losses on society, but theft bore most heavily on individual victims. In Leningrad, lost ration cards would not be replaced before the end of each month, in order to discourage falsely reported losses. In the winter of 1941, the citizen deprived of a ration card early in the month because of theft was unlikely to survive without the support of family or friends. All food crimes were punished severely, and, in Leningrad at least, usually by shooting.[31]

The link from food to civic morale was complex, with many intervening factors. Loss of morale was not invariably the result of food shortages. For example, whole communities in the western territories annexed in 1939–40, in eastern Poland, and in the Baltic, welcomed the invader without any prompting of material deprivation. At the other extreme lies Leningrad; in the winter of 1941, the whole city was dying on its feet, and individuals suffered every kind of physical and moral degeneration; but civic morale did not crack. There was no panic, no looting, and no surrender.

There were many intermediate cases. An instructive case is that of the Moscow 'panic' of October 1941, which was prompted not by material deprivation, but by the near approach of German forces combined with the evacuation of main government offices. Then, looting and other breaches of public order were the product not of food shortage, but of the fear that the people's leaders had deserted them.

In order to unify Soviet society for war, the Stalinist regime softened or abandoned pre-war themes of internal class war and the purging of the enemy within. This took several main forms. Campaigns against the pre-war oppositions of left and right were played down, and a limited number of victims of the pre-war purges were rehabilitated, especially military and economic leaders.

There were also important concessions to Russian national feelings, which were led by Stalin himself in his speeches and decrees. In the autumn of 1941 there began a restoration of the role of the Army in Imperial Russian history, changing its image from an instrument of imperialist oppression to an agent of national liberation; this trend would culminate in the summer of 1942 with the return to a unified military hierarchy (abolishing supervision of professional army officers by political commissars), and the restoration of privileges of rank. Meanwhile, there was a strong promotion of anti-German feeling.

The other side of the coin was Moscow's persistent distrust of civilian morale and values. Soviet leaders behaved as if they believed that public order was always on the verge of breakdown. This is shown by Stalin's reluctance to allow the evacuation of noncombatants from Leningrad in face of enemy advance, and his willingness to incur the resulting casualties, rather than signal a retreat. This pattern would be repeated in 1942 with the refusal to evacuate Stalingrad of noncombatants, which also resulted in heavy civilian losses.

Uncontrolled economic mobilization

What was the historical significance of 1941? It was the year in which the Soviet Union staved off military and economic collapse. This postponement was of such importance because it derailed Hitler's timetable, placed the achievement of his strategic goals in doubt, and ensured that to continue the struggle for a doubtful victory in Russia would now cost Germany ten or twenty times as much in men and *matériel* as had been anticipated. German defeat before Moscow marked the first time in the history of the Third Reich when the Wehrmacht lost ground to a defending army, and when Berlin failed to decide the outcome of a clash of forces. Moreover, Hitler's strategy of *Blitzkrieg* depended upon Germany's holding the initiative continuously for its success.

At the same time, this was not yet the true turning-point of the war. For another year, the two sides would struggle to gain or regain the initiative. On the Soviet side, 1942 would mostly be worse than 1941. Not until after Stalingrad would the Soviet war effort be placed on a relatively stable footing, and in some particular respects (for example, in food supply) 1943 would be even worse than 1942.

There were two reasons for deterioration of the Soviet position in 1942. One was the partial success of German strategic plans, which deprived Moscow of further rich economic assets in the south of the country and additionally disrupted the war economy of the interior regions. The other reason lay in the nature of the Soviet economic mobilization in 1941.

What was the character of this mobilization? In 1941, Soviet defence industries were saved, and munitions production soared, but everything else was left to look after itself, and plunged into an appalling shambles. Over this mess presided the system of informal management at the highest level, described above – the uncoordinated system of economic leadership by individual members of the war cabinet and Politburo.

The war effort could not be long sustained on this basis. The intolerable strains in the civilian economy in 1942 were not just consequences of successful German offensives, but had been worsened by the uncontrolled pattern of mobilization in the previous year. Uncontrolled mobilization had saved the country's immediate military-economic capacities, but at the same time stored up huge problems. The heart of the war economy had been shifted bodily hundreds of kilometres to the east, and now lay in the Urals and western Siberia, where the western and southern factories for making tanks, guns shells, and aircraft had been relocated. This in itself had cost huge resources of civilian transport and construction. Moreover, the remote regions of the interior were utterly unready for such accelerated exploitation. They lacked most things necessary for recommissioning the evacuated war factories – additional workers, housing and food supplies, transport links, electric power, sources of metal products and components, and any kind of commercial and financial infrastructure.

To make good these shortages would cost the economy dearly. Most of the cost was met straightaway, in the immediate creation of a supportive infrastructure, by huge Soviet civilian sacrifice. Later on, some costs were borne by the United States through Lend-Lease shipments, which acquired a massive scale in 1943. Other costs have been realized only in the present day, in the ecological crisis of the Urals and Siberia.

To sustain the war effort, the uncoordinated system of informal management by individual members of the war cabinet and Politburo eventually had to give way. It lasted until the end of 1942. At about the same time, workforce controls were centralized in a single government agency, while personal war production responsibilities of individual war cabinet and Politburo members were devolved upon a new powerful cabinet subcommittee, the Operations Bureau. After this there were fewer crash programmes and panic measures, and formal planning procedures were progressively restored.[32] The administrative rationalization, aided by the enlarged flow of Allied resources through Lend-Lease, would eventually bring the stabilization of the Soviet war economy.

Notes

1 The leading Soviet demographer B. Urlanis, *Wars and Population*, Moscow, 1971, p. 294, gave total worldwide premature deaths as 50 million, on the basis of a Soviet figure of 20 millions. The figure of 26.6 million emerged recently from a study of the long-term demographic record carried out by E. Andreev, L. Darskii, and T. Khar'kova, 'Otsenka lyudskikh poter'' v period Velikoi Otechestvennoi

voiny', *Vestnik statistiki*, No. 10, 1990, pp. 25-27. This figure may or may not include net wartime emigration. The highest scholarly estimate was supplied by V. I. Kozlov, 'O lyudskikh poteryakh Sovetskogo Soyuza v Velikoi Otechestvennoi voiny 1941-1945 gg.', *Istoriya SSSR*, No. 2, 1989. For further discussion of this and other results of the war, see Mark Harrison and John Barber, *The Soviet Home Front, 1941-1945: A Social and Economic History of the USSR in World War II*, London, 1991, pp. 39-44.

2 M. A. Moiseev, 'Tsena pobedy', *Voenno-istoricheskii zhurnal*, No. 3, 1990, p. 14.

3 Jonathan R. Adelman, *The Tsarist, Soviet and U.S. Armies in the Two World Wars*, Boulder, Colo, 1988, pp. 171-3.

4 On 22 June 1941, Germany deployed 153 divisions on the Soviet front, compared with 63 divisions in Germany and in other occupied territories, and 2 divisions on other fronts. These proportions were unaltered six months later: *Velikaya Otechestvennaya voina Sovetskogo Soyuza 1941-1945: Kratkaya istoriya*, 3rd edn, Moscow, 1984, p. 502.

5 German military sources, cited by Alexander Werth, *Russia at War*, London, 1964, p. 259.

6 According to Moiseev, 'Tsena pobedy', p. 15, 20 per cent of 8.7 million wartime deaths among Soviet armed forces personnel were suffered in the second half of 1941.

7 On Soviet rearmament in comparative perspective, see Mark Harrison, 'Resource mobilization for World War II: the USA, UK, USSR and Germany, 1938-1945, *Economic History Review*, Vol. 41, No. 2, 1988.

8 Alan S. Milward, *The German Economy at War*, London, 1965, pp. 26-27.

9 Mark Harrison, *Soviet Planning in Peace and War, 1938-1945*, Cambridge, 1985, pp. 53-63.

10 'Iz tetradi zapisi lits, prinyatykh I. V. Stalinym. 21-28 iyunya 1941 g.', *Izvestiya TsK KPSS*, No. 6, 1990, pp. 216-22.

11 Dmitrii Volkogonov, *Triumf i tragediya. Politicheskii portret I. V. Stalina*, Vol. II, Part 1, Moscow, 1989, p. 169.

12 Nikolai Pavlenko, 'Tragediya i triumf Karsnoi Armii', *Moskovskie novosti*, No. 19, 1989, pp. 8-9. Pavlenko cited Marshal Zhukov as first-hand witness to this attempt, initiated by Stalin on 7 October 1941. Volkogonov, *Triumf i tragediya*, Vol. II, Part 1, pp. 172-73, places the episode as early as July 1941, but in this he is apparently mistaken.

13 Sanford R. Lieberman, 'The evacuation of industry in the Soviet Union in World War II', *Soviet Studies*, Vol. 35, No. 1, 1983: Sanford R. Lieberman, 'Crisis management in the USSR; The wartime system of administration and control', in: Susan J. Linz (ed.), *The Impact of World War II on the Soviet Union*, Totowa, NJ, 1985; Harrison, *Soviet Planning in Peace and War*, pp. 63-100.

14 *Isoriki sporyat. Trinadsat' besed*, Moscow, 1988, p. 314; Kozlov, 'O lyudskikh poteryakh', p. 132.

15 Mark Harrison, 'The volume of Soviet munitions output, 1937-1945: A reevaluation', *Journal of Economic History*, Vol. 50, No. 3, 1990, Table 8.

16 Derived from Harrison, *Soviet Planning in Peace and War*, pp. 110-15.

17 Williamson Murray, *Luftwaffe: Strategy for Defeat, 1933-1945*, London, 1988, p. 371.

18 Vitali Shlykov, 'On the history of tank asymmetry in Europe', *International Affairs*, No. 10, 1988.

19 Harrison, *Soviet Planning in Peace and War*, pp. 250-51.

20 Ibid., pp. 92, 251.
21 According to N. A. Voznesensky, *War Economy of the USSR in the Period of the Patriotic War*, Moscow, 1948, p. 91, in 1942 the industrial worker's hours exceeded those worked in 1940 by 22 per cent.
22 Harrison, *Soviet Planning in Peace and War*, pp. 185-91.
23 Rogachevskaya, *Sotsialisticheskoe sorevnovanie v SSSR. Istoricheskie ocherki. 1917-1970 gg.*, Moscow, 1977, pp. 175-212.
24 Chernyavsky, *Voina i prodovol'stvie. Snabzhenie gorodskogo naseleniya v Velikuyu Otechestvennuyu voinu, 1941-1945 gg.*, Moscow, 1964; A. V. Lyubimov, *Torgovlya i snabzhenie v gody Velikoi Otecestvennoi voiny*, Moscow, 1968; William Moskoff, *The Bread of Affliction: The Food Supply in the USSR during World War II*, Cambridge - forthcoming.
25 Yu V. Arutyunyan, *Sovetskoe krest'yanstvo v gody Velikoi Otechestvennoi voiny*, 2nd edn, Moscow, 1970, p. 361.
26 John Barber, 'The role of patriotism in the Great Patroitic War', paper to Conference on Russia and the USSR in the XX Century, Moscow, 1990.
27 Catherine Andreyev, *Vlasov and the Russian Liberation Movement: Soviet Reality and Émigré Theories*, Cambridge, 1987, pp. 47-50.
28 Yu L. D'yakov, 'Promyshlennoe i transportnoe stroitel'stvo v tylu v gody Velikoi Otechestvennoi voiny', *Istoricheskie zapiski*, No. 101, Moscow, 1978, p. 60.
29 Moskoff, *The Bread of Affliction*, Chapter 8.
30 See K. S. Karol, *Solik: Life in the Soviet Union, 1939-1946*, London, 1986, pp. 94-95.
31 Harrison E. Salisbury, *The 900 Days: The Siege of Leningrad*, London, 1970, p. 533.
32 Harrison, *Soviet Planning in Peace and War*, pp. 175-85.

CHAPTER 14

World War II and Social Change in Germany

MARK ROSEMAN

I

At first sight, total war would seem likely to have had a greater impact on Germany between 1939 and 1945 than any war on any other nation. Surely the war waged by Germany was the most total ever? Was it not a German, Josef Goebbels, who, alone of all the statesmen involved in World War II, presented a total war not as a necessary evil but as something heroic and desirable: '*Wollt ihr den totalen Krieg?*' And surely the Germans experienced the destructive capacity of modern war as intensively as any people has ever done? Yet if this is so, it is striking how little of the historical research concerned with social change in Germany has concentrated solely on the war years or on the impact of war. The emphasis has been on the Nazi period as a whole; 'fascism' or 'Nazism', rather than 'total war', have been seen as the transformative experience for German people.[1]

Why is this? One point is, of course, that when democracy re-emerged in West Germany after the war it did so to a society for whom total war was merely one of a series of powerful shocks. Democracy was suspended in Germany not, as in Britain, simply by five or six years of war but twelve years of fascism and a further four of occupation. So to understand the new features of post-war society it will not do to look at the war alone. In addition, many German observers, whether explicitly or implicitly, have seen war and wartime measures essentially as a continuation of the Nazis' pre-war policies. In the German context, therefore, analysis of the impact of total war must be accompanied by at least some investigation of the changes wrought by the Nazis before 1939 and by the Occupying Powers after 1945. This is a truly massive subject, and one on which a lot of the research remains to be done. In the present chapter, which can do little more than touch on some of the most important issues, attention is focused on two aspects of German society.

One is social policy in a broad sense. It has been frequently argued that total war irrevocably advances the frontiers of state intervention in society and encourages social reforms and social engineering; the question is to what extent and as a result of what factors this applies to Germany both during and after the war. The other aspect is the position of the working class in West German society. If there is one striking contrast between the Weimar and Bonn republics it is the absence in the latter of the tensions and polarization of the former, the diminution of class-conflict and the disappearance of left- and right-wing radicalism. To what extent – that is the question here – were fascism or war responsible for this change?

II

When the war came to Germany in 1939, its impact on National Socialist policy was rather limited. True, the call-up proceeded relatively quickly and by May 1940 over 4 million men had been called to arms. But in general the outbreak of war did not precipitate major changes in the state's role in society.[2] One reason for this was that many of those features of wartime experience – particularly the mobilization of society and economy – that were novel in, for example, Britain and the USA had already been im- plemented or at least prefigured by the six years of Nazi rule prior to 1939. Germany had, as it were, already experienced a rather 'total' peace.

Consider the example of industrial relations. In both World Wars, the advanced industrial nations have felt obliged, with greater or lesser degrees of consultation or coercion, to intervene in the relations between capital and labour. The primary motivation has been to prevent strikes that might en- danger vital production and to ensure that wage settlements are in alignment with established economic priorities. In Germany, the state had already arrogated the necessary powers to itself in 1933 and 1934. The unions were forcibly dissolved and state commissioners, '*Treuhänder der Arbeit*', ap- pointed to fix wage levels.

Beyond industrial relations, the Four-Year Plan in 1936 created the machin- ery and procedures to institute widespread controls over the economy. Although, as we now know, there were many limits to the competence and coherence of the Four-Year Plan organization, it is a fact that before war broke out in 1939, Germany's occupational structure, investment activity and raw materials allocation had already undergone substantial modification in prep- aration for the needs of war.[3] Many analysts speak of a 'peacetime war econ- omy' (*Kriegswirtschaft im Frieden*). Apart from the specific achievements of the Four-Year Plan, there were other signs of a general encroachment of the state economy. Compulsory labour directions were implemented in the 1930s; there was the *Reichsarbeitsdienst* for young men and a compulsory year's work on the land for young women. The result was that the outbreak of war required far fewer new measures than in the democracies – the relationship of state and society had been sufficiently redefined, liberty suf- ficiently curtailed already.

Many of these changes, particularly the restrictions on group and individual liberty but also, to a certain extent, the organizing of economic life were not designed primarily to meet the needs of a future war. It is not in dispute that the Nazis in general and Hitler personally gave military and economic preparations for a war high priority; the notion of an eternal struggle between nations was central to Hitler's ideology. And what the advance calculation of military requirements certainly did do was to ensure that those anti-modernist elements of the National Socialist programme which initially hindered rearmament – the support given to the small businessman and the farmer, for example – were speedily removed. But elsewhere the role of war preparations is less direct. The increasingly intimate co-operation between the state and leading industrialists in planning and controlling the economy manifested (and encouraged) a grander conception which it was intended should outlast any future conflict. With growing clarity, leading industrialists and Nazis promulgated the notion of a highly centralized and organized economy, an authoritarian corporatism, which it was intended should provide a German rival to American-style capitalism.[4] Similarly, the Nazis' attack on the parties, the unions and political liberties (which, of course, went far beyond what the Western Allies deemed necessary for their war effort) was designed to consolidate the Nazis' power in peacetime and to impose the Führer-Prinzip on both politics and the economy. The Nazis certainly hoped and believed that society thus remodelled would be effective at waging war. Nevertheless, the changes implemented by the Nazis were intended to be permanent, creating a new order in peace as well as war.

It is therefore hard, and perhaps also unnecessary, to determine how far the extension of state activity and the mobilizing of society and economy before 1939 were a sign that war was already asserting itself in peacetime and how far they manifested other National Socialist goals and ideals. Having said that, there is no doubt that from 1936 onwards the direct impact of the rearmament drive became ever more obvious as armaments and autarky projects absorbed ever greater resources and the occupational structure of the labour force shifted towards war production.

The other key reason for the lack of change in 1939 was that, as most historians agree, Germany waged a far from total war, at least until 1942.[5] In the field of economic mobilization, from having been so far ahead in 1939, the Nazis were slow to consolidate their control. If the economy prior to 1939 was the 'peacetime war economy', the economy between 1939 and 1942 was just as much the 'wartime peace economy' (*friedensähnliche Kriegswirtschaft*). For example, it was not until the labour registration law of January 1943 that the Nazis laid the basis for total mobilization of labour – and even then the full potential of the law was never exploited. Similarly, it was not until 1942–3 that the Nazis began to ensure that industry was thoroughly combed for inessential employment. Particularly in the first half of the war (although in fact throughout the war years) Germany harnessed its population to the war effort less effectively than Britain or the USA.[6]

The limits to wartime mobilization can in part be explained by the fact that, for the first two years of the war, Germany pursued a type of campaign brilliantly suited to its state of half-preparedness. The strategy of lightning war was a deliberate attempt to avoid the need for armament in depth. But, as is well known, Germany was not properly prepared even for the *Blitzkrieg*. The three-week campaign against Poland in 1939 completely exhausted the supply of spare parts and key munitions. Germany in 1939 presents the curious picture of a nation in which centralized planning and the reorientation of society and economy to wartime needs was already well advanced and yet one in which basic requirements for sustained military effort were lacking.[7]

Another part of the explanation is that the Nazis were unwilling to impose too many sacrifices on the population. This was already apparent before the outbreak of war when, particularly after 1936, the economy began to overheat and suffered from an ever more acute labour shortage. Despite the absence of trade unions, key labour groups were able, on an individual basis, to exploit their scarcity value and negotiate wage increases, a tendency which the Nazis did not resist, despite the costs involved to the war effort.

Once the war started, the Nazis remained very sensitive to public opinion. During the first two years of the war, a whole series of government measures were attempted which were then withdrawn completely or only very half-heartedly implemented. As late as 1943 moves, for example, to revise piece-work rates in order to stimulate higher productivity were made very half-heartedly.[8] Even when new rates had been determined they were often not implemented. The Nazis.' reluctance to upset the established wage structure stemmed from the fear that any change would open a Pandora's box of resentment about existing wage differentials. It is perhaps ironic, but certainly comprehensible, that Germany's fascist leaders felt less assured of their legitimacy and thus less able to mobilize society than were the democratic governments of the Western Allied powers.

In addition to the nervousness of the Nazis, there was also the fact that the confusing proliferation of competing authorities, special plenipotentiaries and powerful interest groups made the regime susceptible to a whole variety of pressures. For example, even before the war, the quest of the DAF (German Labour Front) for power had led it to espouse workers' demands and encourage the drive for higher wages. Business interests found spokesmen at every level and were often able to oppose mobilization measures. Even when a policy had been decided upon by the body nominally responsible for a particular area, it was perfectly possible for it to be sabotaged by some other organization.[9]

In the case of the mobilization of women, these two factors were joined by a third: the reluctance of important sections of Nazi leadership to involve German women – the mothers of today and tomorrow – in the rigours of war production. The upshot was an amalgam of traditional cosy bourgeois views on women's place at the hearth and a new racist social-eugenic stress on the importance of optimum conditions for reproduction. One result of this ideology was that wives of enlisted men were given a very high income supplement, so that many stayed at home or even left former employment. All later attempts to reduce these supplements so as to encourage female employment failed in the face of ideologically motivated resistance and fear of a deleterious impact on soldiers' morale. As a result the number of German women in the economy actually fell between 1939 and 1941 and in 1942 was still lower than in the pre-war period. Whereas in 1943 almost two-thirds of British women were in employment, the equivalent figure for Germany was only 46 per cent.[10]

The regime's reluctance to extend or intensify social and economic mobilization at home encouraged it to exploit the occupied countries. They were to bear the full brunt of Nazi tyranny in order to protect the German population from the ravages and demands of war. Thanks to the massive confiscation of foodstuffs, manufactured and luxury goods abroad, living standards at home remained remarkably stable until towards the end of the war. After a drop in 1942, rations, for example, did not fall again significantly until the summer of 1944. Even more important than the importation of material resources was the recourse to foreign labour. By August 1944 there were over 7.5 million foreign workers on German soil, making up around one-quarter of all employees. By resorting to conscript labour, the Nazis were able to avoid or defer a whole range of unpleasant measures in relation to the German population such as the diversion of labour from inessential plants, enforced rationalization and retraining, the mobilization of women and so on.

The general point is that, for a variety of reasons, wartime social and economic policy relating to the *German* population was very often simply a continuation or a modest extension of peacetime policies. What the war did bring about, however, was the cessation or suspension of a number of social experiments in which the Nazis had been engaged during the 1930s. Not all of the Nazis' social engineering was sacrificed to the war effort; racial policy, as is well known, became more and more radical and there was also the continued reluctance to mobilize women. But, generally, social political goals were shelved for the duration. During the 1930s there had been, for example, various attempts to integrate the working class into the *Volksgemeinschaft.* Employers had been encouraged, particularly by the Nazi labour organization – the DAF – to improve their social policy provisions. Some employees had been given the chance to become owners of their own homes. Opportunities for upward mobility had been consciously created by the Nazi organizations. The Strength Through Joy movement had given considerable numbers of workers the chance to be tourists for the first time. All sorts of symbolic gestures had been made to indicate that the old class divisions no longer applied in the new Germany, the employers, for example, joining the DAF. But during the war, the DAF, though it continued to suggest possible post-war social reforms, became little more than an adjunct of the Nazis' productivity policy. It was no time for *sozialer Klimbim.*[11]

As the war drew on, the severity and intensity of the measures taken to sustain the war effort increased. The impetus came from the failure of the Russian campaign in the second half of 1941 which galvanized Hitler and the Nazi leadership to take mobilization more seriously. Hitler's directive, 'Armaments 1942', which appeared in January of that year, the appointment of Speer as Armaments Minister in February, and the elevation of the Gauleiter Fritz Sauckel to General Commissioner for Manpower, all indicated and encouraged the change in approach that was taking place. Between May 1941 and 1943, the number of industrial workers called to arms doubled; by mid-1944, 40 per cent of the industrial work-force had been enlisted. By then almost half of all German adult males were in the army or had died in combat. In the reorganization of the economy, the Nazis were much less successful than in the call-up and many of the restraints noted above continued to apply. Nevertheless, such measures as retraining labour for work in the armaments industry met with considerable success. A considerable, although not quantifiable, shift took place in the occupational and qualification structure of the German work-force. From mid-1942 onwards, Sauckel was increasingly effective at preventing undesirable, voluntary labour mobility, while at the same time labour direction increased and in the course of 1942 over a million German workers were transferred to war production. The mobilization of German women, on the other hand, remained half-hearted and brought only limited results.[12]

These policies were augmented and supported by the expansion of the police state as the strains of total war increased the Nazis' anxieties about their position. State terror became an increasing part of everyday life. By 1944, death sentences were being imposed on 14–16-year-olds. Between 1940 and 1943, the annual number of executions increased from 926 to 5,336. The Gestapo also took an ever more active role in enforcing discipline at work. In 1942, 7,311 workers were arrested by the Gestapo for breaches of labour discipline, but by 1944 the figure had risen to 42,505.[13]

The growing use of terror had yet another rationale. For alongside and sometimes in direct opposition to the mobilization of society's energies for the war effort, the Nazis were engaged in increasingly radical racist and imperialist policies. The war encouraged such policies in a number of ways. Wartime occupation provided, for the first time, the opportunity to create the European empire of which Hitler had already dreamt in the 1920s. Industry was quick to exploit the opportunities and comprehensive plans were drawn up in 1940–1 for the creation of a closed European economy, dominated by Germany. In the East, the occupation of vast tracts of Russian and East European territory allowed the Nazis to initiate their Utopian plans for racial resettlement and the subjugation of the Slavic peoples. The war against the Soviet Union exposed and unleashed that hatred of the Russians that was deeply ingrained in substantial sections of the military elite. The war also forced a new solution to what the Nazis regarded as the Jewish problem. It became impossible to get rid of the Jews through emigration and, in addition, the occupation of Poland presented the Germans with millions of additional Jews to dispose of. Under cover of war and unrestrained, as in the 1930s, by the desire to maintain goodwill in the West, competing Nazi agencies tried various means of removing the Jewish element culminating in the extermination camps.[14]

Much of this activity impinged on German society only indirectly, or only on small proportions of it: on those German minorities unlucky enough to be the victims; on the sections of the business, political and administrative elites involved in planning and extending the racial and economic empire; on the SS units charged with dirty work. It is true that most of the millions of German soldiers who at some point or other fought on the Eastern Front had at least some experience or involvement in National-Socialist policies towards Russian citizens, whether prisoners of war or civilians. How could they not? In the three months November and December 1941 and January 1942 alone, for example, *half a million* Russian POWs died in German captivity. A British investigation of German soldiers' wallets discovered that they generally contained three categories of photo: mother and girlfriend, pornographic, and atrocities.[15] Yet such experiences, important, shocking or brutalizing though they may have been, were usually short-lived episodes and had no systematic character.

The one area of Nazi racial policy which did involve the extended participation of a substantial proportion of the German population was the use of conscript labour. In its scope and social impact, this was unquestionably the most significant innovation in domestic wartime policy. At the beginning of the war, substantial sections of the leadership had been hostile to the use of large numbers of foreign workers on German soil. Some had been concerned about the threat to internal security, others about the implications for national hygiene and racial purity. Yet from the early months of the conflict, labour shortages combined with the resistance to total mobilization of the German population made pressing the recruitment of foreign labour. Once this had been acknowledged, all those sections of the Nazi leadership that had viewed the use of foreign labour with suspicion now set to work to create the conditions which would avert the ostensible dangers of employing racially inferior foreigners and would remind the German population of its role and responsibility as the racial elite of Europe. As the number of different nationalities amongst the conscript labour grew, the Nazis developed an ever more complex and comprehensive hierarchy of rules which dosed payment, nutrition, freedom, living standards and severity of punishment according to the racial 'calibre' of the group involved and their status as civilians or POWs. German workers were drawn into a series of complex relationships with the forced labour. It was a deliberate aim of the Nazis to make the workers active participants in the regime's racist and imperialist policy, to practise in *Kleinformat* in the factory that racial imperialism which would be enacted on a grand scale in Europe after the war.[16]

In their forced labour policy as in many other of their wartime measures it is evident that the solutions adopted to the problems posed by the war were influenced as much by pre-existent features of the Nazi regime as by any inherent characteristics of total war. The Nazis' imperialist and racial ideology, their ruthlessness but also their insecurity all left an indelible stamp on wartime policy. And after 1945, when the Nazis had fallen, it was the continuities, the specifically National Socialist elements in wartime policy, which left an abiding impression on German and foreign observers alike.

III

Total defeat, when it came, provided the opportunity to create a new society. The war had so drained Germany's military, social and psychological resources that the way was open for the victorious powers to reshape the nation as they wished. This is clearly manifested by Soviet occupation policy which, in the space of a few years, totally reorganized society and economy within its influence. In the Western Zones, however, the underlying trend was restorative. A capitalist democracy was created on the same lines as Weimar. True, the new constitution was more overtly federalistic, most of the major parties had experienced some change in identity and a change of name, and the economy was subjected to a certain amount of decartelization and reorganization. Yet there was a great deal of institutional and even personal continuity. In politics and the labour movement, the leaders of the Weimar era returned to their former positions. In industry and administration only a few top Nazis were removed, otherwise there was little change.[17]

The war had little positive influence on economic and social policy in the post-war era. In many Western countries, the close involvement of the state in wartime mobilization created a precedent for continued involvement in peacetime economic affairs and for a more managed economy generally. In such cases, wartime not only enlightened the state as to the role it might play in the economy but also increased the 'fiscal capacity' of the nation – i.e. the psychologically acceptable proportion of national income appropriated through taxation. In Germany, war's impact was rather the reverse. With the support of the USA, a school of economic thought became dominant which argued from the experience of Weimar and fascism that both political and economic stability depended on the vigorous removal of all constraints on free market activity. Cartels were to be broken up, all state bureaucracies removed and taxation was not to be used for demand management. For these theorists, wartime experience simply underlined the negative character of a state-run economy. Industrialists too had grown more wary than ever of state intervention as a result of the war; industrial figures who were too closely associated with Albert Speer, for example, found it hard to gain positions in post-war industry. The result was that the post-1948 economy was less cartelized and concentrated than in Weimar years, with far less state intervention.[18]

In most spheres of social policy, too, the war had only limited impact, often serving merely to underline anxiety about an interventionist state. It had, of course, created a number of new, though temporary, problems for the legislators, above all that of integrating and compensating the expellees. But war did not stimulate or promote innovative solutions or responses to established social problems. In health and pensions policy, in housing and in education, the authorities returned to the established practices of the pre-war era. It is well known that in Britain, victory brought considerable pressure for social reform in the aftermath of both World Wars, I and II, but in Germany the idea of making a 'home fit for heroes' hardly applied. The nation was far too concerned to restore the basic features of normal life to attempt major innovations in social policy. In the chaotic conditions of the immediate post-war period, the authorities chose to focus on familiar and established practices. In any case, whatever Germany's politicians and citizens thought in private, it was not possible in the early post-war years to celebrate Germany's soldiers as returning heroes, nor could they harbour any expectations of reward for their military service.[19]

Some innovations from the *pre-war* fascist period survived into the post-war era, particularly when they had themselves built on achievements or developments of Weimar. The promotion of owner-occupied homes in the 1930s, for instance, was considerably extended in the 1950s. The reconstruction of German towns was much facilitated by the extended powers the planners had gained under the Nazis. The 1950s saw a flowering of the type of company social policy so beloved of the DAF. But on the whole, neither fascism nor war left many positive institutional or political legacies in the post-war period.

On the other hand, there is no doubt that the general attitudes towards both democracy and labour on the part of Germany's administrative and managerial elites had been profoundly affected by the experience of fascism. One of the most reactionary elements of Germany's elite, the *Junker*, had been completely eliminated from the political scene by Nazi purges and the Soviet Occupation. And for the rest, the excesses of the fascist state and the proximity of the Soviet threat combined to create a new awareness of the attractiveness of the Western democratic model, of the need to avoid extremes, of the virtues of a representative political system and the desirability of institutionalized collective bargaining. In other words, what was new was not the institutions – they had been largely created in Weimar – but the commitment to these institutions of those whose job it was to run them and work within them.

IV

What was the impact of war on the wider German population and on the working class in particular? We should start by looking at the effects of the Nazis' attempts to control, mobilize and reshape German society during the 1930s.

The first point must be that by 1939 Germany had become a repressive society, full of fear and suspicion. The majority of the population were not overtly subject to direct terror. But everyone knew certain things were best left unsaid, actions best left undone. Through analysis of dreams, through the exaggerated fervour with which Germany's middle classes threw themselves into their private amusements, we can detect the undercurrent of fear that ran through German society. Workers in particular had to be careful, former activists were sent in hundreds of thousands to concentration camps, the individual workers were isolated and political communication became too dangerous in all but the most close-knit of neighbourhoods.[20]

At the same time it was a society that seemed to be working again. That feeling of being on the brink of disaster that had haunted much of the 1920s and early 1930s was replaced by a new confidence in the social order. Criminality seemed to be decreasing. After the war, even left-wingers and liberals felt bound to acknowledge that the Nazis had appeared capable and purposeful, harnessing social energies in a productive way. The Nazis drew respect from almost all sections of the population for the skill and finesse with which they organized public spectacles and for their success in getting the economy to work.[21]

It was also a society in which class relationships were visibly changing. Though changes in class composition were far from dramatic, there is evidence that mobility from manual to white-collar positions increased considerably in the 1930s.[22] Furthermore, quite a number of workers, particularly youngsters in the Hitler Youth, experienced a sort of informal upward mobility outside work by taking on positions of responsibility in Nazi organizations. The status hierarchy had been made more complicated: party ranking offered an alternative status calibration. In addition, the Hitler Youth, sports groups and other organizations were, to a certain extent, able to bring the classes together. Everywhere there was the characteristic and peculiar mixture of Führer-Prinzip and egalitarianism. There are indications that Nazi policy, in conjunction with the spread of mass culture through radio and the cinema, was beginning to change the younger workers' social and self-perceptions. For instance, young miners in the Ruhr abandoned the traditional Sunday dress of an open-necked shirt and cap and opted for the collar and tie. In a small way, they were manifesting the weakening of a working-class subculture and a desire to be citizens in the wider community.[23]

Yet the Nazis were clearly far from winning the loyalty and obedience for which they had hoped. The accelerated rearmaments programme, though it initially benefited from the way the Nazis had disciplined and terrorized the labour movement, actually began to undermine the Nazis' control and integration strategy. The increasing demands placed on the labour force and the awareness of their own power in the tight labour-market led to growing criticism of the regime and a new aggressiveness in wage and other demands. Absenteeism increased and productivity suffered while wages in key economic sectors drifted upwards. By 1939, there were signs that the Nazi labour strategy was crumbling into a familiar pattern of (albeit informal) wage bargaining and material gratification.[24]

These trends and patterns were initially little affected by the outbreak of war. For substantial sections of the population, particularly those not subjected to military call-up, it took a long time for war to make significant changes in their way of life. New features of wartime, such as rationing, had little impact on the general standard of living; real wages held up until 1944.

In 1943 there was official opposition to the idea of introducing an evacuation programme for women and children because, it was argued, this would be to disrupt a private sphere hitherto little affected by the war.

For many of those on the home front, it was only in 1942 and 1943 that the war began to bite, partly because of intensified mobilization, but even more because the destructive and disruptive capacity of war began to reach home. German casualties rose steeply in the course of the Russian campaign after two years of relatively bloodless combat. In the beginning of 1942, consumers were shocked by a sudden fall in rations. True, they then revived somewhat and stabilized until the closing months of 1944. But other articles began to run short and everyday life became increasingly dominated by shortages. In the winter of 1942–3, for example, areas outside the coal-producing districts received less than a third of their coal requirement. It was above all the increasingly frequent and intensive air raids that disrupted every aspect of normal life. In 1943 there were three times as many bombs as in 1942, and in 1944 five times as many as in 1943. Travel became difficult and time-consuming after bombs disrupted public transport. Many families became homeless. For all this, there was as in Britain, a determination to go on living as normal a life as possible and it was only in the closing months of 1944 that the normal fabric of social life began to disintegrate.[25]

One important effect of the war was to maintain and indeed increase the comparatively high level of geographical and social mobility of the 1930s. On the home front, while most labour directions did not involve moving home, a considerable number of workers found themselves drafted to new areas. Many women and children in the big cities were evacuated to rural communities. For enlisted men, of course, there was a great deal of travel involved. Many accounts of the first years of the war sound – until they reach the Eastern Front – very much like recollections from an extended holiday, a welter of vivid scenes and impressions from strange and colourful countries; the parallel with tourism extends even to the cheap bargains that were to be had at the exchange rates imposed by the Nazis.[26] To paraphrase Clausewitz: war as the continuation of tourism by other means. Much of this mobility was of a temporary nature, yet it seems to have had some long-term significance for those groups which had previously been rather self-enclosed and isolated: the rural communities and also substantial sections of the working class. The War extended the way in which the Nazis in peacetime had already begun – through the media, tourism and mobilization – to break through the barriers of local consciousness.

At the same time economic mobilization during the war created new job opportunities and the chance of upward mobility. Retraining programmes, for example, enabled a considerable number of unskilled or semi-skilled workers to obtain a new qualification and better rates of pay. The army itself offered considerable opportunities for advancement. Such advances were not always easily transferable to the civil sphere but in practice a good war career proved advantageous at most levels of the post-war job market. For the many workers who became non-commissioned officers and the few who went further, holding positions of authority and responsibility was often a new and important experience which was to inform post-war behaviour.[27]

The influx of foreign forced labour created a form of collective upward mobility for German workers. Since foreigners made up one-quarter of the work-force by the end of the war, many German employees now found themselves elevated to the position of overseers and foremen. In some cases, solidarity developed, particularly where German workers were training their own replacements, as it were, before being sent off to the front. In such cases, the unwilling draftees had an interest in making the training proceed as slowly as possible and needed the foreign trainees' help in doing so. But in general, the Nazis were successful in actively involving an increasing number of German workers in the control and repression of the forced labour. From interviews we know that many workers did perceive their new responsibility as a sort of promotion and, just as for their counterparts in the army, the experience of authority was often a significant and lasting one. These experiences of formal and informal social mobility reinforced those of the pre-war period.[28]

At the same time total war meant the intensification of repression and terror and strengthened the tendency to withdraw into the private sphere and to remain guarded and non-committal in public. The individual was isolated and social groups became fragmented.

Another consequence of the war was that labour's attitude to work and the firm begins to shift. Whereas in the late 1930s discontent manifested itself in climbing rates of absenteeism, the war years see astonishingly stable levels of productivity and absenteeism despite increasingly unfavourable conditions. The more disordered everyday life became, the more attractive was the dependable regularity of the work itself. Even for the conscript labour, the work-place became increasingly a sort of haven and from 1943, the productivity of Russian labour actually rose, amidst deteriorating conditions. For a number of reasons, the interests of labour and employers moved closer together. Both had an interest in protecting plant from call-up and from labour transfers. German labour was given a new role as overseers of the foreign conscripts. And as the employers saw defeat approaching, many were at pains to mend bridges with the labour force.[29]

In general we can say that the war undermined the Nazis' own appeal while reinforcing many of the social changes which they had initiated in the 1930s. It was the increasingly obvious hopelessness of the war that cost the Nazis the last remnants of what limited support they had enjoyed amongst German labour. Yet through isolation and terror, through collective and individual mobility and through the forging of new loyalties and solidarities, the war confirmed the Nazis assault on class traditions.

As the conflict approached its conclusion, all these changes paled increasingly in relation to the fight to survive. From the autumn of 1944 gas and electricity supplies were often missing for large stretches of time in the major cities. In the following spring rations fell below starvation levels. Sybil Bannister wrote in her book, *I Lived under Hitler,* that 'within a few months, with the Allies advancing on all sides, town-dwellers were reduced from a finely organised community to primitive cave-dwellers'. And for the troops, the initially comfortable war on the Western Front and in Africa had been replaced on all sides by an increasingly hopeless and bitter struggle.

In August 1944 the Red Army entered German territory for the first time and from December onwards the mass exodus of refugees from the East began. By the end of the war two-fifths of the German population were on the move – soldiers, evacuees, refugees, 'displaced persons' (d.p.'s), former Nazis and so on. Thus the major consequence of the war in the immediate post-war period was the hardship and dislocation that resulted from the destruction of the cities, from economic collapse and from the massive population mobility. The destruction itself was unbelievable. Over 50 per cent of housing in the big cities had been destroyed. Production fell to almost zero in April 1945. In 1946, production in the Western Zones still had not exceeded 25 per cent of pre-war figures. Rations remained little above starvation levels until 1948. For three years after the end of the war, life was one long struggle for the ordinary citizen.[30]

Though they dominated the immediate post-war period, the hardship and the disruption of normal life were shortlived. Malnutrition disappeared rapidly after 1948. By the mid-1950s unemployment was waning rapidly and living standards exceeded pre-war peaks by a comfortable margin. Enormous strides were made in the housing market. The speed of economic recovery was such as to restore a normal way of life within a few years.

The pace of recovery revealed that, destructive as the war had been, it had left the country's industrial capacity relatively undamaged. Despite bomb-damage and post-war dismantling, the value of industrial plant in 1948 was higher than in 1936. The supply of labour had been harder hit – no less than 25 per cent of the male population in the age range 35–50 had been killed by the war – yet here total war had created its own solution: the refugees and expellees from the East. By 1948 there were getting on for 20 per cent more people available for work in the Western Zones than there had been in 1936.[31]

On the back of economic recovery, the massive number of expellees – by 1950 there were 10,000,000 of them in West Germany – were integrated rapidly. Initially, they faced severe problems of adaptation and were particularly hard hit by the high unemployment that followed the currency reform. Yet the tensions between the newcomers and the established community were for the most part temporary and the expellees were quick to find employment. Their party, the BHE, reached its highpoint in the 1953 election with less than 6 per cent of the vote and soon dwindled to insignificance.[32] In other words the destructive and disruptive impact of total war did not present post-war German society with problems it could not solve. Of greater long-term significance for the German working class were the subtler changes to perceptions, behaviour and relationships, above all the weakening of traditional class identities and antipathies which had been wrought by fascism and war.

Yet this is to look into the future. In the immediate post-war period there was good reason to believe that the working class would conform to the Weimar mould. The effect of the capitulation had been to create a power vacuum within Germany and the surviving leaders of the working-class movement were keen to realize that synthesis of parliamentary and economic democracy which had already been outlined by labour theoreticians in the Weimar era. The experience of fascism merely underlined the urgency of introducing such a system. True, the fascist experience also convinced the different political groupings within the trade unions of the need to form a united organization, an innovation which was to be realized in the following years. But otherwise the stage seemed set for a repeat of the political struggles of the post-World War I era. However the Allies saw to it that the goal of economic democracy was largely stifled. Labour was prevented from exploiting the collapse of authority within Germany. Just as important was the fact that it was not the German employers who prevented it from doing so. It was American power, American intentions and the clear dependence on US aid that made most labour leaders accept fairly rapidly that a capitalist restoration was inevitable. Here and elsewhere the effect of the Allies was to prevent the bitter conflicts between labour and capital that had resulted after 1918 and would otherwise probably have resulted after 1945.[33]

Once the Allies had restrained the reforming impulses of the immediate post-war period and helped to undermine the radical element in the working-class movement, it was Germany's labour leaders themselves who (often unwittingly) ensured that the depoliticization of everyday life and the diminution of working-class identity achieved by the National Socialists was sustained and strengthened. Nervous of the Communists, uneasy about recreating a divided society and sensitive to the criticism that as a mass organization they were liable to extremism, labour leaders were at pains to avoid rebuilding a conflict-oriented labour movement. The old workers' cultural organizations were not re-built, a concerted effort was made to keep politics out of industrial relations and a co-operative, conciliatory approach towards the employers was adopted. The Social Democrats moved towards the centre and tried to win a middle-class following.

Under these conditions, the integrative, depoliticizing tendencies of the Nazi era were able to survive into the post-war period. What emerged, as we know from many surveys in the 1950s, was a hardworking, consumer–oriented, sceptical and unpolitical working class. A strong suspicion of the bosses coexisted with the feeling that labour's status had collectively improved. The boom economy of the 1930s with its possibilities for individual advancement and the toughening experiences of soldiering and surviving the hardships of the Occupation years had encouraged in many workers a confidence in their ability to stand up to those in authority and to profit from the capitalist system. Such individual experiences and the chaos of the pre-1948 rationing system fostered a resigned acceptance of the capitalist system and a recognition of the need for continual rationalization and modernization of production. The language of class conflict lost much of its appeal and younger workers in particular did not even understand terms such as 'proletariat'. In their dress, leisure habits and taste younger workers differed little from their bourgeois counterparts. Despite large inequalities in wealth, German society was probably more culturally homogeneous than at any time before or since. In short, even before the economic miracle had had its effect, fascism, war and Allied policy had together created in the working class a far more solid social and ideological base for a democratic capitalist system than had existed in Weimar.[34]

V

It is evident that 'total war' is not an independent cause of social change. Its influence on German society was shaped decisively by the nature of the regime which waged it and that of the regime which followed it. It is true that certain features of the war would have impinged on society no matter what regime was in power. Any political system would have faced the need to mobilize all possible reserves of labour, materials and energy for the war effort. No regime could wish away the destructive capability of the enemy's weapons. But the way the Nazis responded to such challenges and opportunities and the way the Allies' post-war policies refracted and channelled the experiences and wishes that were the legacy of war were as important in shaping its impact as any such 'objective' features of war itself. This would be a point of lesser interest in a country where, as in Britain, the only changes in the political system were those brought about by the needs of war. But in Germany, the political discontinuities make it of crucial importance.

Partly because of these discontinuities, total war does not stand out as a revolutionary impulse in the way that it perhaps does in some other countries. Even where it stimulated or impelled the Nazis to introduce quite new policies, it is often the specifically National Socialist flavour of these measures that is striking and that carried the greatest potential for social change. In any case, war was slow to bring any changes at all. Many of the innovations necessary for a nationally co-ordinated and concerted war effort had been carried out already, in some cases in advance calculation of wartime requirements, in others because mobilizing society's energies for the national cause was a central goal of the National Socialists.

Nevertheless, the war did have a specific impact which differed from the preceding period. In the first place, it intensified the Nazi assault on established milieus, the fragmentation of social groups and the isolation of the individual. Second, for the German workers, the experience of destruction and dislocation and of common interests with the employers – *vis-à-vis* the Nazi state and later the Occupying Powers – prepared the way for the pragmatic acceptance of the capitalist system. Thus war was preparing the ground for Western Germany's return to capitalist democracy even before total defeat brought the fall of the Nazi regime.

Notes

1 Footnotes are intended to provide an indicative bibliography only and no attempt at comprehensive or systematic references has been made. For general accounts of social change in this period see David Schoenbaum, *Hitler's Social Revolution: Class and Status in Nazi Germany*, New York, 1966; Detlev Peukert, *Volksgenossen und Gemeinschaftsfremde: Anpassung, Ausmerze und Aufbegehren unter dem Nationalsozialismus*, Cologne, 1982; Werner Conze and M. Rainer Lepsius (eds) *Sozialgeschichte der BRD*, Stuttgart, 1983; R. Dahrendorf, *Society and Democracy in Germany*, London, 1968.

2 On wartime social policy see Marie-Luise Recker, *Nationalsozialistische Sozialpolitik im 2. Weltkrieg,* München, 1985. For labour policy specifically, see Wolfgang Werner, *Bleib übrig: Deutsche Arbeiter in der nationalsozialistischen Kriegswirtschaft*, Düsseldorf, 1983.

3 The most comprehensive account of German mobilization is Ludolf Herbst, *Der Totale Krieg und die Ordnung der Wirtschaft: Die Kriegswirtschaft im Spannungsfeld von Politik, Ideologie und Propaganda 1939-1945*, Stuttgart, 1982.

4 See Volker Berghahn, *The Americanisation of German Industry*, Leamington Spa, 1986, introduction.

5 For a view which places more emphasis on changes in the 1939-41 period, see Richard J. Overy, 'Hitler's war and the German economy: a reinterpretation', *Economic History Review*, XXXV, 2, 1982, 277-91.

6 See Recker, *NS Sozialpolitik* and Werner, *Bleib übrig.*

7 Timothy W. Mason, *Sozialpolitik im Dritten Reich: Arbeiterklasse und Volksgemeinschaft*, Opladen, 1977, passim.

8 Werner, *Bleib übrig*, pp. 220ff.

9 On the competition between the DAF and other elements of the Nazi regime, see for example, Gunther Mai, 'Warum steht der deutsche Arbeiter zu Hitler? Zur Rolle der Deutschen Arbeitsfront im Herrschaftssystem des Dritten Reiches', in *Geschichte und Gesellschaft*, 1986, 12, 2, 212-34.

10 On women in Nazi Germany see Jill Stephenson, *Women in Nazi Society*, London, 1975, and Dörte Winkler, *Frauenarbeit im 'Dritten Reich'*, Hamburg, 1977.

11 On social political initiatives towards labour see Schoenbaum, *Hitler's Social Revolution*, and the essays by Reulecke and others in Detlev Peukert and Jürgen Reulecke (eds) *Die Reihen fast geschlossen. Beiträge zur Geschichte des Alltags unterm Nationalsozialismus*, Wuppertal, 1981. See also Günther Mai, 'Warum steht der deutscher Arbeiter zu Hitler'.

12 Werner, *Bleib übrig*, esp pp. 277ff.

13 Richard Grunberger, *A Social History of the Third Reich*, Harmondsworth, 1971, contains a useful description of the impact of Nazi terror. A systematic account can be found in Hans Buchheim *et al.* (eds) *Anatomie des SS-Staates*, 2 vols, Munich, 1967.

14 See Berghahn, *Americanisation*, introduction; Hans Mommsen, 'Die Realisierung des Utopischen: Die Endlösung der Judenfrage im "Dritten Reich" ', in *Geschichte und Gesellschaft*, 9, 1983, 381-420.

15 Grunberger, *A Social History*, p. 63.

16 The standard work on forced labour is now Ulrich Herbert, *Fremdarbeiter: Politik und Praxis des 'Ausländer-Einsatzes' in der Kriegswirtschaft des Dritten Reiches*, Berlin, Bonn, 1985.

17 For a good general discussion of the balance between restorative and innovative elements in the post-war settlement see Jürgen Kocha, '1945: Neubeginn oder

Restauration', in Carola Stern and Heinrich August Winkler (eds) *Wendepunkte deutscher Geschichte 1848-1945*, Frankfurt, 1979, pp. 141-68.

18 See here Berghahn, *Americanisation,* passim.

19 See for instance Hans Günther Hockerts, *Sozialpolitische Entscheidungen im Nachkriegsdeutschland 1945-1947*, Stuttgart, 1980.

20 Detlev Peukert, *Volksgenossen und Gemeinschaftsfremde*, passim.

21 See Ian Kershaw, *Der Hitler-Mythos: Volksmeinung und Propaganda im Dritten Reich*, Stuttgart, 1980.

22 See the discussion of mobility in Josef Mooser, *Arbeiterleben in Deutschland 1900-1970*, Frankfurt/M, 1984, pp. 113ff.

23 On class and status, see Schoenbaum, *Hitler's Social Revolution*; Michael Zimmermann, 'Ausbruhshoffnungen: Junge Bergleute in den Dreißiger Jahren', in Lutz Niethammer (ed.) *'Die Jahre weiß man nicht, wo man die heute hinsetzen soll'. Faschismuserfahrungen im Ruhrgebiet* Berlin, Bonn, 1983, pp. 97-132.

24 These trends are well documented in Mason, *Sozialpolitik.*

25 See Werner, *Bleib übrig*, and Lutz Niethammer, 'Heimat und Front. Versuch, zehn Kriegerinnerungen aus der Arbeiterklasse des Ruhrgebietes zu verstehen', in Niethammer (ed.) *Die jahre weiß man nicht*, pp. 163-232.

26 See Niethammer, 'Heimat und Front'.

27 There is no satisfactory account of the impact of war-time experience on postwar labour. See Niethammer. 'Heimat und Front', and my Ph.D. thesis, 'New labour in the Ruhr Mines', Warwick University, 1987.

28 In addition to Ulrich Herbert's study referred to above, see also his essay 'Apartheid nebenan. Erinnerungen an die Fremdarbeiter im Ruhrgebiet', in Niethammer (ed.), *Die Jahre weiß man nicht*, pp. 233-66.

29 Both Herbert and Werner draw attention to the factory's role as a refuge. On employers' changing attitudes, see Günther Mai, 'Warum steht der deutsche Arbeiter zu Hitler', esp. p. 232. See also John Gillingham, *Industry and Politics in the Third Reich*, Methuen, 1985.

30 For an introduction to conditions after the war, see Manfred Overesch, *Deutschland 1945-1949: Vorgeschichte und Gründung der Bundesrepublik*, Königsten/Ts, 1979.

31 The standard work on the recovery is Werner Abelshauser, *Wirtschaft in Westdeutschland 1945-1948: Rekonstruktion und Wiederaufbaubedingungen in der amerikanischen und britischen Zonen*, Stuttgart, 1975.

32 For a good survey of recent work on the refugees, see Wolfgang Benz (ed.) *Die Vertreibung der Deutschen aus dem Osten: Ursachen, Ereignisse, Folgen*, Frankfurt/M, 1985.

33 An excellent introduction to the post-war labour movement is to be found in Lutz Niethammer, 'Rekonstruktion und Desintegration: Zum Verständnis der deutschen Arbeiterbewegung zwischen Krieg und kaltem Krieg', in Winkler (ed.) *Politische Weichenstellungen in Nachkriegsdeutschland 1945-1953*, Göttingen, 1979, pp. 26-43.

34 Among many other studies, see H. Popitz and P. Bahrdt, *Das Gesellschaftbild des Arbeiters*, Tübingen, 1961; H. Schelsky, *Die skeptische Generation,* Düsseldorf, 1963; Helmuth Croon and K. Utermann, *Zeche und Gemeinde: Unter suchungen über den Strukturwandel einer Zechengemeinde im nördlichen Ruhrgebiet,* Tübingen, 1958; Frank Deppe, *Das Bewußtsein der Arbeiter: Studien zur politischen Soziologie des Arbeiterbewußtseins,* Köln, 1971. In English, see Angi Rutter, 'Elites, Estate and Strata: Class in West Germany since 1945; in Arthur Marwick (ed.) *Class in the Twentieth Century,* Brighton and New York, 1986, pp. 115-64.

Total War in the Twentieth Century

HEW STRACHAN

The proper strategy consists in inflicting as telling blows as possible on the enemy's army, and then in causing the inhabitants so much suffering that they must long for peace, and force the government to demand it. The people must be left nothing but their eyes to weep with over the war.[1]

Although this was advice given in a war fought by Germany, these were not the words of a German but of an American; not of Adolf Hitler but of Phil Sheridan. Politics, geography and even strict chronology favour the wars of German unification as the precursor of the two world wars. But Sheridan's suggestions as to Bismarck's best policy after the battle of Sedan make it impossible to consider the idea of total war solely within the context of a German *Sonderweg*. Sheridan was, after all, speaking from experience. His own campaign in the Shenandoah valley in 1864 had been based on the same principles. Nor was he the only Union general to portray war in such graphic terms. The conduct of William Tecumseh Sherman's campaign in Georgia, also in 1864, had prompted the Confederate general, John S. Hood, to voice his objections. Sherman replied: 'You cannot qualify war in harsher terms than I will. War is cruelty, and you cannot refine it'.[2]

Arguments based on the notion of transatlantic cross-fertilization, particularly in the realm of military ideas, have struggled to command acceptance. Geoffrey Parker has probably been most successful. He has alerted seventeenth- and eighteenth-century historians to the interrelationship between the Old World and the New, between warfare within Europe and conflict outside it.[3] But an older thesis, R. R. Palmer's linking of the American and French revolutions, which possessed a military dimension, has attracted trenchant criticism.[4] Similarly those seeking to explain total war in the twentieth century by reference to Sheridan, Sherman and the American Civil War have not been assured of an easy passage.[5] The prompt reduction in the size of the Union army after the Civil War, and its resumption of frontier campaigning, make specific connections even within America hard to trace.[6] In Britain, G. F. R. Henderson's enormously influential study of Stonewall Jackson, published in 1898, highlighted the early phases of the war, and in France and Germany any precepts to be gleaned from the American Civil War were overshadowed by Prussia's triumph in 1871.[7]

More recent historiographical trends have not helped. The pivot of total war has become less the conduct of war itself and more its cultural and political baggage. The Holocaust and the Russo-German conflict in the Second World War favour Eurocentricism. The current but questionable orthodoxy of strategic studies is that liberal democracies do not fight each other, implying that if they do go to war the need is defensive and the cause just.[8] In the story of triumphant liberalism, the role of the New World has not been to instruct the Old in ways of making war but to rescue it from the consequences of having done so.

But, if the twentieth century is taken as a whole, the USA fought more wars than did Germany (and the UK would probably be ahead of both of them). Sheridan and Sherman serve to show that liberalism has not been as uncomfortable with the concepts of total war as contemporary nostrums might suggest. Moreover, their dicta are revealing in regard to another aspect of late twentieth-century conflict. The wars that afflicted eastern Europe, Africa, and south-east Asia in the late 1990s can be characterized as civil wars. Both Sheridan and Sherman make clear that much of the vocabulary of total war finds its origins in such conflicts, and not in wars between nation states.

In 1948 John Bennett Walters wrote a seminal article entitled 'General William T. Sherman and total war'. It reflected this particular 'Atlantic thesis'. He was especially concerned with Sherman's readiness to use military force against the civilian population of the enemy. This, he explained, had become 'a part of the present concept of total war'. Although he accepted that breaching the principle of non-combatant immunity was only one aspect of total war, he wrote at a time when the attacks on Hiroshima and Nagasaki gave it particular significance. The presumption that underpinned his article was that war had become progressively – if tautologically – 'more' total since 1864. 'Within recent years', he explained, 'the term "total war" had been . . . definitely accepted as part of everyday vocabulary'.[9]

In the wake not only of the atomic bomb but also of the Second World War, Walters' sense of inevitable progression (if progress is the right word to associate with the advent of total war) was uncontroversial. The melding of past and present was common not only to historians but also to political scientists. In *The Century of Total War* (1954), Raymond Aron asserted that the American Civil War 'offered a fairly good preview of what we call total war, with regard particularly to the relentless mobilization of national resources and the competition over new inventions'.[10] He went on to devote a chapter to what he called 'the dynamism of total war', in which he spoke of the expansion of the Second World War as illustrating 'the irrepressible dynamism of modern war with its strategic bombing, guerrilla warfare, deportation of civilians, and death camps'.[11]

Aron, born in 1905, a French Jew who taught in Germany between 1930 and 1933, saw his own life shaped and conditioned by the two world wars and by the advent of nuclear weapons. He put the problem of war at the centre of his understanding of international relations. One of his last and most important books, *Penser la Guerre* (1976), was devoted to his study of Clausewitz.

Clausewitz's *On War* sustains a dialogue between theory and reality, between the ideal and the practicable. His concept of 'absolute war' belongs in the former category. In explicit and graphic descriptions, he makes quite clear that there is no inherent limitation in the conduct of war: violence and bloodshed are at its centre. War consists of three elements, Clausewitz's 'trinity': its basic violence, associated with popular passions; the play of probability and of chance, which fall within the general's purview; and the political direction of the government. At the second level, the constraints inherent in war's conduct, which Clausewitz called 'friction', foil its participants' efforts. But it was the third component which became particularly important to Clausewitz's mental baggage, which served to provide a unifying purpose to *On War* and which served to restrain 'absolute' war. Famously, Clausewitz argued that the achievement of political objectives determines, shapes and ultimately (because Clausewitz, in this context at least, was a rationalist) limits its course. The problem for subsequent critics is that this insight was only incorporated in the first and last books, I and VIII, of *On War*. With its central tensions unresolved, *On War* has become a vehicle for the preoccupations of Clausewitz's successors.

Some see 'absolute war' not so much as an ideal but as a reality, which Clausewitz himself glimpsed through his experiences in the Napoleonic wars. In 1942 Gerhard Ritter, the outstanding historian of German militarism, refused to interpret the Clausewitzian idea of absolute war as a prefiguring of total war. Clausewitz, he pointed out to General Ludwig Beck, only knew of wars between armed forces.[12] Ritter's interpretation is tendentious in itself, but its date makes the point that, for some commentators at least, not even the Second World War could give absolute war contemporary relevance. For many it required nuclear weapons to do that. For Aron's generation, absolute war had become a possibility by 1945, and armed with that insight they imposed a teleological view on the development and growth of modern war that stretched back to Napoleon.

Clausewitz did more than shape their perspectives on war; he also provided them with ways out of their dilemmas. Aron's *Penser la Guerre* extended what Clausewitz did write to suggest what he might have written had he completed *On War*. In particular Aron argued that what he called Clausewitz's 'formula', the relationship between war and politics, was at odds with the concept of absolute war. Aron contended that if Clausewitz had lived to complete the revision of his entire text, he would have jettisoned 'absolute war' as a definition reflecting war's mean rather than its ends. To take *On War* at face value, and to suggest that Clausewitz saw an implicit drift up the scale to 'absolute' (or even total) war, was – in Aron's view – completely to misinterpret Clausewitz's final intentions. Thus Clausewitz the warmonger became Clausewitz the peacemaker. Aron's basis for this intellectual leap was an extrapolation of book VI of *On War*, the section which argues for the strength of the defensive in purely military terms. Aron revised book VI in the light of books I and VIII, and so clothed it in the vocabulary of conflict resolution.[13]

Few cold war strategists went as far as Aron, but most joined him in elevating the third element of Clausewitz's trinity, political understanding. The belief that war did not pursue its own objectives but was subservient to political rationality underpinned the logic chopped in the name of nuclear deterrence. Fed by the fluency of Michael Howard's and Peter Paret's translation, which also appeared in 1976 (truly an *annus mirabilis* for Clausewitz studies), thinkers in the West ceased to categorize *On War* as repetitive, obscure and ambiguous. The cold war provided a framework within which admiration of Clausewitz could flourish.

But with the end of the cold war some of that veneration dissipated. In 1991 Martin van Creveld declared, in *On Future War*, that the Clausewitzian world picture was both obsolete and wrong.[14] Two years later, in 1993, John Keegan began *A History of Warfare* with the provocative statement: 'war is not the continuation of politics by other means'.[15] They argued, essentially, that Clausewitz was a European white male, concerned with the problems of the nation state, and that his discussion of war, because it is rooted in these cultural assumptions, cannot be universally applicable. Martin van Creveld's view of war was protean. Just because he saw conventional war between states as obsolescent, he did not then conclude that war itself was also obsolete; it would be replaced by sub-state violence waged by terrorists, guerrillas and bandits. John Keegan was more positive. He concluded that, by rejecting the western view of war, by repudiating the notion 'that politics and war belong within the same continuum', we could rediscover the patterns of war prevalent in other cultures and other times; 'there is a wisdom', he pointed out, 'in the principles of intellectual restraint and even of symbolic ritual'.[16] In the last of his 1998 Reith lectures he posed the question, 'Can there be an end to war?' His answer, though mixed, was certainly not negative.[17]

John Keegan was no more isolated in his optimism in the late 1990s than was John Bennett Walters in his pessimism 50 years before. The norm in the mid-twentieth century was to assume that total war had become the dominant pattern in warmaking. The norm at the end of the same century was to argue that major war was now obsolete. Note, however, the caution implicit in the change of nomenclature. The absolute 'total', employed by Walters, had given way to the relative and comparative, 'major'.

In 1998 Michael Mandelbaum, professor of American foreign policy at Johns Hopkins University and the author of important works on nuclear deterrence, observed that all those countries capable of fighting 'major' war seemed disinclined to do so. He told the International Institute for Strategic Studies that this was because they could not see major war as fulfilling a political purpose.[18] His conclusion, that major wars were therefore obsolete, reflected a growing orthodoxy among defence planners, developed even before the end of the cold war by John Mueller. Mueller's book, *Retreat from Doomsday*, published in 1989, was subtitled *The Obsolescence of Major War*. Mueller argued that the horrors of the First World War had convinced most powers that war was neither heroic nor useful. The consensus of the inter-war period, embodied in the Kellogg-Briand pact of 1928, and put into practice with appeasement, was that war should be avoided. It required a maniac like Hitler to break that assumption. Nonetheless it was revalidated by the experience of the Second World War. For Mueller, neither NATO nor the Warsaw Pact had resorted to arms because their members (and particularly the Soviet Union) knew only too well the awfulness and waste of modern European war. The argument of *Retreat from Doomsday*, therefore, was that major war's obsolescence began with the two world wars; nuclear weapons did no more than confirm a process that was already in train.[19]

The neglect of nuclear weapons and nuclear deterrence after the end of the cold war served to confirm Mueller's hypothesis that their significance was at best marginal. Nuclear arsenals retained the potential to inflict damage on a scale as great as any threatened before 1990. Moreover, in 1999, arms control agreements remained unratified, the US Senate refused to endorse the Test Ban Treaty, the Russian *Duma* postponed the START II agreement, and both India and Pakistan entered the ranks of nuclear weapons-owning powers. And yet in the last decade of the twentieth century the heat went out of the debate about nuclear disarmament. For western publics, the shadow of nuclear war was lifted. When in October 1999 Margaret Gimblett, Sheriff of Dunoon, briefly thrust the British ownership of Trident missiles back onto the front pages by accepting as a legal defence that their possession was contrary to international law, Magnus Linklater was prompted to write in *The Times* that, 'Ban the bomb is as outdated as semolina pudding'.[20]

Nor was it only nuclear war that seemed less threatening. As Martin van Creveld argued in *On Future War*, armed forces clung to a view of war that put themselves at the centre, and assumed clashes of like versus like. Of course, during the 1990s, they increasingly recognized their role as peace-keepers and peace-enforcers, and the voguish phrase 'asymmetric war' acknowledged that the enemy could be not only radically different in organization and structure but also in methods of fighting. In explaining the British *Strategic Defence Review* of 1998, the chief of the general staff argued that an army configured for conventional war could undertake gendarmerie roles, but that gendarmeries could not engage in 'all arms warfare'.[21] Essentially, the mental image of 'real war' remained a lineal descendant of the Second World War; a conflict between sophisticated armies, navies and air forces, fighting for high stakes and willing to accept high casualties.

The practice of the wars waged by the West after the end of the war in Vietnam suggested something rather different. Both the public and politicians were re-educated to expect wars that were short, victorious and comparatively bloodless. Between 1982 and 1999 Britain was involved in three significant wars in three different continents: the Falklands, the Gulf, and

Kosovo. All were fought far from home, with the result that their conduct carried no direct threat to the continuing tempo of daily life within the UK. In none of them did the burden of casualties have a significant impact on public perceptions. In part this was because the wars' conduct was in the hands of small, professional forces which were already semi-detached from civilian society. But the overwhelming reason was that the casualties were light, and became successively lighter. Deaths in the Falklands totalled 239. In the Gulf, the commander of 7th Armoured Brigade, Patrick Cordingley, reflecting the expectations of high intensity warfare, told the press that he anticipated losses of up to 15 per cent per day of the forces engaged. Some US estimates expected 8 per cent per day.[22] In the event total deaths across all three British services were 24, and those that impinged on the public consciousness were the result of 'friendly fire'. *Time* magazine concluded that the members of the US forces in the Gulf, given the fact that they were young men and women ready to take risks, were probably less likely to die in the Middle East than they would have been at home on the roads or in the bars of America.[23] Two members of the British forces were killed in Kosovo. The press's argument that the foreign policies of the western powers in general, and of the USA in particular, were restrained in the use of armed force by the so-called 'body-bag factor' bore little relation to the actual practice of conflict. Over the last quarter of the twentieth century the western powers devised means of waging war with comparative impunity. Technically they retained the means to fight 'total' war but culturally they no longer felt threatened by it.

As the twentieth century ended, therefore, total war no longer seemed to be a concept as appropriate to Europe's and America's present predicaments as it had at its mid-point. Instead it was a passing phase, a phrase descriptive of a specific period in the past. Moreover, its duration contracted. For Walters' and Aron's generation the evolution of total war could be extended back to the French Revolution and the advent of industrialization. For van Creveld's and Keegan's it was specific to the era of the two world wars. Colin Gray, in *Modern Strategy*, published in 1999, located it between the dates 1916 and 1945. In doing so, he classified the second half of the First World War as total war, principally because of the scale of economic mobilization.[24]

In fact, total war was a concept rarely invoked in the First World War. After all, the static nature of the fighting, although the embodiment of many of its connotations of awfulness, protected the civilian population from direct physical attack.[25] Clemenceau's 1917 government talked about *la guerre intégrale* to indicate its intention of abandoning all restraint in mobilizing French society for war.[26] In 1918 Léon Daudet published a summons to national mobilization called *La Guerre Totale*, in which he defined total war as the extension of the struggle into the realms of politics, the economy, commerce, industry, intellectual life, the law and finance.[27] Daudet was the editor of the right-wing journal, *L'action Française*, and his book was directed as much at the internal opponents of mobilization – Joseph Caillaux, Almereyda and *Le bonnet rouge* – as at Germany.

Daudet's assumption was that Germany had prepared for 'total war' from the war's outset. But this was not how Germany itself saw the war. After 1918 Germany concluded that it had been defeated not in the field but by the impacts of blockade at sea and revolution at home. Its failure was less a military one, at least in traditional terms, and more one of economic and social mobilization. It had lost the war because, despite the Auxiliary Service Law of 1916, its manpower had not been fully incorporated or rationally allocated; because its industry had not been fully converted to war production; and because its population had not entirely subordinated their aspirations to the needs of the nation. It was therefore more the lessons derived from the First World War, rather than the war itself, which gave rise to the concept of total war. Erich Ludendorff's *Der Totale Krieg*, published in 1935, was both its fullest and most perverse expression of this; it was also the book that for the first time gave the phrase 'total war' common currency.[28]

Der Totale Krieg says virtually nothing about the nuts and bolts of fighting, about the conduct of operations, or about the impact of new weaponry. The scholar seeking the latest thinking on mechanized warfare or strategic bombing in 1935 must look elsewhere. The crux of *Der Totale Krieg* is civil-military relations. As first quartermaster general between 1916 and 1918, Ludendorff had been at the centre of a four-way struggle for power – between the Kaiser, the chancellor, the Reichstag and the German supreme command. By 1935 he had formed the conclusion that Germany had lost the First World War because it had failed to establish a military dictatorship. For Ludendorff, as for Daudet, the enemy had been within as well as without. 'The man who is Commander-in-Chief', he wrote at the beginning of his final chapter, 'must hold first place. Anything else is unsound and dangerous. Only with complete power can the Commander-in-Chief maintain unity and force in his actions, which are designed to defeat the enemy and preserve the nation. In all fields of activity the Commander-in-Chief must decide, and his will must be obeyed'.[29]

The German connotations of Ludendorff's choice of title, *Der Total Krieg*, did not serve to clarify his message. Ludwig Beck, the chief of the general staff when the book was first published, welcomed it because he saw it as a call for national mobilization. But by 1938 he had realized that its central point was that the military commander should dominate the state; the Clausewitzian in Beck therefore rejected it.[30] The English edition, which was called *The Nation in Arms*, was more revealing. It translated '*Der Total Krieg*' not as 'total war' but as 'totalitarian war'. In other words, it made clear that the book was less about the means of war, and more about the structure of the state designed to conduct war.

'Totalitarian war', not 'total war', was also the phrase used by J. F. C. Fuller in his commentary on the Italian campaign in Abyssinia, *The First of the League Wars*, published in 1936. What Fuller meant by totalitarian war was much the same as what Ludendorff meant: 'Totalitarianism in war means that when war begins all private life comes to an end, and the nation has only one concern – war'.[31] Fuller cited Ludendorff, as well as Hitler. But Fuller's model was of course Mussolini's Italy. The Italian soldiers in Abyssinia were described in terms which owed more to his own Mosleyite convictions than they did to any detached personal observation of the campaign. Their principal quality was 'a profound faith, not so much in the righteousness of their cause, as in the righteousness of Fascism'. 'Living like anchorites', he went on, 'they fought like Crusaders'. Such hyperbole was never far from absurdity: 'a few handfuls of macaroni a day were all that was necessary to maintain the physical life of these spiritually excellent men'.[32]

The main thrust of the book was, however, deeply serious, as well as remarkably accurate. Fuller saw Abyssinia as the first clash between Fascism and the League of Nations, between nationalism and internationalism, between totalitarianism and democracy. The second such confrontation would result in a totalitarian war, which would be fought for values that were not material and therefore finite, but spiritual and therefore infinite: 'It will be an absolute war in which the political lives of the nations will be staked in a death struggle between two contending ideas'.[33]

But Fuller was interested in Mussolini's Abyssinian campaign not only because of his own political beliefs but also because of his tactical ideas. Much of *The First of the League Wars*, unlike Ludendorff's *Der Totale Krieg*, was concerned with the mechanization of war, and even more with the impact of bombing from the air. These he classified as 'totalitarian tactics'. The nomenclature reflected a confusion in Fuller's own mind: he saw mechanization as an alternative to the mass army, and a means to shorten war and even limit it.[34] But it was a confusion that helped propagate ambiguity in the English language. In the shift from totalitarian war to total war, the phrase lost the specific application which Ludendorff, and Fuller himself, had given it. In the Second World War the democracies responded with more vigour and greater unity than their Fascist critics had allowed for. By 1945 'total war' had become a generalization used to describe the destructiveness of war more than a description of the sort of war conducted by a Hitlerian or Stalinist dictatorship. Two of the standard histories of the Second World War, at least until the appearance of Gerhard Weinberg's *A World at Arms* in 1994, used 'total war' in their titles. Neither Gordon Wright's *The Ordeal of Total War*, published in 1968, nor Peter Calvocoressi's and Guy Wint's *Total War* published in 1972, felt any need to define what they meant by total war. What their titles obscured was a conflation of two concepts.

In 1943 Winston Churchill told a joint session of the Congress of the United States, 'Modern war is total'.[35] At the time this seemed to be no more than a statement of the obvious. The same assumption underpinned John Bennett Walters' article in 1948. But none of Keegan, van Creveld, Mandelbaum or Mueller would agree. As they approached the year 2000, they were apparently confident that modern war did not need to be total.

Total war as Ludendorff defined it is an observation about the power of the state, about its right to conscript its citizens not only for directly military purposes but also for those of economic and social mobilization. Its roots lie in the rhetoric of the French Revolution, and the Committee of Public

Safety's presumption, acting in the name of the general will, of the power of the state over the individual. Its driving force lies in the realm of ideas and ideology.

Modern war, by contrast, is a statement about the means of fighting. The wars of the French Revolution were fought with technologies that had been familiar, at least in their broad outlines, for over a century: they were not modern wars. The two world wars were fought with the fruits of industrialization and technological innovation: they were modern wars.

In conflating modern war with total war, strategic thought of the mid-twentieth century not only got itself into a muddle, but it also left its successors with a conceptual legacy which they have been slow to disentangle. A total war need not be modern, and a modern war need not be total. Economic mobilization demonstrates that distinction. The economically more backward belligerent has to make a greater effort to mobilize its society in order to engage a more advanced and more industrialized opponent on equal terms. In other words total war is an option more likely to be exercised by the less modern state. By the same token, the more advanced state will engage in a war that is certainly modern but possibly not total.

The American Civil War makes this point exactly. The Union spent 74.4 per cent of its 1859 output over the four years of the war while the Confederacy spent more than the entire value of its 1859 output.[36] The Confederacy had gone to war to defend the rights of the individual states against a centralizing government, but in the event the requirements of economic mobilization meant that it was the administration that had to centralize more.

In the Second World War Japan fought the USA with a zeal and fanaticism which we continue to find, frankly, frightening. But the technologies with which the Japanese army was equipped were obsolescent. Its tanks were few, small, under-gunned and thinly armoured; it lacked anti-tank guns; its infantry rifle was a 1905 model and its heavy machine gun a 1914 Hotchkiss.[37] The USA engaged the Japanese almost single-handedly in the Pacific, and yet it devoted only 15 per cent of its total war effort to Japan's defeat.[38] After the battles of the Coral Sea and of Midway in 1942, America could make its greater commitment to the war in Europe. The Second World War was total for Japan because Japan was insufficiently modernized; the USA could fight a limited war in the Pacific precisely because it was modernized.

Moreover, the distinction goes further. The burdens of engaging in total war could have demodernizing effects, but they did not prevent the war from continuing to be total. Having lost the sea battles of 1942, Japan was deprived of raw materials, and, having come under direct bombing attack in the last year of the war, its industrial production slumped. Tank output, which peaked at 1191 in 1942, fell to 790 in 1943, 401 in 1944 and 142 in 1945. Even in those weapons in which Japan increased output, its achievement lagged behind the USA. It produced 49 major vessels in 1941 to America's 544; in 1943, when it needed to make good the losses of the Coral Sea and Midway its output was 122 to the USA's 2654. The Japanese built three new aircraft carriers in 1943 and four in 1944; the Americans produced 90 over the same period.[39] The phenomenon of the *kamikaze* pilots encapsulates the trend exactly. Short of fuel for training, and short of materials for sophisticated and durable aircraft types, the Japanese opted for a tactic that mitigated the defects of technological backwardness but optimized the moral commitment of their young men.

The idea of demodernization has been applied with comparable conviction to the German army on the eastern front. Even in June 1941 the German army was not a mechanized force. Ninety per cent of the divisions earmarked for the invasion of the Soviet Union were dependent on horse-drawn transport; that proportion remained constant for the rest of the war. And the number of tanks in the mechanized elements, the Panzer divisions, declined as the war went on. In 1939 the established strength was 299 tanks per division; with the doubling in number of the Panzer divisions in 1941 the average tank strength tumbled to 141, and at Kursk in July 1943 it stood at 73; in March 1945 it was 54. Production could not keep pace with the loss of equipment. By 31 August 1943 the Luftwaffe's front-line units were operating at 71 per cent of their establishment for fighters and 56 per cent for bombers.[40] The *Wehrmacht* therefore became less well-equipped, less modern, as the war progressed. But if we have any grasp on the reality of total war, as opposed to the concept, it is located here on the eastern front, at Stalingrad, Kursk, and ultimately, Berlin. Conventions about non-combatant immunity, about the handling of prisoners of war, or about proportionality became the victims of what Omer Bartov has called the 'barbarization' of the eastern front. The conduct of war and the implementation of genocide overlapped. Moreover, what underpinned the intensity and ferocity of the struggle were less the dynamics of small-group loyalties intrinsic to western armies' self-definitions and more the ideologies of two competing systems. Total war in so far as it was experienced in the twentieth century was more about the willingness of the individual to subordinate himself to the demands of the state than it was about the destructive effects of modern weaponry.[41]

Establishing the distinction between total war and modern war is particularly important in relation to the wars of European imperialism. When Charles Callwell wrote the first English-language manual on the subject in 1896, he called it *Small Wars*. Until recently, the presumption implicit in his title has tended to stick. But current scholarship has begun to revise that view, detecting in colonial warfare the origins of total war. The effect is both culturally and linguistically significant. The liberal powers of the West have escaped the opprobrium of bellicosity despite the frequency with which they have gone to war because the majority of their wars were 'small wars'. But if these campaigns are now brought within the pale of total war the hands of the USA and Britain, to name only the most obvious, look less clean. The trouble with the argument is that, self-evidently, the wars of imperialism were not total for the colonial powers. Only by unravelling the concepts of totality and modernity can a satisfactory synthesis emerge. Eurocentricism, the product of a focus on Germany and its incipient militarism, is what conflates total war and modern war; globalism, if that is the rendition of the

'Atlantic thesis' appropriate to the twentieth century, makes their separation mandatory.

In the decade after the American Civil War, Sheridan and Sherman continued to apply the principles of war they had formulated in the struggle against the Confederacy to the suppression of the Indian. The distinction between combatant and non-combatant was hard to sustain in wars where the former relied on the latter to be sustained in the field, and where the warrior did not necessarily deem it prudent strategy to accept battle on the terms familiar to conventional armies. The US cavalry targeted the food supplies and villages of the Indian population. In 1901, when confronted with similar difficulties in the Philippines, Brigadier-General Jacob H. Smith reacted in terms as extreme as those of Sherman. 'I want no prisoners', he said. 'I wish you to kill and burn. I want all persons killed who are capable of bearing arms in actual hostilities against the United States'.[42]

At exactly the same time, Britain was being criticized, both at home and abroad, for the adoption of a strategy which required the forceable resettlement of the Boer population as well as its incarceration in concentration camps. Kitchener, the British commander-in-chief in South Africa, had earned a reputation for brutality at the other end of the continent, in the Sudan. In fact, by the standards prevailing in Africa, the Boer War was conducted with remarkable restraint. In wars against native populations, the burning of villages and the destruction of crops were customary, and the taking of prisoners not.[43] During the Zulu War of 1879 Lord Chelmsford told the government that 'I am satisfied that the more the Zulu nation at large feels the strain brought upon them by the war, the more anxious will they be to see it brought to an end'. As one of his subordinates pithily put it: 'War is war and savage war is the worst of the lot'.[44] The Boers were at least treated as Europeans; since the Indian Mutiny the British army had been persuaded that restraint in regard to other ethnic groups could only be interpreted as weakness.

Colonial war was total war only in the sense suggested by Sherman. It regularly and indubitably breached the principles of non-combatant immunity. Therefore, its effects could be truly devastating for the native population. But its purposes were the advancement of European civilization not the implementation of genocide. Jacob Smith was court-martialled; Kitchener was castigated by the British radical press. Public dissent and disapprobation themselves serve to make the obvious point. Colonial war was not total war for the populations of the USA or of Britain. To all intents and purposes, the patterns of civilian life on the American eastern seaboard or within the UK remained uninterrupted. The armies which were implementing national policies were small and professional. Moreover, the very fact that colonial war did not require national mobilization, that colonial war was not total war for the colonial power, required that the colonial army should have the trappings of modernism. Deprived of any superiority in manpower, the soldiers of the USA and Britain compensated with the material advantages. Science, technology and industrialization underpinned the patterns of conquest through prophylactic medicine, the breech-loading rifle, the machine gun and the steam engine.

By contrast, colonial wars did tend to totality for the native population. Lacking the resources of modernism, the tribes of the North American plains or of Africa fell back on the infrastructure of their own societies and on the maximization of geography. The wars they fought were total. They eroded any civil-military distinctions, they undermined the principle of non-combatant immunity, their conduct was frequently barbaric, and their ends – from the resistance of invasion to the achievement of political independence – absolute. Exactly the same points could be made about guerrilla and insurgency operations in the second half of the twentieth century. And, like the wars against colonialism, these later conflicts were often characterized by the use of weaponry, at least on the part of the insurgents, that was crude and primitive.

One consequence, therefore, of modern war is that it enables the more advanced state to choose to fight not total, but limited, war. After the end of the cold war, the USA's advocacy of the so-called 'revolution in military affairs' made this an explicit strategy. The 'revolution in military affairs' enjoyed many definitions, but their common thread was the exploitation of information technology for military purposes. At one extreme this involved making existing conventional forces even more effective through the use of 'smart' weaponry: the Gulf War writ large. Current structures and platforms would remain in place but their kill probabilities, particularly in the application of airpower, would be near-perfect. At the other extreme 'cyber war' would overtake warfare currently defined. Opposing powers would 'hack' into each other's networks, causing not only the operational fragmentation of their enemy's armed forces but also the collapse of the civilian infrastructure, of public utilities, of hospitals and of government: a form of total war.[45] However interpreted, the 'revolution in military affairs' was a programme set by the USA and resting on the presumption of continuing American global supremacy. Lawrence Freedman defined it as a means by which a lone superpower could use professional forces 'in a form of combat, with a high political pay-off, yet a low human cost'.[46] In other words the USA would engage in what would be a modern war for itself but a total war for its enemy.

The obvious question that arises from the disaggregation of modern war and total war – at least for the historian – is how the two concepts became conflated in the first place. There are a couple of explanations. The first revolves around the principle of national self-defence, and the second around the deliberate use of terror as an instrument of war.

The ability to demand the full mobilization of a nation's resources, economic and social as well as political and psychological, was dependent on the belief that the war in hand was defensive rather than aggressive. Neither dynasticism nor territorial aggrandizement could underpin a total war in a democratic society – and, in a circular process, a society needed to possess at least some of the trappings of democracy, in the shape of mass education, literacy and political awareness, for it to have the capacity to wage total war in the first place.

All the belligerents in 1914 were persuaded that they were under attack. Germany, the linchpin of so much of the argumentation over total war, was persuaded it was threatened by Russia, and the latter's prompt invasion of East Prussia gave substance to the fear. Even German socialists, many of them committed to pacifism, could rally to the Kaiser when confronted by the apparent alternative, a police state under tsarist rule. Germany became the bulwark of European civilization against the Slavic hordes. The Russians were caricatured as sub-humans, a status made clear when the beliefs of 1914 were reworked and revived in the Second World War.[47] The evils of the Nazi regime should not blind us to the fervour with which Germans cleaved to an anti-Bolshevik crusade. The loyalty of the German soldier to Hitler, and the doggedness of his resistance in the last year of the war, when by any rational measurement the conflict was over, rested in large part on his determination to defend home and hearth against the depredations of the barbarians from the East.

Perceptions of 'the other', a demonization of the 'enemy', generated a fear so great that an unreserved commitment to the regimes of total war was its consequence. But terror *per se* has more frequently been the product of new technology's impact on warfare itself. Even the advocate of the tank, J. F. C. Fuller, argued that it would achieve its greatest effects through its blows to the morale of the enemy.[48] The deliberate use of terror as an instrument of war has, however, largely rested on the interaction of new technologies with targets that have been civilian not military. The bomber and the nuclear missile have justified their threat to the home front on the grounds that domestic productive effort is crucial to the maintenance of armies in the field. Terror, therefore, purposely threatens to breach a cardinal principle of 'just war' thinking, that of non-combatant immunity, and, as Sherman and Sheridan made clear, this for many is a key component of total war.

But there is no inevitable link between terror and total war. The threat to kill civilians is not the same as actually doing so, and the threat may be sufficient. Indeed terror has been used as a means of limiting war, of shortening it, and even of preventing it.

Sherman's rhetoric about total war was largely just that. What he said was not what he did. Our own knowledge of what was to follow has led us to endow the generals of the American Civil War with a greater grasp of modern concepts than they actually possessed. Most of the damage Sherman did was to property, and lay within the parameters of traditional scorched-earth strategy. His actual infringements of the principle of non-combatant immunity seem to have been both few and justified. His purpose in threatening the people of Atlanta with what Hood called 'studied and injurious cruelty' was, Sherman retorted, to convince them that 'the only way [they] can hope once more to live in peace and quiet at home, is to stop the war'.[49] Sherman's goal was the war's termination, not its intensification.

This is not to say that rhetoric could not become reality. Between 1904 and

1909 Jackie Fisher, the First Sea Lord in the British Admiralty, embraced an approach to the blockade of Germany that rested on the breach of non-combatant immunity. 'The mills of our sea power', the director of naval intelligence reported in 1908, '(though they would grind the German industrial population slowly perhaps) would grind them "exceedingly small" – grass would sooner or later grow in the streets of Hamburg and wide-spread dearth and ruin would be inflicted'.[50] But the declared purpose of this policy was deterrence. 'My sole object', Fisher protested in 1905, 'is PEACE in doing all this! Because if you "rub it in" both at home and abroad that you are ready for instant war with every unit of your strength in the first line, and intend to be "first in" and hit your enemy in the belly and kick him when he's down and boil your prisoners in oil (*if you take any!*) and torture his women and children, then people will keep clear of you'.[51]

Blockade, at least as defined in the unratified declaration of London, did try to distinguish between what was contraband, in other words material directly related to the war effort, and what was not. But it was not a distinction that Britain observed in the First World War. If the blockade had a significant impact, it was less on the production of munitions and more on the supply of food, and those who came last in the queue for rations were those of least military value – the very old, the very young, the chronically infirm and the insane.[52] In other words Britain breached the principle of non-combatant immunity, and what Fisher had said for rhetorical effect for the purposes of deterrence became a fully-fledged objective in the actual waging of war. The beauty of blockade for London was that its implementation rested on seapower, and thus its implications, while total for the enemy, were limited for Britain. In the inter-war period both Germany and Britain colluded in persuading themselves that blockade had been decisive in the outcome of the First World War. The result was that, by making blockade central to its strategic planning for the next war in Europe, Britain could embrace a policy of limited liability.[53]

In practice, of course, the civilian populations of the belligerent powers in the Second World War were hit less by seapower and blockade, and more by airpower and strategic bombing.

The early theorists of air power had never intended that bombing civilians should be only a threat, a means of preventing war rather than fighting it. The most famous of all, Giulio Douhet, was an Italian Fascist, but what he said differed little from the arguments of a British liberal, Basil Liddell Hart. Marked forever by his experiences in the trenches of the western front, Liddell Hart wrestled with the need to contain war for the rest of his life. His answer in *Paris or the Future of War* (1925) was that of vertical envelopment by bombing the sources of production. Through destroying civilian morale, aeroplanes could end wars in short order. Thus, although the terror of air attack was designed to intensify war, it was also intended to limit it.

Nuclear weapons were the logical, if even more ambivalent, consequence of this sort of thought. At least during the period of the USA's nuclear monopoly (not just in relation to the bomb itself, but also in regard to delivery systems), the actual use of nuclear weapons could be construed as a means of limiting war. A nuclear war would be short, and it would be total only for the USA's enemies. Nor would it be manpower-intensive; with the security of nuclear weapons, NATO could ignore the force goals of its 1952 Lisbon conference (96 divisions) and Britain could abandon conscription in 1957.

By the early 1960s the balance of forces expressed in the strategic absurdity of mutually assured destruction made any arguments that nuclear war could be limited for at least one of the belligerents unsustainable. But through deterrence theory nuclear weapons were still compatible with the general objective of controlling conflict. Although a means of fighting total war, their declared purpose was to prevent it from occurring. Deterrence acquired a complicated and esoteric vocabulary that implied that it was a more subtle instrument than in fact it was; its central proposition was the killing of civilians and the destruction of property on a scale totally disproportionate to any possible political ends. Terror was no longer deployed as a means of waging war but of preventing it.

Deterrence's credibility rested, however, not on its central tenet, which made nuclear weapons unuseable, but on its refinements, which granted nuclear weapons war-fighting roles. Thus a mechanism that was primarily political, and whose focus was on ends, expressed itself in terms that were predominantly military. Through deterrence the means of modern war became conflated with the threat of total war. American political scientists defined the steps in escalation to nuclear war not in terms of their political or even operational objectives, but in terms of the capabilities and effects of the weapons employed. Potential conflicts were classified as conventional wars, tactical nuclear wars, theatre nuclear wars and strategic nuclear wars. These divisions reflected the ranges and kilotonnages of the weapons systems. They also referred to whether the nuclear weapon had been fired in the course of a conventional battle along the inner German border (a tactical use in a theatre context) or whether it had been released from a submarine deployed in the middle of the ocean (which made it strategic even if it had a narrowly military and even tactical purpose).

American deterrence theory therefore confirmed an interpretation of twentieth-century war which could be extended backwards to the era of the two world wars, elements of which have persisted beyond the end of the cold war and the apparent irrelevance of nuclear weaponry. It is essentially anti-Clausewitzian. It saw war as a phenomenon shaped by the means employed to carry it through, not by the ends for which it was fought. Indeed war lacked political utility, because its awful and self-sustaining dynamic would ensure that any rational objectives would be usurped in the course of its conduct.

The First World War underpinned this set of beliefs. The idea that the war was futile, a waste, and an end to European civilization, was near-contemporary in its origins. But the rejection of Clausewitz has given it added force. For John Keegan, the First World War demonstrated the irrelevance of Clausewitz because the war was not subordinated to political direction and failed to offer realizable and worthwhile goals. Instead its means became an end in themselves. In 1998 Niall Ferguson endorsed this sort of thinking in *The Pity of War*.[54]

The efforts to limit war in the inter-war period duly concentrated on the means and methods of fighting, not on the reasons for resorting to war in the first place. The Kellogg-Briand pact failed because although it outlawed war, it did not address its causes. In Geneva, the League of Nations debated the abolition of conscription, the limits on submarines and the control of bombers. What preoccupied the powers was the machinery of modern war, not the causes of its employment.

Because the Second World War was essentially Hitler's war, it possessed a clear and consistent political objective. Here indeed the end justified the means. Nonetheless, the Allies' war aims did not enjoy a high profile. The adoption of the policy of unconditional surrender reduced the salience of politics rather than enhanced it. Any closer and tighter definitions of the objectives for which the Allies were fighting could only disrupt their fragile coalition. Thus in practice the bigger debates both then and since – about when to open the second front, about the policy of strategic bombing, about the decision to employ the atomic bombs – were about means, not ends.

This tendency to define war in terms of the means employed, not in terms of the objectives to be attained, persisted after the end of the Second World War. Nuclear deterrence theory was only its most obvious manifestation. The classification of non-nuclear war into high-intensity and low-intensity operations proved almost as persistent. The 1998 British Strategic Defence Review, with its insistence that Britain should retain a capability for 'all arms warfare', gave no indication as to whom such operations were likely to be conducted against, or for what reasons. The same point can be made about the 'revolution in military affairs'. The fact that its putative enemy remained undefined might be one reason why the response it generated among the USA's allies proved so dilatory.[55] Neither high-intensity warfare nor the 'revolution in military affairs' seemed of much relevance to powers that were committed to conflicts whose objects were limited and whose objectives were defined as those of peace enforcement or of counter-insurgency.

During the cold war this determination to categorize wars according to methods and capabilities was not reproduced on the other side of the Iron Curtain. The principal contributors to Soviet thought on nuclear weapons were soldiers, and their objective was to reintegrate the Strategic Rocket Forces with conventional military formations. Much of the published debate therefore treated nuclear weapons solely as a means of fighting rather than as an end of – or to – war. This is not to say that Soviet strategic thought remained totally unaffected by western concepts of deterrence: under Khrushchev this was clearly not the case. But the typology of war remained shaped by Marxist-Leninism, and focused on a war's political characteristics not on the weapons systems used to carry through its objectives. Whether a war was total or not depended, in the first instance, less on any decision regarding the use of nuclear weapons and more on the socio-political characteristics of the belligerents. A clash between the Soviet Union and the USA might well have involved an exchange of nuclear weapons, but its totality would already have been determined by the fact of war between irreconcilable political structures. The strategic thought of the Soviet Union made explicit what that of the USA submerged – that wars have the potential to become total first because of the ends at stake and only second because of the means employed.[56]

The ideological underpinnings of total war were therefore in place before the advent of modern war. We would not now see the Peninsular war as a total war, or at least not for France or Britain, both of whom were simultaneously engaged on other fronts. It has also been the contention of this chapter that the Napoleonic wars were not modern because they were essentially pre-industrial: the Iberian peninsula certainly was. But Goya's series of etchings, 'The Disasters of War', with their depictions of the mass execution of civilians, grieving children and fighting mothers, affirm the capacity of guerrilla war to acquire aspects of totality, at least for the guerrillas and their compatriots. The founding father of military doctrine, A. H. Jomini, served in Spain and embodied his observations in his classification 'national wars' in his textbook, the *Précis de l'art de la guerre*. National wars, he explained, 'are waged against a united people, or a great majority of them, filled with a noble ardor and determined to sustain their independence'. And he went on to warn his readers that, 'The consequences are so terrible that, for the sake of humanity, we ought to hope never to see it'.[57]

For Jomini the ideological underpinnings of total war were in place before the means were available to put it into full effect. The First World War, characterized as a machine war, a war of material, a war in which the courage of the individual was subordinated to the tyranny of the artillery timetable, was in many respects a modern war. But the internal combustion engine did not yet have a major operational effect, and strategic bombing was more an idea than a practice. Thus the war's static nature, at least in western Europe, confined its geographical spread; the fighting barely touched Germany or Britain, and even in France restricted itself to the north-east.

The connotations of waste and futility derived in large part from the experience of trench warfare were the consequences of its modernity. But they also served to dent the notion of its totality, because they imply that the objectives of the war were not proportionate to the means. The debate over war aims, sparked by Fritz Fischer for Germany, serves to confirm this image. However extensive their scope, German ambitions in Poland or Belgium hark back to the tradition of cabinet wars, of territorial ambitions, rather than point towards a clash of ideas. The elements of popular engagement, national independence, liberty – even equality and fraternity – which Jomini associated with the war in Spain 100 years previously do not seem significant in current debates on the First World War.

But, if the First World War has a claim to be total, it is because it was a clash of ideas. If it had been a war only about Germany's claims to suzerainty over

Belgium, or about France's desire to recover Alsace-Lorraine, however non-negotiable those two particular objectives might have been, the scope for an early peace settlement might have been greater. These territorial war aims, for all the efforts of Fischer and others to trace their pre-war origins, do not explain why the war broke out. They were developed after the war was an accomplished fact. The issues in 1914 were far more extensive: the war was, in the words of Alfred Zimmern, an Oxford classics don, 'a conflict between two different and irreconcilable conceptions of government, society and progress'.[58]

Allied propaganda portrayed the war as a struggle between liberalism and militarism. This was not just propaganda in the narrowly defined sense of a government-inspired manipulation of public sentiment; it was what people believed. After Germany's breach of Belgian neutrality, Zimmern and those like him were entirely clear that Britain was fighting for the rule of international law. France saw the struggle not just as one of national self-defence (grand enough objective in itself) but as something that went beyond the bounds of statehood to 'civilization' – a concept which embraced the universalist legacy of the French Revolution.

These ideas, perhaps in part because in the end the *Entente* did win the war, have continued to carry an emotional charge. But by the end of the twentieth century Germany's comparable commitment to militarism has become much harder to comprehend. Even in 1914 British intellectuals saw a distinction between the values embraced by German universities, in the creative arts and in the applied sciences, and those typical of the monarchy, the army and the *Junkers*. But this was not a wedge that either side within Germany would admit. *Kultur* stood four-square with militarism. On 16 October 1914 a manifesto, addressed 'to the world of culture', was published, which bore the signature of almost every professor at every German university. It included those of Max Weber and Albert Einstein, both sceptical about the war itself, but both ready to affirm that the future of European culture was dependent on the victory of German militarism. Germany was fighting against capitalism, against the pursuit of economic self-interest, and against liberalism in the sense of individual freedom. What Germany stood for not only elevated the things of the spirit over the veneration of mammon but also embodied the notion of community. Militarism, defined in this context as the institutionalization of compulsory military service, linked army and society.[59]

The First World War was thus explained by big ideas, *civilization* and *Kultur*, terms that were essentially open-ended. Germany's problem was that it had embarked on a battle for existence with resources that were in aggregate inferior to those of the *Entente*. Its hopes of victory therefore rested on a conviction, born as much from desperation as from reality, that quality could triumph over quantity. The inner strength of Germany's soldiers became the bulwark of its commanders' hopes of victory. Thus materialism was not so much an asset, with the potential to underpin modernity in the conduct of war, and more a danger.[60] Its softening effects could undermine the warrior ethos. Germany embarked on a war that was total in terms of ideology with attitudes that were essentially pre-modern.

Much of Germany's story between 1914 and 1933, or even 1941, is the story of the effort to bring the so-called 'ideas of 1914' into harmony with the economic and material ability to put them into effect.[61] The process began immediately in August 1914 with Walther Rathenau's establishment of the War Raw Materials Office (*Kriegsrohsoffsamt*). Its rationale, whether provided by Rathenau himself or by his AEG (Allgemeine Elektrizitäts-Gesellschaft – General Electric Company) colleague, Wichard von Moellendorff, constituted a form of state-led centralized economy. Through the allocation and distribution of raw materials, Rathenau and Moellendorff promoted a third way, a combination of the best of capitalism and socialism, designed to minimize duplication of effort and maximize output.[62] They aspired to establish through wartime practice the principles of peacetime regulation. But for Fascism the summons to national mobilization found it hard to sustain the distinction. Rathenau, a Jew and a capitalist, provided a vocabulary which was employed not only by Ludendorff in *Der Totale Krieg*, but also by Hitler and the Nazis.

The notion that the Second World War, as opposed to the First, was a struggle between competing ideologies – of liberalism against Fascism, of Fascism against Communism, and implicitly of Communism against liberalism – is one with which historians have been much more comfortable. Furthermore, all three sets of ideas were used as justifications for each state's full mobilization of its national resources for the purposes of war. The Second World War was therefore the nearest the world has come to total war because the ideas of total war and the means of modern war were simultaneously deployed. But when the war was 'demodernized', on the eastern front or in the Pacific, it did not cease to be total in an ideological sense.

Goebbels's so-called 'total war' speech, delivered in the *Sportpalast* in Berlin on 30 January 1943, at the height of the Stalingrad battle, exactly illustrates the point. In the year in which Churchill equated total war with modern war, Goebbels made no reference to modern war *per se* and mentioned tanks and 'new weapons' only in passing. In its complete neglect of the mechanics of economic mobilization his speech represented a step back from the precepts of 1914, but its thrust reinvoked their inspiration. Goebbels deemed the war to be one of national self-defence, but all that he offered the soldier on the eastern front was fanaticism, determination and idealism. Germany would win because its cause was better and its self-belief more profound. Spiritual quality, in other words, would triumph over material quality. The struggle was itself a test of Germany's faith in ultimate victory. Its opponents were plutocracy to the west and Bolshevism to the east, and the source of its resolve would be a renewal of its inner victory over both in 1933. '*Your revolutionary elan*', he declared, 'which is not *dead, which lives*, will determine the tempo of this process of conversion'.[63]

The cold war sustained this ideological tension, by pitting democracy against Communism. But in this case the capacity to wage modern war – in other words, the nuclear arsenals possessed by the two global power blocs – had the effect of preventing total war, not promoting it. Although few recognized it at the time, the concepts of total war and modern war had already begun their disaggregation.

International law tends to be met with cynicism from both practitioners and students of war, but it has in its evolution shown itself remarkably sensitive to the distinction between total war and modern war. In the nineteenth century one of the definitions of nationhood was precisely the right to go to war; the international community – in so far as it existed – did not impugn a state's motives for doing so. Instead, international law focused on regulating the means with which a war was conducted once it had begun. Both the American Civil War and the Franco-Prussian War are indicative of efforts, even if retrospective, to regulate the treatment of prisoners of war, to preserve non-combatant immunity, and to define contraband in order to enforce maritime blockade. In other words, the law dealt with the consequences of modernity in wars between industrialized powers.

It did not deal with the problem of total war because the great powers did not consider themselves to have confronted a total war between 1815 and 1914. In the twentieth century, and particularly after 1945, the focus of international law shifted from the management of modern war to curtailing the threat of total war. The law condoned practices within war that nineteenth-century jurists would have seen as expanding its scope not containing it. The principles of non-combatant immunity and of proportionality – that the means should not outweigh the ends – worked against the deployment of nuclear weapons, but no international treaty specifically outlawed their use. Moreover, the recognition of the rights of the guerrilla in the 1977 Geneva protocol 1 dented the demarcation between uniformed armed forces and the civilian population. Protocol 1 enhanced the powers of the insurgent *vis à vis* the state. He was justified in his resort to war by virtue of his struggle against colonial domination or racism or foreign occupation.[64]

The key issue in determining the rights of the belligerent was therefore no longer *ius in bello* (justice in conduct of war) but *ius ad bellum* (justice in deciding to go to war), the legality of the decision to go to war in the first place. The 1945 United Nations' charter had already made it illegal for the state to declare war except for the purposes of national self-defence. It implicitly recognized that the state's ability to command the popular support necessary for mobilization for total war resided in public perceptions of the justice of its cause. By appropriating to itself the custodianship of the big ideas of international politics, the United Nations curtailed the state's claim on total war as an instrument of policy. The coalition which ousted Iraq from Kuwait in 1991 did so with the authority of a United Nations' resolution. The fact that NATO had no such sanction when it bombed Serbia during the Kosovo crisis of 1999 became the basis for challenging the legitimacy of NATO's actions.[65] NATO's justification for its use of force against Serbia was humanitarian need. It therefore appropriated the vocabulary of the United Nations, even if it simultaneously undermined the UN's authority.

The deployment of concepts of internationalism in support of offensive action presented the law of war with major dilemmas. International law had chipped away at the authority of the nation state at both supranational and sub-national levels, but the nation state remained the law's principal building block. Kosovo was part of Serbia; this was the basis of Belgrade's claim to the International Court of Justice in the Hague. A paradox emerged: the state's authority to go to war had been curtailed but the state remained the engine of mobilization in the event of war.

The definition of total war offered in this chapter rests on assumptions that are traditional. It accepts Montesquieu's proposition that men fight wars not as individuals predisposed to violence but because they are social beings. Killing in war is as absolute in its consequences as is murder, but it is not the same thing. Man can be more moral than the community of which he is a part; not all Germans supported what was done in Germany's name on the eastern front or in Auschwitz. Man can also be less moral than the community; even in wartime some armies, although admittedly not all, punish murders and rapes committed by their troops against the enemy's civilian population.

In defining war in general, and total war in particular, as a state activity – a proposition which Clausewitz endorsed but which neither John Keegan nor Martin van Creveld do – we also accept an element of control. Fighting in primitive and tribal societies may in some cases have become ritualized, as John Keegan has argued. But it also had the potential for totality – the expulsion of entire peoples, the appropriation of their territory and the slaughter or enslavement of the survivors.[66] The nation state, by virtue of its powers of organization, carries the principle of control even into the conduct of total war. James Turner Johnson goes so far as to conclude 'that total war should be conceived as rational political activity'. Total war is not to be understood in terms of 'a sadistic bent to make the weak suffer' or of 'a mad frenzy that will overcome reason'. Instead it embodies 'the idea that there exist certain values, perceived as ultimate, in defense of which individuals and nations must be prepared to fight with no observance of restraints'.[67]

The idea of total war therefore tells us much more about the emergence and subsequent solidarity of the nation state than it tells us about modern war. The confusion about the meaning of total war in the 1990s was less a product of the end of the cold war, and the consequent reduction in the danger of an all-out nuclear exchange, and much more a consequence of the decline of the nation state.

To talk of a decline may seem paradoxical when the number of independent nation states in the world rose from 60 in 1938 to 144 in 1983, and to 191 in 1995.[68] But the nineteenth-century state defined itself not least in terms of its international position; it rested on a continuum of threatening its neighbours and being threatened; it had robust armed forces as part of its national identity; and international law did not curb its freedom to employ those forces. The most conspicuous additions to the ranks of the nation states in nineteenth-century Europe were Germany and Italy, both of which were created by unification rather than division, and so implicitly acknowledged the need for critical mass. Secession was squashed, not least in America. Even the multinational empires – Russia, Austria-Hungary and Turkey – hung together with a resilience that surprised their critics but validated their international standing.

The collapse of all three in the First World War inaugurated a pattern in which states were formed more by division than by unification. The military capabilities of the emergent nation states of the second half of the twentieth century have as a consequence been less than those of their predecessors. The principles of self-determination and self-defence may give them both the ideology and the legal right to wage total war, but they lack the resources to do so. Neither Iraq in 1991 nor Serbia in 1999 was able to strike back at the USA; nor in 1982 did Argentina take its war over the Falklands to mainland Britain. The defence policy proposed for an independent Scotland by the Scottish National Party (SNP) demonstrated the bifurcation between sovereignty in domestic affairs and independence in international security. The armed forces of a Scottish state might total at most 20,000 men. Such negligible numbers, even if equipped with Smart weapons, would probably not be sufficient to sustain national self-defence. They would only have value as part of an international organization, and yet the SNP rejected membership of the alliance organization to which its neighbours belong – NATO – on the grounds that it could not condone the possession of nuclear weapons.[69] The lack of a coherent policy for independence in international terms was not however seen as an impediment to Scotland's claim to statehood in a domestic context.

By the 1990s two consequences for the concept of total war emerged from this weakening of the nation state. First, modern states tended to go to war as part of an international alliance. This was true even for the one power that unequivocally retained the means to fight both a total and a modern war, the USA. The polities of the West espoused ideologies as extensive and far-reaching as those which underpinned the two world wars. The vocabulary of British security policy and of NATO in its intervention in Kosovo was as replete with absolutes – liberalism, democracy and humanitarianism – as were the summons to arms of the belligerents of 1914 or 1939. But, unlike the two world wars, the means were not willed to carry these grand objectives to fruition. The conflicts in which the USA and Britain were engaged were not wars of national self-defence; they were not fought in the national interest. Therefore, the conflicts fought on behalf of internationally accepted values, although the means were modern, were not total wars.

However, this did not mean that bitter battles for ideas were not being fought. The second consequence of the declining robustness of the nation state has been the proliferation of civil wars. Competing religions or competing conceptions of government within a single state have produced conflicts of unbridled viciousness, not least because it has been easier to legitimate a war fought for objectives that are unlimited – such as freedom of conscience or the rights of minority groups – than it has been to legitimate wars whose objectives have been defined in territorial terms. International law was configured to deal with the problems of over-mighty states and their ambitions; it has much less to say about the fissiparous tendencies of its community's weaker members.

The wars for the definition of the state, and for the state's religion, fought in the seventeenth century provided much of the impetus for the Enlightenment's effort to manage and institutionalize the conduct of war. The Fronde in France, the civil wars in Britain, and, above all, the Thirty Years' War in Germany cast a long shadow. Paul Lentsch, reflecting on the intensity of the First World War, could only liken it to the Thirty Years' War. The difference was that ideas were appropriated not by different classes or groups within a single community, as in the European civil wars, but by different nations within a single continent.[70] The civil wars of the late twentieth century, in the former Yugoslavia, in parts of Africa and in Indonesia, were often fought without the means of modern war: rifles, land mines and machetes have been sufficient. But the casualties have demonstrated the power of ideas to remove restraints on combat.[71]

Aspirant and weak states, therefore, have the capacity to promote total war. They can do so in at least three ways. First, in forging their own identity, they rely on combatants who are not uniformed members of the existing armed forces, and so serve to breach the principle of non-combatant immunity. The fact that over 90 per cent of the world's casualties in conflicts between 1995 and 1999 can be classified as civilians[72] may say as much about the use of non-uniformed combatants as about the deliberate killing of non-combatant innocents. Second, the newly formed state can face difficulties in subordinating its own armed forces, which may be predisposed to seek international conflict, not least to legitimate their own domestic political status. If we follow Clausewitz (and Ludendorff), such a war is unlikely to be subject to the restraints imposed by clear political aims. Third, an economically weak state, if it goes to war, has to radicalize its objectives in order to mobilize all its resources. In 1995 one in two of the world's states had a population of less than 7 million and a GNP (gross national product) of less than $10 billion, equivalent to the economy of Luxemburg.[73]

The comparative international security of the western powers at the end of the twentieth century therefore rested on the fact that the states predisposed to fight total war lacked the means to engage in modern war. But that did not mean that they had renounced military modernization. Nuclear weapons, whose comparative cheapness commended itself to the western powers in the 1950s, appealed on similar grounds to states like Pakistan and India in the 1990s. In the 1950s the owning of nuclear weapons was an indication of great power status, and those that did so were committed to the maintenance of the status quo. In the 1990s their acquisition was driven by a desire to change the balance of power, they were therefore a source of instability in international relations, and those that wanted them saw them as instruments of military utility, not of deterrence.[74]

The western powers, which already had the capacity to wage both total war and modern war, had not persuaded others not to seek the marriage of the two. The triumphalism of democracy with the end of the cold war was a challenge to alternative cultures, whether political or religious. It assumed a worldwide uniformity and an inherent resilience in liberalism which it did not possess. It cloaked a political credo with the baggage of westernization, but in so doing it weakened liberalism because westernization was contracting, not advancing. The decline of empires made that true in territorial terms, but it was also true in the key indices of cultural influence – the numbers who spoke English as a first language (rather than solely as a means of communication), and the numbers who professed Christianity. 'Western belief in the universality of Western culture', Samuel Huntington warned in 1996, 'suffers three problems: it is false; it is immoral; and it is dangerous'.[75]

Huntington's proposed solution was a community of civilizations: a global order based on the recognition of cultural difference and on the tendency of small states to group together for international purposes. In 1995 Philippe Delmas, a former member of the French foreign ministry, advocated an alternative – the reinvigoration of the state. This would include the recognition that a strong authoritarian state posed less danger to the international system than a weak democratic one.[76] In 1999 Russia reasserted its statehood in its war against the Chechens. In criticizing Moscow's actions, the West did little for the Chechens, but rather more – according to the interpretations of Huntington and Delmas – to weaken the principle of national sovereignty. Moreover, NATO's action in Kosovo confirmed how fundamentally different the West's view of the international community was: it both promoted intervention on humanitarian grounds, which itself ran the risk of being seen as the indirect advancement of western values, and simultaneously undermined the idea of statehood.

There is here both a contrast to, and a connection with, the American Civil War. In 1863 the Union produced, in Francis Lieber's drafting of General Order no. 100, the first significant effort to compile the laws of war since Emmerich de Vattel's *Le Droit des Gens* over 100 years previously. In other words, the two sides in the American Civil War agreed to conduct the war as though it were, to all intents and purposes, a conflict between two different states. Herein is a further reason for disputing the connection between the American Civil War and total war: the effect was to dampen the intensity of civil war, not stoke it. But the Union still claimed the monopoly of statehood: it denied the right to secede of peoples possessed of different cultures and values. In 1999 the USA was not only less concerned by the rights of statehood, but also less enamoured of the principles of *ius in bello*. It was prepared to bomb civilian infrastructures in the pursuit of NATO's aims in Kosovo: the war was limited for itself, but less so for its opponent.

The contrasts were therefore clear, if ironic. The connections, however, were equally telling. Both the Civil War (at least in retrospect) and the action in Kosovo justified themselves through reference to human rights. In this context, the specifically American links between Sherman's advocacy of 'total war' and the idea of total war in the late twentieth century looked more solid rather than less so. Americans have justified their wars through big ideas.

Totality is therefore implicit in the American approach to war. Nonetheless America did not fight a total war between 1945 and the century's end, and even the Second World War was 'less' total for the USA than for its other belligerents. This was the benefit of modernity: the USA's economic strengths enabled it to fight without the need for full mobilization. It was also the product of geography: the only major threat to its own territorial integrity which the USA confronted throughout its history came from Britain. Therefore, as the twentieth century ended, the power that most obviously possessed the capacity to wage modern war had effectively renounced total war as a policy option. But in foregoing that option, it inhibited the realism of its own foreign policy. It built for itself a system of international relations which depended on those powers possessed of the will to wage total war continuing to lack the capacity to wage modern war. The equation was insufficiently robust to be the grounds for so much optimism.

Notes

1 Michael Howard, *The Franco-Prussian War*, London, 1961, p. 380. What follows had its first airing in the National Museums of Scotland Evening Lecture Series 1999-2000, on 28 October 1999; I am most grateful to those who attended for their comments and questions.

2 Cited by Michael Fellman, 'At the nihilist edge: reflections on guerrilla warfare during the American Civil War', in Stig Förster and Jorg Nagler (eds), *On the Road to Total War: The American Civil War and the German Wars of Unification 1861-1871*, Cambridge, 1997, p. 534. I must acknowledge the stimulus given to what follows by the series of conferences on total war organized by Stig Förster, Roger Chickering, and others. The proceedings of the first two, held in Washington in 1992 and Augsburg in 1994, have now been published as *On the Road to Total War* and as *Anticipating Total War: the German and American Experiences 1871-1914*, Cambridge, 1999, edited by Manfred F. Boemeke, Roger Chickering and Stig Förster. Those on the First World War, *Great War, Total War: Combat and Mobilization on the Western Front, 1914-1918*, and on the inter-war period, *The Shadows of Total War*, in both of which I participated and which were held in Münchenwiler in 1996 and 1999, will form the basis of two further volumes; the fifth and final conference will cover the Second World War.

3 Geoffrey Parker, *The Military Revolution: Military Innovation and the Rise of the West, 1500-1800*, Cambridge, 1988; Jeremy Black, *War and the World: Military Power and the Fate of Continents 1450-2000*, New Haven, CT, 1998.

4 R. R. Palmer, *The Age of the Democratic Revolution*, 2 vols, Princeton, 1961-4: Peter Paret, 'Colonial experience and European military reform at the end of the eighteenth century', *Bulletin of the Institute for Historical Research*, XXXVII, 1964, pp. 47-59; this article appears in a revised form in Paret, *Understanding War*, Princeton, NJ, 1992.

5 See, for example, in addition to Förster and Nagler, *On the Road to Total War*, John Terraine, *The Smoke and the Fire: Myths and Anti-myths of War 1861-1945*, London, 1980; Edward Hagerman, *The American Civil War and Modern Warfare: Ideas, Organization, and Field Command*, Bloomington, IN, 1988.

6 David Trask, 'Military imagination in the United States 1815-1917', in M. F. Boemeke, R. Chickering and S. Förster, *Anticipating Total War*, esp. pp. 332-3.

7 Jay Luvaas, *The Military Legacy of the Civil War: The European Inheritance*, Chicago, 1959; Brian Holden Reid, 'British military intellectuals and and American Civil War: Maurice, Fuller, and Liddell Hart', in *Studies in British Military Thought: Debates with Fuller and Liddell Hart*, Lincoln, NE, 1998.

8 See, for example, Spencer R. Weart, *Never at War: Why Democracies Will Not Fight One Another*, New Haven, CT, 1998.

9 John Bennett Walters, 'General William T. Sherman and total war', *Journal of Southern History*, XIV, 1948, pp. 447-8.

10 Raymond Aron, *The Century of Total War*, London, 1954, p. 19.

11 ibid., p. 39.

12 Klaus-Jürgen Müller, *General Ludwig Beck. Studien und Dokumente zur Politisch-militärischen Vorstellungswelt und Tätigkeit des Generalstabschefs des Deutschen Heeres 1933-1938*, Boppard am Rhein, 1980, p. 56.

13 Raymond Aron, *Penser la Guerre: Clausewitz*, 2 vols, Paris, 1976, esp. I, pp. 240-77. The English translation, *Clausewitz: Philosopher of War*, London, 1983, presents problems: see Hew Strachan, 'Policy continued by other means', *Times Higher Education Supplement*, 6 January 1984, p. 16. Aron's essays on Clausewitz have been collected by Pierre Hassner and Raymon Aron, *Sur Clausewitz*, Brussels, 1987.

14 Martin van Creveld, *On Future War*, London, 1991, p. ix.

15 John Keegan, *A History of Warfare*, London, 1993, p. 1. For a criticism of Keegan, see Charles Bassford, 'John Keegan and the grand tradition of trashing Clausewitz: a polemic', *War in History*, I, 1994, pp. 319-36. Van Creveld and Keegan were primarily concerned with Clausewitz's identification of war with the nation state. For a sustained and effective critique of Clausewitz as a thinker on the operational level, see Shimon Naveh, *In Pursuit of Military Excellence: The Evolution of Operational Theory*, London, 1997, pp. 32-98.

16 Keegan, ibid., p. 392.

17 John Keegan, *War and Our World: The Reith Lectures 1998*, London, 1998.

18 Michael Mandelbaum, 'Is major war obsolete?', *Survival*, XL, winter 1998-9, p. 20.

19 John Mueller, *Retreat from Doomsday: The Obsolescence of Major War*, Basic Books, 1990; first published 1989.

20 *The Times*, 28 October 1999.

21 General Sir Roger Wheeler, 'The British Army after the SDR: peacemakers know that Britain will deliver', *RUSI Journal*, CXLIV, April/May 1999, p. 5.

22 *The Times*, 30 November 1990.

23 Christopher Coker, 'Post-modern war', *Time*, June 1998, p. 8.

24 Colin Gray, *Modern Strategy*, Oxford, 1999, p. 189.

25 Hew Strachan, 'From cabinet war to total war: the perspective of military doctrine 1861-1918', in R. Chickering and S. Förster (eds), *Great War, Total War: Combat and Mobilization on the Western Front, 1914-1918*, Cambridge, 2000.

26 Roger Chickering, *Imperial Germany and the Great War 1914-1918*, Cambridge, 1998, p. 65.

27 Léon Daudet, *La Guerre Totale*, Paris, 1918, p. 8.

28 An English translation by A. S. Rapoport appeared in various editions as *The Nation at War*. For discussions of the text, see Hans Speier, 'Ludendorff: the German concept of total war', in Edward Meade Earle, *Makers of Modern Strategy: Military Thought from Machiavelli to Hitler*, Princeton, NJ, 1943; Roger Chickering, 'Sore loser: Ludendorff's total war', in R. Chickering and S. Förster, *The Shadows of Total War*, Cambridge, forthcoming.

29 Erich Ludendorff, *The Nation at War*, London, n.d., p. 169.
30 Müller, op. cit., pp. 33–4, 55–8.
31 J. F. C. Fuller, *The First of the League Wars: its Lessons and Omens*, London, 1937; first published, 1936, p. 167.
32 Ibid., pp. 63–4.
33 Ibid., pp. 7–8, 165.
34 Anthony John Trythall, *'Boney' Fuller: The Intellectual General*, London, 1977, p. 193; Brian Holden Reid, *J. F. C. Fuller: Military Thinker*, Basingstoke, 1987, p. 215.
35 Harvey DeWeerd, 'Churchill, Lloyd George, Clemenceau: the emergence of the civilian', in Earle, op cit., p. 296.
36 Stanley L. Engermann and J. Matthew Gallmann, 'The Civil War economy: a modern view', in Förster and Nagler, op. cit., pp. 220–1.
37 Richard Overy, *Why the Allies Won*, London, 1995, pp. 221–2.
38 Ibid., p. 321.
39 Ibid., pp. 43, 331–2.
40 Ibid., p. 215; Hew Strachan, *European Armies and the Conduct of War*, London, 1983, pp. 162, 184; Williamson Murray, *Luftwaffe*, London, 1985, pp. 174, 248; see also R. L. DiNardo, *Mechanized Juggernaut or Military Anachronism? Horses and the German Army of World War II*, Westport, CT, 1991.
41 The literature on this topic is vast, and growing. Two collections of essays provide summaries by some of the key contributors. Paul Addison and Angus Calder, *Time to Kill: The Soldier's Experience of the War in the West 1939-1945*, London, 1997, has chapters by Jürgen Förster and Theo J. Schulte. Förster also contributed to David Cesarani, *The Final Solution: Origins and Implementation*, London, 1994, as did Christian Streit, Omer Bartov and Christopher Browning. Omer Bartov's two books, *The Eastern Front, 1941-45: German Troops and the Barbarisation of Warfare*, Basingstoke, 1985, and *Hitler's Army: Soldiers, Nazis and War in the Third Reich*, Oxford, 1991, put the argument most succinctly and forcefully. Stephen G. Fritz, *Frontsoldaten: The German Soldier in World War II*, Kentucky, 1995, pp. 187–218, and ' "We are trying to change the face of the world" – ideology and motivation in the Wehrmacht on the eastern front: the view from below', *Journal of Military History*, LX, 1996, pp. 683–710, paint a more nuanced picture.
42 Glenn Anthony May, 'Was the Philippine-American War a "total war"?', in M. F. Boemeke, R. Chickering, and S. Förster, *Anticipating Total War*, p. 445; see also the essay by Robert M. Utley, 'Total war on the American Indian frontier', in the same volume, and Utley, *Bluecoats and Redskins: The United States Army and the Indian 1866-1891*, London, 1975; US edition, *Frontier Regulars*, 1973.
43 Bill Nasson, *The South African War 1899-1902*, London, 1999, p. 9.
44 Michael Lieven, ' "Butchering the brutes all over the place": total war and massacre in Zululand, 1879', *History*, LXXXIV, 1999, pp. 620–2.
45 Accessible if Anglicized (and Britain itself has barely begun on the RMA path) surveys to the debate include: Lawrence Freedman, 'The revolution in strategic affairs', *Adelphi Paper* 318, International Institute for Strategic Studies, April 1998; Colin S. Gray, 'The American Revolution in Military Affairs: an interim assessment', *Occasional paper* 28, Strategic and Combat Studies Institute, 1997; 'The future of warfare', *The Economist*, 8 March 1997, pp. 17–26; Gray, *Modern Strategy*, pp. 243–54.
46 Lawrence Freedman, 'The changing forms of military conflict', *Survival*, XL, winter 1998-99, p. 44.

47 On the links with August 1914, see Fritz, ' "We are trying . . ." ', pp. 700–2; Peter Fritzsche, *Germans Into Nazis*, Cambridge, MA, 1998; Jeffrey Todd Verhey, 'The "spirit of 1914": the myth of enthusiasm and the rhetoric of unity in World War I Germany', PhD thesis, University of California, Berkeley, CA, 1991.

48 Holden Reid, *Studies in British Military Thought*, pp. 18, 75, 84.

49 Michael Fellman, 'At the nihilist edge', p. 534; Mark E. Neeley, Jr., 'Was the Civil War a total war?', in Förster and Nagler, op cit., argues it was not, and Fellman and Hermann M. Hattaway in the same volume agree; James M. McPherson does not.

50 Avner Offer, *The First World War: An Agrarian Interpretation*, Oxford, 1989, p. 232.

51 Arthur J. Marder, *From the Dreadnought to Scapa Flow: The Royal Navy in the Fisher Era, 1904–1919*, 5 vols, London, 1961–70, I, p. 112.

52 Anne Roerkohl, *Hungerblockade und Heimatfront. Der kommunale Lebensmittelversorgung in Westfalen während des Ersten Weltkrieges*, Stuttgart, 1991, pp. 113–35, 297–315.

53 Hew Strachan, 'War and society in the 1920s and 1930s', in Chickering and Förster, op. cit.

54 Niall Ferguson, *The Pity of War*, London, 1998.

55 Gordon Adams, 'Defence planning: what are forces for, and how much is enough?', *Survival*, XL, winter, 1998-9, pp. 184–91, esp. pp. 186–7.

56 V. D. Sokolovsky, *Military Strategy: Soviet Doctrine and Concepts*, New York, 1963, pp. 166–204; H. S. Dinerstein, *War and the Soviet Union: Nuclear Weapons and the Revolution in Soviet Military and Political Thinking*, New York, 1962; P. H. Vigor, *The Soviet View of War, Peace and Neutrality*, London, 1975.

57 A. H. Jomini, *The Art of War*, Philadelphia, PA, 1862, p. 26; see also National Touring Exhibitions, *Disasters of War: Callot, Gova, Dix*, London, 1998.

58 R. W. Seton-Watson, J. Dover Wilson, Alfred E. Zimmern and Arthur Greenwood, *The War and Democracy*, London, 1915; first published 1914, p. 318.

59 Bernard von Brocke, ' "Wissenschaft und Militarismus. Der Aufruf der 93 "an die Kulturwelt!" und der internationalen Gelehrtenrepublik im Ersten Weltkrieg', in Wm. M. Calder III, Hellmut Flashar and Theodor Linkin, *Wilamowitz nach 50 Jahren*, Darmstadt, 1985, pp. 649–64.

60 Antulio J. Echevarria, 'On the brink of the abyss: the warrior identity and German military thought before the Great War', *War and Society*, XIII, 1995, pp. 23–40.

61 P. Fritzsche, *Germans into Nazis*, Harvard, 1998; J. Verhey, *The Spirit of 1914: Militarism, Myth and Mobilization in Germany*, Cambridge, 2000.

62 Lothar Burchardt, 'Walther Rathenau und die Anfänge der deutschen Rohstoffbewirtschaftung im Ersten Weltkrieg', *Tradition*, XV, 1970, pp. 169–96; Hartmut Pogge von Strandmann, *Walther Rathenau: Industrialist, Banker, Intellectual, and Politician: Notes and Diaries 1907-1922*, Oxford, 1985, pp. 157-9; Wolfgang W. Michalka, 'Kriegsrohstoffbewirtschaftung, Walther Rathenau und die "kommende Wirtschaft" ', and Dieter Krüger, 'Kriegssozialismus. Die Auseinandeersetzung der Nationalökonomen mit der Kriegswirtschaft 1914-1918', in Michalka, *Der Erste Weltkrieg. Wirkung, Wahrnehmung, Analyse*, Munich, 1994.

63 Helmut Heiber, *Goebbels-Reden* (2 vols, Dusseldorf, 1992), II, pp. 158–71; here p. 166, with emphasis in the original.

64 See George J. Andreopoulos, 'The age of national liberation movements', in Michael Howard, George J. Andreopoulos and Mark R. Shulman, *The Laws of War: Constraints on Warfare in the Western World*, New Haven, CT, 1994, p. 191. A brief general introduction to the laws of war is Christopher Greenwood, 'In

defence of the laws of war', in Robert A. Hinde, *The Institution of War*, Basing-stoke, 1991. Geoffrey Best, *Humanity in Warfare*, London, 1980, and *War and Law Since 1945*, Oxford, 1994, are fundamental.

65 See, for example, Simon Jenkins, *The Times*, 24 September 1999, and reply by George Robertson, 30 September 1999; also Mark Littman, ibid., 16 November 1999; Marc Weller, ibid., 24 November 1999.

66 Trutz von Trotha, ' "The fellows can just starve": on wars of "pacification" in the African colonies of Imperial Germany and the concept of "total war" ', in M. F. Boemeke, R. Chickering and S. Förster, op cit., pp. 417–19.

67 James Turner Johnson, *Just War Tradition and the Restraint of War: A Moral and Historical Enquiry*, Princeton, NJ, 1981, pp. 276–7.

68 Philippe Delmas, *Le Bel Avenir de la Guerre*, Paris, 1995, p. 139.

69 Jack Hawthorn, 'Some thoughts on an independent defence force for Scotland', *Occasional Paper* 1, Scottish Centre for War Studies, 1997.

70 Rolf Peter Sieferle, 'Der deutsch-englische Gegensatz und die "Ideen von 914" ', in Gottfried Niedhart, *Das kontinentale Europa und die britischen Inseln. Wahrnehmungsmuster und Wechselwirkungen seit den Antike*, Mannheim, 1993, pp. 153–4.

71 Jean-Marie Guéhenno, 'The impact of globalisation on strategy', *Survival*, XL, winter 1998–99, pp. 5–13; Delmas, *Le Bel Avenir de la Guerre*, esp. pp. 3–11, 139–73, 206–7.

72 Rosemary Righter, *The Times*, 13 December 1999.

73 Delmas, op cit., p. 141.

74 Samuel P. Huntington, *The Clash of Civilizations and the Remaking of World Order*, New York, 1996, pp. 187–9.

75 Ibid., p. 310, and *passim*.

76 Delmas, op cit., pp. 268–9.

Brief Guide to Further Reading

1 General history; social change

Berghahn, V. R., *Modern Germany*, London, 1982; second edition, 1987. (High-quality text book.)

Clark, Martin, *Modern Italy 1871-1982*, London, 1984; new edition 1996. (Very rich text book, strong on the post-1945 years.)

Macmillan, James F., *Dreyfus to De Gaulle: Politics and Society in France 1898-1969*, London, 1985. (Very sound text book.)

Marwick, Arthur, *A History of the Modern British Isles, 1914-1999: Circumstances, Events and Outcomes*, Oxford, 2000. (Two out of the six chapters discuss the impact of the two wars on Britain.)

Middlemas, Keith, *Politics in Industrial Society: the Experience of the British System Since 1911*, London, 1979. (Famous application of the corporatist thesis - associated in this collection with Maier - to Britain.)

Perkin, Harold, *The Rise of Professional Society: England Since 1880*, London, 1989. (The central thesis about the triumph of the professional class is controversial, but the general coverage of social change is excellent as is the attention to the effects of war.)

Roberts, John, *Europe 1880-1945*, revised edition, London, 2000. (The general history selected by the Open University A318 Course Team as being the most thorough and comprehensive for the study of war, peace and social change.)

Schmitt, Bernadotte E., *The World in the Crucible*, New York, 1984. (Slightly old-fashioned but comprehensive study of Europe and the First World War.)

Smith, Paul, *Feminism and the Third Republic: Women's Political and Civil Rights in France 1918-1945*, Oxford, 1996. (A detailed account of the difficulties faced by women in seeking equality in France from the close of one war to the close of the next.)

Wright, Gordon, *The Ordeal of Total War 1939-1945*, New York, 1969. (Comprehensive study of Europe and the Second World War with a fair attention to war and social change.)

2 War, revolution, the dictatorships

Barber, John and Harrison, Mark, *The Soviet Home Front 1941–1945: A Social And Economic History of the USSR in World War II*, Longman, 1991.

Bessel, R. (ed.), *Fascist Italy and Nazi Germany*, Cambridge, 1996.

Bosworth, R. J. B., *The Italian Dictatorship: Problems and Perspectives in The Interpretation of Mussolini and Facism*, London, 1998.

Bourke, Joanna, *An Intimate History of Killing: Face-to-face Killing in Twentieth-century Warfare*, London, 1999. (An uncompromising attempt by a social historian to put the killing back into war and to emphasize that not all soldiers in twentieth-century wars have been victims.)

Browning, C. J., *The Path to Genocide: Essays on Launching the Final Solution*, Cambridge, 1992.

Burleigh, M. and Wippermann, W. (eds), *The Racial State, Germany 1933–1945*, Cambridge, 1991.

Calvocoressi, Peter and Wint, Guy, *Total War: Causes and Courses of the Second World War*, revised edition, London, 1989. (Particularly useful for the military campaigns.)

Conquest, Robert, *The Great Terror*, London, 1968. (A detailed study of the Stalin purges.)

Dunn, John, *Modern Revolutions: An Introduction to the Analysis of a Political Phenomenon*, Cambridge, 1972; second edition, 1989. (An important and stimulating introduction to the subject which ranges from Europe to the Third World.)

Ferguson, Niall, *The Pity of War*, London, 1998. (A provocative, highly readable account of the First World War with particular reference to Britain.)

Ferro, Marc, *The Russian Revolution of February 1917*, London, 1977. *October 1917*, London, 1980. (These two volumes constitute a thorough and important study of the Russian Revolution by one of France's leading historians.)

Figes, Oliver, *A People's Tragedy: The Russian Revolution 1891–1924*, London, 1996. (Full of rich details.)

Fitzpatrick, Sheila, *Everyday Stalinism, Ordinary Folk in Extraordinary Times, Soviet Russia in the 1930s*, New York, 1999.

Friedländer, S., *Nazi Germany and the Jews. The Years of Persecution, 1933–1939*, London, 1997; paperback edition, 1998.

Gros, Jan T., *Revolution from Abroad: The Soviet Conquest of Poland's Western Ukraine and Western Belorussia*, Princeton, NJ, 1988. (A very useful addition to the growing literature on Stalin's 'terror', particularly interesting since the lands considered here have been so little explored by historians in this context.)

Herwig, Holger H., *The First World War: Austria and Germany*, London, 1996. (An up-to-date survey of the war from the point of view of the Central Powers; good on both military and internal aspects.)

Kershaw, Ian, *The Nazi Dictatorship*, London, 1985. (Rightly regarded as one of the best studies of an overworked period, it ranges widely over the Nazi control of Germany including popular responses to the regime.)

Kershaw, Ian, *Hitler, 1889–1936: Hubris*, London, 1998. (More than a splendid biography; a rounded history.)

Leed, Eric J., *No Man's Land: Combat and Identity in World War I*, London, 1979. (Original work on how soldiers were themselves affected by waging war.)

McInnes, Colin and Sheffield, Y. D. (eds), *Warfare in the Twentieth Century: Theory and Practice*, London, 1988. (Contains other important essays apart from the Beckett one reprinted in this collection.)

Overy, Richard, *Russia's War*, London, 1998.

Peukert, Detlev, J. K., *Inside Nazi Germany: Conformity, Opposition and Racism in Everyday Life*, London, 1989. (An important study of how the Nazi regime affected everyday life in Germany and how the regime itself dealt with those that it considered to be undesirable and/or deviant.)

Pipes, Richard, *The Russian Revolution 1899-1919*, London, 1992.

Pipes, Richard, *Russia Under the Bolshevik Regime, 1919-1921*, London, 1994.

Service, Robert, *A History of Twentieth-Century Russia*, London, 1997.

Stone, Norman, *The Eastern Front*, London, 1974. (Classic account of the front too often neglected in British studies.)

Whittam, J., *Fascist Italy*, Manchester, 1995.

Williamson, D., *Mussolini: From Socialist to Fascist*, London: 1998.

3 The causes of wars

Bell, P. M. H., *The Origins of the Second World War in Europe*, London, 1986; second edition, 1997. (A valuable introduction to, and assessment of, the current debate.)

Berghahn, V. R., *Germany and the Approach of War in 1914*, London, 1973. (One of a series of single-country studies of the origins of the First World War designed for students and providing an introduction to the current literature as well as analysis.)

Fischer, Fritz, *Germany's Aims in the First World War*, London, 1966. *War of Illusions: Germany's Policies from 1911 to 1914*, London, 1975. (These are the two volumes in which Fischer outlines in detail his challenging view of the German responsibility for the First World War.)

Herwig, Holger H. (ed.), *The Outbreak of the First World War. Causes and Responsibilities*, sixth edition, London, 1991. (A useful collection of articles from authors who have contributed to the debate.)

Hiden, J., *Germany and Europe 1919-1939*, London, 1977; second edition, 1993.

Hiden, J., *Republican and Fascist Germany*, London, 1996.

Joll, James, *The Origins of the First World War*, London, 1992. (An excellent introduction to the current debates and controversies, in the same series as the book by P. M. H. Bell.)

Koch, H. W. (ed.), *The Origins of the First World War: Great Power Rivalry and German War Aims*, London, 1984. (A useful collection of readings on the Fischer debate.)

Langdon, John W., *July 1914. The Long Debate, 1918-1990*, New York/Oxford, 1991. (An excellent summary of the debate.)

Lentin, A., *The Versailles Peace Settlement. Peacemaking with Germany*, London, 1990; reprinted, 1993.

Martel, G. (ed.), *The Origins of the Second World War Reconsidered: The A. J. P. Taylor Debate after 25 Years*, London, 1986. (The debate rumbles on.)

McDonough, F., *Neville Chamberlain, Appeasement and the British Road to War*, Manchester, 1998.

Mombauer, Annika, *The Debate on the Origins of the First World War*, Cambridge, 2000. (Traces the development of the debate from 1914 to the 1990s.)

Purdue, A. W., *The Second World War*, Basingstoke, 1999. (Useful comprehensive text book.)

Roberts, G., *The Soviet Union and the Origins of the Second World War*, Basingstoke, 1995.

Robertson, Esmonde M. (ed.), *The Origins of the Second World War*, London, 1971. (Readings making a companion volume to Koch.)

Stevenson, David, *The Outbreak of the First World War. 1914 in Perspective*, Basingstoke, 1997. (Contains a useful chronology and an excellent bibliography.)

Taylor, A. J. P., *The Origins of the Second World War*, London, 1961. (A challenging, some would say infuriating, account of Hitler as a diplomat, and why Britain and France finally decided to oppose him over Poland.)

4 The consequences of wars

Addison, Paul, *The Road to 1945: British Politics and the Second World War*, London, 1975; new edition 1994. (Authoritative study which demonstrates a shift to the left in British politics caused by the experiences of war.)

Becker, Jean-Jacques, *The Great War and the French People*, Leamington Spa, 1986. (Richly documented from the French local archives.)

Bessell, Richard, *Germany After the First World War*, Oxford, 1993. (Taken with Chickering, provides a comprehensive account.)

Cadwallader, Barry, *Crisis of the European Mind*, London, 1981. (This and Cruickshank are concerned with the intellectual and cultural impact of the First World War.)

Chickering, Roger, *Imperial Germany and the Great War*, Cambridge, 1998.

Cruickshank, John, *Variations on Catastrophe*, London, 1982.

Dockrill, M., *The Cold War 1945–63*, Basingstoke, 1988.

Ellwood, David, *Rebuilding Europe*, London, 1992. (An excellent history of post-war western Europe that unifies political, economic and cultural perspectives.)

Ferro, Marc, *The Great War*, London, 1973. (Particularly strong on the war's effects on attitudes and perceptions.)

Fridenson, Patrick, *The French Home Front 1914-1918*, Oxford, 1992.

Fullbrook, Mary, *The Two Germanies, 1945-1990: Problems of Interpretation*, London, 1992. (To be read in conjunction with the chapter by Roseman.)

Fussell, Paul, *The Great War and Modern Memory*, New York, 1975. (Widely praised study of the effect of the First World War on English literature.)

Harris, Frederick J., *Encounters with Darkness: French and German Writers on World War II*, New York, 1983. (Extremely useful.)

Kettenacker, Lother, *Germany Since 1945*, Oxford, 1997. (The most authoritative treatment in English.)

Kocka, Jürgen, *Facing Total War: German Society 1914 to 1918*, Leamington Spa, 1984. (Written philosophically, though not politically, from a Marxist perspective.)

Lask, Vera, *Women in the Resistance and the Holocaust: The Voice of Emptiness*, West Port, CT, 1983. (One of the most important contributions in the growing literature on women's role in war.)

Marwick, Arthur, 'Painting and music during and after the great war: the art of total war', in Roger Chickering and Stig Förster (eds), *Great War, Total War: Combat and Mobilization on the Western Front*, 1914-1918, Cambridge, 2000.

Marwick, Arthur, *The Deluge: British Society and the First World War*, London, 1965; new edition, 1991. (The new introduction contains the most up-to-date brief summary of the ideas about war and social change referred to in Beckett's chapter.)

Marwick, Arthur, *War and Social Change in the Twentieth Century: A Comparative Study of Britain, France, Germany, Russia and the United States*, London, 1974.

(An older, but fuller, statement of the ideas about war and social change referred to in Beckett's chapter.)

Marwick, Arthur (ed.), *Total War and Social Change*, London, 1988. (Essays by leading authorities on France, Britain, Germany and Russia.)

Marwick, Arthur, ' "War and the arts – is there a connection?": the case of the two total wars', *War in History*, vol. 2, no. 1, 1995, pp. 65–86. (To be read in conjunction with the chapter by Josipovici.)

Milward, Alan, *War, Economy and Society, 1939–1945*, London, 1977. (One of several important studies by a distinguished economic historian.)

Naimark, Norman, *The Russians in Germany: A History of the Soviet Zone of Occupation, 1945–1949*, Cambridge, MA, 1997. (The best book on the division of Germany based on research in German, Soviet and American archives.)

Naimark, Norman and Gibanski, Leonid (eds), *The Establishment of a Communist Regime in Eastern Europe, 1944–1948*, Boulder, CO, 1998. (A useful, if uneven, collection of essays that contains – in summary – all the most useful recent research on post-war Eastern Europe.)

Smith, Harold L. (ed.), *War and Social Change: British Society in the Second World War*, Manchester, 1986. (Contains the fruits of much recent research; the editor insists strongly that the war had no effect on British society, but the individual essays do not always seem fully to support this contention.)

Waites, Bernard, *War and a Class Society 1910–1920*, Leamington Spa, 1987. (Authoritative study of changes affecting the working class.)

Wall, Richard, and Winter, J. (eds), *The Upheaval of War: Family, Work and Welfare in Europe, 1914–1918*, Cambridge, 1988. (Indispensable collection of thoroughly researched chapters by individual experts.)

Winter, J. M., *The Great War and the British People*, London, 1986. (Points to wartime improvements in British health and nutrition.)

Index

ISSCW   940
        .5
        T717

TOTAL WAR AND HISTOR-
ICAL CHANGE : EUROPE
1914-1955   PAPER

ISSCW   940
        .5
        T717

HOUSTON PUBLIC LIBRARY
CENTRAL LIBRARY